The Sublime Post

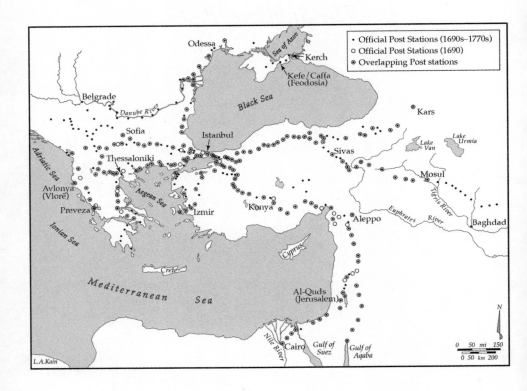

Official Post Stations (1690s–1770s)
Official Post Stations (1690)
Overlapping Post stations

Odessa
Sea of Azov
Kerch
Kefe / Caffa
(Feodosia)
Belgrade
Danube River
Black Sea
Kars
Sofia
Istanbul
Lake
Van
Lake
Urmia
Thessaloniki
Sivas
Adriatic Sea
Avlonya
(Vlorë)
Aegean Sea
Mosul
Tigris River
Preveza
Izmir
Konya
Euphrates River
Baghdad
Ionian Sea
Aleppo
Cyprus
Crete
Mediterranean   Sea
Al-Quds
(Jerusalem)
N
Nile River
Cairo
Gulf of
Suez
Gulf of
Aqaba
0   50 mi 150
0   50 km 200

L.A.Kain

The Sublime Post

HOW THE OTTOMAN IMPERIAL POST BECAME A PUBLIC SERVICE

Choon Hwee Koh

Yale UNIVERSITY PRESS

New Haven & London

Published with assistance from the Kingsley Trust Association Publication Fund established by the Scroll and Key Society of Yale College.

Yale University Press books may be purchased in quantity for educational, business, or promotional use. For information, please e-mail sales.press@yale.edu (U.S. office) or sales@yaleup.co.uk (U.K. office).

Set in Garamond Premier type by Westchester Publishing Services.
Printed in the United States of America.

Library of Congress Control Number: 2023947494
ISBN 978-0-300-27053-2 (hardcover : alk. paper)

A catalogue record for this book is available from the British Library.
This paper meets the requirements of ANSI/NISO Z39.48-1992 (Permanence of Paper).

10 9 8 7 6 5 4 3 2 1

Frontispiece: Official post stations in the Ottoman Empire, 1690s–1770s. The map is derived from Bozkurt, *Osmanlı İmparatorluğunda Kollar, Ulak ve İaşe Menzilleri,* which combines information gleaned from several fiscal registers. The set of official post stations in 1690 is based on the current author's reading of one fiscal register, BOA, MAD 4030. All dots were manually plotted onto the base map by the author using Figma.

Dedicated to Koh Piak Huat, Chin Ngiok Pah,

and

the years five of us spent

together in Bukit Panjang

Contents

Note on Transliteration and Sources

In this book I draw on source materials in Ottoman Turkish, Arabic, and Persian, as well as several East Asian and western European languages. Foreign terms that have entered standard English dictionaries (such as "pasha") are written in their anglicized forms. Modern Turkish spelling has been used for administrative and fiscal terms (such as *guruş* and *akçe*) and Hijri month names (thus: Muharrem instead of Muharram, Rebiülahir instead of Rabīʿ ath-Thānī). For the sake of readability, diacritics have been omitted as far as possible in the body of the text. Dates are primarily given according to the Common Era. As far as possible, I use the modern Turkish spelling for personal names and for place-names, which are followed by their modern place-names (for example, Niş/Niš in modern Serbia). In transliterating from Ottoman Turkish, I have followed the system recommended by the *International Journal of Middle Eastern Studies*. However, if transliterations are cited from published works and secondary sources, the system used in the source is retained. Due to the multilingual nature of the Ottoman Empire and its successor states, and due to the range of sources used in this book, I cannot claim consistency in my choices and must seek the reader's indulgence. All translations are my own unless otherwise indicated.

When citing archival sources, I provide one or more identifying labels, such as page numbers, folio numbers, .jpg (.tiff) numbers, and/or *varak* numbers (for court records). My main reason for doing so is to provide interested readers with enough information to locate the relevant archival source. As fellow researchers will know, archival documents may be inconsistently paginated, may contain odd-sized pages (hence with page numbers such as 1a, 1b, 1c etc.), or be damaged. Digitization conventions may also differ across different archival collections. To help those who wish to investigate further, I have given more than one identifying label where possible.

Earlier versions of portions of Chapters 4, 6, and 8 appeared in "The Ottoman Postmaster: Contractors, Communication and Early Modern State Formation," *Past & Present* 251, no. 1 (2021), 113–152; "The Mystery of the Missing Horses: How to Uncover an Ottoman Shadow Economy," *Comparative Studies in Society and History* 64, no. 3 (2022), 576–610; and "An Ottoman Liquidity Crunch: Immediate and Deferred Payments at Post Stations (*menzilḫāne*), 1713–1763," *Turcica* 54 (2023): 355–375. I thank these journals for giving me permission to use modified versions of these publications in this book.

Abbreviations

BOA — Türkiye Cumhuriyeti Cumhurbaşkanlığı Devlet Arşivleri Başkanlığı, Osmanlı Arşivi [Presidential State Archives of the Republic of Türkiye, Ottoman Archives], Istanbul

For all abbreviations used with BOA—MAD, HAT, etc.—consult Yusuf Sarınay, *Başbakanlık Osmanlı Arşivi Rehberi* (Istanbul: Devlet Arşivleri Genel Müdürlüğü, 2010).

GRGSA IAM OJC 001 — Greece General State Archives, Historical Archives of Macedonia (Thessaloniki), Ottoman Islamic Courts

ISAM — Islam Araştırmaları Merkezi [Centre for Islamic Studies], Istanbul

AŞS — Amasya Şer'iye Sicilleri [Amasya Court Register]
DŞS — Damascus Şer'iye Sicilleri [Damascus Court Register]
HŞS — Hama Şer'iye Sicilleri [Hama Court Register]
KŞS — Konya Şer'iye Sicilleri [Konya Court Register]

The Sublime Post

Introduction

In the 1840s information traveled at roughly the same speed as it had in 840 BCE.[1] Before the telegraph and the steamship, relay postal systems were the premier technology for long-distance communication. Powered by horses, these overland relays were more reliable than boats and more secure than carrier pigeons, and they could transmit messages more complex than the most elaborate smoke signals. After all, boats could capsize, pigeons could be devoured, and smoke signals could be ruined by rain or the slightest shift in wind direction.[2] Hence, for over three millennia, the empires of the Assyrians and the Romans, the Mongols and the Russians, the Manchus and the Ottomans, all converged on a common solution to long-distance communication.

While the core motor of horse power barely changed, the forms of human organization that harnessed it varied across space and transformed over time. Different communities adapted the same technology in different ways to accommodate regional geographies, political values, and other factors. This book is about one way of organizing relay communications in world history: the Ottoman postal system, circa 1500 to 1840.[3]

For centuries, bureaucrats in the "Sublime Porte"—a term used by contemporary European powers to refer to the Ottoman government—coordinated with local officials from Belgrade to Baghdad, Crimea to Cairo, to manage a vast network of over two hundred official post stations.[4] These stations served government correspondence exclusively and, in principle, functioned as ever-ready nodes across the empire's assorted landscapes—mountain, desert, coast, and forest. Through rain, sun, or snow, mounted couriers galloped from station to station, delivering everything from imperial decrees and appointment letters to bills of exchange and petitions. Villagers provisioned these stations with food, water, and, most importantly, fresh horses to substitute tired ones as part of their tax obligations. Postmasters used those resources to serve couriers with coffee and food while stabling, feeding, and shoeing their horses. In the eighteenth century, postmasters began to record the names of these couriers, including their ranks, entourage sizes, number of horses taken, dates of arrival and departure, and final destinations. They compiled this information into registers and submitted them at regular intervals to bookkeepers based in the imperial capital. In turn, bookkeepers used these registers to calculate the annual expenditures of every post station in the empire. This series of connected efforts across the social hierarchy powered the everyday processes of administration—this was empire, in microcosm.

Unlike the Mongols and the Romans, the Ottomans left behind voluminous documentation that detailed these postal operations. Read carefully, these records yield a rich repository of stories. There are stories of bookkeepers puzzling over the cost of a horseshoe, of ambitious postmasters who competed for contracts, of neighboring villages embroiled in disputes over post station responsibilities, of imposters masquerading as official couriers by donning their uniforms in order to obtain post horses for personal use, of widows petitioning the state for financial assistance after their courier-husbands were murdered by highway robbers. There is a story of a bereaved mother learning that her courier-son froze to death with his horse in a snowstorm.

Complementing the official archive of the Ottoman bureaucracy is the unofficial archive of travelogues, chronicles, and memoirs. There are stories of swimming with horses across rivers using inflated goat skins, of singing loudly in the deep of the night to intimidate lurking bandits, of drunken nights in post stations that end in rashly drawn sabers and displays of machismo. These are stories, above all, about life in the Ottoman lands.

This book examines the Ottoman postal system to study state formation. It decomposes this vast system into the perspectives of eight small-scale actors, animate and inanimate. Collectively, the Courier, the Tatar, Imperial Decrees, the Bookkeeper, the Postmaster, the Villager, Money, and Horses enabled the postal system's expansion during the eighteenth century and participated in its transformation from an exclusive government network into a public postal service open to all subjects in 1840. Previously, only Ottoman officials had the status required to access post stations, while common subjects were forbidden due to their low tax-paying status. After 1840, tax-paying subjects became legitimate customers who could legally pay money to use post horses.

The explanation for this arc of change may be found in the process of Ottoman state formation, which is conventionally narrated using the de/centralization framework. This framework views the Ottoman Empire as possessing a centralized state in the fifteenth and sixteenth centuries, a decentralized state in the seventeenth and eighteenth centuries, and finally a modernizing centralized state in the nineteenth. It assumes that a centralized state was a powerful state and, conversely, that a decentralized state was a weak state.[5] However, this assumption is derived from outdated theories of war-driven state centralization in European history. Recent scholarship has uncovered empirical evidence that war-making in early modern Europe often involved private military contractors who were not directly controlled by the state. These findings carry profound implications for state formation theories: instead of focusing narrowly on the state as previous generations of scholars did, present scholars now focus on how states delegated authority and fostered effective principal-agent relationships with local contractors.[6] To be a pre-industrial empire is to delegate governance; the enforcement of imperial policy always required working through local intermediaries. This was indeed the case for the Ottoman bureaucracy, which expanded significantly in scale and complexity over time.[7]

Instead of the de/centralization framework, I argue that the paradigm of "thickening governance" not only offers a more precise account of Ottoman state formation, but also explains symbiotic developments in the Ottoman social order. Thickening governance, a metaphor first developed by the historian Molly Greene, refers to the pattern of imperial bureaucrats and provincial officials recruiting more and more common subjects as local intermediaries to do the work of local governance. This process, which intensified in the seventeenth and eighteenth centuries, enabled imperial bureaucrats to increase their monitoring capacity, to expand the local impact, and to extend the reach of imperial policies. By the same token, participating in local governance enabled many common subjects who served as local intermediaries to attain the status of minor officials and, consequently, petty notables. These common subjects gained important experience from governance work and learned how to organize themselves effectively as collective groups. Consequently, they developed new expectations of imperial authorities. Thickening governance was thus a coevolutionary process where bureaucrats, officials, and common subjects interacted with and adapted

to each other. Over time, this process altered the boundaries of Ottoman officialdom (the "state") and loosened the prevailing social hierarchy. All this set the
stage for the profound social transformations, ruptures, and reforms during the
Tanzimat era (1839–1876) and, more broadly, during the nineteenth-century Ottoman Empire—including the transformation of the exclusive government
communications network into a public pay-per-use postal service.[8]

The thickening governance paradigm therefore focuses analytical attention
on the process of delegation: on different strategies of delegation, the diversity
of local intermediaries, and the variety of outcomes. *This*, I argue, is where the
story of Ottoman state formation is found—in the evolving set of relations between imperial bureaucrats and myriad local intermediaries. State formation cannot be understood apart from the evolution of the social order in which its
processes are embedded.

The postal system, by offering a rare view of the whole empire as one coherent analytical unit, is a suitable proxy to examine these twinned processes. Spatially, the postal system cut across the Ottoman Empire's bewildering diversity
and imposed a relatively uniform and circumscribed bureaucratic context. Language, faith, climate, and diet, as well as legal and tax arrangements, varied from
province to province, as was the case in other Eurasian empires.[9] Yet the Ottoman postal system was, by design, operationally standardized. It had to be. The
system's raison d'être was speed, and the speed of a courier depended on the ease
with which he could flow through each post station and reach his destination.
Predictability and simplicity were key. In other words, it didn't matter which language you spoke, which faith you practiced, or which food you ate. Each post
station had to work the same way as the next in order for the whole system to
work at all.

Temporally, the horse-run relay system endured as an important medium of
communication from the early days of the empire in the fourteenth century until
after the arrival of the telegraph. The earliest sources used in this book date to
the 1380s, when whole villages were granted special tax statuses in exchange for
providing horses to imperial couriers. In 1902, almost half a century after the advent of the telegraph, the deputy judge in a small town near Amman (modern
Jordan) still requested confirmation of the official end of Ramadan by horse-run
post, rejecting the telegram notification.[10] The postal system thus offers historians a practical lens with which to contemplate the entirety of empire over a very
long time.

The Ottoman postal system was a pre-industrial infrastructure. Social scientists have long understood infrastructure as a bundle of relations.[11] Just like the

large technological systems of today, the Ottoman postal system comprised interacting, interconnected components that cannot be studied in isolation from
each other.[12] Just like the large logistical networks of today, the Ottoman postal
system aimed to maintain steady circulation across uneven terrain and mutable
seasons, albeit at a much more modest scale and velocity.[13] In transposing social
science insights on industrial infrastructure backward in time to the pre-industrial
Ottoman world, it becomes clear that theoretical convergences exist between the
scholarship on early modern state formation and on Science and Technology
Studies (STS). This is what makes the Ottoman communications infrastructure
suitable for the study of the state formation process.

One important STS theme that has informed this book's analysis is breakdown. Like large technological systems, the postal infrastructure grew, developed
new problems, and broke down from time to time. Records from the seventeenth
century show that courier traffic and horse usage began to strain the Ottoman
postal system's capacity, resulting in significant delays in government communication as couriers were stranded for weeks at post stations, waiting for horses with
which to continue their journey. To solve this, successive generations of Ottoman bureaucrats implemented reforms to fix horse shortages and to prevent communication lags.

These attempts at fixing chronic breakdowns show what the thickening of
imperial governance looked like in concrete terms. First, imperial authorities enhanced their monitoring *capacity* of local postal operations. They did this by
setting up a new bureau dedicated to postal affairs, expanding the job scope of
postmasters to include administrative duties, and developing new accounting
routines and quantification methods. Second, imperial authorities increased the
weight or impact of their intervention in the provinces. They did this by recruiting more common subjects to participate in local postal operations. Third, authorities extended the territorial *reach* of their policies and, more literally, of their
imperial couriers. They did this by reducing the friction of horse procurement
at relay stations so that couriers could smoothly deliver messages to the limits of
Ottoman territories and then return. These three dimensions of capacity, weight,
and reach have been used to measure state infrastructural power, defined by the
sociologist Michael Mann as the capacity of the state to penetrate its territories
and logistically implement decisions. Here I use them to capture three aspects
of thickening governance, which shares conceptual affinities with Mann's notion
of infrastructural power.[14]

The outcomes of these reforms were striking. During the sixteenth century,
bureaucrats in the imperial capital could not see the different stages of couriers'

journeys and their mail delivery processes. In contrast, during the eighteenth century, these same bureaucrats had regular and meticulous records of every single post station in the empire, as well as of the identities of every single official who visited each post station, how many horses he took, and when he took them. At the other end of the social hierarchy, sixteenth-century common subjects could expect to have their horses confiscated by couriers while traveling—these violent seizures were legal and were the dominant mode of horse procurement for couriers. During the eighteenth century, violent seizures were no longer the norm of horse procurement. Instead, they had been transmuted into mundane bureaucratic procedures—couriers now exchanged tired horses for energetic ones at fixed post stations by showing their papers to local postmasters for authentication. On their part, common subjects (the villagers) maintained these post stations as their tax obligations; they signed collective contracts with imperial authorities, stood as sureties for each other, and complained about the unreasonable behavior of couriers via petitions. And then, in 1840, another transmutation took place—these common subjects transformed into customers of a public postal service where, for a fee, official couriers would deliver their mail for them.

As a common, pan-imperial denominator, the postal system as infrastructure allows a tight focus on a lean institution that crisscrossed the uneven terrain of geography, threaded through the social hierarchy, and survived the vicissitudes of time. By tracking the developing capacity, reach, and weight of Ottoman postal administration, *The Sublime Post* elucidates the expansion of governance through delegation, thereby offering a new account of Ottoman state formation and its social order (fig. 1).

Envisioning the Ottoman Empire as a coherent unit is challenging due to the profound legacies of its collapse at the end of the First World War. The Ottomans began as a small frontier principality in northwestern Anatolia sometime in the fourteenth century. With the conquest of Constantinople in 1453 and the absorption of Egypt and Syria in 1517, the Ottomans created a transregional empire that was heir to Turco-Mongol, Islamic, and Roman-Byzantine imperial legacies. In the twentieth century, the empire unraveled dramatically, and a social order that had endured for centuries completely collapsed. Presently, the empire's more than thirty-five successor states and their cities, from Kosovo to Kurdistan, are more likely to evoke images of genocide, civil war, and destruction than any memory of a united empire that had ruled for six hundred years.[15] The breakup of the Ottoman Balkans into smaller polities fiercely antagonistic to one

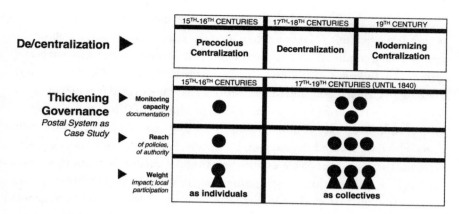

De/centralization ▶	15TH-16TH CENTURIES	17TH-18TH CENTURIES	19TH CENTURY
	Precocious Centralization	**Decentralization**	**Modernizing Centralization**

Thickening Governance *Postal System as Case Study*		15TH-16TH CENTURIES	17TH-19TH CENTURIES (UNTIL 1840)
▶	Monitoring capacity *documentation*	●	●● ●
▶	Reach *of policies, of authority*	●	●●●
▶	Weight *impact; local participation*	♟ **as individuals**	♟♟♟ **as collectives**

Figure 1. Two approaches to Ottoman state formation: de/centralization and thickening governance. Chart by author; refined by Mitchell Tan Wei Liang.

another was so novel a phenomenon that the term "balkanization" was coined to name it.[16] This term has since entered the general lexicon and has been used to describe contexts as varied as cloud computing technology and U.S. political parties.[17] Lamentably, the balkanization of Ottoman lands reproduced the balkanization of its histories, entrenching historiographical views of a hopelessly decentralized and fragmented empire.[18]

Historically, however, the Ottoman Empire was not balkanized. It was a coherent imperial unit linked by its polyglot culture and diversity of faiths, by the continuous movements of administrators and animals, by the regular exchange of luxury goods and grain, by the establishing, maintaining, and extending of basic infrastructure such as roads, bridges, mountain passes, and post stations. Imperial coherence did not mean constant peace and unwavering stability; rebellions were common across its history, just as they were in the contemporaneous Qing and Mughal Empires—and in eighteenth-century France, where a revolution toppled the king and the entire social order of the ancien régime along with him.[19] Undergirding these centuries-long patterns of exchange and circulation, of uprisings and suppression, were the living traditions of Islam in the Ottoman lands. Whether subjects were Jewish, Christian, or Muslim, there was a place for them in the empire, which recognized them legally, fiscally, politically, and socially, even if unequally and inconsistently. Ottoman Islam, as it was lived and practiced, was at once a common baseline and a changing constellation of vernacular cultural codes, laws, and beliefs.[20]

As an object of historical study, the vast size of the Ottoman Empire has led pioneering generations of scholars to undertake smaller studies at the scale of the province, city, community, or neighborhood. Scholarship on the Ottoman postal system has followed this trend. Colin Heywood, Cengiz Orhonlu, Yusuf Halaçoğlu, Cemal Çetin, and other historians have uncovered precious archival documents pertaining to the postal system, producing detailed studies of a single post station or a set of post stations over a long period of time.[21] Like their peers who have studied the Roman, Byzantine, Ayyubid, and Mamluk postal systems, these pioneers have established foundational information, such as locating the relay stations, aggregating their findings into valuable lists, and constructing the first modern maps of such systems.[22] Their painstaking scholarship has greatly facilitated the work of the present generation of researchers, allowing us to attempt a synthesis, to understand the postal relay system as system, in order to achieve a view of the empire as one unit.

The history of the Ottoman postal system cannot be understood apart from the history of the Ottoman Empire writ large. In particular, it was during a period known as the Second Ottoman Empire (ca. 1600–1800) that a profusion of fiscal registers and documents began to be produced about the Ottoman postal system. According to the historian Baki Tezcan, the Second Ottoman Empire emerged when the Ottoman ruling elite (including the vizier and provincial elite households) had consolidated power at the expense of the royal dynasty (the House of Osman). The struggle was violent and costly for the losing side: the royal dynasty suffered one regicide and six dethronements out of nine sultans between 1603 and 1703.[23] As elite power structures were reconfigured, many aspects of Ottoman administration, too, underwent significant changes.

Two new trends characterize these manifold changes brought about by the Second Ottoman Empire, which went beyond the imperial administration and affected all levels of society: an opening up and an enclosing. The empire opened up socially, culturally, aesthetically, architecturally (the historian Shirine Hamadeh refers to this trend as *décloisonnement*).[24] The imperial capital was awash with imports, trends, and fashions from abroad, including from the New World. Tomatoes, artichokes, and cauliflowers appeared in the Ottoman diet; European architectural styles were selectively incorporated in the design of sultanic mosques, producing an "Ottoman Baroque"; new paintings were imported from India and Iran, and floral-patterned textiles from eastern lands furnished Ottoman homes and became Ottoman clothes.[25]

Across the empire, formerly exclusive elite spaces expanded to include newcomers. Barbers and "middle class" persons engaged in literary production; newly consolidated communities such as the Greek Orthodox in the Balkans and the 'Alawis of Syria participated in Ottoman governance; and new groups of traders, forwarding agents, muleteers, and medium-distance merchants participated in commerce as older trading routes faded and yielded to new ones.[26] Urban space came to host a new kind of sociability in major cities such as Istanbul and Damascus as rural migration proceeded apace. Men and women smoked tobacco openly in gardens and coffeehouses, along the rivers, and in the streets, even during the fasting month of Ramadan.[27] Poetry leapt out of two-dimensional pages and came to be inscribed in stone and marble, dotting the urban landscape.[28]

These shifting boundaries produced material consequences. In sixteenth-century Istanbul, only the royal family, grand viziers, and grand admirals endowed buildings. Two hundred years later, the pool of patrons had expanded to include bureaucrats, lower-ranked aghas, and even craftsmen who sponsored mosques, libraries, and fountains—hundreds of the fountains were established across the capital. This urban revival has been described as the "second conquest" of Constantinople, three centuries after Mehmed II's triumph in 1453.[29] A similar mushrooming of construction may be found elsewhere in the empire: in seventeenth-century Aleppo, monumental buildings concentrated in the urban center from an earlier era gave way to the establishment of smaller neighborhood mosques and dervish lodges that spread throughout the city.[30] Libraries, previously clustered within a few big cities, began to be established in a wider range of Ottoman provinces.[31]

The second important trend of this era was an enclosing: historians have described this variously as corporatism, group formation, or communalization.[32] As urban and social spaces were opening up, corporate groups were also coalescing all along the power hierarchy. These groups included professional associations organized along occupational lines and rank (drummers, druggists, money-changers, sardine-sellers, butchers, bakers), associations along lines of identity (blind men, emancipated slaves), and religious groups, as well as whole villages and individual neighborhoods.[33] At the upper end of the social hierarchy, new powerful groups emerged, ranging from pasha-led dynasties (such as those of Ali of Ioannina and Mehmed Ali of Egypt) and provincial households (the Karaosmanoğlus and the Çapanoğlus of Anatolia, the 'Azms of Damascus) to smaller-scale valley lords (*derebeys*) and landowning clans.[34]

The behavior of these corporate groups varied depending on the kind of power they had. Powerful dynasties and households created a "new order of notables" who were "servicers" and contractors of the empire, rather than its "servants."[35] From Albania to Anatolia, from Bosnia to Baghdad, each region produced its own local strongmen who differed from their predecessors by their successful insinuation into governance structures, making them legitimate "partners of empire."[36] Less powerful corporations and groups undertook collective oaths and public vows and established neighborhood endowments at village levels to meet collective expenses and tax obligations. Urban guilds created ways to regulate membership, including licenses to practice a craft (*gedik*).[37] To regulate immigration into Istanbul, the government imposed guarantorship (*kefâlet*) duties on neighborhood communities, which facilitated the integration of newcomers but also consolidated group identities.[38] As corporate groups congealed, social differentiation among them increased and acquired more diverse stakes, creating more contentious publics.[39]

As more and more taxpaying subjects participated in the local work of delegated governance, this experience engendered new expectations of subjects' relationship with imperial authorities, prefiguring the local councils of the Tanzimat era as well as the shift from an exclusive government postal system to a public postal service. In other words, the Tanzimat era of reform, so often presented as a westernizing, modernizing rupture from the preceding period, may also be seen as simply a new phase in the development of thickening governance in the Ottoman Empire.

The story here begins before the Second Empire, starting in Chapter 1 with a historical overview of the ad hoc postal system where imperial couriers were empowered to snatch horses from subjects whom they encountered on the road. During the late sixteenth century, this arrangement of arbitrary confiscations transitioned to become a system of fixed post stations where, in principle, couriers would exchange horses for fresh ones. Chapter 1 shows that the way the Ottoman postal system operated depended intimately on factors unique to the Ottoman geography and its social order. Select examples from other relay communications systems, including the Mongol, Russian, Roman, and Chinese systems, illustrate the variations in how the same technology could be implemented, as well as the common challenges faced by pre-industrial empires.

In Chapter 2 I undertake an "infrastructural inversion" approach to foreground the usually hidden background role of the Ottoman courier in the work of imperial governance during the seventeenth century. Combining a rare, first-person account of an Ottoman courier together with reticent archival records, I show that life on the road meant that the courier often faced dangers from bandits, mercenaries, and rebellious peasants, that he sometimes forged alliances with political rebels and even provided them with cover. The courier played a critical role in moving paper around the empire and enabling the everyday work of administration.

Although couriers held different ranks and titles in the seventeenth century, their jobs became more institutionalized by the eighteenth century when they came under the authority and organization of the Tatar Corps. Chapter 3 continues the exploration of the courier as tatar, extending the discussion chronologically into the Second Empire. The institutionalization of the couriers took several forms. Tatars now had to wear special uniforms; many of the oral messages they conveyed informally were now documented in formal tatar reports; their deaths on the job now meant that financial compensation could go to their surviving family members. All this contributed to the profusion of written records and the coalescing of the tatar couriers into an identifiable group.

The argument of expanding monitoring capacity, weight, and reach is developed in the next three chapters. Chapter 4 introduces two imperial decrees issued in 1696 to fix the problem of rising costs and insufficient horses at stations. However, these decrees did not achieve their goals. A close reading reveals the gap between the bureaucracy's aspirations and their lack of knowledge about the system's realities on the ground. Nevertheless, these two decrees left behind an important legacy: they set in motion new documentary routines and quantification practices that endured over the next century.

In Chapter 5 I examine the bookkeeper and his authorship of one of these new fiscal registers, the Comprehensive Post Station Register. Bookkeepers initially had very little knowledge about how the postal system worked, lacking even basic information about the locations of post stations and the cost of a horseshoe. Over the eighteenth century, bookkeepers had to learn on the job and establish the workflows for the new realm of postal administration.

Bookkeepers could not compile these fiscal registers on their own. Instead, they relied on hundreds of postmasters across the empire to provide information at regular intervals. In Chapter 6 I look at the role of local postmasters in contributing to this documentary profusion. During the Second Empire, postmasters began to be recruited from among common subjects, who were newly able to enter the previously exclusive space of Ottoman officialdom. It was they who produced many of these documents that make up the official archive. By reverse engineering the circuits of fiscal administration, the chapter tracks the information recorded at the local post station by the postmaster and follows it on its journey through various fiscal registers into the heart of the bureaucracy in the imperial capital.

The increased weight of imperial intervention in local spheres is seen most clearly in how villagers were recruited to do governance work during the Second Empire. Chapter 7 surveys the range of new mechanisms used in collective organization, such as multiparty round-robin petitions, collective oaths and contracts, and a new kind of collective liability mechanism that I call nested suretyships. These experiences of local participation in the work of horse provision and post station maintenance facilitated the territorial reach of the state. At the same time, they engendered among villagers the ability and desire to shape imperial agendas. Sometimes villagers organized to defend their interests against a neighboring village; at other times, they allied with neighboring villages to jointly petition imperial authorities to protect shared interests. Here, too, I reflect on the limitations of archival sources and hypothesize that a large part of village-level collaboration and organizational work eluded the written record. Historical examples of how communities beyond the Ottoman Empire used common resources collectively and sustainably bolster this hypothesis.

Thickening governance over time did not mean omnipotent governance. The postal system did break down from time to time. But thickening governance enabled imperial authorities to engage in the repair and maintenance work needed to address breakdowns in more tenacious and dogged ways than would have otherwise been possible. In Chapter 8 I examine two kinds of breakdown that disrupted postal operations—lack of coin and lack of horses—and how authorities addressed them. Breakdowns offer windows onto aspects of the past that are not usually documented. This was the case with the lack of coin: a liquidity crunch forced bureaucrats to describe the postal payments system, which had not been explained previously, in order to reform it. These descriptions provide rare insights into a monetary history that is almost never commented upon and that is taken for granted in other, more routine bureaucratic documents.

Breakdown and its partner, repair, are also mundane maintenance processes by which systems learn, adapt, and grow.[40] This was the case with the lack of horses. Although imperial monitoring capacity had expanded over the course of the eighteenth century, bureaucrats were plagued by chronic reports of inexplicably missing horses. Bureaucrats' evolving policies exhibited their responsiveness to problems on the ground, but structural blind spots prevented them from conclusively solving the problem of missing horses. Drawing parallels with the contemporary Qing bureaucracy, which also faced problems in synthesizing large volumes of incoming information, I argue that the Ottoman bureaucracy struggled to translate the increased information it received into meaningful knowledge. This prevented bureaucrats from perceiving that the problem of missing horses was not about individual infractions by disobedient officials. Rather, if viewed collectively, these individual infractions reflected a connected economic landscape where a strong market demand for post horses systematically diverted them from government work toward profit-making ventures.

In 1840, the Ottoman postal system that once had been an exclusive government service became a public, pay-per-use postal service nominally open to all, regardless of status or rank. In the concluding chapter, I bring together the arguments developed in all the preceding chapters to show that underpinning this transformation of the postal system was a fundamental change in the common subjects' relationship with imperial authorities. The nineteenth-century Ottoman subject was not the same as the eighteenth-century Ottoman subject; through generations of experience in local governance, nineteenth-century subjects developed different expectations of how they should be governed. External factors played an important role too. By the nineteenth century, the Ottomans had suffered costly military defeats, been forced to sign humiliating treaties, and could no longer set the terms of their relationship with European powers from a position of strength, as in the past. The Ottomans began to adopt and adapt European models and institutions with more openness and urgency, notably with respect to education and the military. Such external dynamics likely played a role in influencing the official decision to make the Ottoman postal system a public service: major European postal systems had long served common subjects who were able to post personal letters, and Ottoman officials traveling in Europe had observed such postal services in action and written about them.[41]

Three centuries ago, it took eleven days for a horse rider to send a message from Aleppo to Istanbul, and another seven days for a rider to go from Istanbul to Belgrade. Today, the distance has been alchemized into a click. The average person rarely experiences the friction of distance in their everyday communications. Enabling this user experience of seamless communications is a densely industrial, resource-intensive material infrastructure that has been tucked out of sight and rebranded in disembodied, ethereal terms like "cloud," "cyberspace," or "metaverse."[42] Put differently, the friction of distance has not disappeared; it has merely transmogrified into other kinds of cost to be borne by the environment and those less fortunate.[43] Instead of horse power, computing power; instead of highway bandits and murdered couriers, computer hackers and phishing attacks; instead of horses and provisions, thousands of gallons of fresh water, fossil fuels, and rare earth metals.[44]

This book reaches across the yawning gap separating the pre-industrial world from the post-industrial present. It reconstructs the friction of distance and the organizational solutions that humans had once collectively undertaken to make long-distance communication possible. To this end, this history of empire through the aperture of infrastructure outlines a mode of thinking in systems, of the actors the systems contain, and of the responsibilities each link owes the other. Some have suggested that the locus of imaginable futures is intimately dependent on the kinds of histories we allow into our frame of analysis. By bearing witness to how the sprawling, Ottoman postal system worked for centuries, this book participates in that act of collective imagination.[45]

CHAPTER I

The Ottoman Postal System

In 1920, London had more than fifty small power plants distributed across the city, while Berlin had only six large power plants. The historian of technology Thomas P. Hughes used this contrast to exemplify the idea of variation in technological style. In his telling, this variation had nothing to do with the quantitative output of power generated but instead had everything to do with the way power was generated, transmitted, and distributed. And this, in turn, was due to the different political values that underpinned different regulatory legislation in both cities: while the City of Berlin was the principal regulatory authority of light and power, that same regulatory authority was delegated to multiple municipal boroughs at the sub-city level in London.[1]

The kind of observation made about Berlin, London, and their power plants has rarely been made about large technological systems in the pre-industrial world.[2] But a closer look shows that, like electrical infrastructure, relay communications systems across world history also varied in technological style. For instance, while the Ottomans used horse-mounted couriers, others (like the Tibetans, Swedish, and Incas) used human runners, and still others (like the Tassis dynasty of the Imperial and Spanish Postmaster Generals) alternated among cart, mule, ferry, and foot.[3] And while the Ottomans issued paper permits to travelers who wished to use relay stations, the Mongols issued tablets of authority made from wood or precious metals like iron, silver, and gold.[4] Deeper insights about variation in social or political organization have yet to be gleaned from stylistic variations in relay communications systems.

In this chapter I make a modest attempt in this direction by asking: What can Ottoman postal operations tell us about its society's politics and values? Furthermore, what can a change in the mode of horse procurement (from arbitrary confiscations to a heavily documented system of fixed post stations) tell us about the changing nature of imperial authority in the Ottoman Empire?

The Ottoman postal system began without any fixed post stations. Couriers simply seized horses from commoners, whether they were traveling merchants or peasants tending to their fields. Sometimes couriers swiped extra horses just in case of the accidental injury or death of a horse. Such violent confiscations had the blessings of imperial authority, for couriers were empowered by courier orders: pieces of paper issued in the name of the sultan.[5] Some orders were as brief as a line. Others were lengthier, stipulating both the origin and destination of the courier's journey and even the number of men in his retinue to ensure that only a suitable number of horses and guides was procured.[6] The oldest known courier order dates to 1482, during Bayezid II's reign (1481–1512).[7]

Sometimes couriers did not need to confiscate horses themselves. Local officials would seize horses for them. In certain provinces, officials maintained a stable of horses for circulating couriers and supervised informal arrangements to return confiscated horses to their original owners.[8] However, such arrangements did not always succeed despite the best of intentions. A sixteenth-century police superintendent from Baghdad complained that he had obtained 850 horses for courier usage, but none of the couriers brought them back.[9] This lamentation suggests that, in some quarters at least, there was a prevailing expectation that requisitioned horses should be returned.

In principle, there were laws governing how, where, and what kinds of horses could be confiscated, and from whom. Sultanic law codes (ḳānūnnāme) stipulated that couriers could only confiscate horses that were of medium value and not costing more than a certain price.[10] Moreover, couriers were not allowed to confiscate horses just anywhere they pleased. For instance, mountain passes were a special zone where no confiscations were allowed because the owners of horses would be left without transportation and be vulnerable to bandits. Nor were couriers allowed to accept bribes in return for not confiscating horses.[11] They could not confiscate horses from certain imperial subjects who held special legal statuses, such as Eastern Orthodox priests holding the rank of metropolitan and members of non-Muslim mining communities in the Balkans.[12]

Certain villages enjoyed immunity from horse confiscations because of their founding constitutions; in the late fourteenth century, Ottoman princes and sultans awarded these privileges as an incentive to populate newly conquered lands.[13] Though such laws were numerous, it is not clear how familiar couriers would have been with them.

In 1539–1541, fixed post stations were established along the roads where couriers could exchange horses for new ones. Lütfi Pasha, the grand vizier during this period, claimed to have implemented this new system to alleviate the burdens placed on commoners.[14] Instead of accosting the unwitting traveler or the villager, the courier would now be served by post station personnel at fixed locations.

Unsurprisingly, neither these laws nor Lütfi Pasha's policy of fixed post stations appears to have been consistently honored. Writing in the late sixteenth century, the bureaucrat and chronicler Mustafa Ali kept a record of badly behaved officials. In his accounts, we find Ottoman officials appropriating high-quality brood mares in the Arab provinces and bringing them to Anatolia for breeding, ignoring the injunction that prevented the confiscation of valuable horses. Couriers also snatched horses from travelers in dangerous mountain passes. If a traveler protested, these couriers would "beat him rudely, tie him up, and leave him on the road." Even if couriers had enough horses, they might extort several gold pieces from travelers. Finally, in every town where couriers passed through, they would, "solely in order to insult the 'ulema and to pester the judge," give them a good clubbing while demanding horses from them.[15]

If Mustafa Ali is to be believed, couriers were a rather malicious bunch of bullies.[16] Some contemporaries corroborated his views, suggesting that, at the very least, the malice of couriers appears to have been a common literary trope. Another sixteenth-century chronicler, Qutb al-Din al-Nahrawali, described routes full of couriers who would assault a traveler, snatch his horse, ride it until it expired, and then abandon it while confiscating another traveler's horse.[17] Faqiri, a sixteenth-century poet, lamented the bad luck of anyone who happened to run into a courier.[18] In addition to existing courier traffic emanating from the imperial capital, provincial governors reportedly dispatched more and more of their own men as couriers over the sixteenth century, thereby licensing the practice of arbitrary requisitions on a broader scale.

Ottoman sharia court records also show that confiscations continued to occur even after fixed post stations were nominally established. In the 1590s, half a century after Lütfi Pasha's tenure as grand vizier, villagers appeared before their local postmasters to claim confiscated horses that were later returned to the postmasters. In these cases, villagers had to demonstrate knowledge of their horses' identifying marks to the postmasters in order to make a successful claim. The court records of Üsküdar show, for instance, that "a white stallion with a shortened tail" and a "red stallion with a patch on its forehead" were successfully returned to their owners.[19]

In fact, arbitrary confiscations never completely ceased as a mode of horse procurement. Nineteenth-century British adventurers who traveled with couriers remarked on the violence with which couriers descended upon villages to seize horses and other resources. Sometimes these British travelers also participated alongside couriers, forming an augmented band of invaders.[20] However, confiscation did cease to be the dominant mode of horse procurement in the late seventeenth century, during the Second Empire. By that time, records show that couriers regularly obtained their horses at fixed post stations.

But, why did confiscations work in the first place? How should routine, violent confiscations of horses be understood? The usual answer is corruption. Allegations of corruption are not only found in contemporary chronicles (cited on previous pages) but are also a formidable and hardy trope in the modern historiography of the Ottoman Empire.[21] However, this answer is wrong and misses fundamental aspects of Ottoman society and the pre-industrial world more generally.

In the first place, arbitrary and violent confiscations, forced labor, onerous obligations, and other abuses in the service of long-distance government communications were common beyond the Ottoman context. Examples abound from the Mongol Empire, Timurid central Asia, Imperial Russia, and nineteenth-century Nepal.[22] By definition, a relay communications infrastructure was sustained by, and depended on, exploitation—or at least what would be considered exploitation using the standards of today. Officials serving in the Ottoman or Mongol, Timurid or Russian Empires were entitled to the resources and labor of common subjects, especially when carrying out government duties.

The reason for this entitlement is that inequality was a default condition of pre-industrial society. Social order was underpinned by a status hierarchy. One's position in the status hierarchy determined legal privileges, economic rights, and occupational possibilities and structured the pre-industrial "labor market." Thus, "a woman in fifteenth-century Florence was permitted neither to inherit nor bequeath her dowry . . . a Muslim captive in seventeenth-century Valencia was not entitled to payment for his or her work, and a Jewish man in eighteenth-century Metz could not join a craft guild."[23] In the Ottoman Empire, a "multilayered system" of enslavement comprised varieties of "free" and "unfree" labor. Galley slaves (*forṣa*), a sultan's servitors (*kul*), serfs, sharecroppers, and contract farmers were involved in different kinds of relations of production and received different types of compensation, if at all. Such unequal labor practices, rights to compensation, and life possibilities were the norm beyond Ottoman lands as well.[24]

The status hierarchy also pervaded language and culture at all levels of society. One's rank determined the words you could utter. In languages such as Persian and Japanese, specific sets of verbs were assigned to speakers according to their relative rank and station. Status informed royal protocols, determining the seating plan at a royal banquet and the standing plan at an imperial ceremony. Courtiers, scribes, and eunuchs served as repositories of such politically sensitive knowledge. Status underpinned the hierarchical position of sovereign polities in the premodern interstate order, whether within a Westphalian system or beyond in "universalist" empires such as the Ottoman, Safavid, and Qing.[25]

As a general rule, Ottoman society was traditionally divided into two groups: the elite, tax-exempt *'askerī*, who comprised the military, administrative, and religious ruling class, and the common, tax-paying subjects (*re'āyā*), who included traders, craftworkers, and peasants. Certain groups of *re'āyā* formed a third, intermediary group that received privileges and exemptions in return for providing special services; the previously mentioned mining communities in the Balkans who received exemptions from courier requisitions are examples of this third group. As in many pre-industrial societies, every individual was expected to remain within a social group and to marry, live, and work among their own in order to uphold the social order. And yet, as elsewhere around the world, marriages and partnerships across groups did nevertheless occur.

Over time, this two- or three-part social order became more elaborate. From the late fifteenth century, common tax-paying subjects found ways to achieve the status of the tax-exempt (*'askerī*). Tax-exempt elites, too, became increasingly involved in trade and commerce, which were once the realm of commoners.[26] These trends intensified during the Second Ottoman Empire, which also witnessed a more dynamic differentiation of status hierarchy.

It is in this context of a status-based and status-conscious Ottoman social order that the custom of couriers snatching horses from common subjects has to be understood. As Ottoman officials, couriers were entitled to the resources of common subjects. Conversely, common subjects were obligated to surrender their horses for imperial use. The crucial point is this: chroniclers may have clutched at their pearls and decried such abuse, but they profited from this unequal social order—not unlike many in our day who enjoy same-day delivery services but feel bad about underpaid labor. Corruption does not explain routine violent confiscations of horses by couriers; status does.[27]

Agency was still possible in such a hierarchical world. Thus, a beautiful slave who met a willing patron could become a freewoman or even a queen. A marginalized community could negotiate its standing within a kingdom by providing a rare, but necessary, service. A frontier vassal state could go to war to change its standing in the regional order.

In the Ottoman Empire, common subjects could resist arbitrary confiscations from couriers and government officials. What common subjects felt entitled to was not equality but a sense of justice according to their status.[28] When justice was not forthcoming, common subjects had the option to run away. During the seventeenth century, the subjects of the village of Sviloš in the district of Ilok (in the border region between modern Croatia and Serbia) fled their village when officials took away their food, including honey, and imposed too many services. The fact that the village was alongside a public road facilitated their escape. Similarly, the villagers of Komluš in the same district of Ilok threatened to flee should officials continue taking their food, wagons, money, and sheep.[29] These are examples of how a modicum of agency could be exercised by the least powerful members of a hierarchical premodern society.

The status hierarchy could also change. This was what happened when the Ottoman postal system changed its mode of horse procurement from arbitrary confiscations to a fixed post station system. Common subjects transformed from passive owners of a coveted resource (the horse) to local agents whose help and participation were needed to maintain and operate an extensive logistical network (the relay infrastructure). In this way, many common subjects attained the status of provincial official, thereby moving up the status hierarchy.

Imperial authority, too, changed with this new mode of horse procurement. At first, it was a privilege bestowed upon individual couriers, empowering them to confiscate horses from passersby. With the transition to a fixed post station system, imperial authority became quasi-institutionalized. It was delegated to the local postmasters and villagers who helped with postal operations. The physical space of post stations, too, became akin to little bastions of imperial power that dotted all across the landscape.

The idea that relay stations were loci of imperial power was not uniquely Ottoman but a feature of early modern empires. In the fourteenth century, the Goryeo king ordered an attack on eight Mongol (Yuan) relay stations as a way of attacking Chinggisid rule.[30] A few decades later, the Ming emperor Hongwu took offense with a Korean ambassador and denied him access to Ming relay stations; the ambassador was forced to walk all the way back to Korea from the imperial capital, Nanjing.[31] In both cases, relay stations, including the right of accessing relay stations, were proxy sites of imperial power, to be bestowed and withdrawn at the sovereign's pleasure.

In the Ottoman Empire, the sultan and his proxies reserved the right to issue travel documents (*menzil / ulak / yol hükmü*) for those wishing to use imperial relay stations. Courier orders were issued only to official messengers delivering government correspondence; other kinds of travelers could obtain normal travel passes.[32] Foreign couriers delivering mail in Ottoman lands received passes allowing them to use relay stations; the same courtesy was paid to Ottoman couriers delivering mail in other empires.[33]

However, the vastness of Ottoman territories meant that, at times, sovereign power over the imperial landscape was uneven and dependent on specific local agents. In 1738, the governor (*hospodar*) of Moldavia told a traveler that he unfortunately did not have the authority to allow him to journey to Constantinople; the traveler would have to go to Bender (in modern Moldova) to seek permission from the chief military commander there.[34] Mirza Abu Taleb Khan, a Lucknow-born traveler, faced a similar challenge of patchwork sovereignty. In 1802, he received three separate imperial orders ("*firmauns*") as he journeyed from Istanbul to Iraq. The first imperial order was a general one addressed to all pashas, governors, and commanders; the second imperial order was addressed specifically to the governor of Mardin to arrange cavalry escorts for the route between Mardin and Mosul; and the third imperial order was directed to the viceroy of Baghdad to oversee the traveler's pilgrimage from Baghdad to Kerbala and Bussorah.[35] In other words, a single imperial order did not suffice; rather, imperial authorities were cognizant that separate, targeted imperial orders to specific officials in different locations were necessary.

In some cases, letters of recommendation from local strongmen were more effective than imperial orders from the capital. In the 1810s, an officer in the East India Company, Sir John MacDonald Kinneir, purchased a travel pass from the Sublime Porte that allowed him to procure horses during his journey.[36] While in Central Anatolia, however, Sir Kinneir also obtained letters of recommendation from the local powerholder, Süleyman Bey (leader of the Çapanoğlu dynasty), to help him procure horses in the region, for Süleyman Bey had more sway in Central Anatolia than did the distant Ottoman sultan.[37] A similar dynamic occurred with other European travelers in the Greek and Albanian regions. Here, the imperial order was "little respected."[38] Instead, a writ from the local powerholder, Tepedelenli Ali Pasha, held more sway than one from the Ottoman sultan.

In an exceptional case, Mehmed Ali Pasha, the governor of Egypt, established his own overland relay network in Syria. This was during the Egyptian invasion and occupation of the province from 1831 to 1840 that had threatened the Ottoman throne and the integrity of the empire. This network included almost seventy post stations (Ar. pl. *maḥaṭṭāt al-barīd*) that were separate from the Ottoman postal network. It offered the Egyptians an important alternative to sea communications, which were seen as less secure due to the presence of patrolling Ottoman and British fleets.[39]

In a pre-industrial age, postal networks and individual relay stations were sites of political power. Access to a particular station required permission from the relevant authority. In specific regions of the Ottoman lands, the permission of local powerholders may have been more effective than the sultan's authority. This corresponds to scholarly observations that the geography of imperial power was not at all like the "monochrome shading of imperial maps."[40] Depending on the relationship of a particular province to the larger empire at a particular point in time, travelers had to seek permission from different authorities to access post stations.

In the Ottoman Empire, relay stations were located along the six main routes of the road network, three of which radiated outward from Edirne into Rumelia (the Balkan Peninsula) and another three from Istanbul toward Anatolia. They were called the left, middle, or right (*sol, orta, sağ*) arm (*kol*). These "axes of movement" structured "entire mental maps of the Ottoman Empire."[41]

Ottoman administrative and accounting practices adhered to this tripartite spatial order. For instance, pastoral tribes like the Bozok had sub-groups that were referred to as the "right and left wing tribes" according to where these sub-groups dwelled.[42] The fiscal records of Istanbul's meat provisioning system, too, used the same geographical logic. Bookkeepers calculated the number of sheep extracted from the provinces according to the specific route on which these sheep traveled to reach the capital—the left, middle, or right arm. Thus, there were 233,460 sheep that arrived via the right arm of Europe for the years 1580–1583 but only 208,621 that arrived via the left arm.[43] The postal system was fiscally administered in this same way, where annual expenditures were calculated according to each of six main arms of the Ottoman road network. These right, middle, and left axes structured not just movement and space but also the Ottoman fiscal order and bookkeeping practices.

There were three main patterns of post station establishment: imperial initiative, gradual settlement over time, and bottom-up initiative. An example of

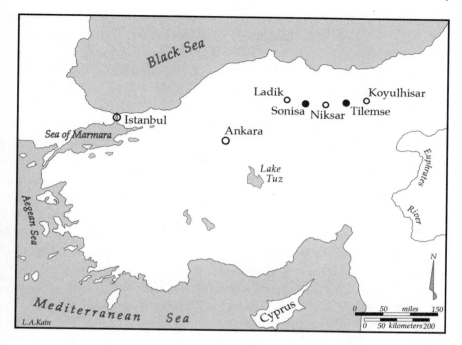

Figure 2. The establishment of post stations at Sonisa and Tilemse, 1724.

the first pattern dates to the sixteenth century, when the chief royal architect, Sinan, oversaw the establishment of relay stations that provided running water, a bazaar, a mosque, and bathhouses for travelers, with many clustering along the Istanbul-Edirne route. He supervised teams who repaved the roads, repaired bridges, and built new mosque complexes between these halting stations, which were spaced a day's journey apart for the regions closer to the capital.[44] All this construction, together with land grants and tax incentives, spurred the growth of settlements along these routes, which, in turn, enhanced road security.[45] Another example of imperial initiative was the establishment of post stations at Sonisa and Tilemse in 1724, done in order to decrease the travel time for horses moving through Ladik, Niksar, and Koyulhisar (fig. 2).[46] This was undertaken during the war with Iran, when courier traffic increased tremendously and caused horse fatigue and deaths. Intermediate stations at Sonisa and Tilemse were aimed at stemming horse losses.

Gradual settlement of new regions also encouraged new routes and stations to form. For instance, monasteries that were established in the Pindus Mountains spurred the establishment of mountain passes and villages. These were followed

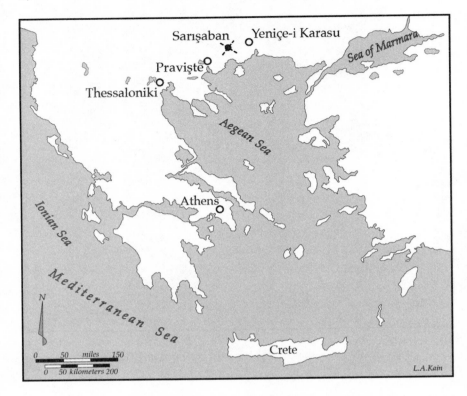

Figure 3. The abolishment of the Sarışaban post station, 1741.

by bridges and post stations, which facilitated movement in the region that now covers northern Greece and southern Albania.[47]

Bottom-up initiatives, such as a village's petition, could establish new stations that cut the traveling distance between two existing ones.[48] They could also ensure the failure of a post station. For instance, sometimes the villagers responsible for operating a station simply refused to obey imperial orders, rendering imperial bureaucrats no choice but to abolish it—this was the case in Sarışaban (Chrysoupoli, Greece) in 1741 (fig. 3).[49]

Other reasons could account for the relocation or abolishment of post stations. Sometimes urban overcrowding forced authorities to relocate post stations to less dense neighborhoods.[50] Sometimes natural disasters could permanently destroy the landscape, rendering villages and their associated post stations uninhabitable.[51]

The frontispiece to this book gives an overview of Ottoman post stations and their changing locations across time. The solid dots represent all the post stations recorded in thirteen fiscal registers across several decades in the eighteenth century; the empty dots represent post stations recorded in one fiscal register from the 1690s; the dots with a dot inside represent the overlap, indicating that these were the post stations that appear to have endured through time.[52] With developments in architectural history and archaeology, a more temporally and geographically precise dataset of Ottoman post stations may be obtained in the future.[53]

While the specific locations of relay stations could change, routes tended to enjoy a greater longevity. The Orient Express, on which Agatha Christie traveled and which provided the setting for *Murder on the Orient Express*, plied the old postal route connecting Constantinople to Belgrade. The trip took twenty-four hours by train but seven days for a swift, horse-borne courier.[54] Further back in time, after the collapse of the Neo-Assyrian Empire in the seventh century BCE, its road system survived and passed into the hands of the Neo-Babylonians (612–539 BCE), who developed it further.[55] Sections of the Persian Royal Road network were paved by the Romans, and Roman routes such as the Via Egnatia and the Via Militaris, as well as the Trabzon-Bayezid road, later became integrated into the Ottoman road network.[56]

One reason for the enduring nature of these ancient "desire paths" was that using them entailed lower costs for governments.[57] Instead of constructing completely new routes, which would have included leveling paths and clearing them of boulders and other obstructions, governments needed only to improve upon existing routes. Built infrastructure such as bridges, guardhouses, and mile markers also encouraged "path dependency." Moreover, word-of-mouth and hand-me-down knowledge meant that the routes, passes, and fords used by travelers, merchants, and caravans became standard over time, which, in turn, helped long-distance travel become more predictable.[58]

The Ottoman postal system was amphibious and included sea routes. The Istanbul-Cairo route was one important example. Routine courier communication typically used the overland route that reportedly took 450 hours (a little over seven days' time).[59] The conveyance of the treasury from Egypt could take place by land.[60] The sea route between Istanbul and Egypt was usually used for the shipping of heavy resources like wheat and for travel by state dignitaries. Communications between Egypt and the Hijaz, just like communications with Ottoman islands, were typically made by sea.[61] By the nineteenth century, sea navigation technologies had advanced significantly; the powerful provincial dynast of Egypt Mehmed Ali Pasha had a brig purchased in 1823 to carry mail swiftly to and from his agents and informers in Istanbul.[62] Thus, while imperial couriers embarking from Istanbul still plied overland routes in the nineteenth century, parallel, private communication channels for powerful provincial leaders could have been seaborne. However, as discussed earlier, Mehmed Ali Pasha preferred overland communication during the Egyptian-Ottoman war and subsequent occupation of Syria for security reasons.[63]

The Danube and Black Sea regions also had amphibious routes. The sharia court records of Vidin, a town along the banks of the Danube River, show that in the early 1700s, local officials were ordered to promptly provide long narrow rowboats called caiques (*menzil kayığı*) to couriers.[64] Along the Danube, a string of piers (*iskele*) facilitated these couriers.

The Crimean khans managed the post stations along the western and northern coasts of the Black Sea, stationing about sixty horses at each stage; a French diplomat described these posts as offering better service than the post stations of Turkey.[65] Sea options were also available (fig. 4). Couriers who arrived overland to the port of Varna were provided sea passage for their onward journey to Özi (modern Ochakiv in Ukraine). Entrusted with urgent messages, these couriers had the option of boarding an eight-seat or a ten-seat caique or a larger ship.[66] Both land and sea options were also available to those traveling between Samsun and Trabzon along the southern coast of the Black Sea. This southern coast was home to many ports—such as Hopa, Rize, and Araklı—where caiques were constructed; large boats were still being constructed by hand there as late as the 1960s.[67]

As a general rule, couriers chose land travel over sea travel whenever they had the option.[68] This was largely due to the unpredictability of sea travel before the nineteenth century. Prior to that, sea navigation was "a matter of following the shoreline, moving crab-wise from rock to rock," and avoiding the open sea.[69] Moreover, piracy was rampant, and hostage taking and exchange were profitable business. In the 1590s, couriers were sent overland to Trablusgarb (Tripoli, in modern Libya) to avoid ongoing sea battles.[70] Not just couriers, but Ottoman judges, too, preferred land travel: judges appointed to serve on the island of Cyprus traveled as far as they could overland and undertook as short a sea journey as they could in order to minimize their risk of being kidnapped by pirates.[71] Sea travel could also be more logistically onerous. To travel from Constantinople to Cairo by sea in the 1580s entailed sailing to Alexandria, arranging an overland transit to Rosetta (Rashid), and then taking a trip up the Nile toward Cairo while on a boat being pulled along the shore by men.[72] But sea travel was unavoidable at times; sending mail to Ottoman islands required at least some travel by sea.[73]

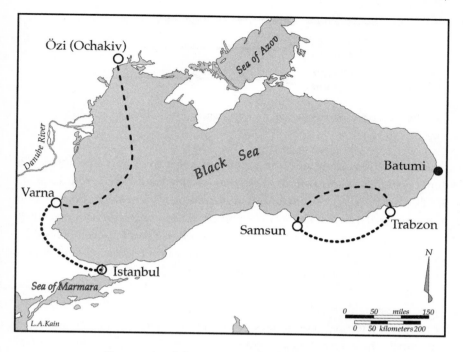

Figure 4. Amphibious routes in the Black Sea region.

The distinction between water routes and land routes was not absolute; a range of rivulets and rivers in the middle of this spectrum could be easily waded through or swum across. Larger rivers, like the Tigris River, had bridges.[74] If the bridge broke, couriers and travelers would cross by boat.[75] At other times, as with the Great Zab River that flows through Turkey and Iraq into the Tigris, caravans and couriers alike used "sheep skins filled with air" as buoys.[76] A British traveler described it thus: "The horses and camels swim across, three or four at a time, being led by a man who swims buoyed up by a goat's skin inflated with wind, which he keeps under his breast."[77] Humans and merchandise crossed on a platform that was buoyed by similarly inflated goat skins.[78] (The documentary film *Grass: A Nation's Battle for Life* [1925] shows how the Bakhtiari tribe used these inflated goat skins.) Humans and animals could also simply swim across rivers; in one case, a horse made an attempt to turn back and ended up drowning, but the British traveler remarked that crossing the river was overall a success given that only one horse was lost.[79]

The Ottoman postal system was not the only amphibious relay system in world history.[80] The Mongol relay system, for instance, comprised over two

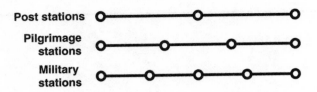

Figure 5. Varieties of relay stations showing relative distances apart. Chart by author.

thousand stations along land and water routes that were served by horses and donkeys but also barge handlers (水夫) and stable hands (馬夫; Old Uyghur: *ulagči*; also 烏駱子 in Chinese Turfan documents).[81] In Ming China, station masters offered different kinds of waterborne transportation services, providing red barges for large rivers as well as "fast-as-a-horse" barges, each crewed by ten people, for small canals.[82] Besides land and sea routes, pigeon-courier networks reportedly existed in the Abbasid and Ottoman Empires.[83]

There were roughly two hundred post stations in the eighteenth-century Ottoman Empire. However, postal stations were not the only type of relay station in the empire. There were other kinds of station, such as the military station (*askeri menzil*) and the pilgrimage station (*hac menzili*). One of the key differences among these three types was the distance between any two stations (fig. 5). The historian Cemal Çetin has pointed out, for instance, that during the eighteenth century there were fifty military stations and thirty pilgrimage stations but only twenty-four official post stations between Üsküdar and Antakya.[84]

The distance between each station corresponded to the speed of travel. Over the same distance, there would be a small number of post stations, a greater number of pilgrimage stations, and the greatest number of military stations. Since couriers were in superior physical shape and carried a light load, they traveled most swiftly and required fewer stops. This meant that a relay post system would have the least number of stations and the greatest distance between each. In contrast, military troops had to transport large amounts of provisions and equipment and would move much slower than couriers and thus needed stations that were much closer together. Consider that in a given fiscal year, a late seventeenth-century military relay station consumed 32,000 *kıntar* of straw (*ṣamān*) valued at roughly 10,000 *guruş*, while a post station consumed only about 10 *guruş* worth of straw (see fig. 10 in Chapter 5).[85] Pilgrims, who typically traveled in organized caravans, could move faster than military troops but were slower than couriers.[86]

In principle, Ottoman archival documents distinguished among military, pilgrim, and post stations. In practice, however, it is not clear that these distinctions mattered to travelers. Narrative sources show that different kinds of travelers used the same buildings. Indeed, many Ottoman relay stations were likely refurbished Seljuk caravanserais, which had served as guesthouses, as prisons, and also as post stations.[87]

Ottoman and European travelogues depict Ottoman relay stations as multi-purpose buildings that accommodated all kinds of travelers. The variety of names that pop up across centuries and across travelogues indicate the flexible nature of travel lodgings. European travelers, whether ambassadors, traders, or military men, lodged in Ottoman stations that they referred to variously as *menzel, cane,* or *khan, Munzil Khana, post-house, caravanseray,* and *konak.*[88] The authors each had their own definitions. For instance, a Swiss traveler described how the "menzel" was a type of "khan" that was "found in almost every village through which there is a frequented route."[89] An English traveler described a "caravanseray" in Diyarbekir as a building "attached to the pasha's palace for the accommodation of public messengers."[90] Sir Kinneir described the "Munzil Khana" as "the traveller's room," the "post-house" as typically a filthy, dirty or hole-like abode, and the term "konak" as usually referring to a home-stay situation, as when Kinneir and his companions lodged in a Christian merchant's house in Antakya or in an Armenian priest's house in Kastamonu.[91] (It was common for travelers to stay in the homes of local residents, local officials, or local merchants.)[92] These different attempts at definitions suggest that both travelers and the providers of hospitality were incredibly flexible. Indeed, whether in the sixteenth century or the nineteenth, travelers also sometimes camped overnight out in the open or in a tent when no proper accommodation was available.[93]

If official relay stations represented islands of sovereign power in the imperial landscape, this motley collection of unofficial rest stops demonstrate the limits of such power. The reality of overland travel in the pre-industrial era involved navigating geographical and social elements beyond the consistent control of any one political power. Like a traveler journeying across a desert by moving from oasis to oasis, from water point to water point, those who traversed the Ottoman lands moved from official relay to official relay—but they had to rely on their own resourcefulness in the myriad in-between stages. Despite bureaucratic distinctions among postal, military, and pilgrimage relay stations, therefore, travelers of the premodern world likely shared the same lodgings whether they were couriers or pilgrims, soldiers or merchants.

The postal system began as an ad hoc arrangement of confiscations. Routine, violent confiscations worked not because of an endemic culture of corruption in Ottoman lands, but because of the prevailing and unequal social order where officials were entitled to the resources of common subjects. Examples from relay communications systems in world history demonstrate that the Ottoman postal system was not unique in exploiting tax-paying subjects or having violence involved.

In the sixteenth century, the Ottomans began to establish fixed post stations across the empire. These stations acquired symbolic sovereign authority, and the privilege of access to those stations could be bestowed, denied, or revoked. However, imperial authorities also depended on common subjects to maintain and provision these fixed post stations. This change in the mode of horse procurement therefore inaugurated a slow shift in the manifestation of imperial authority, from a special privilege that was vested in individual couriers and empowered them to violently seize horses to a partible authority that was delegated to multiple actors, including local postmasters and villagers. This slow shift evolved over centuries, undergoing an intense turn toward documentation in the late seventeenth century. The rest of this book continues tracking this shift and continues to relate postal organization to the changing Ottoman social order.

CHAPTER 2

The Courier

It was a late summer's morning in the year 1649.[1] At a post station in Central Anatolia, a man of about forty years of age named Evliya Çelebi was performing his morning ablutions when he noticed somebody in the distance. An exhausted figure riding atop an equally fatigued horse was heading toward the station. Evliya recognized this weary traveler; it was Çomar Bölükbaşı, a rebel leader. Çomar Bölükbaşı had recently been defeated in a cavalry uprising in Istanbul, which Evliya had witnessed while on official business in the Ottoman capital. Like other onlookers, Evliya had been impressed by the rebel's bravery and fighting skills.[2]

This was the age of the Celali rebellions, when disaffected Ottoman army officers and brigands revolted and plundered the Anatolian countryside. Desperate, the imperial authorities neutralized these rebels by incorporating them into the ruling establishment, offering them promotions and provincial governorships.[3] It was in this atmosphere of blurred loyalties, where an officer-turned-rebel could swiftly become appointed as governor, that Evliya greeted Çomar Bölükbaşı as he approached the station. Embracing the weary rebel, Evliya commanded the postmaster to serve them both coffee immediately, along with whatever food remained in their saddle bags. The rebel was reluctant, but his host was insistent. Evliya introduced himself as being in the employ of Murtaza Pasha, the vizier of Damascus, and explained that he was currently returning to Damascus from Istanbul with letters and imperial orders from the grand vizier. Evliya generously offered Çomar Bölükbaşı a new horse and even invited him to travel together with his retinue, but the rebel hesitated. Reassuring him, our host said, "Brother, for your sake let's travel station by station [*menzil menzil gidelim*]. If your horses are falling behind, I will give you a new horse. Come on, let's go!" Çomar Bölükbaşı acquiesced, and they headed southward together.

At Seyyid Gazi post station, they fed their horses by filling their nose bags with food (fig. 6).[4]

From there, they passed Bolvadin and came upon an open field where a thousand troops were stationed with their tents. Immediately, five to ten rough-looking mercenaries from among the troops came up to confront the travelers, and, looking pointedly at Evliya, they asked: "*Ulak mısız? Are you a courier?*"

Evliya Çelebi recounts this scene in his ten-volume travelogue, *Seyahatname,* a work that has been described as the longest travel account in Islamic literature, even world literature.[5] Born to a palace goldsmith father and an Abaza tribeswoman mother, Evliya (1611–1682) was known for wearing many hats. He served several pashas in the empire, including the grand vizier Melek Ahmed Pasha, a maternal relation, and worked variously as a secretary, a prayer-leader (*imam*), a caller-to-prayer (*müezzin*), and a boon companion (*muṣāḥib*). Above all, Evliya viewed himself as a professional traveler.[6] While Evliya's travelogue is a well-known source and has been used to shed light on a range of historical issues— from Turkish dialects and circumcision customs to the dynamics of married life among the elite—his account has not been properly examined as a first-hand account of an Ottoman courier (*ulak*), as the opening scene demonstrates it to be.[7]

But how reliable is the *Seyahatname*? For many scholars, Evliya's account is useful, but not because his stories are believed to be the unvarnished truth. In fact, much like the writings of his fellow world-travelers Ibn Battuta and Marco Polo, Evliya's stories carry embellishments. Yet even embellishments are shaped by their time and place—there is no view from nowhere. Evliya's exaggerated tales are constrained by the limits of a seventeenth-century Ottoman imagination. Perhaps Evliya did not actually order the postmaster to serve coffee, and perhaps he did not really invite Çomar Bölükbaşı to travel with his own entourage, but to the seventeenth-century reader, these two details would not have been unbelievable. This plausibility is precisely the historian's payoff—it was plausible that

Figure 6. Horse eating from a nose bag in Cappadocia, 1996. Yelkrokoyade, "Une paysanne et son cheval avec sa musette mangeoire. Les vendanges en Cappadoce—Turquie." https://commons.wikimedia.org/wiki/File:Cheval_Cappadoce.jpg. Wikimedia Commons. CC BY-SA 2.5, https://creativecommons.org/licenses/by-sa/2.5/legalcode.

post stations served coffee, and it was plausible that couriers spontaneously invited fellow travelers they encountered on the road to journey with them.[8] Over a century later, nineteenth-century British travelers observed many of the same practices while traveling alongside Ottoman couriers, which corroborates Evliya Çelebi's accounts.

Here I use Evliya's narrative, together with archival records and European travelogues, to reconstruct the experiences of an Ottoman courier. Couriers were once ubiquitous. They were essential workers in the age of embodied communication, before information could travel independently of a human (or animate) messenger. They moved paper around the Ottoman Empire, such as reports submitted from provinces to the capital and imperial decrees issued from the capital to the provinces. Much of the Ottoman archive exists today because of couriers. From the perspective of sedentary bureaucrats in the capital and administrators in the provinces, couriers were infrastructure—they were the background system that enabled the activities of bureaucrats and administrators. As social scientists have perceptively observed, one person's infrastructure is another's job.[9]

Despite this infrastructural omnipresence, couriers themselves left a relatively light paper trail before the eighteenth century. Documents rarely mentioned the names of the couriers who delivered them; an imperial decree issued from the capital would be copied into the judicial register of a distant province with little explanation of how it got there. This is not surprising. Couriers' work and labor were taken for granted. Akin to the squat toilets that were regularly utilized in the most elite of palaces as well as the most modest of villages, the Ottoman postal system was so embedded in everyday imperial operations that it was often assumed rather than explained. Many things that power our lives today appear similarly opaque and invisible—how many of us know the identities of the postal workers who deliver our mail, or the names of the various chips, wires, and protocols that enable our electronic mail to be delivered?

In this chapter, I make couriers visible by inverting the infrastructure, that is, by foregrounding what was usually in the background.[10] Evliya's intimate, first-hand account makes this "infrastructural inversion" possible, especially when used alongside archival records that present the sedentary bureaucrat's perspective. As I will show, "courier" was not an official title but a function fulfilled by a range of Ottoman officials with different ranks. By the eighteenth century, however, Ottoman couriers had become reorganized into a corps, and all messengers became known as tatars.

The mercenaries asked, "*Ulak mısız*? Are you a courier?"

"Yes," Evliya Çelebi replied. "We are coming from Istanbul."

"And what about this wretched mercenary beside you who looks like he came from the Üsküdar battlefield?"

Evliya Çelebi responded with a lie, calmly and nonchalantly. "He is Murtaza Pasha's captain. He was coming from Amasya and we bumped into each other on the road, and so we are now headed to Damascus together."

"Well then, come on in," they said. "The inspector pasha [*teftīş paşa*] will see you."[11]

An Ottoman courier was called an *ulak*, a term related to an old Inner Asian term, *ulagh*, which referred to a postal relay horse or beast of burden.[12] The earliest written evidence of the Turkic word *ulak* is in the Chinese script (鄔落); this term appeared in a chronicle about the journey of the seventh-century Buddhist pilgrim Xuanzang to India. Xuanzang is better known in the Western world as the lead character in the Ming-era literary work *Journey to the West*, along with its popular fictional character the Monkey King. In real life, it wasn't the Monkey King but *ulak* horses that helped transport Xuanzang to India to find Buddhist scriptures.[13] The term had an enduring currency across space and time. In the late nineteenth century, for example, an American Orientalist and diplomat, William W. Rockhill, encountered the Manchu term *ula* in southern Mongolia and Tibet, where it referred to both "relay horse" and "relay post."[14]

In the Ottoman context, *ulak* referred to the human messenger, not the beast of burden. (It was Evliya Çelebi who was the *ulak*, not his horse.) During the seventeenth century *ulak* was a function that could be carried out by a range of Ottoman officials and was not itself an official rank. For instance, Evliya presented himself as an *ulak* to the mercenaries but not to Çomar Bölükbaşı, to whom he had presented himself as the agent of Murtaza Pasha, the vizier of Damascus.[15]

Evliya's choice to disclose different parts of his identity in different situations suggests a few things. First, an agent could also be a courier; that is, delivering messages was a function, not an official rank. Second, the term *ulak* was a general category—like introducing oneself as a doctor rather than an endocrinologist, or as a teacher rather than a professor of Ottoman history. This may be inferred from how Evliya represented himself as a courier (*ulak*) to the mercenaries but as an agent of Murtaza Pasha to Çomar Bölükbaşı, somebody whom Evliya wanted to befriend.[16]

In his travelogue, Evliya frequently used a phrase which underscores how transposable the functions of a courier were, at least in that era: "to be with a courier's duty" (*ulaklığıyla* or *ulaklık ile*). The expression suggests that the courier function was portable and transferable, not inherent in an individual's identity. For instance, when Evliya Çelebi invited Çomar Bölükbaşı to travel with him and his retinue, the rebel demurred. Çomar Bölükbaşı felt it would not be possible for his war-weary self and battle-stricken horse to be suitable travel companions for Evliya Çelebi, since the latter "was with" a courier's duty.[17]

Over two decades later, in the ninth volume of his travelogue, Evliya Çelebi recalled events from the summer in 1649. When referring to the two trips he made to Istanbul, he described himself as being "with a courier's duties," charged with delivering his then-patron Murtaza Pasha's letters. Elsewhere in the *Seyahatname,* other officials, including an agha and a gatekeeper, were sent "on a courier's duty" to deliver messages and were referred to by their titles rather than as couriers.[18]

Archival documents corroborate Evliya's travelogue on this point, notably copies of courier orders that use the term *ulak* as a function that could be carried out by a range of officials of different ranks and titles. Although very few original courier orders have survived, many copies of these orders are preserved in Registers of Important Affairs (*mühimme defteri*). These registers contained copies of decrees issued by the sultan to officials, as well as copies of letters addressed to foreign dignitaries.[19]

Some copies were extremely concise, such as this example from 1630–1631:

> Menzil: A courier order has been written for Hasan from the Cavalry Corps and two men for [their] journey from Istanbul to Skopje and back.[20]

In this abbrieviated copy of a courier order, only the identity of the courier, his title, the number of men accompanying him, and his destination are recorded. Here, Hasan was a member of the cavalry corps who was issued a courier order, presumably to deliver messages on behalf of the state.

Courier orders could also be very detailed. The following is a template with the name of the courier and the number of men in his entourage left blank. Hundreds of such templates may be found in the registers, suggesting that Ottoman scribes prepared them in advance in order to expedite the issuing of courier orders.

> To all the judges, governors, lieutenant-governors, fortress wardens, aghas, and port superintendents along the road from Istanbul to Damascus and Aleppo, and back:

> I have sent [__<name to be filled in>__] marshal [*çavuş*]—paragon among the most eminent and [their] peers—from among the marshals of my throne as a courier [*ulağla*] with some important matters.

> With my honorable order, should he enter any of your areas of jurisdiction:

> in places where post horses are available, please provide them to him and to his [__<number to be filled in>__] men;

and in places where post horses are not available, without adding to his travel load, provide usable post horses from the locals;

and in places that are frightening and dangerous, provide a sufficient amount of people to accompany [him] in order that he may reach each of your stations safely and reach the afore-mentioned place in an expedited manner.

The afore-mentioned matter is an important one; please be strongly warned against dawdling, delaying, ignoring or negligence.[21]

In contrast to the earlier abbreviated copy, this long and detailed courier order included formulaic pleasantries, such as the chancellery title for the marshal (paragon among the most eminent and peers), formulaic exhortations to provincial officials along the courier's travel route to provide him with horses, and formulaic warnings against ignoring the commands it contained. Although the identity of the courier is not yet determined, his rank of *çavuş* (marshal) had been confirmed.[22] Significantly, the *çavuş* is being dispatched "as a courier" (*ulağla*) to deliver important mail. This corroborates the use of the term *ulak* to refer to a function rather than a rank as found in Evliya's travelogue.

Apart from copies of courier orders, Registers of Important Affairs contained copies of other documents issued to the provinces, such as imperial decrees. Sometimes the marginalia recorded the identity of the courier who was ordered to deliver said document. Such marginalia would contain short phrases such as "this was given to Mehmed the marshal" (*Mehmed Çavuş'a virildi*).[23] These marginalia are more readily found in Registers of Important Affairs from the sixteenth century; they became less common by the seventeenth century.[24]

A brief survey of such marginalia and courier orders reveals a range of officials who had to deliver messages. They include gatekeepers (*kapıcı*), marshals (*çavuş*), cavalry officers (*sipāhī*), head gatekeepers (*kapıcıbaşı*), and aghas, as well as men without titles, such as "two persons named Mehmed and Abdi" (*Mehmed ve Abdi nām kimesneler*); some are simply referred to as "men" (*ādem*).[25]

Çomar Bölükbaşı was reluctant to accompany Evliya Çelebi for good reason—the rebel was in no physical condition to travel at the pace of a courier. This was not explicitly articulated in this passage but may be inferred from Evliya Çelebi's response: "For your sake, we will go station by station [*Seniñ hātırın içün biz dahi menzil menzil gidelim*]." This implies that under normal circumstances, Evliya Çelebi would not have gone station by station. Rather, he and his men would have skipped stations, traveling faster and traveling longer distances with fewer breaks in between than an ordinary traveler would (see fig. 5).

To be an Ottoman courier required a few key attributes. The courier had to have physical endurance and a phenomenal stamina. He also had to be street-savvy, to have knowledge of local terrain, and to be attuned to the possibility of lurking bandits. He had to know how to use violence to extract necessary horses and food from the common folk. After all, life on the road was a matter of survival, and delivering messages in the shortest time possible for the Ottoman state was a matter of duty and obligation. He also typically traveled with an entourage and had to manage the dynamics of group travel.

If the Ottoman courier's strength and stamina were only implicitly mentioned in Evliya's travelogue, they were explicitly extolled by foreigners who were positively amazed by these couriers. (These couriers were known as tatars by the late eighteenth century.) According to the foreign accounts, tatar couriers could ride continuously for days with no food.[26] They could sleep while on horseback.[27] They could sleep on the bare ground in the open air.[28] They were such excellent horse riders that terrain meant little to them, and they galloped uphill and downhill indifferently and with ease.[29] The constant exposure to sun, wind, and rain meant a hardy physique and a tough set of skin cells. One British traveler who journeyed as part of an entourage of couriers wrote, "From my long exposure to the sun, the skin had come off both my hands and face." His Ottoman courier companions, in contrast, did not have the same problem of peeling skin.[30]

Matching this physical prowess was couriers' appetite for alcohol. Ottoman couriers drank excessively. They could also ride horses while drunk or hungover. As a British traveler described, "We set out, a very large party, from Tocat [Tokat] at half past four o'clock this afternoon, and being all badly mounted, and the greater part drunk, made a curious figure as we rode through the town. The streets being much crowded, the Tatars roared like so many bulls for the people to clear the passage, every one being obliged to give way to them, as in England to the mail coaches; and if they were not very quick in getting out of the road, they were sure to feel some of the Tatars' long whips." Drinking parties sometimes escalated into brawls, as in the case of Suleyman, a tatar from Sivas, who attempted to shoot another tatar. Fortunately, the rest of the traveling party prevented him from succeeding.[31] Ottoman couriers' enthusiastic drinking customs were not so different from late-Timurid drinking culture in the fifteenth and sixteenth centuries. In his diary, Babur, the founder of the Mughal Empire, noted that being a good drinker meant that one could drink nonstop for twenty or thirty days. Nor was there a contradiction between drink and piety—Babur once described a good Muslim man of orthodox Hanafi belief who would never miss the five daily prayers, even while drinking.[32]

The whip (*kamçı*) was the courier's primary tool. It was applied to beast and human alike to extract resources. As one British traveler observed, "In the poorest villages, where there was not so much as a chicken to be found, I have seen the comchee [*kamçı*] produce a dozen full grown venerable hens. Where a blade of grass could not grow for a single sheep to feed upon, whole flocks have been suddenly presented to our choice." Even horses that appeared to be utterly exhausted could, upon the application of the whip, spring to life again to make "the most extraordinary exertions."[33] Of course, sometimes the whip did not work, and villagers successfully resisted couriers, pelting them with stones and rubbish.[34] Evliya Çelebi recounted how it was difficult to obtain horses while traveling in Wallachia because at each village, rebellious villagers would attack couriers with scythes, pikes, and swords.[35] For the most part, however, the whip worked. Depictions of couriers in seventeenth-century Ottoman costume albums testify to the whip as a quintessential part of their identity (fig. 7).[36]

Couriers needed to be savvy and knowledgeable about local conditions. They had to be constantly vigilant, on the watch for lurking bandits or tribes or for a change in weather. Sometimes a change in season prompted an expedient detour. During the spring and summer months, for instance, trees in certain mountainous regions provided leafy cover for bandits and highway robbers. Couriers were known to have adjusted their routes in these cases to avoid danger.[37]

Couriers' geographical knowledge extended to desert regions as well, as this example from the 1810s demonstrates. Together with a group of tatars and guides, the British traveler William Heude arrived around midnight at a small hill in a desert. The guides discerned on the horizon "a distant cloud driving before the wind." This "distant cloud" was sand and dust kicked up by the hooves of horses, which indicated the impending arrival of an unfriendly tribe. In response to this threat, the tatars and guides began to make a lot of noise, singing a battle song and banging their swords and pistols together. The lone British foreigner attempted to shush everyone, thinking that if everyone kept silent, the unfriendly tribe might not notice their presence. Everyone ignored him and continued singing at the top of their lungs. After about half an hour, a few horsemen separated from the "cloud" and came toward Heude's traveling party. When these horsemen perceived the size of the traveling party, they stopped, gave a greeting (*Salam Alik*), and rode off. Soon after, the "distant cloud" disappeared into the horizon.[38] The threat had passed. Heude noted that he inwardly felt relieved that the group

Figure 7. A Tatar courier holding a whip, 17th century. Claes Rålamb, *Rålambska dräktboken* (*Rålamb Book of Costumes*) (1600), image 105. National Library of Sweden. Retrieved from the Library of Congress, https://www.loc.gov/item/2021668152/.

had not heeded his direction to remain quiet. In this case, the traveling party had spotted the threat in the distance and scared off the attackers by making a racket, thereby demonstrating the size and morale of the group.

Couriers traveled in groups that expanded and contracted on the road, acquiring new members along the way and losing existing ones who were headed in different directions. They were also masters of their own itineraries, which they could and did change to accommodate new travel companions. This was just what Evliya Çelebi did when he wanted Çomar Bölükbaşı to join him; he suggested going station by station to accommodate the latter's physical condition.

Motley merchants, travelers, and couriers sometimes gathered to form a *kafile*, or small caravan, for safety reasons.[39] A British traveler remarked upon the normalcy of having newcomers join his travel party, which hosted "a Turk with a servant and three horses," and, later, some "Diarbekir Tatars and five arabs," making them a group of twenty horses.[40] However, the British traveler put his foot down at one point, protesting against another courier's wish to accompany the party. If a travel party got too big, procuring horses at rest stations became a problem and could delay the journey.[41] Newcomers could also annoy existing members; another traveler complained that a Turkish musician who joined his travel party "sang in a barbarous, inharmonious manner."[42] The trade-offs for having a larger, potentially safer, travel party were speed, potential horse shortages, and interpersonal conflict.

Sometimes bandits and highway robbers succeeded in attacking couriers, rendering their onward itinerary in doubt. In the spring of 1743, three couriers were traveling to Istanbul from Erzurum when they were attacked and robbed of their belongings and horses near a cemetery in Çankırı, northern Anatolia.[43] While the record goes into great detail about the identities and locations of the bandits and exhorts local officials to arrest them, there is no information about the remaining trajectory of this team of couriers and how they continued their travels back to Istanbul. It is reasonable to presume that they might have traveled at a slower pace given their injuries and rested at intermediate relay stations while journeying back to Istanbul.

Travel groups were typically all-male and could be occupationally, religiously, and ethnically mixed. Couriers did not always travel with other couriers. They could travel alongside merchants, whether Jewish, Armenian, or Christian.[44] Armenian merchants sometimes pretended to be the servants of tatar couriers whom they traveled with for security purposes.[45] This masquerade of merchant as servant was believable to outsiders because a hierarchy existed within the courier profession.[46]

The head Tatar was usually the leader of the travel party. He typically rode at the back of the group, where he would use his whip to keep others' horses up to speed. Having your horse whipped by somebody else from behind was perceived as an act of domination and a slight on your physical prowess, at least in the eyes of some British travelers who did not appreciate it.[47] Couriers also received help from the *sürücü*, or guide, an assistant provided by post stations to accompany couriers for a part of their journey for security and navigation purposes. He usually accompanied the tatar and was charged with taking care of spare horses, brought along in the event that a horse was lost or died. If there were no spare horses, these guides were supposed to confiscate the horse of the next traveler they encountered.[48] Sometimes the guide acted as an advance scout, riding ahead to seek accommodations for the larger travel party.[49] Another kind of assistant was the *karakulak*. Dal Taban Mustafa Pasha (d. 1703), who served as the grand vizier for four months between 1702 and 1703, started out his career as a *karakulak* in the entourage of Kara Ibrahim Agha.[50] When entering a village, *karakulaks* would shout out to inform villagers of the arrival of the courier.[51]

In travel parties that were large enough, these guides and assistants could have their own servants. Sometimes postmasters of specific rest stations apprenticed their sons to travel parties to learn the ropes. A British traveler agreed to take on Mustapha, who was the son of the master of the Mosul rest station (*konak*). Mustapha was apprenticed to the head Tatar, so that in time he could become a fully fledged courier. This traveler described Mustapha's role in their traveling party as that of an "upper servant" whose job was to look after the guides as well as to drive the horses as an assistant to the Tatar.[52]

> After verifying their identities, the mercenaries said, "Well then, come on in. The inspector pasha [*teftîş paşa*] will see you."
>
> Evliya Çelebi and his retinue entered the pasha's tent—he turned out to be Baki Pasha, the son of Ketenci Ömer Pasha. "Welcome Evliya Çelebi," Baki Pasha said, and bestowed upon him a horse and twenty gold pieces. They began to converse, and Evliya Çelebi told him about the recent uprising and battle in Üsküdar. Information was exchanged for a horse and money. After having some food, Evliya Çelebi, his retinue, and Çomar Bölükbaşı headed together in the direction of the qibla toward the next post station.[53]

Couriers did not only deliver information contained in the paper mail they carried. In navigating their journeys around the empire, couriers were observers on the ground and incidental vectors of everyday news and goings-on in the vast empire. For Baki Pasha, a horse and some money were probably fair exchange for the information that Evliya Çelebi had relayed about recent events in Üsküdar. The gifts might also have been sweeteners for future favors and tip-offs. It is possible that Baki Pasha's largesse was due to the fact that Evliya used to serve Baki's father, Ketenci Ömer Pasha, who, in turn, was a protégé of Evliya's father.[54] These overlapping ties within an inner circle of Ottoman officialdom, to which

Evliya belonged, meant that Çomar, the rebel on the run, could not have found a better benefactor. The point, however, is that couriers were expected to be information gatherers, even spies, mediators, and diplomats.

As vectors of information, couriers provided context that was especially useful in politically delicate situations. In 1653, the former Celali rebel Ipşir Pasha was appointed the new grand vizier to the consternation of many in Istanbul. Many wondered if the pasha would come to the capital to receive his appointment. More importantly, if he did come, would his mercenary army attack the janissaries, or worse—mount a coup against the sultan?[55]

With so much uncertainty, the leading statesmen all hoped to get in Ipşir Pasha's good graces. Evliya's patron, Melek Ahmed Pasha, dispatched him on a courier's duty to deliver seventy letters. He implored Evliya to hang out with Ipşir Pasha for a few days, get a sense of what he was thinking, make notes of everything he did, and then get letters from him and return to Istanbul. Melek Ahmed Pasha alluded to some enemies who had sown discord by poisoning Ipşir Pasha's opinion against him and emphasized that Evliya Çelebi was the right person for the job of recuperating Melek Ahmed Pasha's image. After all, the new grand vizier was known to be very fond of Evliya. Evliya Çelebi's mission here was not merely mail delivery: it included both diplomacy and espionage.[56]

Not just Melek Ahmed Pasha but also seventy other officials entreated Evliya to put in a good word for them with the incoming grand vizier. They plied him with money and gifts which Evliya deposited with his sister in Istanbul before setting off. These officials wanted to ingratiate themselves with Ipşir Pasha and calculated that enriching the courier who was traveling to meet him in person would be a good strategy. In other words, the written letters were not enough; the human messenger, too, had to be persuaded to augment the written message with an oral one.[57]

Evliya's travelogue sheds light on the embodied nature of message delivery. He describes the ritualistic kissing of the ground by the courier (zemīn-būs) before handing over the letters when in the presence of a high-ranking official. At other times, Evliya kissed the official's hand (dest-būs) instead. Sometimes the courier was present when the recipient read his letters, allowing him to report on the recipient's response to the letters' contents. Before setting off to deliver messages, the courier might also bid farewell to various noble patrons and be bestowed with traveling expenses.[58] The nature and quantity of these gifts could reflect the mood and disposition of the letters' recipients, another useful piece of information in a murky political setting.

In this encounter with Ipşir Pasha, Evliya Çelebi was clearly the medium of choice, at least in his own narrative. After seven days of conversation, Evliya succeeded in persuading a cautious Ipşir Pasha to take up the post of grand vizier in Istanbul. Evliya also succeeded in convincing him of Melek Ahmed Pasha's support for his candidacy.

Ipşir Pasha, too, was interested in extracting information from Evliya Çelebi. He posed pointed questions about other competitors who had been coveting the position of grand vizier and inquired about the strength of support for his own candidacy among the janissary corps. When Evliya Çelebi departed, Ipşir Pasha generously bestowed gifts and money upon the messenger—three purses, two horses, three hundred gold pieces, a suit of armor, some clothes, fifty gold pieces for each of Evliya's slave-servants (gulām), and ninety-five letters.[59] An able, quick-witted courier could win gifts and money.[60]

To mitigate the frequency of lost mail, lost ships, and lost couriers, writers in the early modern world sent multiple copies of texts with different couriers to ensure their messages got to their intended recipients.[61] Ottoman officials did the same. In 1648, couriers arrived in Beypazarı, near Ankara, with letters regarding Evliya Çelebi's father's passing. Three of these letters were addressed to Evliya Çelebi from his family members; another three letters were addressed directly to Melek Ahmed Pasha, entreating him to allow Evliya Çelebi leave to return to Istanbul.[62] All these letters arrived together and appeared to have conveyed the same information.

Generally, the number of letters dispatched with couriers was large. For instance, Melek Ahmed Pasha had sent seventy letters with Evliya. Ipşir Pasha sent Evliya back with ninety-five letters. In another instance, Evliya Çelebi had with him one hundred and seventy letters from a variety of notables and high-ranking officials.[63] It is not known how many of these were repeat copies that had already been dispatched with other couriers or repeat copies sent with Evliya in the expectation that some might be lost, damaged, or stolen en route.

As these examples from Evliya's travelogue show, the paper mail being delivered included official mail, personal mail, and mail that could have been considered both official and personal. Sometimes the items in the paper mail are referred to in the plural as letters (mektuplar) or are described as letters of friendship (mektūb-i muhabbet-üslūblar) between pashas, while at other times they are specifically described as imperial orders (emr-i şerīf) and handwritten decrees by the sultan (hatt-ı şerīf).[64] Contrary to what sultanic law codes suggest, then, couriers delivered not only government correspondence but also personal mail. During the nineteenth century, official couriers performed the same unofficial postal services. A British traveler observed that his Tatar had the travel party go to the bazaar, where he took over two hundred letters from merchants in exchange for presents. The office of the Tatar, the British traveler remarked, was very profitable as the job enabled such side hustles as the delivery of merchants' letters. "The letters are not of any great inconvenience to them, giving no farther trouble than the mere carriage; for when a Tatar arrives at any considerable city, the merchants immediately go to the Conac [*konak*] for their letters."[65] Although such explicit descriptions have not emerged for earlier centuries, it is possible that official couriers had been ferrying merchants' letters within the Ottoman Empire for a long while.

Couriers and circulating officials also exchanged information when they met each other on the road. When journeying to meet İpşir Pasha, for example, Evliya Çelebi mentioned that he bumped into Mercan Ağa, who worked for an Ottoman princess. Evliya noted that Mercan was also on his way to visit İpşir Pasha.[66] This passing detail gestures toward a social dimension of being a courier; there existed a peer network of couriers who knew each other and each other's patrons. Indeed, the movements of couriers were so intimately connected with the flow of intelligence that in 1622 the chronicler Ibrahim of Pec noticed messengers moving between Abaza Mehmed and his own patron, Hafiz Ahmed Pasha, the governor of Diyarbakir, and intuited that an alliance between the two was forming.[67] The bodily movement of the courier indicated the tangible movement and circulation of information, like little speech bubbles moving from one patron to another.

The courier—whatever his official rank—played a vital function in assuaging the frictions among strongmen of the empire, whether between pashas and peers or between the Ottoman sultan and his powerful provincial governors. Couriers were the human infrastructure who powered Ottoman communications, conveying, mediating, or dispelling the tensions among the pillars of the empire. Through persuasion, charm, and wit, they sought to achieve the objectives of their patron while preserving their own lives.

Before the eighteenth century, the job of courier (*ulak*) is best understood as a function fulfilled by a range of officials. A courier was likely to have been a trusted servant of his patron. Such men not only delivered paper mail but also acted as diplomats and offered intelligence to their patrons and to other officials they encountered on the road. Traveling around the empire, couriers traversed diverse provinces and interacted with a wide range of characters, from outlawed rebels to lofty pashas. They had control over their itineraries and traveled in groups that expanded and contracted depending on whom they bumped into on the road. The way in which they socialized and mediated information, both written and oral, constituted a kind of communications infrastructure of empire.

The courier's life offers a glimpse into the messy interplay of social relationships and political allegiances. In the hundreds of post stations across the empire, rebel and official sojourned together, often in isolated settings. For them, friendship, honor, and the shared goal of surviving the precarity of life on the road might have more immediate meaning and value than the intricate vicissitudes of power in distant Istanbul. As Evliya Çelebi's embrace of the rebel Çomar Bölükbaşı reveals, the logic of loyalty to the House of Osman interfaced in complex ways with the solidarity of the road.[68]

CHAPTER 3

The Tatar

On the night of Wednesday, January 6, 1864, a courier and his guide froze to death on the road to Tekirdağ. They had been delivering government correspondence during an especially harsh winter when the horse of Tatar Küçük Mustafa got stuck in a muddy, snowy ditch. The two men tried to rescue the horse and dislodge its legs in vain. At some point, they decided that the guide should go to a nearby village to seek help. Tragically, the guide lost his way in the snowstorm and perished together with his horse. Tatar Küçük Mustafa was later found frozen (*müncemid*) to death (fig. 8).[1]

A week after Tatar Küçük Mustafa's death, his elderly mother and a younger brother petitioned the Ottoman administration for an allowance. They were living in Kütahya, in western Anatolia, over three hundred miles on from where Tatar Küçük Mustafa had died. Their petition was referred to the Supreme Council of Judicial Ordinances (*Meclis-i Vālā-yı Aḥkām-ı ʿAdliyye*), where bureaucrats looked for a precedent in order to determine the appropriate amount of allowance to grant the courier's surviving family members. They found a precedent from two years earlier, in 1862. Another courier had been killed by bandits in the district of İznik, and his surviving widow was granted a monthly allowance of 40 *guruş*.[2] The authorities decided that the same amount of monthly allowance (40 *guruş*) would be granted to Tatar Küçük Mustafa's mother and brother.[3] The logic behind this conclusion was not explained in the memos—

Figure 8. Tekirdağ, where Tatar Küçük Mustafa perished on the night of January 6, 1864.

perhaps one surviving widow was entitled to the same amount of compensation as an elderly mother and a younger brother.

In this chapter I piece together available evidence on the Ottoman courier in the two centuries that separate Evliya Çelebi the *ulak* from Tatar Küçük Mustafa. The process of infrastructural inversion begun earlier and described in the previous chapter, a process of foregrounding what had been implicit in the background, is here extended chronologically into the nineteenth century. Seen administratively, the arc from *ulak* to *tatar* is a change in how the Ottoman bureaucracy organized message delivery: from a function performed by officials holding different ranks to a function performed by one type of official, the tatar. Over the course of the eighteenth century, tatars came under closer regulation: they were required to wear uniforms, they were explicitly prohibited from ferrying merchandise while on the road, and many of their oral messages came to be documented in writing. They also enjoyed new benefits: if they died while on the job, their families would be eligible for compensation, which was not an option readily available to couriers in earlier centuries. These new regulations and policies were implemented amid a larger shift in the behavioral and moral order

that swept across the imperial bureaucracy during the eighteenth and nineteenth centuries. They reflected the expanding reach and weight of Ottoman
imperial authority on the lives of officials, an authority that had acquired a new,
normative character.[4]

In what follows I first offer a brief account of the term *tatar.* Then I survey
the changes in workplace culture in the imperial bureaucracy during the eighteenth and nineteenth centuries. This survey provides the context for the transformation of the Ottoman courier into tatar. In tracing the tatar's trajectory,
I use sources that go beyond 1840, the moment when the postal system transformed into a public service. Although the postal service's public-facing and
public-serving aspect was new, the mounted tatar continued to deliver government correspondence, and it is this latter function I focus on.

Were all tatars of Tatar ethnicity? Available sources show no evidence for this.
Tatar messengers did not come exclusively from an ethnic Tatar background. But
the question remains: Why did this ethnic term come to refer to Ottoman couriers in the mid- to late eighteenth century? This remains largely a mystery.

The term "Tatar" is most commonly associated with the descendants of Ch-
inggis Khan via the Golden Horde Mongols. These Crimean Tatars were a formidable military force who served in Ottoman campaigns.[5] From the seventeenth
century on, Ottoman government documents used the term *tatar* to refer to couriers who served the grand vizier.[6] (Couriers who served other officials typically
held different ranks, as shown in the previous chapter.) By the late eighteenth
century, the term *ulak* had fallen out of use in the written record and been replaced
by the term *tatar,* which came to refer to all government messengers, not just
those who served the grand vizier. This transition coincided with the establishment of the Tatar Corps (*Tatarān ocağı*). Although its precise date of establishment
is unknown, this Tatar Corps underwent a reorganization in 1775, suggesting
the corps must have been around for some time before that.[7]

Contemporaries were aware of this semantic overload. An eighteenth-century
British traveler commented that only those who were uninformed assumed that
ethnic Tatars ("people of the Tartar nation") held the office of the courier.[8] Ignatius Mouradgea d'Ohsson (1740–1807), an Armenian Catholic from Istanbul
who published a comprehensive description of Ottoman institutions (*Tableau
général de l'Empire othoman*), explained that tatars were ordinary government
couriers, and made no connection between them and the Crimean Tatars.[9]

Within modern Ottoman historiography, some scholars collapse the distinction between *ulak* and *tatar* and use these terms interchangeably, while others

distinguish among officials (*memur*), couriers (*ulak*), and tatars.[10] The historian
Iwamoto Keiko hypothesizes that, after the loss of Crimea to Imperial Russia,
Crimean Tatar refugees who fled to Ottoman lands may have sought employment as couriers in large numbers. Rather than settle as sedentary dwellers, these
nomads and semi-nomads may have found the life of a courier attractive. In turn,
their demographic majority may have prompted the shift in the conventional
term of reference from *ulak* to *tatar* within bureaucratic circles.[11]

It should be noted that there existed a range of messengers besides the tatars
who worked within the Ottoman bureaucracy. The *kapı kethüdası* (stewards of
the gatekeepers), for instance, handled the correspondence between the capital
and provincial governors. They acted as personal agents of these provincial governors, managing their political and economic interests in the imperial capital,
helping them secure lucrative offices, and managing their investments.[12] High-
ranking officials could also be dispatched to deliver sensitive messages between
Ottoman military commanders stationed at the warfront. The historian and
courtier Ahmed Vasıf (1735–1806) was one such example. When dispatched with
a message, Vasıf was referred to as a messenger (*nāmereslik*) who traveled by way
of a noble and pure-blooded horse (*sevk-i yekrān*).[13] Here I do not address these
special types of messengers, focusing instead on the main, dominant group of
tatar couriers.

In the second half of the eighteenth century, the imperial bureaucracy began to
impose a new behavioral and moral order on its officials. This manifested most
visibly in new regulations governing officials' movements, work hours, and work
attitudes. The new tendency to intervene in normative affairs forms an important context for the shift from *ulak* to *tatar*.[14]

In December 1786, the Ottoman government issued the earliest known decree that defined work hours for its officials. It demanded all officials turn up for
work "early" and specified the time by which they were to finish their duties for
the day. At the moment, the decree noted, most officials were arriving at the office past noon and worked only for a few hours. The government hoped that this
measure would remedy the "tardiness and neglect" of officials, which had resulted
in "low productivity."[15] Imperial authorities continued to regulate work hours
over the next century, issuing dozens of decrees that defined and redefined the
length of the workday.[16]

Spatial discipline accompanied time discipline. For much of the eighteenth
century Ottoman government offices were porous, relaxed spaces. Foreign dignitaries, translators (dragomans) of foreign embassies, messengers, coffee- and

tea-makers, and even peddlers and beggars could freely enter the offices and interrupt the workflow. In 1797, this changed. A strict visitor policy was imposed; no longer could individuals enter and leave Ottoman government offices as they wished. Authorities also reconfigured office space by separating officials who were handling more confidential documents from officials who were handling less confidential ones.[17]

This spatial logic received a further boost in the nineteenth century. For instance, in 1826, the *şeyhülislam*, the head of the Ottoman judiciary, began to work out of a specific office building. Previously, he did not have a dedicated office. Similarly, the Sublime Porte, the apex of the Ottoman government, had historically been synonymous with the grand vizier's residence. Ottoman scribes would work variously in the Topkapı Palace as well as in the grand vizier's residential compound, which had an office section and a residential section (the harem) where the grand vizier's family stayed. In 1839, the grand vizier's residences were moved outside the Sublime Porte. The historian Melis Hafez suggests that this clearer segregation represented a stronger "demarcation between work and non-work" and an increased emphasis on productivity. Even a new writing style called *rik'a* was adopted by bureaucrats because it "could be written quickly and without raising the pen from the paper."[18]

Underpinning this newfound demarcation between work and non-work was arguably a fundamental shift in Ottoman values and how they should be expressed spatially. Ottoman notions of public and private were not congruent with Western ones that have since been normalized today. To the contrary, what informed an older Ottoman spatial logic were the dichotomies of "the privileged and the common," "the sacred and the profane." The inner chambers of a household compound symbolized privilege and sacrality, while the common and profane were kept at a distance, in the outer chambers or even outside the compound. It is this logic that explains why the imperial council, the highest organ of government, met within the walls of the imperial palace inside the sultan's home. In the same vein, the most elite echelons of government did not do work in "public buildings" but in the household compound. In the nineteenth century, however, all this changed. The household compound was no longer associated with prestige and sacrality but instead with unprofessionalism and "non-work."[19]

This new spatial logic was accompanied by a new moral discipline. By the late eighteenth century, laziness had become recognized as an organizational vice and thus as a reason for dismissal. This attitude began as a positive mechanism of reward. In 1791, the grand vizier sought Selim III's approval to reward hardworking bureaucrats as a gesture of appreciation.[20] Bureaucrats who were "no good for work" did not receive any gift but did not receive any punishment either. A century later, they did. Between 1879 and 1914, 171 bureaucrats were punished for being lazy and careless. Offenses ranged from sleeping while on duty or being slow in carrying out one's duties to incompetence and absenteeism. If officials received more than two warnings, they would be dismissed or relocated. Out of these 171 cases, 149 officials were dismissed.[21]

During the eighteenth and nineteenth centuries, the Ottoman imperial bureaucracy was undergoing an organizational shift that was both cultural and moral. This shift manifested temporally as a newfound emphasis on work hours, spatially as a newfound demarcation of boundaries within the office, and behaviorally as a newfound code of conduct for officials. The new regulations governing tatar couriers—ranging from their clothing, their movements, and their behavior to how they carried out their work—have to be understood in this context.

In the seventeenth century Evliya did not wear a uniform that rendered him visually identifiable as a courier. The men in his entourage did not wear uniforms either. This was why Evliya was able to smuggle his rebel friend Çomar Bölükbaşı into his traveling party. This was also why a group of mercenaries whom the two men encountered had to ask Evliya if he was a courier.[22] The mercenaries may have guessed that Evliya was a courier, but they could not be sure just by looking at him.

By the late eighteenth century all Ottoman tatars and their entourages were required to wear uniforms. The uniform was visually distinct. The most prominent item of clothing was the special courier fur cap called a *kalpak*. It was a yellow cap, about a foot high, with a broad and flat top that narrowed toward the bottom to fit the head. Black lambskin covered the lower part of the cap, while the insides were "lined and quilted" and the upper part "stuffed with wool extremely tight." The *kalpak* was a protective covering for the head—much like a helmet—and was very heavy. A British traveler commented that a *kalpak* "feels unpleasantly at first" and that it was easier to wear with a shaved head, in order to keep cool.[23] Imperial decrees noted that the *kalpak* was a defining marker (*'alāmet*) of those in the Tatar Corps.[24]

Other elements of the tatar uniform included "a brown cloth coat trimmed with a broad black silk binding, wrapping quite round the body with short wide sleeves, and hanging down to the calf of the leg"; wide blue Turkish trousers trimmed with black silk binding, "buttoning tight around the small of the leg";

and "strong red boots to pull over the trowsers as high as the calf of the leg." A Turkish gown with long sleeves buttoning close around the wrist was worn underneath the coat, together with an uncollared shirt. A cummerbund, or broad waist sash, was to be tied very tightly around the waist so weapons like pistols and sabers could be affixed there with other accoutrements.[25]

The purpose of this uniform was, in part, to regulate the usage of horses at post stations. This regulation did little to stop imposter couriers, who managed to obtain uniforms and inveigle postmasters into believing that they were bona fide couriers so they could procure horses. However, should any tatar wish to escort a rebel, traveler or merchant, as Evliya did, he would now have to dress them up in the tatar uniform. Tatar couriers coalesced as a visually identifiable group through this sartorial regulation.

Not just Tatar couriers' clothing but their behavior came to be regulated. Late eighteenth-century imperial decrees began to explicitly single out couriers who transported commercial merchandise on the side for censure, although this had been condoned as a customary practice previously.[26] Sometimes decrees targeted couriers plying specific routes for censure. In July 1820, for instance, a decree banned couriers traveling from Istanbul to Baghdad and back from carrying merchandise on behalf of traders as this delayed the delivery of official correspondence. In some cases, the merchandise could be so heavy that the horses carrying it died.[27]

Tatar couriers' movements were also recorded. In 1713, a roll-call register (yoklama defteri) listed every single marshal and tatar courier in imperial service—a snapshot in time of where all marshals and tatars were located physically.[28] This snapshot included the names of 992 couriers, of whom 553 were present in the capital. Thirty-eight were retired. One was found to have been deceased and thus removed from the register.[29] Another 235 had been sent on various delivery tasks in different provinces of the empire—details were given regarding which specific pashas and aghas had dispatched these messengers. The remaining 165 were either arriving in the capital soon or were in distant regions and had not been able to arrive for the roll call; their last known locations were listed.[30]

This roll-call register of tatar couriers resembles the muster lists used in troop mobilizations for war campaigns.[31] Orders were sent out to soldiers to arrive at a specified mustering point, full attendance was taken of those who showed up, and interim roll calls would be made at periodic intervals. The creating of roll-call registers helped bureaucrats check for discrepancies between paper records and actual membership in the Tatar Corps.[32]

From the mid-eighteenth century on, Tatar couriers' oral messages entered the written record as tatar reports (*tatar takrīri*). Typically, tatar reports contained a title that consisted of a one-line summary of the report's contents. These reports were concisely written and offered information about what was transpiring on the ground. They almost never included the elaborate, opening formulas that characterized imperial decrees or other kinds of internal memos. It is possible that these reports were dictated by couriers to scribes in the imperial bureaucracy, which may account for their standardized form, tone, and register.[33] The earliest known example of a tatar report is dated to October 1745.[34]

Tatar reports addressed a range of issues. Some conveyed military intelligence.[35] For example, in 1832, a tatar courier reported that Ibrahim Pasha and his troops were headed for Aleppo and included details about troop strength.[36] At the time Mehmed Ali, the governor of Egypt, and his son, Ibrahim Pasha, had invaded Syria.[37]

Tatar reports were used to corroborate reports from provincial governors. In one instance, in 1798, a tatar report directly contradicted the claims of the governor of Rumeli.[38] While the governor claimed that he had allied with a bandit leader to keep the peace, the tatar reported that the governor had, in fact, lost control of the bandit leader, who was plundering the region around Plovdiv (modern Bulgaria). The tatar further revealed that the bandit was using his relationship with the governor to appoint local officials who would be amenable to his interests.[39] By exposing this web of conflicting interests, the tatar report offered a counterpoint to the governor's narrative.

Tatar reports also helped to maintain the Ottoman postal system itself, as exemplified by reports regarding efforts to recoup stolen or lost mail. In 1826, a tatar had been attacked by bandits from the Arab tribe of Aneze between Hama and Homs, and they took his carrier bag (*torba*) and abandoned it in the desert.[40] Subsequently, the deputy lieutenant-governors (*mütesellim*) of Hama and Homs stated that they would send men to the desert, and if they found the carrier bag, they would hand it over to tatar.[41] This was how a "lost and found" service might have looked like in the nineteenth century.

Mail was not always paper. Sometimes tatars were charged with delivering body parts from the battlefield. In 1789/1790, Tatar Omer and Mehmed Agha had to deliver two hundred heads and a hundred ears (*iki yüz kelle ve yüz kulak*) from the battlefield of Anapa, along the northeastern coast of the Black Sea in modern Russia. Officials were rewarded for obtaining the severed body parts of the vanquished, which would be displayed outside the Topkapı Palace in Istanbul in a symbolic boost for the victorious Ottoman side.[42]

Tatar reports also recorded numerical information regarding manufacturing and production volumes. For example, the villages of Mürefte, Ganos, and Hora in Thrace were well-known tile- and brick-making centers.[43] In the 1790s, information about local factories and their production numbers was sent via tatar to the imperial capital; in this case, 5,540,000 baked tiles and 1,442,000 unbaked tiles had been produced.[44]

The appearance of tatar reports with such diverse contents raises the question of how the kinds of information they conveyed had been transmitted previously. Had they been orally transmitted before the late eighteenth century? Perhaps, as the amount of information flowing to the imperial bureaucracy increased over the years, the oral transmission of some information gradually became written down. These written records might have made it easier for imperial bureaucrats to document, organize, and remember the kinds of information they conveyed. As the bureaucratic corps expanded, documentation became more important for safeguarding institutional memory. Nevertheless, tatar couriers likely continued to convey oral messages after the eighteenth century; there is no documented evidence of this one way or another. What is new, though, is the routine documentation of *some* of their testimonies.

It is against this backdrop that compensation for tatar deaths became institutionalized. Knowledge of the deaths of couriers while on the job has survived because of petitions for compensation by surviving family members included in the archive. Such financial compensation, or at least its formal documentation, was a new development in the nineteenth century.

Tatar Küçük Mustafa, who froze to death with his horse during a snowstorm, was not the only courier to perish while delivering official correspondence. In 1867, Tatar Yusuf Agha was killed by highway bandits while delivering mail from Skopje. This event is recorded because his orphaned son, Muhyiddin Efendi (or an adult guardian acting on his behalf), had petitioned the administration for income.[45] A subsequent report reveals a few more details surrounding Tatar Yusuf's death: he was wounded while carrying mail correspondence, and he had two wives, one of whom was the mother of Muhyiddin. Unfortunately, it is not known how this case was resolved and whether any compensation was awarded.[46]

Sometimes the widows' voices were preserved in the archive. In 1857, Hatice submitted a petition in which she addressed the Ottoman state directly. "My husband, Tatar Mehmed, was killed by highway bandits near Isparta," she began. She complained that while the police (*bāb-ı żabṭiye*) had dealt with the matter, a long time had passed and his property had been taken by the authorities.

"I found myself, a woman [*eksik etek*], going again and again to the office to ask for help."[47] She protested this injustice, sought an imperial decree to set things right, and signed off with her name. In the paper trail that followed, we learn that Tatar Mehmed had been killed near a place called Burdur. Furthermore, the four murderers had been imprisoned by the police but had not yet been judged. The paper trail ends abruptly. It is not known what conclusion was reached or whether she was ultimately awarded compensation.

There is a rare eighteenth-century precedent to this nineteenth-century practice. However, the eighteenth-century request was framed differently from subsequent compensation requests: instead of asking for compensation, the widow requested that her tatar husband's money be returned to her.[48] In June 1765, a tatar's surviving widow alleged that 500 *guruş* had been pocketed by her deceased husband's boss, el-Haj Ahmed Pasha, the former commander of the Vidin fort. The commander had dispatched her husband to deliver some correspondence to the governor of Rumelia in Sofia, where he died. His widow alleged that el-Haj Ahmed Pasha had then pocketed the deceased's money and property that amounted to 500 *guruş*. In response, the judge in Sofia conducted an investigation and declared the widow's claims unfounded. According to the judge, the property and money of the late tatar had not amounted to 500 *guruş*; in fact, it had not even been sufficient to cover the costs of his funeral. This implied that the deceased tatar's family was indebted to the authorities, not the other way round.

Although this widow had only dared to ask for her husband's rightful property and cash to be restored to her, widows and other bereaved family members of later generations went further. They sought monetary compensation for their husbands' deaths directly from the authorities, just like Tatar Küçük Mustafa's family did after he was found frozen to death. These widows of tatar couriers faced similar financial challenges upon the deaths of their husbands and tried to work within the Ottoman administrative system to claw back financial support that they would have enjoyed had their husbands not perished. There was a shared goal of survival.

The risks of overland travel were not new. Neither were pensions and group insurance arrangements. In the sixteenth and seventeenth centuries, retired military officers were eligible for pensions. Provisions were made for orphans and dependents of deceased military officers in some cases.[49] What was new in the nineteenth century was that a wider range of officials became eligible for such benefits.

Tatar couriers were one such group; like their military colleagues, they came to enjoy benefits in the mid- and late nineteenth century.[50] So did police officers. Like tatar couriers, police officers faced many physical threats in their daily work, for they were tasked with securing roads and capturing bandits. One gendarme commented, "Night and day, we pursue bandits in the mountains, forests, valleys, and hills. I have perhaps fought bandits in fifty skirmishes until now. My body has twenty-five wounds."[51] Police officers could be compensated for work-related injuries, and their surviving families would also be compensated in the event of work-related deaths. They were also entitled to retirement pensions upon thirty years of service. In contrast, rank-and-file gendarmes only had the right to a proper burial.[52]

The case of the tatar courier coheres with broader patterns of employment in the imperial bureaucracy, given similar practices across different groups of Ottoman officials. Serving the Ottoman bureaucracy now acquired the form of "employment" more familiar to us today, a contractual relation that came with benefits and compensation. The older notion of being the sultan's slave or servitor (*kul*) had faded.[53] Between 1765, when a widow demanded money to be returned to her, and the 1860s, when Tatar Küçük Mustafa's family won compensation for his death, new workplace norms and expectations emerged. In the nineteenth century, surviving family members were newly entitled to compensation for the loss of their tatar sons, husbands, and fathers.

The transformation of the *ulak* into the *tatar* is a story of organizational change. Out of an amorphous group of *ulak* couriers, comprising officials of diverse ranks and titles, the office of the tatar emerged as a professional corps sometime in the eighteenth century. Tatars began to wear uniforms. At least some of the information they conveyed began to be recorded in standard formats. Their documentary presence proliferated. Their surviving family members began to receive formal financial compensation for their deaths on the job. All this took place against a backdrop of a changing imperial bureaucracy. The workday of an Ottoman official began to be defined. The office space came to be regulated. Laziness began to be penalized.

The next few chapters track the decrees shaping the postal service and the bookkeepers, postmasters, and villagers who collectively sustained postal operations throughout the eighteenth century and beyond.

CHAPTER 4

The Decrees

All the post stations are to be abolished . . . henceforth the post
station keepers shall maintain the horses themselves.

—MUSTAFA II (November 1696)[1]

On November 6, 1696, Sultan Mustafa II abolished (*ref*) the existing Ottoman postal system. He ordered a completely new system to be established in its
place within six months. Escalating costs and horse shortages had reached a critical point, and the sultan decided that drastic measures were needed. This was
the first major overhaul of the postal system since the transition from ad hoc
horse confiscations to the establishment of fixed post stations, which had taken
place over a hundred years earlier.

As technological systems expand, certain components within these systems
may become out of sync with the rest. The historian of technology Thomas
Hughes referred to such lagging components as a "reverse salient." A salient is a
geometric protrusion, a bulging feature on the battlefield that penetrates into
enemy territory; a reverse salient is the opposite of that. It is akin to a bottleneck, but Hughes found the visual of the bottleneck too rigid. He felt that the
idea of a reverse salient was better able to capture the "drag," the "limits to potential," and the "emergent friction" in dynamic, expanding systems undergoing
uneven change. Hughes further observed that in many technological systems,
the need for organization, rather than the need for a new invention or a technological breakthrough, could correct the reverse salient. The holding-company
of the 1920s was one such example. It was a novel organizational form that
could supervise "the construction, management, and financing of horizontally
and vertically integrated utilities."[2]

The Ottoman postal system was an expanding technological system undergoing uneven change in the 1690s. It had already been experiencing difficulties for some time before Mustafa II's decrees. Courier traffic had increased, straining the capacity of the postal system. As a result, couriers frequently found themselves stranded at post stations, unable to find fresh horses with which to continue their journeys. This delayed government communications, frustrating bureaucrats. This was not the first reverse salient in the history of the postal system—I hypothesize that the sixteenth-century transition away from ad hoc confiscations had corrected the previous reverse salient, and the establishment of fixed post stations at that time was able to expand the system's capacity to meet the needs of a growing Ottoman bureaucracy for roughly a century.

In the 1690s, the problem of horse supply exerted a drag on the system again. The seventeenth century was marked by political turmoil and costly military campaigns on multiple fronts, placing pressure on the Ottoman fiscal system and its communications system.[3] This decade saw notable reforms, including the introduction of life-term tax farming (*mālikāne*) and the reform of the *cizye* tax, as well as the settlement and sedentarization of nomadic tribes.[4] The postal system, too, underwent a reorganization during this decade in order to achieve an even, balanced expansion. Sultan Mustafa II's two imperial decrees provided a novel way forward—the decrees may not have been the first attempt at fixing this problem, but they were the most comprehensive attempt.

For decades, scholars have interpreted these two decrees as having introduced a "marketisation and privatisation" of the Ottoman postal system.[5] I argue the opposite—that, in fact, the Ottoman imperial bureaucracy continued to administer the postal system. Nothing was left to the "market," and nothing was privatized. The Ottoman postal system was still an exclusive government communications system run by the state. A nominal fee was introduced for the use of horses, but only officials were eligible to access post stations—common subjects who could afford the fee were still not allowed to do so, not legally in any case. Furthermore, many officials were granted fee waivers, which they simply presented to local postmasters in order to obtain fresh horses for free. For these reasons, Mustafa II's decrees should be understood as initiating a new phase of organizational reform, not a phase of marketization and privatization.

What is tricky, however, is understanding what this reform entailed in practice. What did Sultan Mustafa II mean when he announced that the existing postal system was to be "abolished" (*ref*)? What did it mean for the postmasters to "maintain the horses themselves"? Were they not already doing that? In fact, a close reading of these decrees reveals even more ambiguity and confusion.

It turns out that Ottoman bureaucrats did not have the knowledge about postal operations required to implement Mustafa II's reforms. There was a knowledge gap between sedentary scribes in the imperial capital and couriers circulating in the empire. Strictly speaking, Mustafa II's two decrees did not achieve their dual aim of "abolishing" the entire system and installing a new one in its place within six months. Nevertheless, these reform decrees did leave an important legacy: they shaped new documentary practices and bookkeeping routines in Ottoman postal administration that persisted over a century.

Mustafa II's decrees were two among more than fifty imperial decrees concerning the reorganization of the Ottoman postal system issued between the 1690s and the mid-nineteenth century.[6] This amounted to an average of one reform decree issued every three years.

The earliest known decree dates to 1690, six years before Mustafa II's. Channeling the voice of Sultan Suleiman II (r. 1687–1691), the decree complained that for a few years now, the sultan's orders had been ignored by post stations all over Anatolia.[7] Everyone was taking as many horses as he wished from post stations, leaving official couriers who were charged with delivering important matters stranded for days, unable to find fresh horses with which to continue their journeys. Postmasters were reprimanded for their carelessness in inspecting courier orders. They were urged to check the sultan's monogram for its authenticity— courier orders without an authentic monogram were not to be accepted (fig. 9). This request suggests that imperial bureaucrats had information about expired or counterfeit (sāhte) courier orders in circulation.

Barely a year and a half later another decree identified a new culprit: couriers. This time, not "everyone" but instead couriers specifically were blamed for taking more horses than they were allowed.[8] Issued in December 1691 by Sultan Ahmed II (r. 1691–1695), this decree complained that a range of Anatolian officials had continued to disobey Sultan Suleiman II's earlier decree by issuing stamped papers for their subordinates to obtain horses at post stations despite not having the authority to do so, which resulted in a shortage of horses.[9]

Another few years later, in 1696, Mustafa II (r. 1695–1703) issued the two reform decrees in which he took up the same issues of crippling costs and shortages of horses, alleging that horses were being "worked to death" and that villagers who serviced the post stations were being "ruined." The decrees also identified a range of officials who used post horses for trivial matters and "even for their own affairs."[10] Given this situation, Mustafa II abolished (ref') all existing post stations and commanded that a new system (tertīb-i cedīd) be established within six months' time.

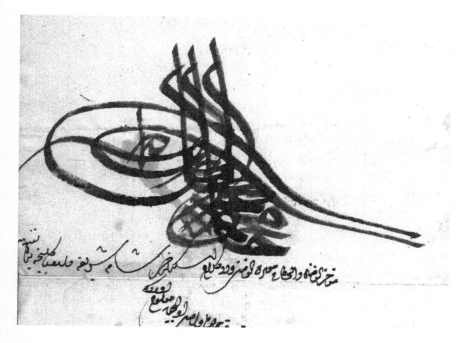

Figure 9. Example of Sultan Mahmud I's monogram (*tuğra*) found on a courier order dated 1743 (AH 1156). BOA, Topkapı Sarayı Müzesi Arşivi, Evrak (TS.MA.e) 891/31).

In this new system, fees would be charged for post station usage. Henceforth, officials and couriers would have to pay for horses, guides, and food at post stations.[11] It now cost 10 *akçe* to use one horse for one hour's travel. Guides (*sürücü*) accompanying official travelers were also to be dispatched at the same rate of 10 *akçe* per individual per hour's travel. Couriers were no longer permitted to eat free meals at post stations. Mustafa II ordered that they take meals at a price corresponding to the cost of the food consumed. As if anticipating resistance, the decree further warned of harsh penalties. Any couriers who sought free or subsidized food were to be penalized. Those who did not pay for horses were to be punished. Provincial governors were to "prevent and restrain such people" and note down the "the names and descriptions and characters of the offenders."[12]

Mustafa II's reforms took aim at precisely the kind of behavior Evliya Çelebi had exhibited when he gaily invited the rebel Çomar Bölükbaşı to travel with him and his entourage. Evliya's socializing had nothing to do with work, was not an important matter, and would have been considered his "own affair." Evliya even traveled at a slower pace, lodging at more stations than was necessary, to accommodate Çomar Bölükbaşı's weakened physical condition. All that occurred

in 1649. Had Evliya been alive in 1696, he might have found himself penalized
for his actions.

> For the operating expenses of each post station in districts which lie on
> main routes, the greater part is provided by the inhabitants of villages;
> some [by] the Imperial Treasury, and some [by] transfers of funds and
> grants-in-aid from districts.
>   ... in districts that are not on the main route, and where there is no
> designated post station ... the people of the district meet the expenses
> among themselves. Hence there is *no entry* for post stations of this type
> in the Treasury Registers, and as a consequence, the total annual cost of
> the postal system is *not known*.

—Mustafa II's first reform decree, November 6, 1696[13]

Despite Mustafa II's intention to abolish an entire system and install a completely new one in its place, his decrees inadvertently reveal that, in 1696, the Ottoman ruling establishment did not know much about the operations of the
postal system. The first decree sketched out broad guidelines for reform that re-
volved around its centerpiece legislation: the levying of fees for the use of horses,
food, and lodging.

But as if cognizant that bureaucrats and officials might not have known how
to execute the reforms and levy fees, the sultan issued a second decree five days
later that addressed the operational details of how the first decree could be implemented. Specifically, the second decree assigned concrete bookkeeping duties
to provincial officials, who had to report the following information to bureaucrats in the capital:

- The number of post horses maintained at each post station, including
  official [*mu'ayyen*] and unofficial [*gayri mu'ayyen*] post stations
- The annual expenses of each post station in *akçe*, including both official
  and unofficial post stations
- The contributions provided by villages to maintain official post
  stations, denominated in *akçe*
- The contributions provided by villages to maintain unofficial post
  stations, denominated in *akçe*
- The distance in hours between each post station and the next[14]

Did you notice that last bullet point? *The distance in hours between each post
station and the next.* Bureaucrats in the imperial capital did not know what these

distances were.[15] How, then, did bureaucrats think they could implement a fee-paying system that charged 10 *akçe* per horse per hour of travel?

Bureaucrats also did not know how many horses were maintained at each station. They did not know where the unofficial post stations in the empire were. They did not know how much each village was forking out to support their local post station. They did not possess what might be considered basic information about the Ottoman postal system, much less what was required to implement ambitious reforms.

But all this information would have been known by couriers. Shuttling between pasha and pasha, post station and post station, Ottoman couriers would have known which routes to take and where they could stop for a rest. They possessed a working knowledge that was not known to sedentary bureaucrats in the capital.

Bureaucrats required all this information in order to implement Mustafa II's reforms, to translate his vision into actionable policy. This need motivated a complete reorganization of the relationships among sedentary bureaucrats and bookkeepers working in the imperial capital, postmasters operating at post stations, villagers provisioning these stations, and couriers circulating through the empire. Now bookkeepers in the imperial capital could no longer remain ignorant of information that typically only a courier would know. Now they had to keep detailed records. Mustafa II's two decrees, which synthesized the concerns of previously issued reform decrees, put in place new documentary processes that endured over the next century.

> The post horses issued to couriers . . . *are to be recorded and listed* by the local judicial authorities. The current postmasters shall exercise trusteeship on behalf of the Treasury . . . and *the accounts of each post station* shall be made up at the beginning of each Ruz-ı Hızır, and the fees which have been collected together *shall be sent and delivered to the Imperial Treasury.*
>
> —Mustafa II's first reform decree, November 6, 1696[16]

The most significant legacy of Mustafa II's decrees was in shaping new documentary routines and creating new quantification practices in postal administration. These decrees did not work alone. Grand viziers, bookkeepers, and other scribes discussed the vision sketched out by Mustafa II's decrees and elaborated upon them. These discussions were recorded in memos, some of which are found in the prefaces of fiscal registers.

Among the memos elaborating on Mustafa II's vision was one dated May 7, 1698, which received approval from the grand vizier, Köprülü Amcazade Hüseyin Pasha.[17] If, as the decrees instructed, bookkeepers and postmasters were to keep records of the horses issued to couriers, as well as records of the fees received, how were they to do so? The scribe showed how: assume that the hourly fees for the use of each horse was pegged at 10 *akçe* per hour. Then, assume that each horse took ten hours for each trip and took one trip every four days, or ninety trips in 360 days. In a year this would amount to 9,000 *akçe*, or 75 *guruş*.[18] The collected fees would cover over half of the expenses needed for the maintenance of each horse, which he had calculated to be 147.5 *guruş*.[19] The remaining 72.5 *guruş* would be funded from sources other than the fees, meaning tax revenues from assigned villages. In other words, the scribe provided a range of assumed values (ten hours per trip, one trip every four days, ninety trips in 360 days, etc.) that together constituted a standard multiplier.

A large part of bookkeeping would henceforth be based upon the number of horses maintained at a post station; from that single number, a whole array of accounting information would be derived. It is not known whether each horse did take an average of ten hours for each trip. Nor is it known how the scribe came up with his constant values and his variables. But this formula remained in use for much of the following century.

The postal administration's turn to quantification enabled it to build an imperial-scale model that could contain hundreds of geographically dispersed post stations within the same frame. It also enabled bureaucrats to construct an abstract epistemological object: the aggregate annual expenditure of each post station.[20] With this object, all post stations could be easily compared and plotted along the same axes. Fiscal registers listed the aggregate annual expenditure of all post stations found along each of the six main routes they belonged to— an imperial-scale quantitative snapshot was created. As a technology of distance, quantification acted as a language that could commensurate diverse provinces, connecting local-level operational details to an empire-wide system.[21]

The grand vizier also approved new administrative procedures to keep track of post station expenditures. Typically, couriers dispatched from the imperial capital were issued courier orders that entitled them to free horses and access to post station services. Yet there had been reports about governors issuing such courier orders without discretion, thereby stretching the system beyond its operating capacity and resulting in hardship for postmasters.[22] To discourage such indiscretion, postmasters were to keep a record of every imperial courier order they received.[23] With these records, it would be possible to match provincial records (of courier orders that were *used* to obtain free horses) with records in the imperial capital (of courier orders that were *issued* to entitle holders to obtain free horses). Together, provincial officials and imperial bureaucrats would, in principle, be able to track the issuing of every single horse from post stations and verify whether each transaction was an authorized one. The paper flows that the decrees and the grand vizier had set in motion became routine for decades to come, engendering thousands of pages of paper records that remain in the archives today.

Mustafa II's decrees were issued during a volatile period of elite politics. Traditionally, the sultan's household and the military provided the primary training ground for recruits to high administrative office. Over the seventeenth century, vizier and pasha households had gradually replaced those venues to become the new training ground for elite administrators in the Ottoman government. In other words, the House of Osman changed from being the sole center of power to being one among several—this marked the transition to the Second Ottoman Empire. By 1695, the start of Mustafa II's reign, more than half of high office appointments went to members of vizier and pasha households. The Köprülü household, which had produced several grand viziers, was an important example. This household was credited with exerting a stabilizing impact on imperial administration and, for certain periods of time, elite politics, as it controlled the office of the grand vizierhip and oversaw an extensive and effective network. But these were still volatile times. Grand viziers, sultans, and jurists plotted to overthrow each other in a game of shifting alliances. Amcazade Huseyin Köprülü, the grand vizier from 1697 to 1702, fell victim to the intrigues of Mustafa II's tutor and advisor, Feyzullah Efendi. Mustafa II himself was eventually deposed by a jurist whose grandfather had deposed the sultan's own grandfather.[24]

In any case, reforms persisted despite such political turbulence, and the imperial bureaucracy continued to expand. From the sixteenth to the nineteenth century, the scribal service (*ḳalemiye*, or "men of the pen") expanded from 50 clerks and 23 apprentices to between 50,000 and 100,000 men, including nominal affiliations. After the 1830s, the scribal service became known as the civil bureaucracy (*mülkiye*).[25] Career lines for individual scribes became more consolidated, and the scope and definition of tasks became narrower, just as a tap root produces smaller secondary roots that, in turn, produce even smaller tertiary roots.[26] In contrast to the scribal service, the military-administrative establishment and the religious establishment (*ʿulemā*) did not experience the same trajectory of expansion over these three centuries.[27]

Amid this expansion in the number of bureaucratic personnel, new bureaus emerged, such as the Post Station Bureau, the Office of the Reisülküttap (Chief of Secretaries), and the Office of Protocols.[28] Accompanying the creation of new bureaus was the creation of new genres of administrative documents. For instance, the Office of Protocols was established as a separate unit in the final decades of the seventeenth century. The earliest known protocol register (*teşrifāt defteri*) was compiled at the same time.[29] This protocol register chronicled important technical details regarding accession ceremonies, funerals, and the reception of foreign envoys. Such details concerned delicate distinctions in the status hierarchy and the symbolic language of diplomacy, and their recording provided a model of reference and precedent for later ceremonies.

Other examples of documentary specialization abound. The Complaints Register (*şikāyet defteri*) had an interesting journey: it began life as a section within another kind of register, the Register of Important Affairs. In 1649, it was peeled away to become an autonomous Complaints Register. Over a century later, in 1752, the Complaints Register spawned provincial clones through administrative mitosis such that each province in the empire had its own dedicated Provincial Complaints Register (*aḥkām-ı şikāyet*).[30] This "specialization of the provincial paper trail" is also exemplified by the emergence of provincial registers of imperial rescripts (*vilāyet aḥkām defteri*) as well as standardized compilations of legal rulings (Tr. sg. *fetva* / Ar. sg. *fatwā*) by provincial muftis in the seventeenth and eighteenth centuries.[31]

Viewed collectively, the expansion of the imperial bureaucracy in the Second Empire involved a greater specialization in record-keeping at imperial and provincial levels. Sometimes this was aided by the establishment of specialized, dedicated bureaus; sometimes the initiative came from provincial officials.[32] The reforms of the postal administration fit within this wider trend, as the establishment of the Post Station Bureau spurred the production of new genres of post station registers by bookkeepers in the imperial capital, as well as by postmasters in the provinces.[33]

There is, however, a puzzling move by Mustafa II that is difficult to explain. In the 1696 decrees, Mustafa II granted a general permission to private persons to use the Ottoman postal system without any *firman* but with the payment of a prescribed fee. Postmasters were obliged to maintain a number of horses that could cater to this private (non-government) demand.[34] At first glance, this general permission is striking: by authorizing non-official usage of the Ottoman postal system, Mustafa II opened up the exclusively official communication service to all imperial subjects. Despite this nominal authorization, however, subsequent decrees either ignored or expressly walked back this declaration. From 1696 to the 1830s, decrees emphatically insisted that those without official courier passes were not eligible to use horses at post stations.[35] The decrees maintained that post horses served Ottoman officials and government correspondence exclusively. Private usage of post stations was vehemently denied, contradicting Mustafa II's 1696 decrees.

It is difficult to account for this abrupt reversal. Perhaps Mustafa II's two decrees were ahead of their time in anticipating the idea of a postal service that ordinary individuals could use, an idea that entailed a different kind of relationship between the Ottoman imperial bureaucracy and the empire's subjects. Perhaps this prescient quality of Mustafa II's decrees provoked internal opposition from elite bureaucrats that escaped written documentation. Or perhaps this was simply an early modern typo, a gaffe, a trivial blip in the world of early modern policy-making and administration.

Over a century later, Sultan Mahmud II (r. 1808–1839) undertook a major reform of the Ottoman postal system. In the nineteenth century, viziers and bureaucrats were still trying to solve the same problems of rising costs and insufficient horses. Again they called for the "abolishment" of the existing system. Again they argued for the imposition of a (higher) fee. In the nineteenth century, however, Mahmud II introduced new nomenclature: post stations were henceforth to be converted into "rent stations" (*kirahāne*), all postmasters were to be known as "renters" (*kiracı*), and all post horses and animals were to be known as "rent animals" (*kira ḥayvanātı*).[36]

Still, the basic principles of Mahmud II's reforms matched those of Mustafa II's reforms, despite the new terminology. Mahmud II shared his ancestor's concern for escalating costs and the burdens placed on tax-paying subjects, and addressed this in the same way that his ancestor did: by implementing fees (now called rents, *kira*) for horse usage. Instead of Mustafa II's rate of 10 *akçe* per horse per one hour's travel, however, Mahmud II raised the fee to 20 *paras* (or 60 *akçe*). In addition, he updated the existing rationing policy, revising the horse quotas allocated to individual ranks. In sum, Mahmud II's reforms did not stray far from Mustafa II's vision of postal reform from a century earlier.[37]

Experiences from other parts of the world suggest that the problem of cost was a chronic and intrinsic feature of a relay communications system. The Roman *cursus publicus* operated by placing burdensome obligations on inhabitants who maintained stations and draft animals. Mongol messengers riding in haste were, it was noted, "an affliction on the people." The Swedish Postal System faced increasing complaints after the wars from the 1610s on, with peasants protesting "the burden of having to offer free food, horses, and transport."[38] Placed side by side, these problems, spanning over a millennium, give evidence of a common affliction of pre-industrial empires. The problem of costs was neither new nor unique to the Ottomans.

If this was a new reverse salient in the 1830s that signaled uneven expansion resulting in a drag on postal operations, the proposed organizational solution looked very similar to that proposed in 1696. Whether in the 1690s or the 1830s, an enduring problem was rising costs, which was likely due to increased traffic. The increased usage of post stations and horses inaugurated a vicious cycle: with the greater demand for horses, existing horses were being worked to death, resulting in an even smaller number of horses and cascading delays in official communications. The crucial difference between the seventeenth and the nineteenth centuries, though, was that new technological breakthroughs and innovations (such as the telegraph) would soon arrive on Ottoman shores.[39]

Regardless, Sultan Mustafa II's reforms can be regarded as having set the template for Ottoman postal administration. Even though they were not the first attempt at postal reform and did not achieve their stipulated aims, they left an important legacy.

Mustafa II's first decree ends thusly:

> I command that on the arrival of [the courier] with My Noble Order, you are to act in conformity with My command replete with authority; furthermore, on the basis of the foregoing, you are to enter [the text of the firman] into the [judicial] Register (*sicill*) in each [district] in which a post station is situated, and to cause copies which you are to authenticate to be put into the hands of the post station keepers. And you are to prevent and restrain anyone from transgression of this My Noble Command.
>
> Thus you are to know; you are to place reliance on the Noble Sign.
>
> Written on the tenth day of the month of *Rebīʿül-aḫir* in the year one thousand, one hundred and eight [1696 CE].

IN THE RESIDENCE OF
EDIRNE
THE WELL-GUARDED[40]

CHAPTER 5

The Bookkeeper

Sometime in the 1690s, an Ottoman bookkeeper wanted to find out the cost of a horseshoe and nail. He had just been transferred to a newly established division called the Post Station Bureau (*menzil halîfesi ḳalemi*).[1] Parked within the Bureau of Contributions in Kind (*mevḳūfāt ḳalemi*), the Post Station Bureau was created to administer the fiscal affairs of the Ottoman postal system. This was a new development. The postal system had not been autonomously administered before. The bookkeeper would have to actively create new protocols, routines, and workflows. Doing so entailed defining even the most trivial of details, such as determining the cost of a horseshoe and nail, which this newly transferred bookkeeper did. He wrote in a fiscal register: "horseshoe and nail—3 *akçe*."

But how did he arrive at this quote? Did the bookkeeper send somebody to check with the Imperial Stables? Or perhaps the bookkeeper asked the farrier himself when he brought his own horses for shoeing? How many sets of horseshoes and nails did 3 *akçe* cover, given that horseshoes are typically changed every four to six weeks?[2] There is no explanation of how the bookkeeper arrived at this number, which would be aggregated into a multiplier that included other post station expenses, such as the costs of barley, straw, horse equipment (nose bag, halter), the salaries of the housekeeper, cook, and so forth. Using the ladder (*merdiven*) accounting style, the bookkeeper added these costs up to calculate the annual expenditure of the post station (fig. 10).

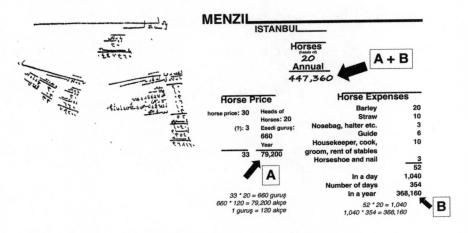

Figure 10. The cost of a "horseshoe and nail" (*na'l ve mıh*) as derived in the ladder (*merdiven*) style of accounting, 1691–1692. BOA, KK 2742, 2.jpg. Diagram by author.

Ottoman bookkeepers were tasked with creating a new arena of postal administration beginning in the 1690s. Previously, postal affairs were administered as a tax matter. After the 1690s, however, postal affairs were "carved out" and administered independently by the newly established Post Station Bureau. I hypothesize that the bookkeepers who were newly transferred to this bureau had previously been working in tax administration, and although they brought with them experience in compiling tax registers, they did not know much about the Ottoman postal system at the outset. This ignorance is reflected in the earliest fiscal registers that bookkeepers produced for the Post Station Bureau—the Comprehensive Post Station Register (*menzil defteri*). In this chapter I line up four such registers produced between the 1690s and 1760s to trace the fitful learning curve of these bookkeepers. As they learned more about the postal system, they refined their approach to administering it. This chapter therefore continues the story from the previous chapter about the two decrees of 1696, showing how the bookkeepers in the Post Station Bureau produced the knowledge necessary to translate Mustafa II's vision of reform into actionable policy.

These four registers are referred to here in chronological order as Alpha (1690), Beta (1691–1692), Delta (1697–1704), and Omicron (1757–1769) and are a gateway to the bookkeeper's world.[3] As a broad category of archival document, such fiscal registers hold a special place in Ottoman historiography. Earlier generations of Ottoman historians used to focus on the analysis of one kind of fiscal register (*defter*)—the Land Deed and Registration Registers (*tapu ve taḥrīr defterleri*)—to understand an important land tenure system known as the *timar*. Many were interested in how Ottoman antecedents could be brought to bear on contemporary land reforms in Turkey. Others were influenced by Marxism and modernization theory and were deeply invested in defending the empire against notions that it was "necessarily corrupt" and "decadent."[4] Working within this subfield of "defterology," these pioneering scholars mined fiscal registers for information on landholding arrangements, agricultural production, and demographic history.[5] While they produced many valuable studies, other scholars were cautious about such approaches given their overwhelming focus on quantitative data and the optimistic underlying assumption that such data provided an accurate representation of historical reality.[6]

More recently, historians have approached statistics and quantification not simply as a technical phenomenon but also as a social and political one.[7] Accounting historians, too, began to approach historical accounting ledgers as a social practice and as a part of culture, rather than as a neutral, technical matter.[8] The doyenne of Ottoman studies, Suraiya Faroqhi, suggested that scholars could perhaps pivot to considering the compilers of such data instead of the data itself to provide a social history or to illuminate the worldviews of the bookkeepers who produced Ottoman fiscal registers.[9]

Faroqhi's suggestion coincided with kindred intellectual trends. Scholars were starting to question the information preserved in archives and to examine how such information was produced. They began to view the archive as the explicit subject of historical analysis rather than as a neutral treasury of information. By paying attention to an archival document's silences, probing its marginalia, and tracing its afterlife, historians and anthropologists alike have attempted to recover occluded social histories beyond the formulaic registers of state-sanctioned scripts.[10]

This convergence of skeptical attitudes toward quantitative historical sources and archives more generally informs my approach to the Ottoman fiscal register and its composers, the bookkeepers. By contextualizing Ottoman bookkeepers as social beings rooted in existing communities who reproduced traditions of practice, I mine the technical language of accounting entries, their marginalia, and their blank spaces for clues about the organizational changes that bookkeepers brought about.[11] If knowledge infrastructures like Euclidean geometry, which underpins how many of us imagine space, may be compared to material infrastructures like aqueducts and roads, which shape how humans live life, then decoding these fiscal registers and how bookkeepers organized accounting information will be key to elucidating material aspects of Ottoman postal operations.[12]

In the 1690s, as we saw, bookkeepers produced a new kind of fiscal register called the Comprehensive Post Station Register under the aegis of the Post Station Bureau. It was a database of all official post stations across the empire arranged in geographical order. The first entry was usually the imperial capital (Istanbul or, before 1703, Edirne), which served as the starting point of the six main roads of the Ottoman Empire, called arms (*kol*). Three arms, the left, middle, and right, stretched across the Balkans, and three others extended across Anatolia and the Arab provinces. The Comprehensive Post Station Register was organized into sections, each of which tracked the routes of these six arms. There were also sub-sections that tracked smaller, secondary routes that branched off these six main arms, including water routes, such as those along the Danube. Within each of section and sub-section, stations were listed in the order that a courier would encounter them if he set off from the capital.[13]

Bookkeepers made extensive changes to the form and content of Comprehensive Post Station Registers between the 1690s and the 1760s. In terms of length, Omicron is almost five times longer than Alpha, with 356 pages compared to 64 pages.[14] In terms of content, bookkeepers recorded different kinds of information about each post station. For instance, they began to record the fees collected at each post station included in Delta, which was compiled around 1697; they did not do so previously in Alpha or Beta. This is probably due to Sultan Mustafa II's decision, in 1696, to impose a fee of 10 *akçe* per horse per hour's travel. The Comprehensive Post Station Registers reflect both the development of postal administration over the eighteenth century and the arc of the bookkeepers' learning journey, beginning with their initial unfamiliarity with the postal system and their eventual mastery of it through the administrative routines they created.

Alpha, the earliest Comprehensive Post Station Register, compiled around 1690, represents the first stage in this long process. The bookkeepers who compiled it were likely recent transfers into this newly established bureau, with very few precedents or senior colleagues to learn from. For these reasons, Alpha stands out among the four extant registers. Unlike later registers, it is replete with blank entries. And unlike later registers, it bears traces of the postal system's close links with tax administration and military administration; these links became less salient over time, especially by the 1760s, when Omicron was produced. Finally, unlike later registers, Alpha references much earlier records of post stations that were kept in the Imperial Treasury.

Alpha contained many blank entries, which suggests that, at the time of its composition, bookkeepers were unfamiliar with many basic features of the Ottoman postal system. They did not know the names of many post stations, and even when they did, they did not know, or were unable to obtain, information about them. These blank entries may be broadly classified into four different types:

1. completely blank entries (without even the names of post stations)
2. blank entries of named stations with a comment that they had "sufficient horses"
3. blank entries of named stations with a comment that they were "unofficial post stations"
4. repeated entries for the same named post station[15]

Completely blank entries typically afflict whole sections of postal routes. All the entries for the post stations between Damascus and Mecca, for example, were left completely blank except for the names of the individual post stations. In figure 11, not just the post stations along the route from Damascus to Mecca but also the post stations along the route from Damascus to Jerusalem, from the Bridge of Jacob (along the upper Jordan River) to Egypt, newly established post stations from Istanbul to Çeşme, and certain sections of the route from Istanbul to Erzurum and Kars have blank entries.[16] Occasionally, individual blank entries occur on otherwise filled-up pages, such as those for the Ismail Geçidi, Tatarpınarı, and Akkerman post stations, which lay on the route between Istanbul and Özi.[17]

A second type of blank entry is for a post station with sufficient horses, a fact made known by a marginal note scrawled above the upper border of the entry: "this post station raises a sufficient amount of post horses" (*Kifāyet mikdāri menzil bārgīri beslerler*). Such entries are scattered all over the post station register.[18]

A third type of blank entry has a note above it stating that the post station in question is not an official post station (*muʿayyen menzil değildir*) or that no post station is at that location (*menzil yokdur*).[19] However, the fact that entries for these post stations are recorded in this register suggests that the locations were already being used by couriers as rest stops, but probably without official fiscal arrangements, meaning that local villages probably bore the costs as a customary practice. The post stations of İnceğiz, Vize, Ladik, and Hacıköy, as well as

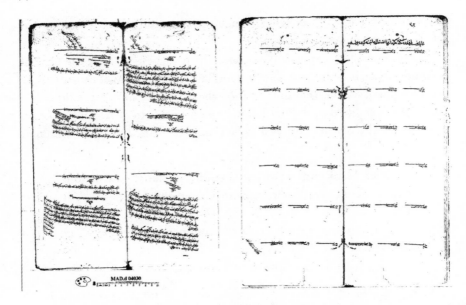

Figure 11. Alpha, the earliest known Comprehensive Post Station Register, 1690.
On the left, a typical "filled-in" page; on the right, a page of blank entries.
BOA, MAD 4030, pp. 10–11 (3.jpg), and pp. 32–33/pp. 10–11, 14.jpg/pp. 32–33.

others with as-yet-undeciphered names, are marked as unofficial post stations.[20]

Finally, a fourth type of blank entry consists of repeated entries for the same post station. These repeated entries typically feature marginal notes instructing the reader to refer to an earlier record within the register ("recorded above," *Bālāda muḳayyeddir*). These entries may be found in clusters, consecutively arranged.[21] This kind of extensive repetition does not exist in later post station registers, which bolsters the theory that Alpha represents one of the first times bookkeepers had to prepare a Comprehensive Post Station Register.

The recurring pattern of these blank entries suggest that in the 1690s, Ottoman bookkeepers were still discovering basic information about the sprawling Ottoman postal system. As I explained in Chapter 1, old post stations were routinely abolished and new ones were routinely established due to war, natural disasters, and human neglect. Before bookkeepers could fill in these blanks, they had to ascertain which post stations were still in use, the number of horses housed at each post station, and whether a station was sufficient for postal service purposes. Later post station registers did not retain many of these idiosyncrasies—repeated post station entries, blank entries with marginal notes indicating sufficiency of horses, or notes on the lack of official status of the station. The composition of Alpha therefore marked the moment when bookkeepers began to learn about and to regularly track the status of post stations. This was the start of a process of knowledge transfer that documented in writing what had previously only been known by couriers. These blank spaces were meant to be filled in.[22]

Bookkeepers compiling Alpha likely drew on their prior experience compiling tax registers. This hypothesis is based on the observation that before the 1690s, fiscal information pertaining to the postal system could be found in tax registers. After all, the postal system was funded by taxes—either by tax revenues or indirectly through tax exemptions.

Let's take the example of the Extraordinary Tax Register. Extraordinary taxes ('avārıż) were a type of tax levied on villages. Accordingly, the Extraordinary Tax Register is a database of individual villages and the extraordinary taxes that each village was obligated to pay. Postal affairs only entered the tax register incidentally, as when villages were exempted from paying extraordinary taxes in return for providing essential services such as post station management. In Extraordinary Tax Registers, these villages had a special label: they were referred to as the menzilciyān.[23]

Conversely, the Comprehensive Post Station Register is a database of post stations, not villages. Unlike the Extraordinary Tax Register, the Comprehensive Post Station Register did not record every single village in each district in each province. Instead, it recorded all the post stations in the empire, and then only the names of villages that were responsible for maintaining those post stations. The Comprehensive Post Station Register was not concerned with the tax obligations of all villages, just villages that financed post stations. It was as if postal matters were "peeled" away from the universe of tax matters and came to be autonomously recorded. To use the analogy of a narrative, the Comprehensive Post Station Register reframes the narrative subject away from the individual village and toward the individual post station.

Traces of the earliest, halting stages of this "reframing" may be found in Alpha, the earliest Comprehensive Post Station Register. Consider the entry for Eskişehir, about 81 miles southeast of Bursa, in Alpha. According to this entry, sometime in the year 1670 its villagers submitted a petition to the Imperial

Council in Edirne in which they explained that historically, they were tasked with rearing four post horses for the post station as part of their tax obligations. In reality, however, they had been obliged to provide up to thirty or forty post station horses. The villagers of Eskişehir implored that their difficult situation be taken into consideration. On October 19, 1670, that sultanic favor was granted. After verifying their contention with older documents stored in the Imperial Treasury, the sultan declared that the villagers of Eskişehir were henceforth required to maintain only ten post horses for the post station, not more, not fewer.[24] All this information occupied the main space of the entry, and it was all about the village's tax obligations. There was not any information about courier traffic or about the use of the post horses and the station. In contrast, later Comprehensive Registers shifted their main focus toward the recording of courier traffic and the use of post horses in the station; information about a village's tax obligations become relegated to the marginalia in these later registers. I hypothesize that recently transferred bookkeepers compiled Alpha using information predominantly drawn from tax registers but reformatted it to accord with individual post station entries. It would take more time for actual postal administrative content to be created.[25]

Extraordinary taxes were just one type of tax obligation. Ottoman subjects faced a range of tax obligations that were undertaken collectively, usually at the whole-village level. Sometimes, specific villages charged with the maintenance of local post stations could get some or all of their tax obligations waived. Alpha shows us, for instance, that villagers from Provadiya, a town located along the Black Sea coast in modern Bulgaria, were exempted from Extraordinary Taxes ('avārıż) in return for supporting the post station and maintaining the local fort.[26] In the western Anatolian town of Iznik, villagers were exempted from paying the Substitute Tax for Saltpeter (bedel-i güherçile) in return for maintaining the Iznik post station, according to a decree dated 1647.[27] (Saltpeter is one of the principal ingredients in gunpowder.) Hacı Hamza village, in northern Anatolia, received exemptions from paying all taxes in return for provisioning its post station.[28]

At other times, villagers did not receive tax waivers; instead, their tax revenues constituted the budget for their local post station. For instance, the post station in Homs, in western Syria, was funded by local tax farm revenues (mukāṭaʿ).[29] Kurdkulağı post station, near Adana in the south of Anatolia, was supported by a combination of tax revenues—Extraordinary Taxes, the Substitute Tax for Provisions (bedel-i nüzül), tax farm revenues (mukāṭaʿ).[30] These examples from the Balkans, Anatolia, and the Levant show the different ways in which post station services could be procured, whether as revenues or as services. Alpha dutifully records all of these details.

Alpha does not only show an institution intimately tied to tax administration; it also shows a relationship with military logistics. For instance, in the entry for Edirne, the seat of government at that time, the bookkeeper recorded that 21,500 pounds of wheat and 108,000 pounds of barley were collected from surrounding villages.[31] These large amounts do not seem to accord with the typical consumption pattern of post stations but instead resemble the quantities usually found for military provisioning. The same entry in Beta, compiled one or two years after Alpha, did include the amount of straw collected, but it was a mere 10 *guruş* worth.[32] Later registers, such as Delta and Omicron, do not record the quantities of wheat and barley supplies. It is likely that the analytical categories of "postal" and "military" were still very much enmeshed in the 1690s and that the autonomy of "postal" as a category distinct from "military" took time to coalesce, at least in the minds of bookkeepers. In reality the physical locations of the post station and the military station in Edirne could have been the same, or they could have been in the vicinity of each other—the sources do not indicate location one way or other—but the two types of stations may have differed in location in other towns and locales. Sultan Murad IV's (r. 1623–1640) Baghdad Campaign Register of Military Stations (*Bağdat Seferi Menzilnāmesi*), for instance, recorded the various sites where the army could stop for rest, the distance in hours between stations, the availability of water and its quality, as well as the road conditions.[33] Presumably, the assessment of water availability and road conditions would have been carried out with the needs of a large mobile army in mind, not those of a light, swift contingent of couriers.

Alpha bore other kinds of traces of the empire's military activites. For instance, the Divane Ali post station was newly established because of war on the Özi front (modern Ochakiv in southern Ukraine).[34] In 1685/1686, the Komanova post station increased its number of horses because of war.[35] Bookkeepers also referenced ongoing wars and implied a likely related shortage of horses in several other post station entries. The exigencies of war undeniably affected the postal system: it could deplete the horse resources needed to operate the post, and it could justify the establishment of a new post station.

Between the 1690s and 1760s, bookkeepers changed the way they recorded information in Comprehensive Post Station Registers as well as the way they categorized this information. Examining the entries for the Üsküdar post station

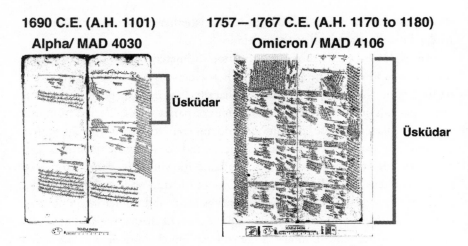

Figure 12. Comparison of the entries for Üsküdar Post Station, 1690 and 1757–1767.
BOA, MAD 4030 2.jpg, MAD 4106 7.jpg; adapted by the author.

through four Comprehensive Post Station Registers from 1690 to 1760 illustrates how bookkeepers changed their recordkeeping practices.

How representative is Üsküdar, and why choose it as an example? As the first station along the Anatolian postal routes, Üsküdar is not very representative of all imperial post stations, especially since it had to maintain more horses than other stations and thus would have had a bigger expense budget. However, its consistently rich records over the years allow us to see change in scribal and accounting practices over time. This is pertinent especially since in the earlier post station registers, blank entries tend to be common, the coverage of information was uneven, and the type of information recorded was different.

A look at the earliest and the latest post station registers presents the most stark differences. When compiling Alpha, bookkeepers recorded information pertaining to one fiscal year (1690). This entry is extremely concise, extending over half a page. When compiling Omicron eighty years later, bookkeepers recorded more than ten consecutive years' worth of fiscal information, 1757 to 1769, all of which covered two folios (four pages) (fig. 12). It may be inferred from this that by the 1750s, bookkeepers had established their accounting routines.

A closer consideration of the routines may be obtained by looking at the contents of these two entries. Alpha's concise entry for the one year is translated in table 1, revealing an annual expense of 240,000 *akçe*. This sum was furnished from tax-paying lands around Üsküdar and from the Imperial Treasury. In contrast,

TABLE 1. ENTRY FOR ÜSKÜDAR POST STATION IN ALPHA (1690 CE / AH 1101)

Üsküdar Post Station, in the charge of Mahmud the Postmaster with the rank of *subaşı* of Üsküdar

Annually	
240,000 [*akçe*]	
From the tax-paying lands of Üsküdar	From the Imperial Treasury
152,000 [akçe]	*88,000 [akçe]*

Source: BOA, MAD 4030.

the twelve-year-long entry from Omicron, translated in table 2, features many more categories of information. Table 3 lists the different categories of information contained in each register, including the two intermediate registers, further revealing the change from Alpha to Omicron. This shift suggests that by the late eighteenth century, bookkeeping had become iterative; it was no longer "creative." Bookkeepers were no longer learning on the job; they did not need to invent form and content. Their work had become routinized.

One to two years lapsed between the Alpha and Beta registers. Despite the short interval, Beta features several new categories of information. It revealed for the first time that eight post horses were stationed at Üsküdar. It also featured the costs of equipment, such as the horseshoe and nail, as well as the salaries of post station personnel, including the cook (*aşçı*) and the guide (*sürücü*). These costs were itemized for Istanbul and Silivri post stations, which were the first entries in Beta but were collapsed into the category of "others" (*sâ'ire*) for subsequent entries, like that of Üsküdar post station.[36]

All these costs were multiples of the number of horses maintained at the post station. For instance, if the post station had one horse, the cost of horseshoes and nails was 3 *akçe*, but if it had two horses, the corresponding cost would be 6 *akçe*. These costs were then multiplied by the number of horses stationed at the post station (twenty) and then again by the number of days in a hijri year (354) to give an aggregated annual expenditure, as shown in table 1. This mathematical relationship at the heart of postal accounting practices reflects the importance of the horse to the postal system.

The compilers of Delta, six years later, introduced two crucial fiscal categories that would remain in future Comprehensive Post Station Registers: aid

TABLE 2. ENTRY FOR ÜSKÜDAR POST STATION IN OMICRON, 1757–1769 CE / AH 1170–1182

Year CE (AH)	Number of Horses	Total Expenditure	Fees	Remaining Expenditure	Aid	Extraordinary Taxes	Fee Waivers: for those traveling from Üsküdar to Gekbuze (akçe)
1757–1758 (1170–1171)	40	5,900	3,000	2,900	3,000	1,797	187,000
1758–1759 (1171–1172)	40	5,900	3,000	2,900	3,000	1,625	135,000
1759–1760 (1172–1173)	40	5,900	3,000	2,900	3,000	1,886	146,450
1760–1761 (1173–1174)	40	5,900	3,000	2,900	3,000	2,055.5	182,970
1761–1762 (1174–1175)	40	5,900	3,000	2,900	3,000	2,441.5	193,841
1762–1763 (1175–1176)	40	5,900	3,000	2,900	3,000	2,817(?)	192,000
1176–1177 (1763–1764)	40	5,900	3,000	2,900	3,000	2,817.5	204,099
1764–1765 (1177–1178)	40	5,900	3,000	2,900	3,000	2,834	197,200
1765–1766 (1178–1179)	40	5,900	3,000	2,900	3,000	1,376 (slightly smudged)	182,000
1766–1767 (1179–1180)	40	5,900	3,000	2,900	3,000	1,386	177,840
1767–1768 (1180–1181)	40	5,900	3,000	2,900	3,000	1,386	287,000
1768–1769 (1181–1182)	37	5,457.5	2775	2,682.5	3,000	1,386	123,079

Source: BOA, MAD 4106, 7–8.jpg.

TABLE 3. CHANGES IN INFORMATION RECORDED IN ALPHA, BETA,
DELTA AND OMICRON, 1690–1769

Information Recorded	Alpha (1690)	Beta (1691–1692)	Delta (1697–1704)	Omicron (1757–1769)
Annual expenditure	x	x	x	x
Number of horses		x	x	x
Equipment costs		x		
Salaries of personnel		x		
Aid			x	x
Fee waivers			x	x

Note: An "x" indicates an entry where information was recorded.

(*imdādiyye*) revenues and fee waivers (*inʿāmāt*).[37] Delta offers more details regarding the sources of funding for Üsküdar post station: a bakery furnished 25,000 *akçe*; there were also extraordinary taxes and aid.[38] Delta also recorded fee waivers (*inʿāmāt*) awarded to couriers traveling from Üsküdar post station to Gekbüze post station. However, Delta is visually very messy, and the information is scattered across different pages.

In contrast to Delta, Omicron, prepared fifty years later, is visually very neat and orderly. Bookkeepers maintained consistent categories of information and an even, standard scribal handwriting. By this time, financial sources for Üsküdar post station included extraordinary tax revenues, aid revenues, and fee waivers; if there continued to be contributions from the aforementioned bakery, it appears that its contributions had been combined with extraordinary tax revenues as an *ocaklık*.[39] In other words, the different sources of contributions had been aggregated and were no longer itemized. As for fee waivers, they were classified in two categories and served as a proxy for horse traffic, either away from the imperial capital to the next post station or toward the imperial capital, which was effectively the adjacent post station to Üsküdar in the other direction. Over the years, bureaucratic oversight increased for hundreds of post stations across the empire; the kind of detail observed in Omicron's Üsküdar post station's entry is mirrored in the entries for remote post stations far away from the imperial capital.

When compiling early Comprehensive Post Station Registers like Alpha and Beta, bookkeepers were concerned with elucidating the specific expenses of each post station, down to the costs of a horseshoe, a halter, straw, and the salaries of cooks and other helpers at the post station. In later Comprehensive Post Station Registers like Delta and Omicron, however, such details completely disappear. Taking their place are aggregated sums like expenditure and revenue that do not give any visibility into their component parts or the way the sums were arrived at. This change suggests that early bookkeepers had to discover the ground realities of post station management and do the foundational translation of these realities into numbers, whereas later bookkeepers likely inherited numbers that had become embedded in accounting formulas and continued to reproduce them. In other words, the earlier bookkeepers had successfully created routine workflows that subsequent generations of bookkeepers would only need to reproduce and reiterate. A new tradition of practice was born.

A close reading of four Comprehensive Post Station Registers has shown how comprehensive databases of the postal system were created, developed, and refined. Bookkeepers first extracted the fiscal histories of individual post stations from older tax documents and copied them into Alpha. In the early days, these Comprehensive Post Station Registers mainly featured tax information. Bookkeepers continued to learn on the job and, over decades, Comprehensive Post Station Registers changed. Beta, Delta, and Omicron came to record postal information about courier traffic, horse usage, and operating costs. Tax information was important insofar as it formed the operating budget for the post station; specific details about tax obligations were generally relegated to the marginalia. Across generations, bookkeepers collectively created a novel postal point of view.

However, this postal point of view was idiosyncratic. The quantitative information recorded in these fiscal registers, like the cost of horseshoe and nail, were most likely estimates. Even if not a faithful representation of reality, such quantitative information reflects attempts to represent that reality, and these attempts provide clues about the bookkeepers' worldviews. The larger point here is that Comprehensive Registers and, more generally, Ottoman fiscal registers should not be used naively as stable representations of actual ground-level operations.

The bookkeepers did not compile Comprehensive Post Station Registers alone; they received help from local officials based in the provinces. To examine how bookkeepers procured information about individual post stations across the empire, we turn to the next chapter, on the postmaster.

CHAPTER 6

The Postmaster

In 1715 the postmaster of Adana died. El-Seyyid Hasan was survived by his wife, daughter, and sister. Among the property he left for them were a few animals (five camels and two water buffaloes), an assortment of utensils (a copper dish, a frying pan, a jug, and a bowl), and a variety of cloths, rugs, and cushions (including used velvet material, prayer rugs, and pillows).[1] The postmaster of Adana also left behind a list of debts; he owed money to roughly twenty individuals, including the farrier and the butcher.[2]

Almost a century later, in 1806, Giridi Hüseyin was removed as postmaster of Üsküdar and Gebze. An inventory was made of the items in both post stations as part of this transition. The list included twenty-one cushions, a wide variety of kitchen utensils, a stool, a cloth specifically for sitting on, a small carpet, several coffee pots and cups, and a range of horse-related tools, from packsaddles to halters and horseshoes.[3]

Judging from the postmasters' material world, they led modest lives as low-level officials who performed menial services for imperial couriers and their horses. Their documentary output, however, suggests that postmasters performed an outsized role. In particular, during the eighteenth century, postmasters began to compile Fee Waiver Registers (*in'āmāt defteri*) that directly served the needs of bookkeepers in the imperial capital. In absolute number of pages, Fee Waiver Registers form the overwhelming majority of the postal documents that have survived. Focusing on the expansion of the postmaster's bureaucratic role will show

how his new bookkeeping duties expanded the imperial monitoring capacity of postal operations and amplified the weight of imperial policy locally, exemplifying the thickening of Ottoman governance during the Second Empire.[4]

There were at least 270 Ottoman postmasters in the empire in the 1700s according to fiscal registers.[5] The real number is likely to have been higher for a few reasons. For one, unofficial post stations were not recorded in fiscal registers. Furthermore, it was common for each post station to be manned by more than one postmaster; it could be jointly managed by two individuals, or, in some cases, running it could be a family trade.[6] For instance, two brothers managed the Adana post station in 1737, while the sons of Hızır Çavuş managed the Konya post station for three decades, even controlling an adjacent post station in Karapınar for a short period of time.[7]

The office of postmaster was not the exclusive preserve of members of any religious faith; Muslims and non-Muslims served as postmasters in the Balkans, Anatolia, and the Arab provinces during the seventeenth and eighteenth centuries. Many times these postmasters are mentioned in the documents only as *zimmi*s, a term that refers to non-Muslim subjects who were "people of the book," such as Jews and Christians. These *zimmi* postmasters have been found in Istanbul, Silivri (an hour's drive west of Istanbul), Edirne, Evreşe (Çanakkale), Lepanto (Inebahtı; in modern Greece), and Kirkuk and Erbil (northern Iraq and Kurdistan).[8] Sometimes the distinctiveness of these postmasters' names reveals the specific non-Muslim communities to which they belonged. Three postmasters in Kirkuk and Erbil, for instance, were Assyrian Christians (Ḥajō son of Veli, Shābō son of Ḥanna, and Quryāqōs son of Junbad) while a fourth was a member of the Church of the East (Jumʿa son of Hormizd).[9] Another *zimmi* postmaster in the Çirpan district (Chirpan in modern Bulgaria) was named Krikor, suggesting that he was Armenian.[10] In rare instances, postmasters were identified in the records by their specific community, such as "the Armenian, Boghos son of Arshak," in Rusçuk (Ruse in modern Bulgaria).[11] Joint management of post stations could also involve partnerships between Muslims and non-Muslims, such as with the Lepanto post station, which was jointly managed by a Greek Orthodox named Christos and a Muslim named Mehmed Yazıcı.[12]

Postmasters were usually drawn from a local pool of candidates and appointed locally. Broadly speaking, there were two types of provincial administrators in Ottoman officialdom: those who received their appointments directly from the capital and those who did not. Ottoman judges (*kadı*) fall into the first category; they typically underwent formal training and served a few years in one district before being rotated to a different district.[13] Postmasters fall into the second category, like the market inspector (*muhtesib*) and the police superintendent (*subaşı*).[14] In the late seventeenth century, appointment deeds (*hüccet* or *temessük*) of postmasters began to be recorded in provincial judicial registers. These appointments were described in contractual terms and usually involved the participation of local elites or notables whose consent was sought.[15] When these appointments were confirmed, the Ottoman judge, as the chief administrator in his district, would notify bureaucrats in the imperial capital.[16]

An extremely concise appointment deed from Amasya dated 1690 reads as follows: "As postmaster Ibrahim has completed a year of his contract on the last day of the month of Rebiülahır 1101, it is recorded that Arslan and Ibrahim were jointly appointed as postmasters for six months beginning from the month of Cemaziyelevvel with a budget of 700 *guruş* and it is recorded that they undertook this responsibility."[17] Other examples from Amasya court records typically mention the postmaster's name, his length of tenure, and the sum of the operating budget.[18] A judicial record from Vidin, in modern Bulgaria, describes the appointment of Hussein Agha and Halil Agha as postmasters for one year beginning in March 1720 (AH 1132).[19]

Postmaster appointment deeds were usually in Ottoman Turkish, but they could be recorded in the Arabic language as well, attesting to a shared contractual idiom and legal culture in the vast empire. In 1732, for instance, al-Seyyid Ahmad ibn Sha'ban undertook the office of the postmaster (*menzilji*) in Hama (modern Syria) with a budget of 3,500 *guruş* for one year.[20] In this case, the key verb, "to undertake," used the Arabic-language equivalent of the usual Ottoman Turkish term (Tr: *ta'ahhüd [etmek]* / Ar: *ta'ahhada;* Tr: *iltizām [etmek]* / Ar: *iltazama*) to denote the undertaking of the office of the postmaster.[21]

In an earlier record from Hama, in 1680, two postmasters acknowledged undertaking this office; the entry in the court register used the Arabic terms *akarra* and *i'tarafa* (he acknowledged/confirmed). The term *akarra* continued to be used in the nineteenth-century western Indian Ocean, where debt-related contracts and acknowledgments (*ikrār*) of debt constituted a "fundamental idiom of commercial society" that bound together merchants and statesmen, moneylenders and planters, caravan leaders and mariners across generations.[22] This "idiom" invoked the power to oblige across linguistically distinct regions of the Ottoman Empire and beyond its boundaries.

Sometimes locals competed for the office of postmaster, suggesting that there was an incentive to hold the office, whether financial or social. In January 1692, for example, Seyyid Mehmed Çelebi and a second Seyyid Mehmed Çelebi were jointly appointed as postmasters (*menzilci*) in Konya with the proposed budget of 3,000 *guruş* for one year.[23] Three days later, two other men stepped forward to undercut the previous bid. Mehmed Beg and Musa Beg counter-proposed a budget of 2,500 *guruş* and won.[24] In the judicial scribe's explanation, Mehmed Beg and Musa Beg had offered the discount out of their compassion for the villagers. The previous appointment of the two Seyyid Mehmed Çelebis was annulled.[25] Fifteen village notables stood as sureties for Mehmed Beg and Musa Beg's fulfillment of their duties for the designated time period.[26]

From this survey of postmaster appointment deeds, it may be provisionally concluded that the office of the postmaster was usually a short-term appointment of six months to a year. Local villagers were involved in the appointment process, usually as sureties. Together with the local judge, villagers witnessed and postmaster-appointees acknowledged receipt of the post station budget, which typically came from local tax revenues. While some appointment deeds were extremely brief, others could be lengthy and stipulate the range of duties and responsibilities pertaining to the management of post stations and horses.

During the eighteenth century, the scope of the postmaster's duties expanded to include administrative duties. Previously, postmasters had mainly served food and drink to incoming couriers and serviced their horses. By the eighteenth century, postmasters had to compile guestbook-like name lists called Fee Waiver Registers, the most voluminous genre of postal documents by number of pages. The postmaster's earlier menial job had acquired an administrative, scribal flavor.

Fee Waiver Registers were crucial for calculating the amount of fees incurred by officials who used post horses. As we saw, Mustafa II had a plan for imposing fees at post stations in 1696, where 10 *akçe* would be charged per horse per hour's travel. In practice, however, most couriers and officials were awarded fee waivers and therefore exempted from paying fees at post stations, making it incumbent upon postmasters to record the name and title of every single official who visited the post station, the number of horses the official took, as well as the date and his direction of travel—these were the contents of Fee Waiver Registers.[27] Postmasters submitted these Fee Waiver Registers to the imperial capital in order to receive reimbursements from the Imperial Treasury, usually at intervals of every six to twelve months. Bookkeepers had to vet the Fee Waiver Registers, which functioned as reimbursement requests. If a register was approved, the bookkeeper would authorize a transfer of funds to reimburse the local postmaster. Bookkeepers recorded all fee-related information from hundreds of such

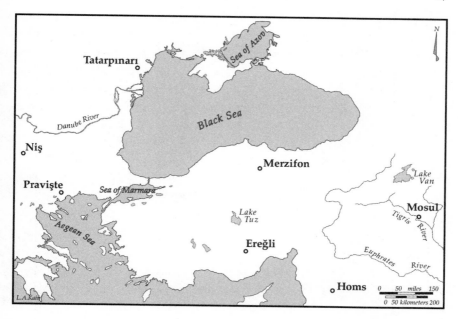

Figure 13. Map showing the seven post stations whose Fee Waiver
Registers are recorded in table 4.

registers, from hundreds of postmasters in the Comprehensive Post Station
Registers.[28] In this way, the postmaster and the bookkeeper kept each other informed of courier traffic and horse usage at local post stations.

A map and a table offer a sense of the scale and longevity of the production
of Fee Waiver Registers by using a sample of seven randomly chosen post stations in the Balkans, Anatolia, and the Arab provinces (fig. 13; table 4). The Fee
Waiver Registers in the table span eight decades, from 1700–1784. However, this
is unlikely to be the full list, as many registers were likely destroyed owing to war
or natural disasters and for other reasons.

Now let's move from the survey of the production of Fee Waiver Registers
across time and space to an examination of their content. The variation in Fee
Waiver Registers in terms of format and content suggests that postmasters across
the empire probably did not undergo formal scribal training, a suggestion that
corresponds with the trend of social mobility and openness (*décloisonnement*)
in the Second Empire. During this period, more and more common subjects who
did not have tax-exempt status (*'askerī*) were allowed to join the imperial bureaucracy as officials.

TABLE 4. FEE WAIVER REGISTERS FROM SEVEN OTTOMAN POST STATIONS (1700–1784 CE / AH 1112–1198)

Year CE (AH)	Niş	Pravişte	Tatarpınarı	Ereğli	Merzifon	Homs	Mosul
1700–1703 (1112–1114)				x			
1703–1708 (1115–1119)				x			
1708–1713 (1120–1124)		x	x	x	x	x	
1713–1717 (1125–1129)					x		
1717–1722 (1130–1134)	x	xx			xx	x	
1722–1727 (1135–1139)	xx	x		xxxx	x		
1727–1732 (1140–1144)	xxx	x	xxx	xxx	xxxx	xx	x
1732–1737 (1145–1149)	xxxxx	xx		xxxx	xxxxxxx	xxx	
1737–1742 (1150–1154)	x	x	xx	xxx	x		
1742–1747 (1155–1159)							
1747–1751 (1160–1164)							
1751–1756 (1165–1169)							
1756–1761 (1170–1174)	xx	xx	xx	xxx			
1761–1766 (1175–1179)	x	xxx	x	xxxx	xxxx		x
1766–1771 (1180–1184)	x	x			xxxx		
1771–1776 (1185–1189)		xx					
1776–1780 (1190–1194)				x	x		x
1780–1784 (1195–1198)							x

Sources: All are in BOA unless otherwise stated.

Niş: AE.SAMD.III.124/12614; C.NF.29/1448; D.MKF.d.28566; C.NF.38/1894 (with Aleppo); D.MKF.d.28800; D.MKF.d.28852; D.MKF.d.28901;
  C.NF.30/1470; D.MKF.d.29150; D.MKF.d.29134; D.MKF.d.29333; C.NF.25/1202; D.MKF.d.29922; MAD.d.21485; C.NF.25/1240; MAD.d.21839;

Pravişte: D.MKF.d.27969; D.MKF.d.28239; AE.SAMD.III.91/9009; D.MKF.d.28533; D.MKF.d.28767; D.MKF.d.29000; D.MKF.d.29130;
  D.MKF.d.29449; AE.SMST.III.132/10361; D.MKF.d.29929; MAD.d.21529; D.MKF.d.30024; D.MKF.d.30055; D.MKF.d.30212; D.MKF.d.30501;
  D.MKF.d.30602

Tatarpınarı: D.MKF.d.28012; IE.DH.24/2150; AE.SMHD.I.229/1829I; D.MKF.d.28650; AE.SMHD.I.229/1427; AE.SMST.III.65/4843;
  D.MKF.d.29933; D.MKF.d.29984

Ereğli: National Library of St. Cyril and St. Methodius, Sofia, Oriental Department, F1.18354; D.MKF.d.27906; D.MKF.d.27956; D.MKF.d.28367;
  D.MKF.d.28446; D.MKF.d.28486; D.MKF.d.28509; D.MKF.d.28620; D.MKF.d.28651 (with Karapınar); D.MKF.d.28677; D.MKF.d.28729;
  D.MKF.d.28855; KK.3034; D.MKF.d.29052; D.MKF.d.29113; D.MKF.d.29356; D.MKF.d.29225; C.NF.30/1458; D.MKF.d.29796; D.MKF.d.29888;
  D.MKF.d.29979; D.MKF.d.29917; AE.SMST.III.302/2416I; D.MKF.d.30076; C.NF.25/1242

Merzifon: IE.DH.22/2001; D.MKF.d.28057; D.MKF.d.28300; D.MKF.d.28368; D.MKF.d.28564; D.MKF.d.28590; D.MKF.d.28626; D.MKF.d.28653;
  D.MKF.d.28723; D.MKF.d.28732; D.MKF.d.28849; D.MKF.d.28896; D.MKF.d.28956; KK.3029; C.NF.29/1422; D.MKF.d.29024; D.MKF.d.29183;
  D.MKF.d.29169; D.MKF.d.29228; C.NF.35/1701; C.NF.46/2274; C.NF.11/508; MAD.d.21482; C.NF.26/1257; C.NF.43/2144; AE.SMST.III.110/8344;
  AE.SMST.III.190/14939; AE.SABH.I.148/10056

Homs: D.MKF.d.27958; AE.SAMD.III.137/1331S; D.MKF.d.28671; D.MKF.d.28847; D.MKF.d.29017; C.NF.28/1381; D.MKF.d.29128

Mosul: D.MKF.d.28616; C.NF.25/1219; C.NF.29/1413; C.NF.35/1724

Note: Each "x" represents one register.

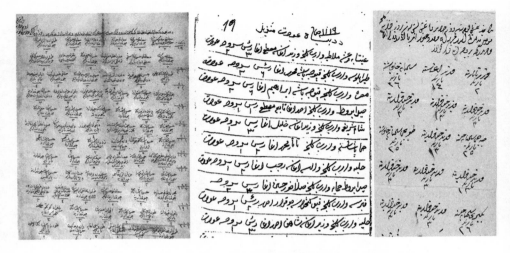

Figure 14. Fee Waiver Registers from Belgrade (left), Konya (middle), and Mosul (right),
early to mid-18th century. Belgrade: BOA, C.NF.14/691, 1.jpg (1701 CE/AH 1113);
Konya: BOA, KK 2998, 9.jpg (s1707–8 CE/AH 1119); Mosul: BOA,
C.NF. 25/1219, 1.jpg (1762 CE/AH 1176).

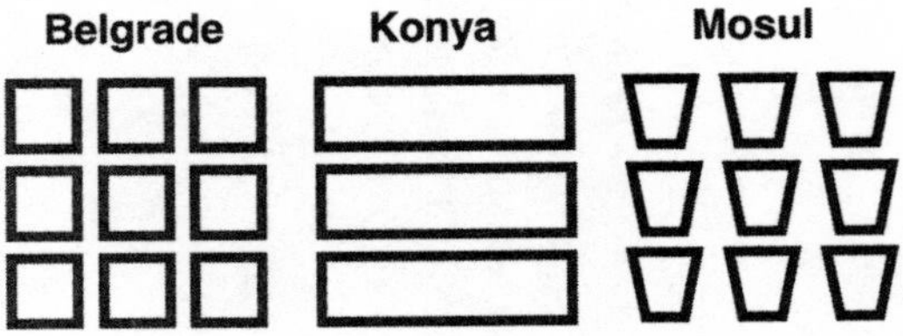

Belgrade   Konya   Mosul

Figure 15. Abstracted forms of the Fee Waiver Registers
depicted in figure 14. Diagram by author.

Figure 14 shows samples of Fee Waiver Registers from Konya, Belgrade, and
Mosul. Visually, the differences in format are salient. The Konya register (1707–
1708) features run-on lines like a prose piece, without any paragraphs; each entry occupies one line that reads from right to left. In contrast, the Belgrade register
(1701) and the Mosul register (1762) both adopt a cellular, grid-like format, like
a Microsoft Excel sheet. All entries read from right to left (figs. 14–15).

As the translations in table 5 show, these three Fee Waiver Registers did not
record the same types of information. All three dutifully noted the number of
horses and guides that officials procured from the post station, but not all of the

TABLE 5. TRANSLATION OF SAMPLE ENTRIES ON EACH FOLIO
FEATURED IN FIGURE 14

Belgrade	Horses given to Hasan Pasha's messenger 2 head [of horses]	Horses given to Hasan Pasha's messenger 3 head [of horses]
Konya	Ibrahim Aga, head of the palace doorkeepers, who was going to and returning from Egypt 6 head [of horses], 2 guides	Mehmed Aga, head of the palace doorkeepers, who was going to and returning from Tripoli 6 head [of horses], 2 guides
Mosul	To the Tatar of the Vizir Horse 2	Vizier Horse 14

registers show the officials' names, ranks, and destinations. The way that the number of horses was recorded also differs linguistically; both the Konya and the
Belgrade postmaster used the classifier or counter word to designate the number of horses: re's, which means head. In contrast, the Mosul postmaster simply
used the term for horses, *bārgīr*. The level of penmanship could also vary widely
across provinces.

The unevenness of local records meant that bureaucrats in the imperial capital had an uneven view of postal operations. If the Mosul postmaster was reticent, then bureaucrats would be none the wiser about where the tatar of the vezir,
who took two horses, was headed or whether he hired any guides.

The format of Fee Waiver Registers changed in the late eighteenth and nineteenth centuries as they began to look like the tables that we use today, with regular rows and columns and with each new entry taking a new row (figs. 16–17;
table 6). The Mosul register features terse entries, indicating only the number of
horses given to, for instance, the tatar couriers of the governor of Baghdad. In
1832–1833, the Üsküdar register maintains the same line-based entry format but
includes the number of hours of the journey and boasts more descriptive entries.
For instance, the Üsküdar register includes details about the mission of the
dispatched couriers (i.e., regarding the matter of provisions), as well as about
the type of imperial correspondence conveyed by these officials (i.e., "illustrious
letters" / *mektūb-ı sāmī*). The type of calligraphy used has also transformed to
the *rik'a* style.

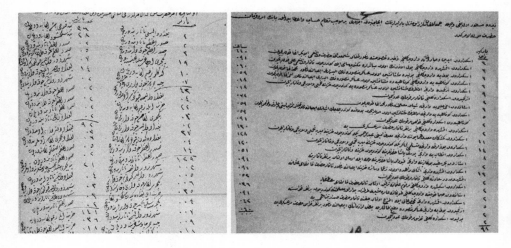

Figure 16. Fee Waiver Registers from Mosul (left) and Üsküdar, late 18th and
19th centuries. Mosul: BOA, C.NF. 29/1413, 3.jpg (1777 CE/AH 1191);
Üsküdar: BOA, C.NF. 36/1761 1.jpg (1832/33 CE/AH 1248).

Mosul   **Üsküdar**

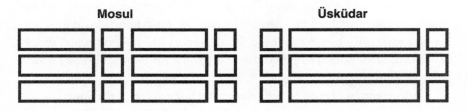

Figure 17. Abstracted forms of the Fee Waiver Registers depicted in figure 16.
Diagram by author.

As mentioned, Fee Waiver Registers supported the production of Comprehensive Post Station Registers in the imperial capital. Bookkeepers routinely extracted data from the former and copied it into the latter. An example from
Antakya, in southern Turkey, illustrates how postmasters in the province and
bookkeepers in the capital collaborated through these registers. In 1758 postmasters and provincial officials in Antakya submitted an eight-page Fee Waiver
Register to the imperial bureaucracy that listed details of every courier and official who had visited the post station from the end of 1756 through 1758.[29] Upon
receipt, bookkeepers in the imperial capital calculated the total number of horses
used by couriers and guides, and from these figures, they calculated the expenses

TABLE 6. TRANSLATION OF THE FIRST TWO ENTRIES ON EACH FOLIO
SHOWN IN FIGURE 16

Mosul			Horses
		Given to the Tatar couriers of the Governor of Baghdad	2
		Given to the Tatar couriers of the Grand Vizier	2
Üsküdar	Hours		Horses
	110	For the men of Ebu Bekir Aga who have been charged with traveling from Üsküdar to Aydın and Saruhan regarding the matter of provisions	3
	91	For the Tatar couriers of agents along the road between Üsküdar and Akşehir who have been issued illustrious letters	3

borne by the Antakya post station. Bookkeepers wrote these calculations in an esoteric accounting notation (*siyākat*) on the final page of the provincial Fee Waiver Register.[30] Other scribes within the imperial bureaucracy copied these sums into the Comprehensive Post Station Register covering the years 1757–1769 (that is, in the Omicron register) under the entry for Antakya (fig. 18).[31] The data shared in both registers for 1757–1758 (AH 1170–1171) is reproduced in table 7.

The costs incurred by courier traffic, including the number of horses and local guides employed, were organized according to the incoming direction of the courier. This was indicated by the penultimate post station he visited (al-Zanbaki, Tenrin, or Bakras) before arriving at Antakya. An exception was made for the Imperial Army, which was on the move. Omicron also contained courier traffic records for Homs (1757–1768 / AH 1170–1181), Mosul (1757–1765 / AH 1170–1178), Ereğli (1757– 1768 / AH 1170–1181), and Merzifon (1757–1769 / AH 1170–1182).[32] While the individual Fee Waiver Registers for these post stations in these years have not been found in the archives, these records probably did exist and were submitted to the imperial capital, but they have been lost or damaged, or I have simply failed to find them.

Other examples of corroboration between Fee Waiver Registers and Comprehensive Post Station Registers do not look as neat as the Antakya example. Information drawn from Ilgın's Fee Waiver Register (1707–1708 / AH 1119), for instance, is written horizontally at a few different places across the page in the

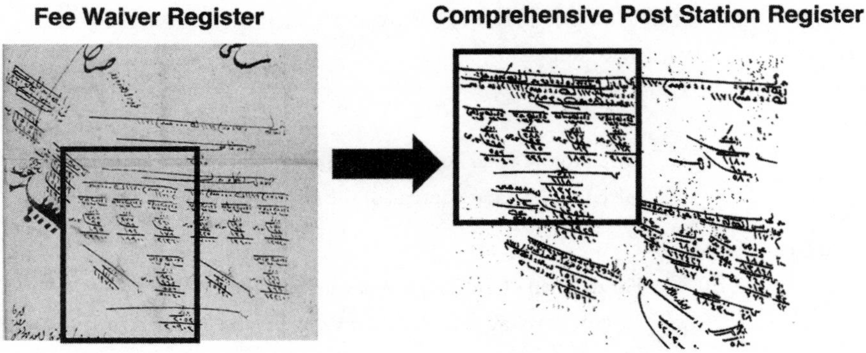

Fee Waiver Register   **Comprehensive Post Station Register**

Figure 18. Bookkeepers' calculations. On the final page of Antakya's Fee Waiver Register
(left), a bookkeeper in the imperial bureaucracy calculated the total expenses borne by
Antakya's post station between 1756 and 1758 (AH 1169–1171). Another bookkeeper then
copied the aggregated expenses for the years 1757–1758 (AH 1170–1171) into the entry for
Antakya in Omicron, a Comprehensive Post Station Register covering the years 1757–1767
(right). The final sum of 209,030 *guruş* is subjected to two more discounts (subtracting
what appears to be a surplus budget amount from the previous year as well as a onetime
treasury grant) to yield the final cost of 191,060 *guruş*. BOA, C. NF. 25/ 1224, p. 5 (5.jpg);
BOA, MAD 4106, p. 142 (55.jpg).

corresponding entry for Ilgın in a Comprehensive Post Station Register.[33] Such
messiness notwithstanding, there are strong reasons to suppose that postmasters
all over the empire submitted Fee Waiver Registers to bookkeepers in the imperial capital with some regularity.

A second purpose of Fee Waiver Registers was simply to keep a record of officials who were legitimately using post horses for free—that is, using authorized fee waiver decrees. An imperial decree issued in 1723 revealed that these
records would be verified (*taṭbīḳ*) with the bureaucracy's own records of courier
orders that had been issued. The imperial decree by itself might have had little
power to enforce compliance, but by insisting on having a paper trail and forwarding papers to imperial bureaucrats, the decree meant that postmasters could
be held accountable for their actions, at least in principle.[34]

Such methods of verification were not new in world history. Fourteenth-
century Milan is said to have had the "earliest 'time sheets' in European history,"
where each courier recorded the receipt of letters and goods at post stations
alongside his name and the time of day.[35] Uyghur texts from the Mongol Empire (thirteenth–fourteenth centuries) show that local administrators kept lists

TABLE 7. POSTAL TRAFFIC INFORMATION AND COSTS FOR ANTAKYA,
1757–1758 (AH 1170–1171)

Direction and time	From Antakya to the Imperial Army (12 hours)	From Antakya to al-Zanbaki (10 hours)	From Antakya to Tenrin (12 hours)	From Antakya to Bakras (9 hours)
Total number of horses used (by guides and couriers with valid passes)	260	277	288	821
Number of horses used by local guides (*sürücü*)	82	88	93	265
The difference (number of horses used by couriers with valid passes)	178	189	195	556
Total cost (at the rate of 10 *akçe* per hour)	21,360*	18,900*	23,400*	50,040*

Total cost	113,700
Total cost for the previous fiscal year (1756–1757 CE / AH 1169–1170)	95,330
Grand total	209,030

Source: BOA, C. NF. 25 / 1224, p. 5 (5.jpg) and MAD 4106, p. 142 (55.jpg).

* That is, the number of hours scheduled for the trip multiplied by the rate per hour multiplied by the number of horses used by couriers with valid passes. For instance, from Antakya to the Imperial Army, that was 12 hours × 10 *akçe* × 178 horses.

of horses provided for different people at a relay station located near Turfan, in today's Xinjiang. Just like Ottoman Fee Waiver Registers, these Uyghur texts record the identity of the officials obtaining horses, the direction of their travels, the number of horses they took, and even the name of the person who provided the horses.[36] In Ming China, the seal and paper tally, or *kanhe* (勘合), authentication method was used to determine who could access official relay stations. This method involved the use of inscriptions and seals stamped equally on two separate paper surfaces, which would later be physically matched to see if the half-stamps and half-inscriptions corresponded with each other in order to determine authenticity. (Despite these elaborate measures, fraud was still rampant.)[37]

Fee Waiver Registers continued to be produced until the mid-nineteenth century; the latest known register was produced by the postmaster of Yeñibāzār (Novi Pazar, modern Serbia) and dates to 1854–1855 (AH 1271).[38] For a century and a half, then, postmasters and bookkeepers worked together to usher in a new era in post station management, one that involved the regular production of figures and records. Previously, scholars have tended to adopt exclusively quantitative approaches to these sources and have generally concluded that traffic volume and expenditure increased over time.[39] However, such increases might reflect more rigorous recording rather than real increases. Focusing exclusively on the numerical data of these registers might detract attention from the fact that these documentary flows existed at all, and, further, that these flows exemplified the thickening circuits of fiscal and administrative maintenance.[40]

This examination of the postmaster offers several new perspectives on a core issue of Ottoman historiography: tax farming. Here, I first discuss terminology and translation before moving on to advocate for a more precise analytical distinction between task delegation and tax farming. Finally, I show variation in the outcomes of task delegation across different administrative contexts in the empire.

The term in postmaster contracts that is conventionally understood and translated in English as tax farming is the Ottoman Turkish term *iltizām* and its verb form *iltizām eylemek*.[41] The terms are used alongside cognates of the word *'ahid,* such as *ta'ahhüd* and *der'uhde. 'Ahid* is usually translated to mean agreement, pact, treaty, or covenant, while *ta'ahhüd* and *der'uhde,* when used with the auxiliary verb *eylemek,* may be translated as "to undertake."[42] In the nineteenth century, the noun form of this verb was recorded as *deruhdeci* in an Ottoman-English dictionary that noted its obsolete usage and translated it as "contractor."[43]

Instead of tax farming, I suggest that a better translation of the term *iltizām eylemek* is "to undertake." The postmaster did not collect tax revenues. He was not supposed to. The postmaster's stipulated duties were to manage the post station and provide horses to incoming couriers. He was given a budget that comprised tax revenues, but it was usually the local treasurer or judge who procured the funds and then handed them over. It is possible that the term *iltizām* shifted in meaning over time, just like the term *ḳānūnnāme* (sultanic law). (As the historian Molly Greene noted, the sultanic law codes of Ottoman Crete contravened actual sultanic law; nevertheless, successive bureaucrats continued to refer to these deviations as sultanic law codes.)[44] As far as the eighteenth century is concerned, however, *iltizām* did not always mean tax farming or even tax collection.

More fundamental to the question of translation is the issue of how historians should classify the range of actions of an eighteenth-century imperial bureaucracy. Here, an analytical distinction between task delegation and tax farming is useful, at least at this point in Ottoman historiography's development. Pre-industrial empires delegated a range of tasks. Tax farming, which entailed the sale of tax collection rights in a certain domain for a period of time, was just one among this range of tasks. This was not unique to the Ottoman Empire; a variety of tax collection arrangements and remuneration systems abounded across the world at that time, from Paris to Bangkok.[45]

The Ottoman imperial bureaucracy delegated many other kinds of tasks, such as the provision of security in certain regions, the protection of *hajj* caravans, and the management of post stations. Often, local tax revenues were used to pay those who carried out these tasks. For instance, the postmasters from Diyarbakır in 1752 and those from Hama in 1680 were appointed to manage post stations using budgets derived from local tax revenues which were collected by others and handed over to them.[46] This transfer of revenues from local sources for local expenditure was known as *havāle*. From an imperial perspective, such an arrangement was efficient; instead of collecting tax revenues in the capital and redistributing them again to the provinces to finance local administrative services, the Ottomans oversaw a quasi-federalized system in which local revenues funded local expenditures and authorized local agents collected their own operating budgets.[47] Many European states used a similar system.[48]

The point here is that tax collection was just one of many tasks that were delegated to local agents. But tax revenues were also used to remunerate delegates who were carrying out other kinds of tasks for the government. This fine but crucial distinction may account for why task delegation and tax farming are often conflated in the scholarship.

Sometimes task delegation and tax farming are difficult to disentangle because the same local agent was tasked with tax collection alongside a range of other responsibilities. In Ottoman Lebanon, for instance, tribal emirs served as government tax agents through the *iltizām* system, which entitled them to a share of tax revenues. However, they were also obliged to provide security and order in designated regions, to protect *hajj* caravans, and to contribute to war campaigns. Describing these tribal emirs as tax farmers is not adequate; they were entrusted with a scope of duties more akin to those of a regional governor.[49]

The struggle to pin down the precise meaning of *iltizām* is not new. In 1955, the historian Lajos Fekete challenged the view that *iltizām* was tax farming, suggesting instead that the *mültezim* (the "agent noun" of the verb *iltizām eylemek*) should be seen as a state employee. This view was, in turn, challenged by other scholars, including Joseph Matuz.[50] Such debates are helpful and generative and perhaps should be revisited by historians today.

What is at stake in this struggle for conceptual precision is a proper understanding of the true scope of Ottoman administrative activity, which affects how the imperial bureaucracy's monitoring capacity, territorial reach, and local impact (weight) are evaluated. During the Second Empire, Ottoman administrators governed more than before with the help of more intermediaries. Lumping this expanding range of tasks under the blanket category of tax farming obscures the burgeoning scope of their work and the deepening interventions in local affairs. Even the category of tax farming can be unpacked, since different kinds of taxes required different skills for collection. A skilled collector of the sheep tax, for instance, might be useless at collecting a *boza* tax (*boza* is an alcoholic drink made from millet). For one, the urban owners of *boza* shops might have had strategies to conceal their true tax liabilities, thus requiring *boza* tax collectors to adopt a particular relationship management style; this skill would likely have been irrelevant for collecting sheep taxes from shepherds who roamed about rolling, verdant pastures.[51]

Better conceptual precision also makes visible the variation in the outcomes of task delegation and contracting across different administrative contexts in the empire. At the elite level, the *mālikāne*, a new life-term tax farming contract issued in the last decade of the seventeenth century, was a way of extracting finances from the uppermost echelons of the Istanbul elite.[52] The life-term tax farmer typically hailed from the Ottoman political and social elite in Istanbul and had networks that extended from the imperial capital to multiple provinces. The very first life-term tax farm contract was issued in 1695 to Grand Vizier Ömer Pasha and his son, and in the late eighteenth and nineteenth centuries, one of the largest holders of life-term tax farms was the sister of Sultan Abdülhamid I, Esma Sultan (d. 1788).[53] While Istanbul elites dominated the life-term tax farming contracts, the maintenance and administration of these tax farms involved a whole ecosystem of provincial elites and subcontractors; the system rendered profits at every level of these elaborate networks and enabled the accumulation of local power by the provincial elites.[54]

At the level of the provincial elites, the aggregation of contracts and offices within powerful households had grave repercussions for imperial authorities.

Throughout the eighteenth century, provincial magnates managed to amass power through the accumulation of offices and contracts.[55] By successfully negotiating with the imperial bureaucracy for the hereditary rights of these offices and contracts, these magnates succeeded in establishing provincial dynasties, or households (*hānedān*). Their power was most saliently reflected in the palatial residential complexes that they built for themselves in the provinces.[56]

In stark contrast to life-term tax farmers and provincial magnates, the postmaster never attained the extensive reach, prodigious wealth, or elevated social status that the provincial and Istanbul elites did. Likewise, the fiscal reforms of the post station system did not cause such aggravated frictions with provincial administration as the life-term tax farming system did. Nor did the Ottoman authorities become so irreversibly dependent on individual postmasters as they did in the case of the provincial magnates, given that postmasters could easily be replaced. Indeed, unlike provincial elites, the low-ranking postmaster posed little existential threat to the empire. On the contrary, if he fulfilled his duties, his grassroots administrative efforts increased the visibility (and hence the monitoring capacity) of local transactions for bookkeepers located in the distant capital, thereby making him extremely productive and beneficial. If he did not fulfill his duties, there was little political cost to replacing him with another local candidate eager to enter Ottoman officialdom. The outcomes of task delegation varied across the administrative spectrum and could strengthen imperial supervision and control in some cases.

Nevertheless, postmasters resembled provincial and Istanbul elites in a few ways. They were rewarded financially for undertaking governance work locally. They also achieved social mobility, attaining the status of minor notables. Evidence of this may be seen in the role they could play as a procedural witness (*şühūd'ül-ḥāl*) in property transactions, repayment of debt cases, debt disputes, the arrangement to finish constructing a school, camel purchases on behalf of the state, inheritance disputes and transactions, as well as general disputes.[57] In imperial decrees, postmasters were addressed as minor officials responsible for various imperial orders not related to the postal system, such as the capture of bandits (*eşkıyā*) and the regulation of alcohol taxes.[58] Even after retirement or after giving up the office of the *menzilci*, postmasters appear to have retained their status locally and to still have been engaged as procedural witnesses; they are referred to in the records as former postmasters (*menzilci-i sābık*).[59]

The office of the postmaster became a hereditary post over time in some parts of the empire, staying within the same household for generations.[60] Unlike the powerful provincial dynasties, however, families who controlled the office of the postmaster never attained regional hegemony. This is because dynastic provincial households operated at a much larger scale and acquired a range of diverse offices and contracts; they were pseudo-states within the larger imperial state. Provincial dynasties became powerful enough to be selective about the government orders they took up, accepting some but rejecting others. They were even able to marginalize the Istanbul-based imperial elite in the provincial administration.[61] In contrast, the case of the postmaster is more akin to the cases of craftsmen within guilds, where a trade and the right to practice that trade remained within a family.[62]

The case study of the postmaster not only shows how Ottoman imperial authorities became more deeply entrenched in local districts across the empire. It also revises the conventional understanding of tax farming in the historiography and shows that it has been conflated with the concept of task delegation. The postmaster was not a tax farmer. He was in charge of managing the local post station. In the eighteenth century, his duties expanded to include bookkeeping duties, and the volumes of fiscal registers he produced helped to increase the monitoring capacity of bureaucrats and bookkeepers in the capital. In return, he received financial benefits and improved his social status. Imperial administration was, ultimately, a systematic distribution of different kinds of rents through different kinds of contracts that formalized the delegation of tasks.

The postmaster was also a member of his village. As a villager, he participated in local society, was subject to village politics, and had aspirations that were shaped by the village's context. The management of Ottoman post stations largely took place within the world of the village. Villagers provided the horses, provisions, and personnel to maintain the relay stations of the Sublime Post. The next chapter explores the important role of these villagers.

CHAPTER 7

The Villager

Ibrahim was the imam of the fortress mosque (*mescid-i ḥiṣār*) in Taraklı, a small town in northwest Anatolia. The year was 1777, and there were ongoing battles along the Ottoman-Iranian frontier. Couriers shuttled between the war-front and the imperial capital with increasing frequency, demanding fresh horses and food wherever they passed. However, these couriers sometimes deviated from the official routes. Instead of passing through the post stations at Hendek, Düzce, and Bolu, for example, some couriers went south, galloping through the quiet towns of Geyve, Taraklı, Göynük, and Mudurnu. In the cold month of January 1777, villagers like Ibrahim decided that they had had enough of this unofficial and unwelcome courier traffic (fig. 19).

The four towns submitted round-robin petitions (*ʿarż-ı maḥżār*) in which they jointly complained about this unusual courier traffic and the burden of provisioning that came with it.[1] Ibrahim was one signatory who had turned up at the courthouse to sign the town of Taraklı's petition (fig. 20).[2]

There were fifty-four signatories to the Taraklı petition. The Geyve, Göynük, and Mudurnu petitions had thirty-eight, fifty-one, and twenty-seven signatories, respectively. The order of the signatories appears to reflect the status hierarchy of the villagers. At the top were religious leaders and teachers, followed by local civil and military administrators. Ibrahim, being the imam at a locally significant mosque, was listed in the second row, where he stamped his seal under his name. Presumably, after stamping his seal, Ibrahim exchanged greetings with

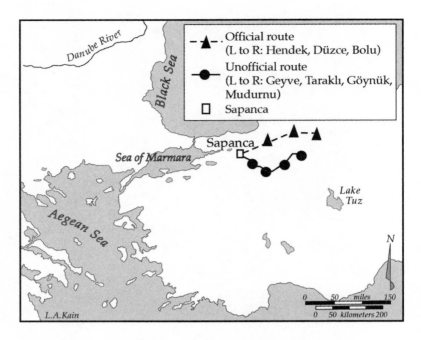

Figure 19. Official and unofficial courier routes in northern Anatolia, ca. 1777.

The Taraklı petition

Close-up of Ibrahim's seal
(red square on left)

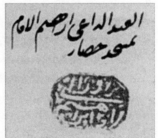

Figure 20. The Taraklı petition and a close-up of Ibrahim's seal, 1777.
BOA, C. NF. 29/1411, 16.jpg.

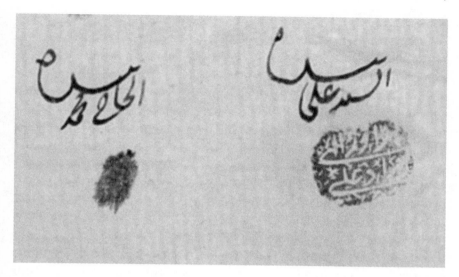

Figure 21. Signatories on the bottom row of the Taraklı petition, 1777: left to right, el-Haj Mehmed with a thumb print and Seyyid Ali with a seal. BOA, C. NF. 29/1411, 16.jpg.

others from the first few lines of signatories, such as Abdulrahman, the imam at the Yunus Pasha mosque; Hasan, the teacher at a local madrasah; and Mehmed, the muezzin.[3]

Appearing in the lines below Ibrahim's signature were the signatures of the elders of the district (*ihtiyār-ı kazā*), several military personnel, and a former postmaster. The signatories at the bottom rows were identified uniformly with the title *bende* (humble servant) and their name, but with no other description. In these bottom rows, individuals typically marked their sign with a thumb print instead of a seal. There was, however, one exception: a certain Seyyid Ali brought his own seal and stamped it (fig. 21). Seyyid Ali may not have held a high status within the social order of the village, but he may have been important in other ways; perhaps he had been wealthy, which might explain why he owned a seal. In any case, judging from the order of signatories, imams and muezzins were still regarded as socially important in the late eighteenth century, at least in the context of an official round-robin petition.

Villagers played a vital role in the Ottoman postal system. I use the term "villagers" to refer to a range of heterogeneous tax-paying subjects, including agriculturalists in rural provinces, merchants and artisans in larger towns, and elders, teachers, and religious leaders. Ottoman scribes used Ottoman Turkish terms such as *ahālī* (the people) and *reʿāyā* (flock) to refer to a similarly heterogeneous range of subjects. In the sixteenth century, villagers typically entered the written record as individuals whose horses had been confiscated by a traveling courier.[4] By the eighteenth century, villagers tended to appear in the written record as collective groups. They signed collective contracts and displayed a greater capacity for collective action across supra-local units than in centuries past. The joint petitions by four towns exemplify this new capacity. After all, substantial communication among these towns must have first taken place about the abnormal courier traffic. Consequently, the villagers would have had to agree upon a course of action and to articulate their shared problem to the imperial bureaucracy. All this resonated with the trend toward corporatism (an enclosing and coalescing of groups along the social hierarchy) that, together with *décloisonnement* (a newfound openness that facilitated social mobility) characterized the Second Ottoman Empire.[5]

Bureaucrats also tapped into this new capacity, mobilizing these collective units in support of their own policy agendas. For instance, bureaucrats in the eighteenth century introduced a new mechanism of collective liability that I call nested suretyships. This mechanism compelled more and more villagers to become stakeholders in postal operations by making them collectively liable for their local postmaster's work performance. But by becoming stakeholders, villagers could also raise grievances and protest policies, within limits. In this way, the work of infrastructural maintenance drew more local participation but also engendered more contention and negotiation.

The thickening governance paradigm that began in the previous chapters on the decrees, bookkeepers, and postmasters reaches completion here.[6] I clarify the dialectical relations among interconnected and interacting components of the postal system—local villagers, local officials (such as the postmaster), and bureaucrats in the imperial capital.

Yet the written record ultimately offers an insufficient account of the true scope of what villagers did. Many of their actions took place beyond the ken of imperial authority and eluded documentation. I thus hypothesize about what might have transpired beyond the visibility afforded by the written record, building upon suggestive clues in the archival sources, empirical literature on how historical communities have managed common pool resources (CPRs), and organizational studies on collaboration in the absence of active authority. I also discuss sources that future historians could consider using which I have not been able to use here.

In the sixteenth century, villagers mostly appeared as single individuals in documents pertaining to Ottoman postal administration, if they appeared at all. As we have seen, the Ottoman bureaucracy did not track postal traffic, official movements, or horse supplies at post stations. Instead, couriers confiscated horses from random passers-by or entered villages along their routes to snatch fresh horses. Sometimes the horses were returned to their proper owners, who had to demonstrate knowledge of their physical features to establish ownership.

Standard examples of horse returns may be found in late sixteenth-century Üsküdar where a villager named Mehmed b. Yusuf claimed that a grey mare (*kır kısrak*) belonged to him; he demonstrated knowledge of the mare's identifying marks to Hasan, the postmaster, before he was able to claim it.[7] In another instance, the same postmaster handed over a red stallion with a patch on its forehead and a white horse with a shortened tail to a man named Ibrahim. Presumably, when Ibrahim came to the postmaster to claim his horses, he had described them; this may explain why the scribe recorded this detailed description in the court register.[8] There are several similar entries recording the handing over of particular horses and mules (whether to their putative owners or to the postmaster); they are typically accompanied by some description of the animal.[9] The care taken to describe each animal and to record these movements of horses in and out of the postmaster's custody suggests that there was a protocol for returning them after they had been used by couriers and that a customary respect for the rightful ownership of animals existed at the time. Recording these returns in the judicial register would also have made it difficult for others to later contest the postmaster's decision.

There were variations on these standard transactions, often with complicating circumstances. Sometimes disputes arose regarding confiscated horses. What is interesting in these cases is that the courier's act of horse confiscation was never in contention. Rather, the point of contention concerned other points of detail or secondary actions surrounding the act of confiscation. While courier confiscations may have been as oppressive as chroniclers and poets decried at the time, this litigative (off-)focus indicates the great extent to which, at a pragmatic level, horse confiscations were very much part of the accepted status quo.

Consider, for instance, the case of Mehmed, a member of the Yörük pastoralists, who owned a grey stallion. One day in 1519, a courier confiscated this grey stallion from Mehmed at a place named Akbıyık. The courier spent the night there but awoke the next morning to find the horse, saddle, and bridle gone. He went to the superintendent (*subaşı*) and accused Mehmed, the original owner of the grey stallion, saddle, and bridle, of stealing them back during the night. This accusation demonstrates the extent of the courier's entitlement to Mehmed's horse, so much so that when the courier found his confiscated horse missing, he accused the original owner of stealing it back. The superintendent launched an investigation, bringing in several witnesses to testify in court. The missing horse, saddle, and bridle were eventually found and returned to the courier-plaintiff. Mehmed, the original owner of the horse, was acquitted of any wrongdoing.[10] To our modern eyes, this may seem unfair and absurd, but in the social order of the sixteenth-century Ottoman Empire, this legal logic prevailed.

Another variation on the courier-confiscated-my-horse court case may be found in 1535. Nasuh b. Abdullah had a horse confiscated by a courier—except that the horse did not belong to him. The owner of the horse, Hızır, lodged a complaint at the courthouse in Üsküdar, alleging that Nasuh b. Abdullah lost a horse that Hızır had entrusted to him.[11] In his defense, Nasuh b. Abdullah took an oath (*yemīn*) and swore that he had committed no wrongdoing, for a courier had taken the horse. The judicial scribe affirmed in his record that Nasuh b. Abdullah had indeed committed no wrongdoing.

In this court case, the courier's confiscation of Hızır's horse was not in contention. Rather, what was in contention was whether Nasuh b. Abdullah had failed to fulfill his duties by losing a horse that had been entrusted to him. Reading between the lines, it may even be suggested that Hızır's intention in bringing Nasuh b. Abdullah to court was to compel him to take an oath affirming that a courier had indeed confiscated the horse and to confirm that Nasuh had not, instead, sold the horse. This reading pivots on the potency of the exculpatory oath, which was treated as a proper legal procedure for determining truth in Ottoman courts. Examples from seventeenth- and eighteenth-century Damascene judicial registers show defendants who publicly insisted on their innocence in court but refused to take an oath; that is, they refused to place a hand on a copy of the Qur'an and swear by their innocence. In such cases, the judge would typically deem the defendant's reluctance to take an oath as an indirect admission of guilt and mete out a penalty.[12] This pattern underscores the power and validity of the oath in the Ottoman court and could be the reason why Hızır sought it when he brought Nasuh b. Abdullah to court. Overall, this incident reveals that in the eyes of the court and villagers, horse confiscations by imperial couriers were a fact of life.

Over a century later, around the 1690s, villagers became increasingly involved in postal administration as collective groups. This involvement manifested in three ways: they were involved as collective sureties in postmaster appointments, they collectively petitioned imperial authorities on a range of operational issues, and they undertook collective contracts with the state to maintain post stations.

Villagers participated in the process of postmaster appointments through a mechanism I call nested suretyships.[13] In Ottoman Turkish, a surety is known as a *kefil*. Its noun form is *kefālet,* meaning suretyship; *kefil* is a loan word from Arabic with the root *k-f-l.*[14] (Today, the same term is used in the *kafala* migrant labor sponsorship system practised in the Gulf states, Lebanon, and Jordan.)[15] Ottoman suretyships were utilized in a variety of situations—for example, during a general levy of military forces (*nefîr-i 'ām*), in business partnerships, in loan guarantees in case the debtor defaulted in payment (*kefil bi'l-māl*), and in ensuring not the loan amount but the "personal availability of a debtor" (*kefil bin-nefs*).[16] From the eighteenth century on, suretyships were also used to regulate immigration into Istanbul. Typically, only local notables or individuals with credible reputations could stand as sureties and have their names recorded in the court register.[17] In other cases, the principle of collective liability and suretyship was applied among ordinary individuals within the local community.[18]

Nested suretyships involved several layers of sureties, where sureties required their own sureties. This gradual increase in layers of suretyship was mandated by imperial decrees issued between the late seventeenth century and the late eighteenth century. Over time, more and more layers of provincial society were drawn into the appointment process of the postmaster and the management of post stations.

In an imperial decree dated January 1698, villagers were instructed to appoint a "trustworthy" (*mu'temedün-'aleyh*) person as postmaster.[19] There is no indication of sureties.[20] The only requirement was that the postmaster be trustworthy.

Four decades later, things had changed. In 1740, an imperial decree expanded the potential pool of postmasters to include common subjects (*re'āyā*)—that is, those who did not have tax-exempt ('askerī) status. In the case of postmasters with a common background, the decree commanded that they should have trustworthy (*mu'temedün-'aleyh*) sureties from among notables and villagers.[21] If the postmaster possessed tax-exempt ('askerī) status, he would not need these sureties.

Another three decades later, in the late eighteenth century, the principle of collective liability was taken to an even more extreme degree. A 1775 decree stated that to appoint the postmaster, trustworthy sureties who received unanimous agreement from villagers must first be chosen.[22] A nested suretyship arrangement had emerged. Before the postmaster could even be appointed, the various sureties for the postmaster would have to first receive unanimous guarantees from the villagers. In this decree, the requisite quality for the sureties was reliability (*mu'temedün-'aleyh kefilleri*). The postmasters themselves were required to be

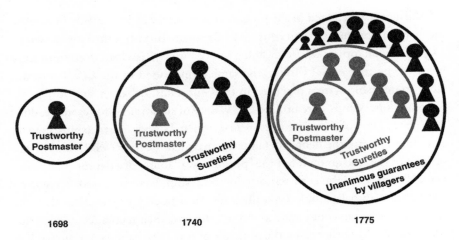

Figure 22. The emergence of nested suretyships, 1698–1775. Diagram by author

skillful (*kārgüzār*) and experienced in their conduct (*mücerrebü'l-etvār*) (fig. 22).[23] Subsequent decrees upheld this same stringent requirement of unanimous guarantees for sureties of trustworthy postmasters.[24]

   From an imperial bureaucrat's perspective, there were several possible reasons to include more villagers in the process of appointing the postmaster. First, this may have been a way to reduce villagers' complaints about incompetent postmasters. Second, making villagers stakeholders in the management of the post station could contribute to smoother operations. Whereas villagers were previously responsible for supplying horses as in-kind taxes to the post station, villagers now had oversight as to how their horses (their taxes) were used or misused. Although the postmaster acquired a new prominence in the bookkeeping side of postal administration, he was dependent on the villagers for horses. The formal inclusion of villagers as sureties entrenched postal operations securely within local communities.

   There were consequences to such inclusion. Imperial bureaucrats could mobilize village collectives for the purposes of postal administration. In turn, mobilization recursively consolidated the village as a collective unit that could challenge bureaucrats or persuade them to take their side in disputes with other villages. Thickening governance thus did not translate into a simplistic teleological trajectory of a strengthened imperial bureaucracy; rather, what appears to have emerged during the Second Ottoman Empire was an increasingly contentious society with increasingly sophisticated communities that were learning to protect their collective interests more effectively.[25]

Villagers fought with neighbouring villagers to protect their interests and to secure an equitable distribution of provisioning burdens. Examples of intervillage conflicts show how villagers provided feedback to imperial bureaucrats through their petitions and how they tried to protect their interests within the system of empire. The conflicts also underscore the structural interdependence of each node in the postal system, as well as the cascading consequences that might ensue from the collapse of any link in the pan-imperial chain.

A conflict between Gedegara (present-day Vezirköprü) and Osmancık shows how villagers in Gedegara educated imperial bureaucrats on locally specific information about their natural environment in order to veto an extra tax burden. In 1686, the villagers (re'āyā) of Gedegara gathered at the local courthouse to make a complaint about a neighboring village, Osmancık, and its post station.[26] The villagers of Osmancık had somehow managed to obtain an imperial order compelling the villagers of Gedegara to pay 150 guruş in aid (imdād) to them. Unsurprisingly, Gedegara villagers protested. According to them, couriers typically avoided the routes leading to Osmancık during the spring and summer because the trees in the mountains foliated (ağaçlar yapraklanub) then, providing camouflage and cover for the bandits and highway robbers.[27] Instead, couriers opted for the safer route, which went through Gedegara. Using the first-person plural, Gedegara villagers took care to emphasize that they meant all couriers coming from the eastern provinces of the empire, from Baghdad, Erzurum, or Kurdistan, as well as those coming from the western side, from Kastamonu: "all these couriers pass by our district."[28] Given that Gedegara was bearing the brunt of summer traffic, Gedegara villagers did not agree that they should fork out another 150 guruş to Osmancık villagers on top of their existing annual tax burden of 500 guruş. The villagers protested that they had absolutely no ability to do so and were financially distressed.

This petition captures the kinds of conflict that could arise between neighboring villages in a relay postal system. In this case, couriers went either through Gedegara or through Osmancık. If the villagers of Gedegara are to be believed, the villagers of Osmancık behaved in bad faith by levying an extra tax burden on them even though Gedegara experienced higher traffic during the summer months. A few conclusions may be drawn from such cases. First, petitions could convey important local information to bureaucrats in the capital about the behavior of couriers beyond what fiscal registers recorded, equipping the bureaucrats with the context necessary to fine-tune policy and distribute post station–related taxes in a just way. While imperial bureaucrats were instrumental in coordinating and mediating among villagers hosting post stations to

ensure that the whole system functioned smoothly, they needed to be educated about local conditions. Second, it may be deduced that villages with savvy
leadership could potentially obtain extra grants and revenue from unwitting
bureaucrats at the expense of neighboring villages. If those neighboring villages
did not respond, the savvy villagers could get away with their ruse; in the case of
Gedegara, neighboring villagers fought back.

Sometimes recalcitrant villagers could shirk all responsibility for post stations. This was the case for Izoli in the district of Malatya. In 1646, a group of
villagers (ahālī) from the district of Malatya sent a petition claiming that although
villagers from Izoli were supposed to contribute an annual amount of 600 guruş
for the maintenance of post station horses, they did not send this amount in full.[29]
Almost a full century later, in 1742, the villagers of Izoli were again accused of
not paying tax dues that would have financed seven post stations in Malatya. An
imperial order to the governor of Malatya and the deputy lieutenant-governor
of Rakka chided the villagers of Izoli for being disobedient ('adem-i iṭā'at) and
for having no desire to maintain the post stations. This imperial order specifically named eight men as being in a perpetual state of rebellion ('iṣyān) and pre-
venting the proper management of post stations. This created difficulties for
villagers in the Harput and Malatya region and for couriers going through that
region. The imperial decree ordered that these troublemakers were to be expelled
and resettled in Rakka.[30]

There are other examples of villagers educating bureaucrats about local circumstances. Sometimes bureaucrats appear to have forgotten about decisions
made by their predecessors, and villagers had to remind them. In 1693, for instance, the villagers of Ereğli, in Central Anatolia, submitted a petition to the
capital regarding a nearby post station at Karapınar that had become defunct
(mu'aṭṭal).[31] This post station was important, for it functioned as an intermediate layover between Ereğli and Konya, which were roughly ninety-four miles
apart. Horses could not make this full distance in one trip; without an intermediate stop, they could become severely fatigued and die en route. However, the
lands whose revenues were supposed to support Karapınar post station had been
converted into hāṣ; that is, they were now lands whose revenues were earmarked
for high-ranking administrators and the royal family.[32] As a result, the poor, suffering villagers (fukarā ve żu'afā) of Ereğli had to pay an extra 1,000 guruş per
month to provide horses because they kept dying en route between Ereğli and
Konya. The villagers, having reached their breaking point, had submitted a petition for the post station in Karapınar to be reinstated. Ultimately, the petition

was successful; instructions scribbled at the top of this petition indicate that an imperial decree was to be issued to rectify the situation.

It is significant that the villagers of Ereğli were knowledgeable about the Karapınar post station, its funding structure, and the reclassification of its revenue source as *ḥāṣ*. This was fiscal information that would typically be recorded in the registers of the imperial bureaucracy. In fact, in response to the petition, a bookkeeper affirmed in the marginalia that, indeed, the tax farm (*muḳāṭaʿ*) whose revenues were designated for the Karapınar post station was now allocated to one of the sultan's consorts (*ḥāṣekī sulṭān*). Clearly, then, local villagers and administrators were knowledgeable of local fiscal arrangements, and, in this case, they were in a position to remind imperial bureaucrats about changes to fiscal arrangements that their colleagues had approved and to inform them about the consequences of those changes on villagers' livelihoods. Here, villagers had "intervened" in imperial administration in their role as ground-level caretakers of the postal system. When the integrity of any part of the chain was under threat, they actively directed the attention of decision-makers in the imperial capital toward those weak links.

Sometimes villagers sought to remove their local postmaster. In 1698, villagers (*reʿāyā*) from the small town (*ḳaṣaba*) of Kızılcaviran submitted a petition directly to the imperial authorities calling for their postmaster, el-Haj Ahmed, to be removed from his position.[33] In their petition, the villagers accused Ahmed of embezzling (*ekl ve belʿ*) the fees that couriers paid to use the post station. Now and then (*gāh gāh*), Ahmed would pressure villagers to fork out more money to cover post station expenses; the extra expense constituted a source of great oppression for them. The villagers hence requested that an imperial decree be addressed to their local judge ordering him to appoint a reliable (*muʿtemedün-ʿaleyh*) postmaster who would benefit the common folk.

Unlike with previous petitions, the villagers of Kızılcaviran were themselves the signatories to this petition, not the local judge. They signed off as a collective: "the villagers of the aforementioned small town" (*ahālī-i ḳaṣaba-i mezbūre*). Reading between the lines, we can see a few possible reasons for villagers to have bypassed their local judge. Perhaps the judge was a close friend of the postmaster. Perhaps the judge could not, for unknown reasons, discipline the postmaster locally but required a higher authority.[34] Luckily for the villagers of Kızılcaviran, their request was granted.[35] It should be noted that in 1698, nested suretyships had not yet been mandated by imperial decrees; they would only be implemented in the eighteenth century. Perhaps incidents like this prompted bureaucrats in the imperial capital to involve more villagers in the postmaster appointment process in order to stave off the need for post hoc removal petitions.

Through collective petitions, villagers voiced grievances, defended their interests, negotiated better deals, and, as a byproduct, offered important local information to imperial bureaucrats. When villagers complained about increases in tax and horse quotas, they gave contextual information to explain why those increases were not warranted and why they could not be supported. Phrases like *tahammülleri olmayub* (unbearable) and *iktidārımız yokdur* (we have no ability to do so) informed imperial bureaucrats when maximum capacity was surpassed, allowing them to monitor operations from afar. The ultimate decision was almost always an approval of the local community's request.[36] A parallel may be drawn with Istanbul's meat provisioning system, where complaints from butchers (*celepkeşān*) to have their quotas reduced were almost always granted; the historian Anthony Greenwood has suggested that this practice of regular approvals indicates that the provisioning system was meant to be "functional, not punitive."[37] The postal system, which depended on horse and food provisions from villagers, was likely managed with the same philosophy.

During the eighteenth century, imperial authorities initiated collective contracts with villagers, requiring residents as a group to guarantee the provisioning of local post stations. Setting up group sureties was a new practice that accorded with the new use of suretyships in the eighteenth century, which saw the profusion of Suretyship Registers (*kefālet defteri*).[38] Confronted with increasing waves of migration into the capital, bureaucrats produced these Suretyship Registers to distinguish legitimate residents, who would have sureties guaranteeing their legitimacy, from illegitimate newcomers in neighborhoods (*mahalle*).[39] Bureaucrats also monitored the influx of migrant laborers to specific sectors. For instance, Bathhouse Registers (*hammāmları defteri*) were supposed to record the identities of legitimate bathhouse workers.[40] In these eighteenth-century examples, the locus of collective liability was applied to groups defined by occupation or residential neighborhood. By recording individuals' names, places of origin, and the names of their local sureties, the imperial bureaucracy tracked the growth of new migrant populations in Istanbul. This impulse to monitor intensified in the early nineteenth century, when a new layer of low-level administrators, the *muhtār*, was created to monitor Muslim and non-Muslim communities in Istanbul.[41]

It is against this bureaucratic backdrop that collective contracts and surety-ship registers began to be employed in postal administration. In 1725–1726, Hasan Agha, one of the sultan's elite mounted escorts (*dergâh-ı ʿâlī gediklü müteferriḳa*), traveled to inspect the imperial post stations in Anatolia.[42] At each post station, which would have been located within a village, Hasan Agha met with the local judge and villagers at the courthouse. In the presence of this visitor from the im-perial capital, villagers undertook collective contracts (*taʿahhüd, tekeffül*) and stood as mutual sureties for each other (*birbirlerine kefīl*) to guarantee that they would provide sufficient horses for the local post station and would offer assis-tance to their postmaster. The judge then composed a report (*ʿarż*) or deed (*ḥüccet*) affirming the villagers' contracts for submission to the sultan and his bu-reaucrats in the capital.[43] Hasan Agha collected the judge's deed and rode off to the next post stations to repeat this routine.[44] When he eventually returned to Istanbul, Hasan Agha handed over all of the deeds he had been carrying with him to the Bureau of Suspended Payments (*mevḳūfât ḳalemi*). There, a book-keeper summarized the contents of these collected deeds, copying them on the back pages of a post station register in neat diagonal lines, all slanted at the same angle, as shown in figure 23.

Not just Hasan Agha but Ismail Aga, Khalil Agha, and Mehmed Agha were also dispatched to different locations along post station routes to procure simi-lar contracts.[45] They did their inspection tours around the same time, in 1726 and 1727. Separately and independently, these men supervised the undertaking of col-lective public oaths in multiple villages, oaths that were entered into judicial statements and deeds. They carried these papers (*kâġıd*) back to the capital, where bookkeepers summarized them on the back pages of the pertinent post station registers.[46]

There was variation in the kinds of collective contracts and mutual sure-tyships obtained at different villages. When Hasan Agha visited Sapanca, a town roughly eighty-seven miles east of Istanbul, he procured a deed that a scribe summarized as follows: The villagers of this district (*ahālī-i ḳażā*) stand as sureties for each other (*birbirlerine tekeffül*) such that couriers traveling through this post station have not previously been delayed and will henceforth also not be delayed.[47] Like public vows, this last clause in the suretyship con-tract is "future-oriented" and "preventative."[48] This act of standing surety was recorded in a legal deed (*ḥüccet-i şerʿiyye*), and the notarization was affirmed in a report (*ʿarż*) that the local judge prepared for Hasan Agha to bring back to the capital.

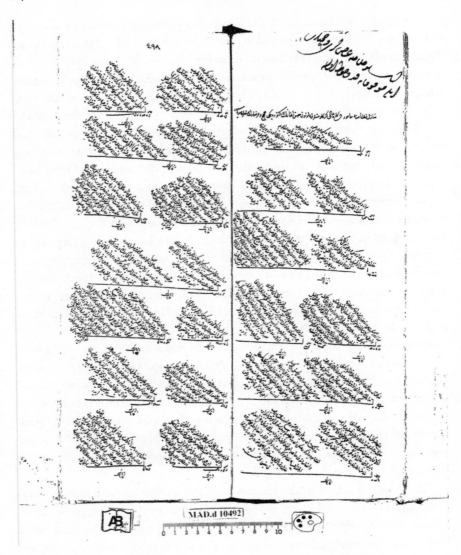

Figure 23. Villagers' collective contracts, 1720s. BOA, MAD 10492, 225.jpg.

Sometimes an extra guarantee of horse provision was included in these contracts. This was the case with Akşehir, whose villagers stood as sureties for each
other (*birbirlerine kefil olub*) and undertook a mutual contract (*ta'ahhüd*) to provide healthy horses for the post station.[49] This guarantee was recorded in the
first-person plural register: "We will provide a sufficient number of horses."

At other times, neither the terminology for suretyships nor that for mutual contracts was used. In Lefke, for instance, villagers gathered at the courthouse simply to affirm that they would put post station affairs in order (*nizām virildüği*) with all their collective skill (*cümle ma'rifetiyle*).[50] However, the fact that these summaries were listed alongside other collective contracts suggests that we should understand them within the same context of collective liability and responsibility.

Sometimes only the postmasters were specified and the villagers were absent from any meeting. For instance, Mehmed Agha visited Karahısar-ı Şarki, where Ivaz Beşe undertook (*ta'ahhüd*) to fulfill his duties as postmaster and also accepted, as co-contractor (*müte'āhid*), the duty of operating within the budget of 1,000 *guruş* each month.[51] There are other similar examples from the same page of this fiscal register.[52]

These collective contracts and mutual suretyships were a novel phenomenon in the eighteenth-century postal administration. Like nested suretyships, they gesture toward an increased bureaucratic desire to institutionalize reliability and trust through a system of mutual guarantees within each locality. Additionally, they reflect a more active and participatory vigor in local governance than prevailed before. Collective contracts could be interpreted as another manifestation of increasing corporatism in Ottoman society. Dispatching imperial officials on inspection tours was one way for the bureaucracy to cultivate and maintain ties with decision-makers in villages. Such missions also created opportunities for collective participation in face-to-face group events that could reinforce the villagers' sense of participating in the larger project of empire.[53]

There was a curious stipulation in some of the aforementioned legal deeds. In one, the villagers at Gerede collectively guaranteed, as sureties, that horses from neighboring post stations would not go beyond their station. In other words, the villagers at Gerede guaranteed that post horses would only shuttle between two stations.[54] How did villagers manage to control the travel range of their horses, and why did they do so? The legal deed does not offer more information, but it is possible to make a few guesses.

There were several good reasons to restrict horses' movements to a certain geographical region. Confining the use of horses to familiar routes helped horses to relax and conserve energy, thereby increasing safety and efficiency for their human riders.[55] Stabling horses within the same group and with the same humans could also fulfill the animals' social and behavioral needs.[56] Humans who lived with animals had a deep knowledge of each animal's personality and feeding preferences, and even the social dynamics among the animals.[57] While research-ing the Yörük of southeastern Turkey in the 1960s, the anthropologist Dan-iel G. Bates observed that these pastoralists could recognize the faces of each of their (several hundred) animals.[58] For millennia, humans who lived with ani-mals engaged with them as individuals, as social beings, and shared emotional and interdependent relations with them.[59] Restricting horses' movements could thus have been for reasons of health, safety, and even emotional attachment.

But the practical aspect of restricting the travel range of post horses would have required substantial work and coordination. It entailed having some means of identifying which horse came from which station, of communicating with ad-jacent villages, of coordinating with villages beyond the immediate range to en-sure sufficient post horses for onward journeys, of enforcing restrictions if couriers decided to skip stations, and perhaps of negotiating with semi-pastoral and pas-toral communities for horse resources.[60] My view is that villagers likely under-took a substantial amount of collective organizing in the absence of active authority, that this work of organizing eluded the written record, and that it constituted an important element in Ottoman postal administration. I base my argument on clues such as that tantalizing stipulation in the legal deed men-tioned above and on ways communities have collectively managed resources across history.

Common pool resources (CPRs) are any kind of large resources, natural or human-made, from which it is costly to exclude free riders. Typical examples of common pool resources include fishing grounds, groundwater basins, grazing ar-eas, streams, lakes, and other bodies of water.[61] Elinor Ostrom, a political scien-tist, collected numerous case studies of how communities, historical and present-day, devised effective solutions for using CPRs sustainably. She observed that these communities were mutually dependent on each other, exhibited learn-ing behavior over time, and produced a diversity of institutional arrangements that used a variety of enforcement mechanisms.[62] With her empirical findings, Ostrom challenged dominant strands of thinking in her day that advocated either "privatization" or "nationalization" of CPRs. She also critiqued widespread mod-els for analyzing CPR problems that assumed that individuals were "only capa-ble of short-term maximization but not long-term reflection about joint strategies to improve joint outcomes" and that individuals needed some "external author-ity [to impose] a solution."[63]

Horse management across multiple post stations likely involved a high de-gree of collective self-governance in the absence of active imperial authority. Post horses were akin to common pool resources; the existing stock of horses was a renewable resource, and, if well maintained, could yield the new horses that were required to fulfill a village's tax obligations. The weakness of this argument is that it is not based on empirical evidence; a mere line in a collective contract that horses not travel beyond the next station is not enough proof. Furthermore, the issue of horse breeding is completely absent in all the archival documents pertaining to the postal system that were consulted for this book, even if it must have been an important consideration for Ottoman villagers. (This absence of an imperial written record may actually strengthen the hypothesis that villagers were engaged in collective self-governance in coordinating horse breeding activities in the absence of imperial authority.) It is my hope that other scholars may, in the future, find source material, both government-produced and private papers, to support this argument. The Registers of Apportionment (*tevzī' defterleri*), which record the communal collection of taxes and expenses at the village level, are especially promising.[64]

For now, I will highlight examples of collective organization in the Ottoman historiography to show that Ottoman villagers had the potential to coordinate in similar ways in the postal context. However, this requires reading against the grain of the archival record. When collective self-governance is successful at the local level, it rarely enters the imperial written record. It is only when collective self-governance breaks down that imperial authorities get involved and a paper trail is created. For instance, one may read a study of water administration in the Damascus hinterland by the historian Astrid Meier as suggesting that the ten or so villages that shared the same water source from the river A'waj had enjoyed a rather successful period of collective self-governance in managing its use.[65] One could argue the Ottoman archival paper trail emerged only when this collective arrangement failed. A dispute had led one of these villages to invite intervention from provincial authorities, which, in turn, created a documentary record. Disputes are not uncommon in collective self-governance arrangements, and parties may resort to incremental escalation. Mediation is first attempted within a small group, and if there is no resolution, the dispute is escalated to a broader circle, radiating outward until a resolution is reached.[66] However, escalation to higher authorities does not always work. This village's solicitation of imperial intervention met with a crisis in 1708, when another village sent fifty armed men to confront the official delegation sent by the judge of Damascus and successfully hindered the delegation's work. A new water redistribution arrangement was only arrived at, according to the documentary trail, five years later. Ultimately, the written record provides an imperial perspective that obscures local negotiation processes and further details of conflicts. The written record would also have omitted all instances of successful collective self-governance arrangements because, by definition, imperial authorities were not needed in those cases.

A second example comes from the southern coast of the Black Sea. The anthropologist Michael Meeker, in his magisterial decades-long study, shows that the local elites of Trabzon were able to form coastal coalitions that could mobilize thousands of armed men by land and sea in order to challenge a provincial governor. These extensive mobilizations were not undertaken to overthrow the imperial order but to contest it and claim a bigger stake in it. Meeker's main thesis is that Ottoman governance worked through concentric circles of interpersonal association such that provincial governors could rely on local elites to reach, via "twig and branch," into the most rural corners of coastal districts. Conversely, locals could work through their elite representatives to participate in and claim a stake in imperial governance. Strikingly, Meeker shows that in one of the smallest towns in the Black Sea region, a local elite family (the Selimoğlu) who had participated in regional governance since Ottoman times continued to hold power after the empire's collapse in the 1920s and the establishment of the modern Turkish republic. This "House of Selim" had outlasted even the House of Osman. The enduring bonds of interpersonal association at the level of local communities thus strongly suggest that at least some Ottoman communities could and did exercise a substantial degree of collective self-organization and that imperial governance would have depended greatly on this capability.[67]

The above discussion gives examples of Ottoman communities' abilities to self-govern. Many examples can also be found beyond the Ottoman context.[68] The Balinese irrigation system serves as one living example of how communities use CPRs sustainably (in this case, water). Combining the use of colonial archives, anthropological research, oral interviews, and computer simulation models, the anthropologist Steve Lansing discovered that water temple rituals, long regarded as having only religious significance, had the practical function of coordinating collective action in irrigation management. These rituals enabled *subak*s (water-user groups of about a hundred or so farmers) to "behave like agents in a complex adaptive system."[69] Complex adaptive or emergent systems are systems where large networks of simple units following simple rules produce complex collective behavior without any central coordination. Such complex systems are found in both the natural world and in human society—examples are ant colonies, firefly swarms, human brains, traffic jams, market economies, and crowds of pedestrians walking efficiently on the same street without constant collisions.[70] In the last case, pedestrians follow simple rules, adjusting their walking speed and direction according to the behavior of the two or three pedestrians closest to them. At scale, the crowd manages to flow without constant collisions.[71]

Pertinently, Lansing does not only give an account of how cooperation occurred; he also explains when and why cooperation broke down due to conflict. In his research team's investigations of multiple *subaks*, they discovered a wide variety of self-governance dynamics. Factors such as customary beliefs, social standing, and leadership styles affected whether *subaks* behaved cooperatively and in unison.[72] For these reasons, Lansing's approach to complex adaptive systems as they apply to real-life communities is not deterministic, but instead involves what he has called "ongoing experiments in self-governance," "spiraling eddies [where] the balance of forces in each *subak* flowed first in one direction and then the other."[73]

The foregoing examples suggest that across cultures, geographies, and time periods, people in an "interdependent situation can organize and govern themselves to obtain continuing joint benefits when all face temptations to free-ride, shirk, or otherwise act opportunistically."[74] The Ottoman postal system created one such interdependent situation for Ottoman villagers, who had to organize and coordinate with villagers in adjacent districts in order to safeguard their horses. I am hopeful that future generations of Ottoman historians will be able to offer robust evidence of such collective self-organizing. Until then, the account here of how the Ottoman postal system worked remains underdetermined.

In the sixteenth century, villagers entered the written record as individual suppliers of post horses. In the eighteenth century, they typically appeared as collective units and displayed a new capacity for collective action. They gave feedback to imperial bureaucrats about local conditions, raised complaints to protect their interests, and, in so doing, "intervened" in postal policy. For their part, bureaucrats harnessed these new, energetic collectives to achieve imperial aims. They used new mechanisms of collective liability such as collective contracts and nested suretyships to draw villagers into the work of infrastructural maintenance.

The involvement of villagers in postal maintenance resonates with the broader trend of corporatism that characterized the Second Ottoman Empire. The Greek Orthodox communities in the Balkans and the 'Alawi communities in Syria, for instance, also increased their participation in provincial governance during the eighteenth century, thus becoming more visible in the written record.[75] The historian Stefan Winter observes that far from being "resilient to Ottoman imperial authority," the 'Alawi community was, in fact, born of and made by that authority; the 'Alawis as community were its very "incarnation."[76] There is a relationship of mutual reinforcement, for, on one hand, imperial authorities delegated governance work to local communities and, on the other hand, local communities consolidated as coherent collectives through the execution of such work. This recursive relationship may be observed across different kinds of collectives, whether geographically bounded villages or geographically dispersed religious communities. This argument thus makes it possible to revise prevailing conceptions of Ottoman social life as "atomized" with "weak mechanisms of aggregation" and little ability for collective action at a supra-local level.[77] These newly consolidating collective groups could and did become minor stakeholders in the empire.

To conclude, villagers were crucial actors in operating the sprawling postal infrastructure. Couriers circulating around the empire depended on the coordinated efforts of bookkeepers and postmasters and on the collective work of villagers. But villagers almost certainly did more work to ensure the smooth operations of the Ottoman postal system than was captured in the archival sources.

CHAPTER 8

Breakdown

It was sometime in the 1760s. A courier and his men were galloping at top speed toward Belgrade carrying high-priority mail from Istanbul.[1] "Get there in one week," the vizier had instructed. Stopping at Plovdiv for a change of horses, the courier fumbled around for small change. The postmaster stood, waiting expectantly. But the courier had run out of coins. What now? The postmaster called in the local judge. Together, they inspected the courier order; it was authentic. The judge agreed to provide paperwork for the postmaster so that he could petition the Imperial Treasury for reimbursement. This would have to do, since the courier did not have enough cash to pay for the horses he and his men needed. Reassured, the postmaster motioned for his stable boys to fetch fresh horses . . . except no horses were available. The courier was enraged. He protested that he was on urgent government business. The postmaster calmed him down and invited him to have some coffee and food. Hand on the courier's back, the postmaster guided the traveling party toward an empty nook in the post station. Then the postmaster sent his men to procure horses from the villagers.

This imagined scenario, extrapolated from written records, showcases two kinds of disruption that plagued Ottoman relay communications from the late seventeenth century to the nineteenth: lack of coin and lack of horses. Like all technological systems and infrastructures, the Ottoman postal system often broke down. Horses could die. Couriers could fall ill. A storm could unleash a landslide, making the road unpassable. These breakdowns could be minor or major, geographically bounded or regionally widespread. All this disrupted government correspondence. Of all the kinds of breakdowns captured in the archival record, the lack of coin and the lack of horses occupied bureaucrats' attention the most. Imperial decrees condemned these two problems in dramatic ways. However, the frequency with which the shortages of coin and horses popped up in the written record throughout the eighteenth century suggest that they were, in fact, ordinary and routine occurrences.

Breakdowns offer a fruitful site for historical study. Scholars of infrastructure have long recognized that societies learn to reproduce themselves through repair and maintenance. They learn to innovate, improvise, and upgrade existing systems, whether buildings, roads, canals, or larger infrastructure.[2] Breakdowns also reveal relations and politics that are usually hidden from view. Catastrophic breakdowns like wars, pandemics, terrorist attacks, labor strikes, and extreme weather or even small-scale breakdowns like a clogged toilet, a blown fuse, and being out of salt can cause disruptions to the seamless circulations that sustain everyday life. These disruptions, big and small, force those affected to confront their dependency on infrastructural circuits they did not know existed, on relations of exploitation they had had the luxury to ignore, on the goodwill of neighbors and neighboring communities they had not realized they needed.[3]

For historians of the pre-industrial world, breakdowns can offer revelatory windows into the past. In the case of the Ottoman postal system, the lack of coin forced bureaucrats to compose imperial orders to diagnose and fix this liquidity crunch. In doing so, they inadvertently described how the payments system was supposed to have worked—providing the only written explanation of this system known to historians. Similarly, the lack of horses forced bureaucrats to develop policies to increase their availability at post stations. In doing so, they inadvertently revealed the extent to which non-officials, including merchants, were siphoning off post horses away from government use and toward the commercial transportation of goods. The recurring pattern of breakdowns across an extensive period of time can also expose long-term transformations. In particular, the chronic lack of horses at post stations was an early indicator of a growing market demand for horse-borne commercial transportation, which in turn reflected larger shifts in the regional socioeconomic landscape.

Piecing together a range of sources, in this chapter I follow two arcs of change across several centuries: the transformation of the courier order from a symbol of imperial authority into "paper money" and the transformation of the post horse from a government-owned resource into a commodity. I argue that because Ottoman bureaucrats did not fully recognize these transformations or their implications, they were unable to solve the problems of coin and horse shortages, even as they tenaciously addressed them.

Infrastructural breakdown completes the argument of this book by showing the limits of thickening governance. Governing more through more local agents could create a secondary demand for more repair and maintenance work, like a "second-order infrastructure."[4] This, in turn, required the recruitment and cooperation of more agents to investigate and to fix things. Thickening governance begot thicker layers of governance—but sometimes these layers formed blind spots.

THE METAMORPHOSIS OF THE COURIER ORDER

Before the 1690s, there was one kind of courier order. It was a piece of paper that primarily functioned as a symbol of imperial authority and empowered its holder, the courier, to confiscate horses as needed from anybody encountered on the road. These were the early days of the Ottoman postal system, when violence was the main currency of horse procurement. Courier orders were the material artifact of imperial authority that legitimized these violent confiscations.

Things changed after fixed post stations were established and fees were imposed on the usage of post horses. Courier orders evolved accordingly. After the 1690s, there were two main types of courier order: those that included fee waivers and those that did not.[5]

Courier orders that included fee waivers were known as Fee Waiver Orders (*inʿāmāt emri*). They functioned as a form of paper money, like promissory notes. Although Sultan Mustafa II imposed a nominal fee of 10 *akçe* per horse per hour's travel in his decrees of 1696, he waived these fees for official couriers delivering government correspondence. Fee Waiver Orders performed that function—couriers used them to procure horses at post stations without any payment. Postmasters would record each use of a Fee Waiver Order in a Fee Waiver Register (*inʿāmāt defteri*), and every six to twelve months, they would send these registers to the imperial capital to obtain reimbursements.[6] In brief, the Fee Waiver system was a deferred payment system.

Courier orders that did not include fee waivers provided access to post stations and their horses but required the additional payment of a fee—this was most likely paid in cash at a post station. This was known as the Immediate Cash (*peşin*) payment system.[7]

To use an analogy, these two kinds of courier order were like having a premium membership or a basic membership in the exclusive club of the Ottoman

	Access to Post Stations	Access to Horses	Fees Waived? (Horses Free of Charge)
Fee Waiver Order (Courier Order with Fee Waiver)	✓	✓	✓
Courier Order without Fee Waiver	✓	✓	✗
No Courier Order, Just Cash	✗	✗	N.A.

Figure 24. Types of courier orders after 1696 (in principle). Chart by author.

postal system. A premium membership entitled couriers to access post horses with no additional payment needed; a basic membership entitled couriers to access post horses but required additional (cash) payment.[8] Officials without any courier order were not permitted to access post horses at all, at least in principle (fig. 24).

During the eighteenth century, a shortage of coin in the Imperial Treasury disrupted payments at post stations. In the ensuing fallout, unnamed bureaucrats composed three exceptionally detailed imperial orders between 1757 and 1763 diagnosing the strengths and weaknesses of the Fee Waiver (or deferred payment) system and the Immediate Cash (*peşin*) (or advance payment) system. The main thrust of all three imperial orders was consistent: the bureaucrat-authors repeatedly recommended that higher authorities abandon the Immediate Cash payment system and adopt the Fee Waiver system.[9] This was because the Immediate Cash payment system was almost three times as costly as the Fee Waiver system: a horse cost 39 *guruş* under the Immediate Cash payment system but only 12.5 *guruş* under the Fee Waiver system, resulting in the loss of 26.5 *guruş* per horse for the Imperial Treasury.[10]

Although the bureaucrat-authors did not explain this discrepancy in costs, I would venture an explanation. Consider the fact that these two different payment systems entailed decision-making at different stages of a courier's travel. The Fee Waiver system incurred costs at the moment of transaction in the post station, when a courier showed his Fee Waiver Order to the postmaster to procure horses. These costs were "unrealized" or "paper" costs, to use twenty-first-century expressions: they were recorded by postmasters in Fee Waiver Registers for future reimbursement purposes. In contrast, the Immediate Cash payment system incurred costs in advance, *before* a courier embarked on his journey. Bookkeepers and bureaucrats in the imperial capital made cost projections by using the official cost (10 *akçe* per horse per hour of travel) multiplied by fixed hourly distances between post stations. (See Chapter 5.) They would then issue the projected amount of cash to couriers before they departed the capital. These costs were thus "realized" in advance of the courier's journey; they were disbursed in hard coin, in specie.

It is perhaps not surprising that the bookkeepers' cost projections overestimated the real costs of courier travel by more than three times. As Chapters 2 and 3 have shown, couriers wielded considerable autonomy in planning their routes given the vagaries of overland travel. This autonomy completely undercut the bookkeepers' static formulas, which were based on fixed hourly distances between post stations. Such assumptions of fixed hourly distances were inaccurate reflections of the reality of overland travel. As travelogues from the seventeenth to the nineteenth century reveal, it was not unusual for couriers to change their itineraries spontaneously. Couriers had to confront risks and threats ranging from inclement weather to lurking bandits, difficult terrain, accidents, and the availability of horses. They might decide to rest overnight under the stars instead of in a post station. They might decide to accompany another travel party for safety reasons or to take a detour. Or, like Evliya Çelebi, they might decide to give cover to a rebel on the run whose valor on the battlefield they respected, and therefore travel at a slower speed and stop at each post station. Furthermore, a component of bookkeepers' static formulas was the fixed costs of horse maintenance, such as the cost of horseshoe and nail of 3 *akçe* described at the start of Chapter 5. It should be noted that these costs did not change over several decades, but were frozen in an aggregated multiplier that was reproduced in the accounting routines of subsequent generations of bookkeepers.

In sum, the bookkeepers' cost projections did not reflect a courier's on-the-ground reality, much less predict in advance what might happen on any given journey. The Immediate Cash payment system was essentially a shift in the locus of decision-making from couriers (who were physically plying these pan-imperial itineraries) to bookkeepers (who were sedentary scribes based in the imperial capital).[11] Instead of couriers having on-the-spot budgetary control over their itineraries and horse usage, bookkeepers in the distant capital with no experience at plying postal routes were the ones making cost projections about couriers' future itineraries and future horse usage before any journey was undertaken. Bookkeepers used a fixed formula that depended on a series of assumptions, and the results were vast overestimates. If my reasoning is sound, then these overestimates were a strong argument for the necessity of delegating decision-making to local actors instead of making plans from the imperial capital. This particular breakdown shows one weakness of thickening governance: the amassed information about postal operations that bureaucrats in the imperial capital had access to motivated (and perhaps emboldened) them to make what turned out to be costly decisions.

These burgeoning costs led the bureaucrat-authors to argue, in an imperial order dated to 1756, that higher-level decision-makers should abandon the Immediate Cash payment system and restore the Fee Waiver system. In any case, the Imperial Treasury was running out of coin (*akçe*).[12] There was a liquidity crunch.

Despite numerous entreaties and despite the lack of coin, however, the Immediate Cash payment system endured for at least seven more years.[13] In 1763, another imperial order repeated the recommendation to abandon the Immediate Cash system, noting that in reality, local officials had effectively reverted to the Fee Waiver system.[14] Substitutes for cash had emerged. Some officials, for instance, were issued papers that acted as fee waivers. Other officials, like the courier in the imagined scenario that opened this chapter, simply turned up without the ability to make cash payments. In these cases, local postmasters obtained another type of documentation—notifications (*i'lām*)—that functioned as premodern IOUs, as acknowledgments of debt. Deputies of local judges (*nā'ib*) produced these notifications for postmasters to use as proof of having provided horses to officials, and they could then be used to seek reimbursement from the Imperial Treasury. This, however, created downstream difficulties for bookkeepers in the capital, who struggled to verify the notifications and opened the door for fraudulent reimbursement claims and even more losses for the Imperial Treasury.[15]

Officially, the postal system was operating with the Immediate Cash payment system, where everyone was paid right away and in cash. In practice, however, the postal system had already returned to the old system of Fee Waivers. In cases where neither cash nor authentic fee waivers were available, postmasters enlisted local judges to create substitute paperwork. In other words, the liquidity crunch had forced the Ottoman postal system into a kind of early modern institutional drift. Although the rules did not officially change, the behavior of actors did.[16] The actors on the ground modified their behavior to cope with the lack of coin. While some Ottoman bureaucrats recognized that these rules were being implemented in ways that deviated from the original intent, they did not, or could not, persuade higher-level decision-makers to change the rules and restore the

Fee Waiver system.[17] This instance of disagreement and debate within different arms of the imperial bureaucracy reflected the internal heterogeneity of what is often assumed to have been an undifferentiated Ottoman "state."

It is not known how the payment situation was eventually resolved. The extraordinarily detailed and revealing paper trail regarding postal payments ends abruptly in 1763, the date of the final imperial order on this matter. However, this paper trail, born out of infrastructural breakdown, reveals both the resilience and the limits of expanded Ottoman governance. On one hand, local officials showed initiative in devising substitutes for fee waivers and money, which allowed postal operations to continue. This may have been a temporary fix that created downstream difficulties for bureaucrats in the imperial capital, but it did allow couriers to continue circulating through the postal system on fresh horses. On the other hand, the institutional drift that widened the gap between the letter of Ottoman policy and the reality of its implementation suggests that high-level decision-makers did not always make the best policy choices. It is possible that there were good reasons to insist on a cash payment system, but the fact remained that there was not enough liquidity to sustain it. Overall, the initiative of local officials was an important aspect of the participatory culture of the Second Empire.

More broadly, this case study poses new questions about Ottoman financial and monetary history. Existing scholarship on this topic focuses on credit relations used by private merchants or brokered by moneylenders on behalf of Ottoman officials. Less attention has been paid to the "credit" relations (or deferred payment mechanisms) used in Ottoman public finance.[18] To that end, it might be helpful to view Fee Waiver Orders alongside other forms of paper money that enabled deferred payments within the context of Ottoman public finance. Understanding the true breadth of financial instruments that were in use can help clarify wider transformations taking place in the empire.

An example of paper money may be found as early as the 1590s in the payroll ticket (*esame*) which was used to pay the wages of members of active military corps. These payroll tickets recorded the holder's membership in a corps as well as his right to payments in cash and kind. Depending on the holder's service and achievements, additional components of his wage could be recorded on the payroll ticket.[19] By the late eighteenth century, these payroll tickets had begun circulating in a secondary market, available for purchase as a form of dividend-bearing investment. As the pool of payroll ticketholders diversified, a wide segment of society came to identify with the interests of the janissaries, creating unexpected alliances that crisscrossed Ottoman society.[20]

The bill of exchange was another form of paper money that was used by the Ottoman authorities. The bills were typically small slips of paper upon which coded scribbles were written; they were used to transfer money to distant locations.[21] European merchants typically facilitated these transactions, issuing bills of exchange to Ottoman governors transferring provincial tax collections to the imperial capital, to Cairene emirs hoping to sweeten their petitions to the sultan in Istanbul and elicit favorable responses, and to a range of private clients, including European and Ottoman merchants as well as Jewish communities in different Ottoman provinces who sent regular donations to the *Pekidim* (officials) in Istanbul for redistribution across a large philanthropic network.[22] In some of these cases, Ottoman couriers were the human vectors delivering these bills of exchange.[23]

Ottomans also used interest-bearing state notes such as the *esham* and *kaime*. In contrast to the bill of exchange, the *esham* was an internal borrowing mechanism created in 1775 by the Ottoman government to borrow money from rich subjects. In return for buying a "share" (*pay, hisse,* or *sehm*), *esham* holders could receive dividends.[24] The *esham* was thus a fiscal product, an instrument of investment. It created the conditions for the launch of the interest-bearing note, the *kaime*, in 1840, and the first non-interest-bearing *kaime* in 1852.[25]

Although the *kaime* is conventionally viewed as the first Ottoman paper money, I argue that it was not.[26] Indeed, the longer history of deferred payments facilitated by paper-based monies, briefly described above, shows that the *kaime* was not the first paper-based money used in the Ottoman Empire. What was novel about the *kaime,* rather, was that it represented the first time state authorities attempted to impose a single medium of exchange across multiple strata of currencies and to exclude local, circumscribed forms of currencies. This was a true rupture in Ottoman monetary policy.

According to the monetary historian Akinobu Kuroda, societies have used multiple currencies for different kinds of exchanges for much of human history. For instance, in late eighteenth-century Jessore (in modern Bangladesh), one currency was used for the rice and grain trade, while another currency was used for the salt trade.[27] In colonial Belgian Congo, one currency was used for buying canoes and another currency was used for buying fish.[28] In the Ottoman case, different kinds of paper monies were used for different purposes; courier orders were used for post horse procurement, while the payroll ticket (*esame*) was used to pay military officers. Kuroda calls this coupling of particular currencies with particular goods a currency circuit. Historically, people lived life across multiple currency circuits, which did not necessarily require state control, coordination, or enforcement. This multiplicity and complementarity of diverse monies only came to an end in the twentieth century, when "the notion of a single currency under a sovereign authority gained common understanding." It then became hard to fathom how societies could have functioned with multiple currency circuits. Nineteenth-century Europeans who were used to a single territorial currency felt frazzled when confronted with what appeared to them to be "chaotic and eccentric" monetary systems—as the British Protestant missionary and sinologist Joseph Edkins felt, for instance, when traveling in China.[29] In this vein, what distinguished the Ottoman *kaime* of 1852 was not that it was paper money but that it was intended by the imperial authorities to replace multiple currencies in use at the time. Therein lies the important break from the past. It was not the materiality of paper that was novel; it was the intended function of the *kaime* to become a single medium of exchange that was.

The Fee Waiver Order is one more case study of paper-based money used in the currency circuit of the Ottoman postal system. It is part of the history of multiple and complementary currencies in the Ottoman world. In this case, it was the lack of coin—a liquidity crunch—that forced bureaucrats to articulate details about how payments worked in the postal system, thereby revealing this currency circuit. Disruption exposed the usual workings of the system, showing blockages and diversions in circulation where there used to be untroubled—and hence unremarked-upon—flows. Local postmasters learned from their experiences in producing Fee Waiver Registers for reimbursements and devised ersatz fee waiver claims to substitute for the lack of coin by couriers alighting at their post stations. Imperial bureaucrats had to deal with these claims, possibly reimbursing even fraudulent ones, because of higher-level decision-makers' insistence on keeping the cash payment system. Given the lack of sources, it is not known what bureaucrats' later decisions were.

THE METAMORPHOSIS OF THE HORSE

From 1690 to 1833, Ottoman bureaucrats repeatedly complained that horses were frequently missing at post stations. Missing horses delayed couriers, and delayed couriers meant delayed communications. Bureaucrats took this disruption very seriously, issuing over fifty decrees in the name of the sultan during these 140 years, all in attempts to fix the issue; this was roughly one decree every three years. But despite over a century of effort, bureaucrats were unable to solve this problem.

Here, I explore the Ottoman bureaucrats' struggles to fix the breakdowns caused by missing horses at post stations. They implemented a horse rationing system that they repeatedly updated over the eighteenth century. They responded regularly to feedback from local provinces and repeatedly recalibrated the enforcement of imperial policies. However, despite their dogged attention, horses remained missing. Couriers continued to be delayed.

Through a close examination of these fifty decrees, I argue that this problem endured because the postal system was serving functions apart from government correspondence. Notably, officials and non-official persons were diverting post horses toward profit-making ventures, such as the transportation of commercial merchandise. Although bureaucrats condemned these individual infractions by officials using horses for "personal affairs," they did not examine, in writing, these infractions collectively, and therefore did not perceive a systemic demand that competed with the imperial authorities' demand for horses. The written record shows that bureaucrats did not perceive that a shadow economy could have mushroomed around the post stations, that post horses had transformed from a government resource restricted exclusively to officials into a commodity available to the highest bidder. Instead, bureaucrats in the imperial capital engaged with reports of missing horses as unconnected and discrete.

The lack of horses caused a different kind of breakdown from that caused by the lack of coin, especially in terms of length of time. Here, the enduring problem of missing horses was a continuous, chronic breakdown that persisted for over a century, revealing more fundamental and long-lived transformations in the broader socioeconomic landscape. The post horse transformed from a government resource mainly accessible by status into a commodity mainly accessible by money, reflecting a shift in the moral order among bureaucrats regarding the boundaries of what officials were entitled to. Bureaucrats, on their part, tenaciously implemented, enforced, and updated their post station policies over the course of the eighteenth century. However, they ultimately lacked the ability to synthesize discrete sources of incoming information within a shared matrix and failed to perceive a unified shadow economy. This challenge was not unique to the Ottoman bureaucracy—the Qing bureaucracy, too, encountered a similarly blinkered informational order.[30]

For Ottoman bureaucrats, the supply of horses—specifically, their breeding and production—was not the problem; rather, it was horse availability at post stations that was the problem.[31] This is because the Ottoman Empire did have a relative abundance of horses. The Crimean, Balkan, and Arab provinces and Anatolia were well endowed with horses. Horses raised on the pasture lands of the Pontic-Caspian steppe were known to be extremely tough and well adapted to wet and cold conditions.[32] An eighteenth-century French diplomat estimated that the horse population there could easily provide for 80,000 cavalrymen; in the nineteenth century, this figure increased to between 96,000 and 130,000.[33] Locals had enough surplus horses to trade them; the Nogais were known to have sold around 30,000 to 40,000 horses annually to the Muscovites.[34] Specialized horse-transport ships regularly took horses from the northern steppe to buyers in Kili, Circassia.[35] In the Balkans, horses from Bulgaria and Bosnia were particularly well regarded; the Bosnian Muslim nobility were known to be experienced horse-breeders.[36] Moldavia and Wallachia sent horses annually as tribute to the Ottomans.[37] The Arab provinces and Anatolia were also rich in horses, many of which were supplied by pastoralists.[38] In 1910, these regions boasted about one million horses in total.[39] The Ottoman administration extracted horses as in-kind taxes from pastoralists; the Atçeken, for instance, were obliged to supply horses annually and were subject to district-specific quotas, while the Muntafiq confederation supplied horses to the Mamluk-dominated Baghdad administration.[40]

The Ottoman Empire's relative abundance of horses is reflected in how it tracked them administratively—that is, without much care or attention. Across thousands of pages of fiscal registers pertaining to the postal administration, horses were typically mentioned in one way: as a quantity attached to a locality. These horses were simply a number. The records did not specify whether any individual animal was a stallion, a gelding, a mare, or even a mule; whether it was young or old; or whether it was locally bred or had been taken from another region in the empire.[41] The same could be said for Ottoman military horses.[42]

Empires suffering from equine deficits paid far more bureaucratic attention to their horses than the Ottoman Empire did. Within the Mughal administration, for example, every single horse in its service had its own identity certificate, branding certificate, and death certificate. The identity certificate provided a brief description of the horse's features, such as the color of its coat, any distinguishing spots, and its sex. When Mughal horses were branded, they received a branding certificate; when they died, they were issued a death certificate.[43] Similar kinds of obsessive, documentary tracking may be found in China during various dynasties.[44] The Song and Ming, for instance, created specialized offices in the government bureaucracy (Horse Trading Office; Tea Tax Office) to supervise the tea-horse trade with pastoralists.[45]

The Ottomans displayed no such active management of horse procurement. It is only in this comparative context that the way the Ottomans documented their horses can be put in perspective and shown to be relatively less granular. This absence of documentary obsessiveness, I suggest, is connected to the Ottoman Empire's relative abundance of horse supplies.

Because horse supply was not a problem in the Ottoman Empire, bureaucrats simply focused their attention on the availability of horses at post stations. Ottoman documents pertaining to postal administration consistently ignore the issue of horse supply; they never afford any visibility to the level of Ottoman villages and their horse breeding or trading activities. Instead, Ottoman villages were assumed to have horses and to be able to provide them to post stations as their tax obligations.

In tackling the missing horse problem, bureaucrats' main response was to ration horse usage among officials according to rank and then enforce access criteria in post stations. Over the eighteenth and nineteenth centuries, they assigned specific quotas to individual official ranks and revised them. Table 8 shows the quotas that were issued to all provinces in the empire in 1717, 1735, 1789, and 1835.[46] This is the strongest piece of evidence that reveals bureaucrats' diagnosis of the missing horses problem as fundamentally one of resource allocation.

Bureaucrats in the capital may have created comprehensive horse-rationing lists, but they faced multiple challenges in enforcing them. They had to strike a careful balance in the wording of imperial decrees that, somehow, had to communicate a single policy agenda to a wide range of postmasters who could interpret that agenda in a variety of ways.

For instance, one decree reminded postmasters that only agents bearing courier orders with the sultan's monogram were allowed horses and that those holding courier orders with expired dates were to be denied horses.[47] Some postmasters rightly obeyed this instruction and, accordingly, denied horses to couriers with expired orders. As a consequence, couriers who were slightly delayed in executing official matters found themselves denied horses at post stations. Such incidents led bureaucrats to walk back on their earlier position. They issued a new command that postmasters provide horses to couriers delivering important messages who were on their return journey even if their courier orders were expired. Bureaucrats even accused postmasters of using the excuse of an expired courier order to charge hourly fees for horses.[48]

Whereas bureaucrats sought flexibility in the case of expired courier orders, they wanted rigorous enforcement in other cases. For instance, some postmasters were too relaxed and would not verify the number of horses stipulated in the imperial decree but instead provided as many horses to incoming officials as they had arrived with.[49] In this case, bureaucrats not only admonished

TABLE 8. HORSE-RATIONING LISTS FOR 1717, 1735, 1789, AND 1835

Rank	1717	1735	1789	1835
First Master of the Imperial Stables (*Mīrahur-ı Evvel*)	12	20	20–30	20
Second Master of the Imperial Stables (*Mīrahur-ı Sānī*)	8	15	13	15
Deputy Chief of the Gates (*Kapıcılar Kethüdāsı*)	10	18	15–30	15
Lieutenant of the Imperial Guards (*Haṣeki Ağa*)	6	10	8	8
Special Cavalry of the Ottoman household (*Haṣṣa Silāḥṣoru*)	4	8	8	6
Head Gatekeepers of the Sultan's Court (*Dergāh-ı mu'allā ḳapıcı başları*)	6	10	12–20	12
Aghas of the Janissaries, first rank (*Ağaların Evvel Ṭabaḳası*)	4	—	12	—
Aghas of the Janissaries, second rank (*Ağaların Ṭabaḳa-i Ṣāniyye*)	3	—	8	—
Esteemed individuals (*Vācibü'r-ri'āye*)	2	—	2	—
Footman (*Çuḳadār*), Tatar courier, imperial band member (*Mehterān*), and others of equivalent rank	1	According to need	1	3
Top-ranking Janissaries sent by the Sultan's Court (*Dergāh-ı mu'allā yeñiçerileri ocağı ṭarafından gönderilen yeñiçeri żabiṭiniñ büyükleri*)	8	—	—	—
Subjects of the Crimean Khan and others according to rank (*Ḳırım Hanı eṭba'i ve gayri dahi ḥaddine göre*)	1–5	According to need	—	—
Middle-rank Janissaries sent by the Sultan's Court (*Orta Ṭabaḳası*)	4	—	—	—
Janissaries of other ranks sent by the Sultan's Court (*Diğer ṭabaḳası*)	2	—	—	—
Aghas of the Janissaries, third rank (*Ağaların Ṭabaḳa-i Ṣāliṣe*)	—	—	6	—
Janissaries at the frontier, members of the elite mounted personal escort of the sultan, and holders of deeds (*gedik*) (*Ba'zı serḥadāt-ı hāḳāniyyeniñ yeñiçeri sālyānecilerine, müteferriḳa ve gedikliyān*)	—	5	5	4–5
Aghas of the Grand Vizier (*Haṣekiyān-ı Hāṣṣa-i ve Ağavāt-ı Ṣadr-ı 'Āliye*)	—	4	3	4–5

(*continued*)

TABLE 8. (CONTINUED)

Rank	1717	1735	1789	1835
Cannoneers (*Ṭopçu*), armourer (*Cebeci*), cavalry (*Sipāhī*), swordbearer (*Silāḥdār*), military cartwright (*Arabacı*), Aghas of the inner court (*Ağayān-ı Enderūn*)	—	—	2	3
Every 10 *kise* worth of treasury money (for the transportation of the treasury)	—	—	1	—
High-ranking functionaries (*menāṣıb-ı sitte*)	—	—	—	20
Middle-ranking functionaries	—	—	—	12

Sources: For 1717: Çetin, *Ulak Yol Durak,* 222–223, KŞS 47, p. 250/29.jpg, and MAD 8464, p. 9/4.jpg. Wherever there are divergences between Çetin's text and the sources, I have followed the copy of the imperial decree preserved in Konya's Judicial Register. For 1735: Yücel Özkaya, *18. Yüzyılda Osmanlı Toplumu* (Istanbul: Yapı Kredi Yayınları, 2008), 297. For 1789: GRGSA IAM OJC 001 F157 6–7.jpg. For 1835: HAT 491 24036.

Note: The list has been rearranged to reflect a general descending order of ranks. In the interest of brevity, I have omitted some offices from the table.

postmasters but also reprimanded couriers for requesting more horses than they were eligible for.[50]

These difficulties not only demonstrate the difficulty of communicating policy to postmasters across the empire. They also demonstrate the difficulty of distinguishing local officials' genuine misinterpretations of new regulations from willful violations. Were postmasters interpreting imperial policy overzealously when they denied horses to couriers with expired passes, or were they using them as an excuse to charge the couriers for horses? Even couriers and officials could be suspect. Why, for example, were couriers dissatisfied with the number of horses they were eligible to have, and why did they pressure postmasters into giving them more? What use did couriers have for extra horses? Were they accompanied by unnamed individuals?

Over the eighteenth century, bureaucrats also condemned other kinds of official misbehavior, especially that of price-gouging postmasters who gave horses to merchants and couriers who transported commercial merchandise. One imperial decree condemned postmasters for being attracted by profits.[51] Another decree scolded postmasters for embezzling post station funds for their own per-

TABLE 9. OFFICIAL HOURLY RATES OF POST-HORSE
USAGE PER HOUR'S TRAVEL

Year (CE)	Hourly rate per horse (*akçe*)
1696	10
1824	60
1826	90
1830	120

sonal use; it named twenty-two different stations whose postmasters were guilty of this charge.[52] A third decree accused postmasters of profit-seeking, bankrupt behavior and treachery; it singled out postmasters who held tax-exempt (*'askerī*) status for these sins.[53] This language that emphasized profits, greed, and embezzlement appeared for the first time in the 1730s. What these comments point toward, collectively, is that postmasters across the empire, from Rumelia to Anatolia and the Arab provinces, were raising prices. There were probably fundamental reasons beyond just individual greed for this broad, transregional convergence of pricing behavior.

One possible reason for the price-gouging behavior was inflation; another was a competing demand for horses. These were not mutually exclusive. Ongoing wars could have created short-term price fluctuations, prompting postmasters across multiple provinces to charge more for horses.[54] The state-mandated hourly rate of 10 *akçe* per horse was probably not keeping pace with actual post station expenditures and living costs. Set in 1696, that nominal rate remained unchanged for well over a century. It was raised to 60 *akçe* (20 *paras*) in August 1824.[55] Over the following decade, it was steadily increased: in 1826 to 90 *akçe* (30 *paras*), and in 1830 to 120 *akçe* (40 *paras*) (table 9).[56] The trend of these price increases—a slow rise followed by a relatively big jump in the nineteenth century—was likely linked to dramatic inflation during the later period.[57] However, the eighteenth century also witnessed gradual inflation, which may have prompted postmasters to take matters into their own hands and raise prices themselves.

A second possible reason for the raised prices was a competing demand for horses. This possibility is strengthened by evidence from other decrees issued in the final decade of the eighteenth century and by a reading of their implications back in time.

In 1793, it was discovered that a private transportation service had been diverting horses from post stations in Rumelia to serve Jewish and Christian merchants. Imperial authorities condemned those behind this service, accusing them of gaining profits through trickery and deceit.[58] Yet these tricksters were not simple bandits; they were former officials, and some were expelled tatar couriers. They procured post horses by wearing the special courier fur caps (ḳalpaḳ) and masquerading as official couriers. Even when postmasters could tell that they were imposters, they reluctantly acquiesced to their demands out of fear. Imperial bureaucrats identified the origins of these imposters: twenty men came from Yenişehir, ten each from Thessaloniki (Selanik) and Sofia, and one or two from unidentified provinces. These networks and services must have existed for some time before the 1790s, since they were unlikely to have emerged overnight as fully formed entities.

Such commercial transportation services that leeched off state horses were also found in the Anatolian and Arab provinces.[59] In November 1794, a decree chided couriers who moonlighted as transporters of merchandise in Anatolia. Two decades later, in July 1820, another decree explicitly banned couriers traveling between Istanbul and Baghdad from carrying merchandise on behalf of traders. Ferrying merchandise on the side not only delayed the delivery of official correspondence; the heavy weight of the merchandise could also cause the horses carrying it to die, which exacerbated the provisioning burdens of tax-paying subjects.[60] By the 1830s, bureaucrats had imposed a weight limit for the carrying loads of horses: 170 pounds (76.8 kilograms or 60 vuḳḳiyye).[61]

In Damascus, Ottoman officials and the men in their service posed as couriers by wearing special courier fur caps in order to obtain fresh horses.[62] Other imperial decrees attest to merchandise transporters, voivodes, and revenue farmers who masqueraded as official couriers so that they could travel fast.[63] These decrees demonstrate that such interlopers—who included genuine officials— were knowledgeable about Ottoman official regulations regarding uniforms and that they were able to procure such clothing. Reports of bandits robbing couriers of their clothes and belongings show one of the ways in which the paraphernalia of authentication could have fallen into the wrong hands.[64] By the late eighteenth century, bureaucrats were aware of such incidents but continued to respond to each as if they were stand-alone cases, at least according to the available sources.[65]

When read together, these decrees reveal the outlines of a shadow economy that depended on the Ottoman relay infrastructure. The participants in this shadow economy included price-gouging postmasters, imposter couriers, organized gangs who provided private transportation services, and legitimate officials who were transporting commercial merchandise on the side while traveling for work, a practice that had become widespread enough that the authorities had to issue an order explicitly banning it.

These broadly defined groups did not necessarily work in tandem, scattered as they were across the empire with its varied geography. What connected their discrete activities was a commonly shared economic landscape, where a strong market demand for horses competed with the official demand that nominally paid the rate of 10 *akçe* per hour per horse. This market-driven demand, which likely came from private merchants, appears to have paid a higher rate to couriers than the government did, thereby attracting both postmasters and couriers.

The enduring lack of post horses over the eighteenth century is suggestive of gradually increasing commercial activity, increasing consumption, and the increasing integration of the Ottoman Empire into the world market.[66] This uptick in commerce affected demand for commercial transportation services, resulting in increased demand for horses and the proliferation of short- and medium-distance overland trading routes. An important source of power and mode of transportation in the pre-industrial world, the horse transformed into an "interlinked" commodity attached to a range of other commodities that it helped to transport, connecting producers to consumers.[67] Like a color dye used to trace flows in scientific and medical experiments, these missing horses help us to see the diachronic diffusion of commercial actors and forces across the empire.

The logistics of commerce transformed significantly during this period. With the rise of Smyrna (Izmir) and Aleppo as trading hubs and with the northward shift in Ottoman trading partners, from Venice, Dubrovnik, and France toward the Russians and the Habsburgs, opportunities emerged for newcomers to participate in regional and longer-distance commerce, in line with the *décloisonnement* that characterized the Second Ottoman Empire.[68] Competition from new groups of overland traders and trade fairs in the Balkans contributed to the demise of the Adriatic port city Dubrovnik after 1700.[69] New kinds of merchants catering to regional trade, rather than long-distance trade, emerged on the commercial scene. These included forwarding agents and muleteers in the Balkans and part-time Aleppine merchants who traded local manufactures such as soap, rice, and cloth. These smaller-scale merchants differed from those managing the large caravans that traded long-distance transit goods such as Iranian silk.[70] They connected the local producers of cotton, olive oil, soap, and textiles in the hinterlands with buyers in the cities.[71] Horses transported these humans and their local wares. The equine transportation offered by moonlighting officials in the shadow economy catered to these new logistical demands. Such domestic trade constituted a sizeable portion of commodity exchanges until the late Ottoman Empire.[72]

Officials had long engaged in commercial enterprise, but their engagement probably acquired a greater scale and intensity in this period. Beginning in the sixteenth century, janissaries became increasingly involved in commerce, while greater numbers of artisans and commoners entered the janissary ranks to gain protection, access to credit, and other privileges.[73] From the mid-seventeenth century, many officeholders faced more acute financial needs since they had to independently finance their large households and retinues, especially while they were between appointments and receiving no income.[74] Examples abound of such entrepreneurial officials, such as a cavalry officer who founded a soap factory dynasty and janissaries who engaged in moneylending and invested in agricultural estates (çiftlik), animal farms (kışlak), and beehives that produced honey for Ottoman and foreign markets.[75] Jurists, dragomans, and governors, too, took part in moneylending while serving in their official roles; they forged business partnerships across religious lines and with European consuls and merchants.[76]

Amid this fervent commercial activity, there was, arguably, a change in the moral order in the Ottoman bureaucracy. Specifically, I maintain that there was a shift over time in the boundaries of what officials were entitled to. This may be perceived in two sets of sources: the writings of intellectuals and the fifty-odd imperial decrees that address the problem of missing horses at post stations.

Should officials be involved in commerce? Above, I gave numerous examples of such officials engaged in commerce, but did such activities acquire cultural acceptance in the eighteenth century? Despite the reality of officials engaged in commerce, the normative view that the realms of officialdom and commerce should remain distinct continued to exert a hold on elite statesmen and intellectuals. The seventeenth-century historian Mustafa Naima defended the commercial activities of Grand Vizier Derviş Mehmed Pasha (ca. 1590–1655). In mounting this defense, Naima inadvertently revealed the powerful grip of the conventional view.[77] In the late eighteenth century, the statesman Ahmed Vâsıf Efendi (ca. 1735–1806), too, outwardly reiterated this classical view by upholding strict boundaries between such distinct professional spheres as commerce and soldiering and by identifying the morality of maintaining such boundaries. However, he contradicted himself when he advised wealthy statesmen to establish a merchant marine to protect the empire's interest.[78] In other words, there was a growing dissonance between older norms and current practice.

This dissonance is also reflected in the language of the fifty-odd imperial decrees regarding the missing horses. Reading the implications of later imperial decrees back in time shows that bureaucrats' mindset apparently underwent a slow shift in attitude toward the proper boundaries of official behavior and whether government officials should be allowed to use government resources (post horses) for personal use and commerce.

In the early eighteenth century, moonlighting officials who used horses for commercial activities on the side were implicitly mentioned in variations of a vague formula: these officials were using horses for "their own personal affairs" (*kendü umūr içün / kendü maṣāliḥiyle*). The first incarnation of the phrase "using horses for personal affairs" appears in the earliest decree examined in this chapter, of 1690. It noted disapprovingly that "everyone was taking as many horses as he wished from the post stations" but did not mete out any punishment.[79] In 1696, the phrase pops up again in a decree issued by Mustafa II, which noted that his officials used post station horses for "unimportant and trifling matters and even for their own affairs." It did not elaborate on the nature of these personal affairs, but it did say that a wide range of officials, including military commanders, viziers, governors, governor-generals, and their deputies, behaved in this way, suggesting that such usage of horses was commonplace.[80] The phrase was used in internal reports and decrees until the 1830s, which repeatedly noted that officials with proper courier orders were using post station resources for their own affairs.[81] None of the decrees specified the nature of those affairs.

Sometimes an unexpected variation of this formulaic phrase exposes the shadow economy. A decree dated 1787 identified those using horses "for their own affairs" as "the sorts of people who were travelers, contractors, and merchants."[82] By inference, these merchants were likely using post horses for commercial affairs.

Since the late seventeenth century, "using post station resources for their own affairs" was the formulaic bureaucratic expression used in imperial decrees that avoided specifying what exactly officials (and non-officials) were using post horses for but affirmed that they were, indeed, using them.[83] Significantly, in the late eighteenth century, the phrase continued to appear alongside decrees that explicitly condemned officials for undertaking commercial activities, suggesting that there was a transitional period during which the categorical distinction of "using horses for commercial activities" was still emerging as something to be censured but had not yet been consolidated.

By the 1830s, imperial decrees were using more direct and explicit language to condemn officials using post horses to engage in commerce. Earlier, I cited a decree from July 1820 that explicitly banned couriers from carrying merchandise on the side. Another internal memo from this time stated that although the postal system was supposed to have been restricted to government correspondence, all kinds of non-officials, ranging from vagabonds to merchants, managed to use post horses. Sometimes they did so with illicitly obtained courier orders, sometimes without, and sometimes with the protection of provincial powerholders. All this contributed to the rising costs of operating post stations.[84]

Increasingly explicit condemnations reflected a shift in the normative views held by Ottoman bureaucratic circles, but this shift was slow and very belated, since the behavior of using post horses to engage in commerce had likely been going on for a long time, from at least 1690. For over a century, an entire social, moral, and economic world had been changing around the recurring phrase "using post station resources for their own affairs" that repeatedly appeared in decrees from the 1690s to the 1830s.[85] This recurring phrase was deceptive in its constancy; it masked sharp discontinuities. As the historian William Sewell Jr. noted, "A new discourse or practice does not appear suddenly in its fullness. It typically incorporates terms or technologies or concepts or materials that were part of the old discourse or practice. . . . The new is often formed by an articulation between two preexisting practices/discourses not previously articulated, and the new articulation takes place over time. The old configurations don't disappear in some instantaneous flash. It typically takes time and repeat performances for the new to congeal into something solid enough to displace the old."[86] The recurring phrase "using post station resources for their own affairs" was a "repeat performance" that replayed for almost a century and a half before a new world congealed into something "solid enough to displace the old."

This is a lean evidentiary base, admittedly. If my interpretation of these scraps of evidence is sound, then in this new world that displaced the old, a slow mindset shift on the part of Ottoman bureaucrats led certain accepted official entitlements to no longer be condoned. Profound economic and social transformations affected not only imperial subjects but also Ottoman bureaucrats and officials and thereby caused the reconstitution of the culture and society of the rulemaking administration itself.

Even though bureaucrats condemned and punished moonlighting officials, they did not connect individual reports of such behavior to view the problem systemically. This segmentation of administrative attention would have been exacerbated by changes in administrative personnel and the ebbing of institutional memory over time. Bureaucrats in Qing China faced an analogous problem of a fragmented informational order, which offers an instructive comparand to the Ottoman case. From 1750 to 1860, the Qing bureaucracy accumulated discrete sets of information about different frontiers in the empire and developed "segmented, regionally specific strategies." However, the lack of a "single language" and "unifying matrix" to parse these localized sets of information would later have grave consequences for the empire's security. Crucially, Qing bureaucrats only belatedly realized that the British trading in Guangzhou, referred to as the "Yingjili" in internal documents, were the same people referred to as the "Pileng" in another set of internal documents from the Indian frontier. Because Qing bureaucrats could not integrate distinct pieces of information from different frontiers, they were slow to react to foreign developments and consequently suffered the unexpected and devastating impact of the Opium War (1840–1842).[87]

In comparison, the stakes were lower for the Ottomans and their missing horses, but there were similar features. In the Ottoman Empire, the 1690s reforms of the postal system catalyzed increased flows of information to the imperial bureaucracy in the capital, but these flows were received, processed, understood, and responded to separately and discretely. This segmented attention, described by one historian as Ottoman scribal officials' "craftsman-like" fixation on "documents as ends in themselves," is also evident in the disjointed narratives advanced by different genres of sources: fiscal registers provide granular information about post station expenditures and show a gradual increase in number of horses maintained there, but imperial decrees tell of chronic horse shortages at post stations and stranded couriers. This discrepancy between what fiscal registers claimed and what decrees revealed points to a gap in the Ottoman informational order whereby bureaucrats did not integrate abundant, discrete information into one unifying framework.[88]

Certainly, one might argue that individual Ottoman bureaucrats were aware of the shadow economy even if they did not put their awareness in writing. Perhaps bureaucrats knew the political costs of eliminating official entitlements but were uncertain how effective such a policy would be in recuperating horses at post stations; this sort of loss aversion and status quo bias could have prevented them from confronting the shadow economy. Perhaps bureaucrats simply did not think that this problem was a priority, despite the severe tone of the imperial decrees; indeed, the postal system consumed about 1 percent of the empire's annual budget, meaning that it was simply not a major institution in terms of cost. Without written evidence, however, all this remains speculation. Hewing closely to the written record suggests that Ottoman bureaucrats simply did not respond to discrete violations as if a broader shadow economy existed, even if they knew it did.[89]

In 1817, the imperial postal system became accessible to private individuals (non-officials) for a fee of 54 *akçe* (18 *para*s) per horse per hour.[90] De facto nonfficial use of post horses finally received de jure status. From an exclusive government service, the Ottoman postal system had transformed into a pay-per-use system open to all, both officials and ordinary subjects. In this social order money had become officially fungible with post horses, which now increasingly resembled a commodity. In practice, such market transactions had already been taking place in the shadow economy. But now, they were legal.

Yet the problem of the missing horses endured. In 1832, an imperial decree complained that couriers were being delayed because they could not find horses.[91] In 1835, another imperial memorandum (*lāyiḥa*) repeated that the problem existed and advocated a total overhaul of the postal system.[92] All this transpired during the reign of Sultan Mahmud II, the one who oversaw a reform of the postal system that renamed post stations "rent stations," raised post horse fees, and recalibrated horse quotas across official ranks. In other words, the century-long bureaucratic struggle to regulate the Ottoman postal system and its horse resources endured; no amount of obsessive policing via monograms, dates, ranks, quotas, passes, or uniforms had succeeded in stemming the seepages. And it is this continual repair and maintenance work, the repeated debugging, the constant work of removing blockages and restoring circulation, that is the strongest testament to the thickening of Ottoman governance.

The relay postal system had a "leaky infrastructure," to borrow the anthropologist Nikhil Anand's metaphor. Horses went missing; coins went missing. These disruptions to the flows of official communication provide a precious opportunity to study how business as usual was supposed to look. I have used two kinds of infrastructural breakdown to show that, although Ottoman governance became more sophisticated during the eighteenth century, recruiting ever more layers of local agents to do the work of governance and using ever more refined tools of administration, bureaucrats still faced challenges that they could not solve. The lack of coin showed that a profusion of information via expanded monitoring capacity could, ironically, lead bureaucrats to undertake suboptimal decisions. The continuous lack of horses showed that bureaucrats were constrained by changes in the socioeconomic landscape, such as intensifying commercial activity and shifting conceptions of what officials were and were not entitled to have and to do. Yet there were creative and vigorous responses. Local officials devised alternative papers to substitute for money. Bureaucrats doggedly enforced the rules of horse use and tracked down missing horses. These were important elements of thickening governance and defy conventional conceptions in the historiography of a weak and increasingly impotent empire. And the continual failure to remedy the lack of coins and horses frustrates easy, teleological expectations of this expanded governance as necessarily being superior governance. After all, organizations of different sizes, scales, and complexity are confronted by different kinds of problems.

Many unanswered questions remain: the payment process is still not fully explained, and the extent of the shadow economy, as well as the nature of the goods being transported, remain a mystery. But even unanswered questions are perhaps a feature of historical research. The point is continuing research, the constant grind of answering small questions and raising new ones.

Conclusion

Elinor Ostrom, the first woman to win the Sveriges Riksbank Prize in Economic Sciences in Memory of Alfred Nobel, once explained that her research methodology was inspired by biologists. Like them, she chose the simplest possible organism in which a process occurs in clear, exaggerated form for empirical observation. The organism was not chosen because it was representative but because it allowed certain processes to be studied effectively.[1] The organism chosen in this book is the Ottoman postal system, and the process captured is state formation.

Instead of framing Ottoman state formation in the usual terms of de/centralization, I have proposed a new paradigm of thickening governance. Between 1500 and 1840, the Ottoman imperial bureaucracy recruited more and more common subjects to do the work of governance, thereby expanding its monitoring capacity, deepening the impact and weight of its policies, and extending the reach of its authority. This was a coevolutionary process whereby bureaucrats, officials, and subjects interacted with and adapted to each other.[2]

The Ottoman postal system began as an ad hoc arrangement where official couriers were empowered to seize horses of random passers-by. In the sixteenth century, fixed post stations were established where official couriers could procure fresh, well-rested horses instead of violently seizing their own. In the eighteenth century, post stations began to be more intensively administered. Reams of paper documentation that survive in the archives today reveal that local officials and bureaucrats in the imperial capital assiduously tracked postal traffic, carefully calculated the annual expenditure incurred by each post station, and deliberately restricted access to post horses to specific officials. All this entailed instituting new documentary routines, creating new bookkeeping practices, and delegating new kinds of tasks to local agents. Between the sixteenth and the nineteenth centuries, the Ottoman state's capacity to penetrate local society and logistically implement policies was enlarged. At the same time, what it meant to be an Ottoman subject also transformed.[3]

Coevolution was not a tidy, recursive loop of mutual reinforcement. Thickening governance was not teleological. There were gaps in the interplay of imperial agenda and local interests. Breakdowns, large and small, could and did occur. Imperial policies could be misunderstood. They could be willfully (mis)interpreted. They could also be incoherent. Sometimes local officials devised ways to cope with the incoherence, and at other times they took advantage of the confusion for personal gain. Bureaucrats in the imperial capital could miss important developments on the ground despite their enhanced ability to extract information from local officials; more information did not always translate into greater knowledge. Despite increasingly detailed fiscal information about hundreds of post stations across the empire, for instance, bureaucrats could not solve the chronic problem of missing horses.

But focusing only on outcomes misses the sea change in Ottoman governance processes. Bureaucrats in the imperial capital doggedly pursued the back-and-forth of policy implementation, enforcement, reward, and punishment. This tenacity was matched by local officials and villagers who continuously maintained relay infrastructure but also doggedly protected their interests. They submitted memos, petitions, and complaints, thickening the flow of information to bureaucrats in the capital and forcing them to consider interests besides their own. As the internal friction of policy-making and implementation increased, so did the viscosity of Ottoman governance.

Thickening governance was thus not only about augmenting the capacity, weight, and reach of Ottoman governance but also about the growth, development, and maturation of resistance to this augmented governance. Local officials and villagers who were recruited to do the work of local governance learned to be good at their jobs. They learned from the experience of entering into collective contracts with imperial authorities, of being party to collective liability arrangements through nested suretyships, and of collaborating with neighboring villages to coordinate shared administrative tasks. All these activities cultivated in villagers an enhanced capacity for collective action; in one case, four neighboring villages coordinated with one another to petition imperial authorities, indicating a considerable degree of local-level brokerage activity to align the interests of all involved.

Between 1500 and 1840, these experiences changed generations of villagers, as individuals and as collectives. As imperial subjects, they acquired new expectations of their relationship with imperial authorities, with local officials, and with fellow subjects in neighboring villages. The historian Hülya Canbakal observed a similar phenomenon through her study of collective contracts and vows, noting that "dynamism in public life coexisted with increased social differentiation" during the seventeenth and eighteenth centuries, gesturing toward the emergence of "more diverse agents with more visibly diverse stakes."[4] All this, I argue, made it possible in 1840 to establish a public postal service where Ottoman officials "served" common subjects as "customers."

The Ottoman imperial post officially ended in 1840, when the first public postal service running from Istanbul to Edirne was established.[5] Certainly, government communications continued beyond 1840, but the exclusive space of post stations and the exclusive access to post horses that had characterized the imperial post were no more. According to a newspaper announcement at the time, couriers plying the new public postal route from Istanbul to Edirne would depart the capital on Mondays and arrive in Edirne on Thursdays; subjects who wanted to send messages could expect a certain arrival time.[6] A few weeks after that, the first public post office opened its doors.[7] A year later, in 1841, the first Postal Regulations (nizāmnāme) were issued.[8] In another decade, the first telegraph lines were established in the Ottoman Empire.[9]

At first glance, the emergence of a public postal service in 1840 is considered late in a world historical context. The United States had a national postal system by the 1820s. It not only boasted institutionalized protections for the privacy of personal communications but also provided substantial subsidies for newspaper circulation.[10] The growth in the number of American post offices was phenomenal (from 75 in 1790 to 13,468 in 1840), as was the number of letters delivered (0.3 million in 1790 to 40.9 million in 1840).[11]

The Habsburgs allowed individuals to send personal letters at an even earlier period. During the sixteenth century, anyone who could afford a small fee could send letters, news, money, and small goods like jewelry, and samples of textiles and spices between Antwerp and Naples, Prague and Madrid.[12] Even in the thirteenth and fourteenth centuries, merchants were regularly using courier operations between Tuscany and the Champagne region of France; in a recent publication a historian has used this as evidence for the growth of capitalism.[13] Whether evaluated in terms of subsidized public service (as in the United States), a pay-per-use regional mail and package delivery service (as in the Habsburg Empire), or a niche courier service catering to non-government individuals (as in merchant communications between Tuscany and the Champagne region), the Ottoman historical experience appears belated. Non-government communications in Ottoman lands must have existed, but thus far evidence of its institutionalization or significance of scale before 1840 is scarce.

Instead of asking big comparative questions, this book has deliberately anchored its analysis of the Ottoman postal system in its domestic context. It has intentionally focused on the long-term processes that created the possibility of 1840, rather than on the moment of 1840 and its significance in world history.

There were a few reasons for doing so. First and foremost, the asymmetry of the research landscape means that while a lot more is known and understood about postal systems in Europe and the United States, relatively little is known about the Ottoman case. A history of the Ottoman postal system anchored in its domestic context thus understands it on its own terms.

This is especially pertinent in navigating the historiography of communications, where scholars have debated the concept of a "communications revolution." These scholars have used different definitions of such a revolution; some emphasize speed, while others highlight public policy, spatial structure, or media revolutions that gave rise to the periodical press and a public sphere.[14] Even when using the same definition (say, speed), they arrive at different conclusions: for instance, a U.S. postal historian contended that the communications revolution did not occur until the 1790s, while a European historian remarked that it took place as early as in fourteenth-century Europe. It turns out that the disagreement is definitional; for the latter, the first "time sheets" were found in fourteenth-century Milan, altering the "perception of speed."[15] Using this logic of the first "time sheets," then perhaps the Uyghur time sheets used in the Mongol Empire during the thirteenth and fourteenth centuries could be considered evidence of a communications revolution.[16] But it is not clear that such comparisons are meaningful. Hence, this book has prioritized an account of the Ottoman postal system's development in its own social and political context. Larger comparative questions can be revisited when the historiographical landscape is less asymmetrical.

Such a focus does have a drawback: by sidestepping both comparative and connected histories of communication, this book cannot comprehensively address the influence of European powers on Ottoman communications. The role of Europe in late Ottoman history is a vexed topic. On one hand, it is well known that Ottoman ambassadors had sent in detailed reports of their diplomatic missions in European cities since the seventeenth century. At least some of these included descriptions of traveling overland, procuring horses, and encountering the local postal system and horse-borne messengers. On the other hand, however, there are no explicit mentions in the archival documents examined in this book that show how these observations in Europe may have been translated into policy-making within the empire. There had to be some degree of European influence, just as there was certainly a considerable degree of Ottoman agency. Future research can address this question.[17]

The Sublime Post's main intervention has been to dislodge the de/centralization framework's grip on Ottoman historiography. For far too long, Ottoman historians have fixated on the rise of local powerholders (whether called partners of empire or local notables) and concluded that the empire was losing its coherence and integrity from the seventeenth century on. But it is not the brute fact of intermediaries that affected the monitoring capacity, reach, or weight of imperial authorities in local contexts. Whether in the sixteenth, eighteenth, or nineteenth century, there were always local intermediaries with whom and through whom imperial authorities had to work to implement imperial agendas.[18] Fixating on prominent powerholders obscures recognition of the proliferation of new kinds of local intermediaries along the power hierarchy who continued to implement imperial agendas until the end of empire. These included minor officials such as couriers and postmasters, who may have enjoyed a "petty" notable status in more circumscribed contexts, as well as common villagers. They did not become "partners of empire" like provincial notables; they remained minor officials and common subjects, but what it meant to be a minor official and common subject had transformed.[19] Their work has to be evaluated alongside the growing autonomy of prominent powerholders. All this took place in the context of broader trends in Ottoman society, namely the opening up (*décloisonnement*) and an enclosing (corporatism) of occupational, cultural, and socioeconomic boundaries that characterized the Second Ottoman Empire.

Ultimately, the postal system was a relatively minor institution in the Ottoman Empire. Preliminary calculations show that it consumed only about 1 percent of the empire's annual budget.[20] It was not as costly as war, and it was not as administratively elaborate as law. Yet, for such a lean institution, the postal system still depended to such a great extent on local intermediaries to function. What more, then, for a heftier institution? Surely, any imperial institution that is even slightly heftier than the postal system would have needed to depend on local intermediaries and local agents as well. The existing Ottoman historiography already indicates as much. Discerning readers will have realized that this study has used terms and concepts created by other Ottoman historians (thickening governance, Second Empire, corporatism, *décloisonnement*, etc.) to build a new paradigm of state formation. These existing concepts already point toward a picture more complex than the de/centralization framework and more meaningful than "transformation."[21] As the historiography of the Ottoman Empire continues to develop, these concepts will and should be cast aside for new ones—like the raft that gets discarded upon reaching the opposite shore. Then, a more precise understanding of the profound transformations experienced by ordinary Ottomans, as well as a true accounting of their contributions, may be achieved.

Like all large-scale infrastructure, humans are at the heart of the story of the Ottoman postal system. Whether a relay network, a vaccine maker, or a cheese production facility, infrastructure purports to serve human ends, is subject to human politics, and is vulnerable to human error.[22] As a technology of communication, infrastructure shapes social conceptions of time and space and defines how humans relate to one another.

This book has told a story of human organization that once existed in an empire that has now been divided into over thirty nation-states. It is hoped that the memory of this shared history can contribute to the possibilities for a shared future.

Notes

INTRODUCTION

1. Richard R. John, "Recasting the Information Infrastructure for the Industrial Age," in *A Nation Transformed by Information: How Information Has Shaped the United States from Colonial Times to the Present,* ed. Alfred D. Chandler and James W. Cortada (Oxford: Oxford University Press, 2000), 56; Thomas Allsen, "Imperial Posts, West, East and North: A Review Article: Adam J. Silverstein, Postal Systems in the Pre-modern Islamic World," *Archivum Eurasiae Medii Aevi* 17 (2011): 271; Karen Radner, "Introduction: Long-Distance Communication and the Cohesion of Early Empires," in *State Correspondence in the Ancient World: From New Kingdom Egypt to the Roman Empire,* ed. Karen Radner (Oxford: Oxford University Press, 2014), 2–4.

2. On acoustical and optical signaling systems that could outpace the fastest horse in specific contexts, including the use of whistling arrows and colored smoke, see Allsen, "Imperial Posts," 248–249. On "talking drums" in sub-Saharan Africa, where "an entire language [was mapped] onto a one-dimensional stream of the barest sounds," see James Gleick, *The Information: A History, a Theory, a Flood* (New York: Pantheon Books, 2011), 13–27.

3. Historians and sociologists of technology have explained such variations as an issue of technological style. Thomas P. Hughes, "The Evolution of Large Technical Systems," in *The Social Construction of Technological Systems: New Directions in the Sociology and History of Technology,* ed. Wiebe E. Bijker, Thomas P. Hughes, and Trevor Pinch (Cambridge, MA: MIT Press, 1987), 68–70; Thomas P. Hughes, *Networks of Power: Electrification in Western Society, 1880–1930* (Baltimore, MD: Johns Hopkins University Press, 1983). A question of true world historical scope will have to contend with the impact of the horse in the Americas, southern Africa, and Australasia post-1492 and

indigenous systems of overland communications before that date. Peter Mitchell, *Horse Nations: The Worldwide Impact of the Horse on Indigenous Societies Post-1492* (Oxford: Oxford University Press, 2015).

4. "Sublime Porte" is a synecdoche, analogous to "White House," which refers to the home and office of the U.S. president.

5. The classic formulation of the de/centralization framework may be found in an article that was pathbreaking in its time: Ariel Salzmann, "An Ancien Regime Revisited: 'Privatization' and Political Economy in the Eighteenth-Century Ottoman Empire," *Politics & Society* 21, no. 4 (1993): 393–423. Despite advances in the scholarship, a longtime, uneven temporal focus in Ottoman historical research, with studies clustering on the sixteenth and nineteenth centuries, has entrenched the de/centralization framework that rigidly associates certain centuries with "centralization" and others with "decentralization." Huri Islamoğlu and Çağlar Keyder, "Agenda for Ottoman History," *Review* 1, no. 1 (1977): 32–37.

Many Ottoman historians do not define what they mean by "centralization" or "decentralization," including in recently published monographs. Among those who do, "de/centralization" is used to mean different things. Some use centralization to describe a concentration of authority, and decentralization to refer to the delegation of authority. For instance, whereas previously the authority to appoint deputy judges was delegated to a range of provincial judges, in the nineteenth century the Şeyhülislam's Office was made the sole authority—this process was described as centralization. Conversely, the seventeenth-century delegation of authority to local notables in matters of provincial governance has been described as a "decentralization of authority." [Jun Akiba, "From Kadı to Naib: Reorganization of the Ottoman Sharia Judiciary in the Tanzimat Period," in *Frontiers of Ottoman Studies: State, Province, and the West*, ed. Colin Imber and Keiko Kiyotaki (London: [A-Z]. [A-Z]. Tauris, 2005), 46, 54–55; Stefan Winter, *A History of the 'Alawis: From Medieval Aleppo to the Turkish Republic* (Princeton,: Princeton University Press, 2016), 120; Halil Inalcık, "Centralization and Decentralization in Ottoman Administration," in *Studies in Eighteenth Century Islamic History*, ed. Thomas Naff and Roger Owen (Carbondale: Southern Illinois University Press, 1977), 27–28.] Some use "centralization" to mean standardization, such as the standardization of European mean time across the Ottoman Empire. [Avner Wishnitzer, *Reading Clocks, Alla Turca: Time and Society in the Late Ottoman Empire* (Chicago: University of Chicago Press, 2015), 13–15, 59–61.] Some use centralization to refer to state involvement in normative areas of life where it did not previously exist, such as in crimes against the individual. [Omri Paz, "Documenting Justice: New Recording Practices and the Establishment of an Activist Criminal Court System in the Ottoman Provinces (1840–Late 1860s)," *Islamic Law and Society* 21, no. 1/2 (2014): 85; and see Canbakal's comment about "the role of the state in the normative domain" in Hülya Canbakal, "Vows as Contract in Ottoman Public Life (17th–18th Centuries)," *Islamic Law and Society* 18, no. 1 (2011): 114.] Many other historians use de/centralization in an oxymoronic way, noting simultaneous "centrifugal" and "centripetal" forces between imperial capital and province. [Choon Hwee Koh, "The Ottoman Postmaster: Contractors, Communication and Early Modern State Formation," *Past & Present* 251, no. 1 (2021): 138–141.]

The problem of semantic overload is not unique to the Ottoman field. For instance, see Sheilagh Ogilvie's discussion of state capacity as a "muddled concept." Sheilagh Ogilvie, "State Capacity and Economic Growth: Cautionary Tales from History," *National Institute Economic Review* 262 (2022): 28–50.

Not all historians use the de/centralization framework to organize Ottoman history; many use the paradigm of "transformation." For a critique of "transformation" as a "catch-all term" that highlights an analytical impasse in Ottoman historiography, see Olivier Bouquet, "From Decline to Transformation: Reflections on a New Paradigm in Ottoman History," *Osmanlı Araştırmaları* 60 (2022): 27–60.

6. For war-driven state centralization theories, see Michael Roberts, *Essays in Swedish History* (London: Weidenfeld and Nicolson, 1967), chap. 7; Geoffrey Parker, *The Military Revolution: Military Innovation and the Rise of the West, 1500–1800* (Cambridge: Cambridge University Press, 1988); Charles Tilly, *Coercion, Capital, and European States, AD 990–1992*, rev. ed. (Cambridge, MA: Blackwell, 1992).

   For state formation theories that focus on principal-agent relationships and contracting, see Irving A. A. Thompson, *War and Government in Habsburg Spain, 1560–1620* (London: Athlone Press, 1976); David Parrott, *The Business of War: Military Enterprise and Military Revolution in Early Modern Europe* (Cambridge: Cambridge University Press, 2012); Jeff Fynn-Paul, ed., *War, Entrepreneurs, and the State in Europe and the Mediterranean, 1300–1800* (Leiden: Brill, 2014); Rafael Torres Sánchez, *Military Entrepreneurs and the Spanish Contractor State in the Eighteenth Century* (Oxford: Oxford University Press, 2016). For instances of military contracting outside of Europe, see Yingcong Dai, "The Qing State, Merchants, and the Military Labor Force in the Jinchuan Campaigns," *Late Imperial China* 22, no. 2 (2001): 68–80; Yingcong Dai, "Yingyung Shengxi: Military Entrepreneurship in the High Qing Period, 1700–1800," *Late Imperial China* 26, no. 2 (2005): 1–67; also see Lawrence Zhang, *Power for a Price: The Purchase of Official Appointments in Qing China* (Cambridge, MA: Harvard University Asia Center, 2022), 21.

   Within Ottoman historiography, scholarship on confessionalism is one space where a more sophisticated understanding of how imperial power worked through local intermediaries, especially with regard to enforcement, may be found. Derin Terzioğlu, "How to Conceptualize Ottoman Sunnitization: A Historiographical Discussion," *Turcica* 44 (2013): 321–322; Ayfer Karakaya-Stump, *The Kizilbash-Alevis in Ottoman Anatolia: Sufism, Politics and Community* (Edinburgh: Edinburgh University Press, 2020), 259, 289.

7. Cornell Fleischer, *Bureaucrat and Intellectual in the Ottoman Empire: The Historian Mustafa Âli (1541–1600)* (Princeton, NJ: Princeton University Press, 1986), 214.

8. Molly Greene, *The Edinburgh History of the Greeks, 1453 to 1774: The Ottoman Empire* (Edinburgh: Edinburgh University Press, 2015), 182. I have borrowed the concept of co-evolution from Ang Yuen Yuen, *How China Escaped the Poverty Trap* (Ithaca, NY: Cornell University Press, 2016), 3; Timothy Mitchell, "The Limits of the State: Beyond Statist Approaches and Their Critics," *The American Political Science Review* 85, no. 1 (1991): 77–96.

9. For instance, inheritance laws could differ widely even between districts that were relatively close to each other (in this case, Nablus and Tripoli). Beshara Doumani, *Family*

Life in the Ottoman Empire: A Social History (Cambridge: Cambridge University Press, 2017).

10. It should be noted that we still use paper mail today, in the age of electronic agreements and signatures. Eugene Rogan, "Instant Communication: The Impact of the Telegraph in Ottoman Syria," in *The Syrian Land: Processes of Integration and Fragmentation,* ed. Thomas Philipp and Birgit Schaebler (Stuttgart: F. Steiner, 1998), 119. I thank Eugene Rogan for generously sharing the original archival document used in his article with me.

11. Susan Leigh Star, "The Ethnography of Infrastructure," *American Behavioral Scientist* 43, no. 3 (1999): 380; Hughes, "Evolution of Large Technical Systems"; Paul N. Edwards, "Infrastructure and Modernity: Force, Time, and Social Organization in the History of Sociotechnical Systems," in *Modernity and Technology,* ed. Thomas J. Misa, Philip Brey, and Andrew Feenberg (Cambridge, MA: MIT Press, 2003), 185–225; Paul N. Edwards et al., "Introduction: An Agenda for Infrastructure Studies," *Journal of the Association for Information Systems* 10, no. 5 (2009): 364–374; Keller Easterling, *Extrastatecraft: The Power of Infrastructure Space* (London: Verso, 2014); Brian Larkin, "The Politics and Poetics of Infrastructure," *Annual Review of Anthropology* 42 (2013): 327–343; Timothy Mitchell, *Carbon Democracy: Political Power in the Age of Oil* (Brooklyn, NY: Verso, 2011); Frederik Meiton, *Electrical Palestine: Capital and Technology from Empire to Nation* (Berkeley: University of California Press, 2019); Katayoun Shafiee, *Machineries of Oil: An Infrastructural History of BP in Iran* (Cambridge, MA: MIT Press, 2018).

12. Hughes, *Networks of Power,* 6.

13. Deborah Cowen, *The Deadly Life of Logistics* (Minneapolis: University of Minnesota Press, 2014), 1–21.

14. Hillel Soifer, "State Infrastructural Power: Approaches to Conceptualization and Measurement," *Studies in Comparative International Development* 43, nos. 3–4 (2008): 231–251; Michael Mann, "The Autonomous Power of the State: Its Origins, Mechanisms and Results," in *States in History,* ed. John A. Hall (Oxford: Basil Blackwell, 1986), 109–136, quote modified from p. 113.

15. Baki Tezcan, "Ethnicity, Race, Religion and Social Class: Ottoman Markers of Difference," in *The Ottoman World,* ed. Christine Woodhead (London: Routledge, 2011), 159; Malcolm E. Yapp, "Europe in the Turkish Mirror," *Past & Present* 137, no. 1 (1992): 134–135.

16. Vesna Goldsworthy, *Inventing Ruritania: The Imperialism of the Imagination* (New Haven, CT: Yale University Press, 1998), ix, 4–5; Maria Todorova, *Imagining the Balkans* (Oxford: Oxford University Press, 2009).

17. This term was also applied to the academic study of English literature. For example, Harold Bloom, the *New York Times* best-selling literary critic, once lamented the "Balkanization of literary studies." Harold Bloom, *The Western Canon: The Books and School of the Ages* (New York: Harcourt Brace, 1994), 517–518.

18. Rifaʿat Abou El Haj, "The Social Uses of the Past: Recent Arab Historiography of Ottoman Rule," *International Journal of Middle East Studies* 14, no. 2 (1982): 185–201; Alexander Vezenkov, "Entangled Geographies of the Balkans: The Boundaries of the Region and the Limits of the Discipline," in *Entangled Histories of the Balkans: Concepts, Approaches, and (Self-)Representations,* ed. Roumen Daskalov et al., vol. 4 (Leiden: Brill,

2017), 115–256; Halil Berktay, *The "Other" Feudalism: A Critique of 20th Century Turkish Historiography and Its Particularisation of Ottoman Society* (Birmingham, UK: University of Birmingham, 1990), chap. 2.

19. To give just a few examples: in the Qing, the Revolt of the Three Feudatories lasted from 1673 to 1681; Qing struggles with the Koxinga dynasty in Taiwan ended only in 1683; and in Mughal India, "succession struggles" marked "every transition of power." In addition, the Mughal-Maratha wars took place over the course of the seventeenth century. See Munis D. Faruqui, *The Princes of the Mughal Empire, 1504–1719* (Cambridge: Cambridge University Press, 2012), 237.

20. A. Kevin Reinhart, *Lived Islam: Colloquial Religion in a Cosmopolitan Tradition* (Cambridge: Cambridge University Press, 2020), especially chap. 3.

21. Jülide Akyüz, "Anadolu'nun Orta Kolu Üzerinde Bir Menzil: Amasya Menzili, İşleyişi, Sorunları [A Post Station on the Anatolian Middle Road: Amasya Post Station]," *Askeri Tarih Araştırmaları Dergisi* 8 (2006): 45–53; Zübeyde Güneş Yağcı, "Hac ve Askeri Yol Üzerinde Bir Menzil: Adana Menzili [A Post Station on the Haj and Military Road: Adana Station]," *Çukurova Araştırmaları Dergisi* 1, no. 1 (2015): 58–74; Ali Açıkel, "Osmanlı Ulak-Menzilhane Sistemi Çerçevesinde Tokat Menzilhanesi (1690–1840) [Tokat Post Station in the Framework of the Ottoman Postal System, 1690–1840]," *Ege Üniversitesi Edebiyat Fakültesi Tarih İncelemeleri Dergisi* 19, no. 2 (2004): 1–33; Hüseyin Çınar, "Osmanlı Ulak-Menzilhane Sistemi ve XVIII Yüzyılın İlk Yarısında Antep Menzilleri [The Ottoman Post Station System and the Antep Post Station in the First Half of the Eighteenth Century]," *Osmanlı* 3 (1999): 627–637; Milka Zdraveva, "The Menzil Service in Macedonia, Particularly around Bitolj, in the Period of Turkish Domination," *Études Balkaniques* 31, no. 2 (1995): 82–88; Mehmet Güneş, "XVIII Yüzyılın İkinci Yarısında Osmanlı Menzil Teşkilatı ve Karahisar-ı Sahib Menzilleri [The Karahisar Post Station and the Ottoman Post Station System in the Second Half of the Eighteenth Century]," *Afyon Kocatepe Üniversitesi Sosyal Bilimler Enstitüsü Dergisi* 3, no. 3 (2008): 35–63; Yaşar Baş, "XVIII–XIX Yüzyılın İlk Yarısında Gebze Menzilhanesi [The Gebze Post Station in the Eighteenth and First Half of the Nineteenth Century]," *International Periodical for the Languages, Literature and History of Turkish or Turkic* 8, no. 5 (2013): 101–126; Cemal Çetin, "XVIII. Yüzyılda Çorum Menzilhaneleri," in *Uluslar Arası Osmanlı'dan Cumhuriyete Çorum Sempozyumu (Bildiriler 23–25 Kasım 2007)*, vol. 3 (Çorum: Çorum Belediyesi Kültür Yayınları, 2008), 1573–1593. Exceptions include Yusuf Halaçoğlu, *Osmanlılarda Ulaşım ve Haberleşme (Menziller)* [Ottoman Transportation and Communications] (Ankara: PTT Genel Müdürlüğü, 2002); Cemal Çetin, *Ulak yol durak: Anadolu yollarında padişah postaları (Menzilhaneler)* [Courier Stops: The Padishah's Post along Anatolian Roads] (Istanbul: Hikmetevi Yayınları, 2013); Yücel Özkaya, "XVIII Yüzyılda Menzilhane Sorunu [The Question of Post Stations in the Eighteenth Century]," *Ankara Üniversitesi Dil ve Tarih Coğrafya Fakültesi Dergisi* 28, nos. 3–4 (1970): 339–367.

22. The existing literature is vast. Here is a sample list of works: Rıza Bozkurt, *Osmanlı İmparatorluğunda Kollar, Ulak ve İaşe Menzilleri* [Roads, Couriers, and Provisioning Stations in the Ottoman Empire] (Ankara: Genelkurmay Başkanlığı Harp Tarihi Dairesi, 1966); Jason Curtis Fossella, "The Emperor's Eyes: The Dromos and Byzantine

Communications, Diplomacy and Bureaucracy, 518–1204" (PhD diss., Saint Louis University, n.d.), accessed July 19, 2022; Richard J. A. Talbert, *Rome's World: The Peutinger Map Reconsidered* (Cambridge: Cambridge University Press, 2010); Kurt Franz, "Handlist of Stations of the Ayyubid and Mamluk Communication Systems," in *Egypt and Syria under Mamluk Rule Political, Social and Cultural Aspects*, ed. Amalia Levanoni (Leiden: Brill, 2021), 295–396.

23. For Baki Tezcan, the Second Ottoman Empire lasted from ca. 1580–1826. Leslie P. Peirce, *The Imperial Harem: Women and Sovereignty in the Ottoman Empire* (New York: Oxford University Press, 1993), 101; Baki Tezcan, *The Second Ottoman Empire: Political and Social Transformation in the Early Modern World* (New York: Cambridge University Press, 2010), 1, 238; See also Joseph Fletcher, "Turco-Mongolian Monarchic Tradition in the Ottoman Empire," *Harvard Ukrainian Studies* 3, no. 4 (1979–1980): 236–251.

24. Shirine Hamadeh originally used the term *décloisonnement* to refer to the increasing openness of eighteenth-century Ottoman Istanbul. Shirine Hamadeh, *The City's Pleasures: Istanbul in the Eighteenth Century* (Seattle: University of Washington Press, 2008).

25. Arif Bilgin, "From Artichoke to Corn: New Fruits and Vegetables in the Istanbul Market (Seventeenth to Nineteenth Centuries)," and Suraiya Faroqhi, "Women, Wealth and Textiles in 1730s Bursa," in *Living the Good Life: Consumption in the Qing and Ottoman Empires of the Eighteenth Century*, ed. Suraiya Faroqhi and Elif Akçetin (Leiden: Brill, 2017), 231; Ünver Rüstem, *Ottoman Baroque: The Architectural Refashioning of Eighteenth-Century Istanbul* (Princeton, NJ: Princeton University Press, 2019); Gwendolyn Collaço, "'World-Seizing' Albums: Imported Paintings from ʿAcem and Hindūstān in an Eclectic Ottoman Market," *Ars Orientalis* 51 (2021): 133–187; Amanda Phillips, *Sea Change: Ottoman Textiles between the Mediterranean and the Indian Ocean* (Oakland: University of California Press, 2021), chap. 6; Hamadeh, *The City's Pleasures*, 8.

26. Aspects of these phenomena have been described variously as "Ottomanisation," localization, and "proto-democratisation" of the Ottoman state. Dina Rizk Khoury, "The Ottoman Centre versus Provincial Power-Holders: An Analysis of the Historiography," in *The Cambridge History of Turkey: The Later Ottoman Empire, 1603–1839*, ed. Suraiya Faroqhi, vol. 3 (Cambridge: Cambridge University Press, 2006), 135–156; Tezcan, *The Second Ottoman Empire*, 10; Nelly Hanna, *In Praise of Books: A Cultural History of Cairo's Middle Class, Sixteenth to the Eighteenth Century* (Syracuse, NY: Syracuse University Press, 2003); Dana Sajdi, *The Barber of Damascus: Nouveau Literacy in the Eighteenth-Century Ottoman Levant* (Stanford, CA: Stanford University Press, 2013); Derin Terzioğlu, "Where İlm-i Hal Meets Catechism: Islamic Manuals of Religious Instruction in the Ottoman Empire in the Age of Confessionalization," *Past & Present* 220 (2013): 86; Greene, *The Edinburgh History of the Greeks, 1453 to 1774*, chap. 7; Stefan Winter, *A History of the ʾAlawis: From Medieval Aleppo to the Turkish Republic* (Princeton, NJ: Princeton University Press, 2016), chap. 4; Christine Philliou, "Communities on the Verge: Unraveling the Phanariot Ascendancy in Ottoman Governance," *Comparative Studies in Society and History* 51, no. 1 (2009): 151–181; Bruce McGowan, *Economic Life in Ottoman Europe: Taxation, Trade and the Struggle for Land, 1600–1800* (Cambridge: Cambridge University Press, 1981), 20; F. W. Carter, "The Commerce of the Dubrovnik Republic, 1500–1700," *The Economic History Review* 24, no. 3 (1971): 389–390;

Suraiya Faroqhi, "The Early History of the Balkan Fairs," *Südost Forschungen* 37 (1978): 50; Traian Stoianovich, "The Conquering Balkan Orthodox Merchant," *The Journal of Economic History* 20 (1960): 261–262, 281–282, 287, 299, 301; Bruce Masters, *Origins of Western Economic Dominance in the Middle East: Mercantilism and the Islamic Economy in Aleppo, 1600–1750* (New York: New York University Press, 1988), 174–175; Beshara Doumani, *Rediscovering Palestine: Merchants and Peasants in Jabal Nablus, 1700–1900* (Berkeley: University of California Press, 1995); Suraiya Faroqhi, "Ottoman Craftsmen: Problematic and Sources with Special Emphasis on the Eighteenth Century," in *Crafts and Craftsmen of the Middle East*, ed. Suraiya Faroqhi and Randi Deguilhem (London: I. B. Tauris, 2005), 90; Mehmet Genç, "Ottoman Industry in the Eighteenth Century: General Framework, Characteristics, and Main Trends," in *Manufacturing in the Ottoman Empire and Turkey, 1500–1950*, ed. Donald Quataert (Albany: State University of New York Press, 1994), 64, 67.

27. James Grehan, "Smoking and 'Early Modern' Sociability: The Great Tobacco Debate in the Ottoman Middle East (Seventeenth to Eighteenth Centuries)," *American Historical Review* 111, no. 5 (2006): 1352–1377.

28. Hatice Aynur, "Ottoman Literature," in *The Cambridge History of Turkey*, ed. Suraiya Faroqhi, vol. 3 (Cambridge: Cambridge University Press, 2006), 497–498.

29. Hamadeh, *The City's Pleasures*, 17, 45, 76–79.

30. Heghnar Zeitlian Watenpaugh, *The Image of an Ottoman City: Imperial Architecture and Urban Experience in Aleppo in the 16th and 17th Centuries* (Leiden: Brill, 2004), chap. 4.

31. İsmail Erünsal, *Osmanlılarda Kütüphaneler ve Kütüphanecilik: Tarihi Gelişimi ve Organizasyonu* (Istanbul: Timaş Yayınları, 2015), 149; for more changes, see 160, 437.

32. Johann Büssow and Astrid Meier, "Ottoman Corporatism, Eighteenth to Twentieth Centuries: Beyond the State-Society Paradigm in Middle Eastern History," in *Ways of Knowing Muslim Cultures and Societies: Studies in Honour of Gudrun Krämer*, ed. Bettina Gräf, Birgit Krawietz, and Schirin Amir-Moazami (Leiden: Brill, 2019), 81–110; Işık Tamdoğan, "The Ottoman Political Community in the Process of Justice Making in the 18th-Century Adana," in *Forms and Institutions of Justice: Legal Actions in Ottoman Contexts*, ed. Yavuz Aykan and Işık Tamdoğan (Istanbul: Institut français d'études anatoliennes, 2018), 9–18; Also known as "communalization," see Halil Inalcık, "Centralization and Decentralization in Ottoman Administration," in *Studies in Eighteenth Century Islamic History*, ed. Thomas Naff and Roger Owen (Carbondale: Southern Illinois University Press, 1977), 37–38; Hülya Canbakal, "Vows as Contract in Ottoman Public Life (17th–18th Centuries)," *Islamic Law and Society* 18, no. 1 (2011): 108–112; Antonis Anastasopoulos, "Imperial Institutions and Local Communities: Ottoman Karaferye, 1758–1774" (PhD diss., Cambridge University, 1999). On a related line of argument, see Albert Hourani, "Ottoman Reform and the Politics of Notables," in *The Modern Middle East: A Reader*, ed. Albert Hourani, Philip S. Khoury, and Mary C. Wilson (London: I. B. Tauris, 1993), 83–109; James Gelvin, "The 'Politics of Notables' Forty Years After," *MESA Bulletin* 40, no. 1 (2006): 19–29.

33. Büssow and Meier, "Ottoman Corporatism, Eighteenth to Twentieth Centuries," 89; Inalcık, "Centralization and Decentralization in Ottoman Administration," 38; Stanford J. Shaw, *The Financial and Administrative Organization and Development of Ottoman Egypt, 1517–1798* (Princeton, NJ: Princeton University Press, 1962), 119–122.

34. Ali Yaycıoğlu, *Partners of the Empire: The Crisis of the Ottoman Order in the Age of Revolutions* (Stanford, CA: Stanford University Press, 2016), chap. 2.

35. Contemporary accounts describe some of these "notables" less charitably, for instance Tepedelenli Ali Pasha (of Ioannina) was one of several "independent freebooters" who nevertheless preserved the "form of subjection" to the sultan by furnishing military men and paying tribute. John Cam Hobhouse Broughton, *Travels in Albania and Other Provinces of Turkey in 1809 & 1810*, new ed. (London: J. Murray, 1855), 99–106, https://catalog.hathitrust.org/Record/101677626.

36. Yaycıoğlu, *Partners of the Empire*, 67–68, 112–113; Dina Rizk Khoury, *State and Provincial Society in the Ottoman Empire: Mosul, 1540–1834* (Cambridge: Cambridge University Press, 1997); Jane Hathaway, *The Politics of Households in Ottoman Egypt: The Rise of the Qazdaglis* (Cambridge: Cambridge University Press, 1997); Canay Şahin, "The Rise and Fall of an Ayan Family in Eighteenth Century Anatolia: The Caniklizades (1737–1808)" (PhD diss., Bilkent University, 2004); Canay Şahin, "The Economic Power of Anatolian Ayans of the Late Eighteenth Century: The Case of the Caniklizades," *International Journal of Turkish Studies* 11, nos. 1–2 (2005): 29–49; Dennis N. Skiotis, "From Bandit to Pasha: First Steps in the Rise to Power of Ali of Tepelen, 1750–1784," *International Journal of Middle East Studies* 2 (1971): 219–244; Andrew G. Gould, "Lords or Bandits? The Derebeys of Cilicia," *International Journal of Middle East Studies* 7 (1976): 485–506.

37. Engin Akarlı, "Gedik: A Bundle of Rights and Obligations for Istanbul Artisans and Traders, 1750–1840," in *Law, Anthropology and the Constitution of the Social, Making Persons and Things*, ed. Alain Pottage and Martha Mundy (Cambridge: Cambridge University Press, 2004), 166–200; Seven Ağır and Onur Yıldırım, "Gedik: What's in a Name?," in *Bread from the Lion's Mouth: Artisans Struggling for a Livelihood in Ottoman Cities*, ed. Suraiya Faroqhi (New York: Berghahn Books, 2015), 217.

38. Tamdoğan, "The Ottoman Political Community in the Process of Justice Making in the 18th-Century Adana"; Betül Başaran, *Selim III, Social Control and Policing in Istanbul at the End of the Eighteenth Century: Between Crisis and Order* (Leiden: Brill, 2014); Madoka Morita, "Between Hostility and Hospitality: Neighbourhoods and Dynamics of Urban Migration in Istanbul (1730–54)," *Turkish Historical Review* 7 (2016): 58–85.

39. Canbakal, "Vows as Contract," 109, 111–112.

40. Stephen Graham and Nigel Thrift, "Out of Order: Understanding Repair and Maintenance," *Theory, Culture & Society* 24, no. 3 (2007): 1–25; Andrew L. Russell and Lee Vinsel, "After Innovation, Turn to Maintenance," *Technology and Culture* 59, no. 1 (2018): 1–25.

41. Virginia H. Aksan, An Ottoman Statesman in War and Peace: Ahmed Resmi Efendi: 1700–1783 (Leiden: Brill, 1995); Benjamin C. Fortna, *Imperial Classroom: Islam, the State, and Education in the Late Ottoman Empire* (Oxford; New York: Oxford University Press, 2002); Veysel Şimşek, "The First 'Little Mehmeds': Conscripts for the Ottoman Army, 1826–53," *Osmanlı Araştırmaları* 44, no. 44 (2014): 265–311; Veysel Şimşek, "Ottoman Military Recruitment and the Recruit: 1826–1853" (Master's thesis, Bilkent Universitesi, 2005); Yirmisekiz Çelebi Auteur du texte Mehmed Efendi, *Relation de l'ambassade de Mehemet-Effendi, a la cour de France, en M. DCC. XXI. écrite par lui-meme, et traduite du turc.* (Constantinople; Paris: chez Ganeau, libraire, rue S. Severin;

à S. Louis, & aux armes de Dombes, 1757), 20; Seyyid Abdürrahim Muhibb Efendi and Seyyid Ali Efendi Moralı, *Deux ottomans à Paris sous le Directoire et l'Empire: relations d'ambassade*, trans. Stefanos Yerasimos (Arles: Actes Sud, 1998), 190–94; Stanford J. Shaw, *Between Old and New: The Ottoman Empire under Sultan Selim III, 1789–1807* (Cambridge, Mass: Harvard University Press, 1971), 185–86; Sociologists have long observed that organizations are influenced by their environment and tend to become isomorphic with them. John W. Meyer and Brian Rowan, "Institutionalized Organizations: Formal Structure as Myth and Ceremony," *The American Journal of Sociology* 83, no. 2 (1977): 340–63.

42. Certainly, the pandemic and its cascading consequences (such as global supply chain disruptions) have done much to render this infrastructural background visible. Nathan Ensmenger, "The Environmental History of Computing," *Technology and Culture* 59, no. 4 (2018): S7–S33.

43. "If the Cloud were a country it would be the sixth largest consumer of electricity on the planet. A typical data center requires hundreds of thousands of gallons of fresh water a day to operate; a single semiconductor fabrication facility requires millions." Ensmenger, "The Environmental History of Computing," S10.

44. These analogies were inspired by Marshall McLuhan's:

> The telephone: speech without walls.
> The phonograph: music hall without walls.
> The photograph: museum without walls.
> The electric light: space without walls.
> The movie, radio, and TV: classroom without walls.
> Man the food-gatherer reappears incongruously as information-gatherer.

"In this role, electronic man is no less a nomad than his Paleolithic ancestors." Marshall McLuhan, *Understanding Media: The Extensions of Man* (Cambridge, MA: MIT Press, 1994), 283.

45. For instance, a growing movement within the design studies and design history community seeks to "Decolonize Design" by looking to the "histories and texts of different cultures." Tristan Schultz et al., "What Is at Stake with Decolonizing Design? A Roundtable," *The Journal of the Design Studies Forum* 10, no. 1 (2018): 81–101; Luiza Prado de O. Martins and Pedro J. S. Vieira de Oliveira, "Designer/Shapeshifter: A Decolonizing Redirection for Speculative and Critical Design," in *Tricky Design: The Ethics of Things*, ed. Tom Fisher and Lorraine Gamman (London: Bloomsbury Visual Arts, 2019), 103–114; Daniela Rosner, *Critical Fabulations: Reworking the Methods and Margins of Design* (Cambridge, MA: MIT Press, 2018), 1–21. I thank Melika Alipour Leili for introducing me to this literature.

CHAPTER 1. THE OTTOMAN POSTAL SYSTEM

1. Hughes, "Evolution of Large Technical Systems," 69–70; Hughes, *Networks of Power*, chaps. 7, 9.

2. A notable exception is Karl Wittfogel's hydraulic thesis whereby labor-intensive irrigation systems necessarily generated absolutist political systems. Karl A. Wittfogel, "The

Hydraulic Civilizations," in *Man's Role in Changing the Face of the Earth*, ed. William Leroy Thomas (Chicago: University of Chicago Press, 1956), 152–164.

3. Petra Maurer, "The Tibetan Governmental Transport and Postal System: Horse Services and Other Taxes from the 13th to the 20th Centuries," *Buddhism, Law & Society* 5 (2019): 4; Magnus Linnarsson, "The Development of the Swedish Post Office c. 1600–1718," in *Connecting the Baltic Area: The Swedish Postal System in the Seventeenth Century, edited by Heiko Droste* (Huddinge, Sweden: Södertörns högskola, 2011), 25–47; John Howland Rowe, "Inca Culture at the Time of the Spanish Conquest," in *Handbook of South American Indians*, ed. Julian Haynes Steward, vol. 2: *The Andean Civilizations* (Washington, DC: U.S. Government Publishing Office, 1946), 231–232 I thank Jorge E. Bayona for this reference. Rachel Midura, "Princes of the Post: Power, Publicity, and Europe's Communications Revolution (1500–1700)" (unpublished manuscript, n.d.), iii, accessed January 27, 2023; I thank Rachel Midura for sharing an early draft of her book manuscript chapter with me. Also see Xiaoxuan Zhao, *Songdai Yizhan Zhidu [The Relay System during the Song Dynasty]* (Taipei: Lian jing chu ban shi ye gong si, 1983), 58–65; Chelsea Wang, "More Haste, Less Speed: Sources of Friction in the Ming Postal System," *Late Imperial China* 40, no. 2 (2019): 94; C. A. Bayly, *Empire and Information: Intelligence Gathering and Social Communication in India, 1780–1870* (Cambridge: Cambridge University Press, 1996), 58–69.

4. Márton Vér, "The Postal System of the Mongol Empire in Northeastern Turkestan" (PhD diss., University of Szeged, 2016), 46–47; Adam J. Silverstein, *Postal Systems in the Premodern Islamic World* (Cambridge: Cambridge University Press, 2007), 142–143.

5. These confiscations were also known as *suhra* (requisitions) and refer to the use of corvée labour. James Redhouse defines it as "man or beast, reduced to subjection or obedience." See Alan Mikhail, *Nature and Empire in Ottoman Egypt: An Environmental History* (Cambridge: Cambridge University Press, 2011), 183; Sir James Redhouse, *A Turkish and English Lexicon Shewing in English the Significations of the Turkish Terms* (Beirut: Librairie du Liban, 1987), 1044.

6. Uriel Heyd noted that courier orders varied in length and detail, and would often be recorded at the end of *Mühimme Defteri* (Registers of Important Matters), at least in his period of study (sixteenth–early seventeenth centuries). Uriel Heyd, *Ottoman Documents on Palestine 1552–1615: A Study of the Firman According to the Mühimme Defteri* (Oxford: Clarendon Press, 1960), 22. For a study on the transformation of the courier order as a documentary form, see Colin Heywood, "The Evolution of the Courier Order (Ulak Hükmi) in Ottoman Chancery Practice (Fifteenth to Eighteenth Centuries)," in *Osmanische Welten: Quellen Und Fallstudien. Festschrift Für Michael Ursinus*, ed. Johannes Zimmermann, Cristoph Herzog, and Raoul Motika (Bamberg, Germany: University of Bamberg Press, 2016), 269–312.

7. Heywood, "The Evolution of the Courier Order (Ulak Hükmi)," 274. For a transcription and German translation of a courier order dated 1497 (issued during Bayezid II's reign), see Friedrich Kraelitz-Greifenhorst, *Osmanische Urkunden in Türkischer Sprache aus der Zweiten Hälfte des 15. Jahrhunderts: Ein Beitrag zur Osmanischen Diplomatik* (Vienna: Alfred Hölder, 1921), 106–108.

8. This may be inferred from Mustafa Ali's writings that indicate an expectation for couriers to hand their horses over to these magistrates. Mustafa Ali, *Mustafa Ali's Counsel for Sultans of 1581: Edition, Translation, Notes I*, trans. Andreas Tietze (Vienna: Verlag der österreichischen Akademie der Wissenschaften, 1979), 33.

9. Mustafa Ali, *Mustafa Ali's Counsel for Sultans of 1581: Edition, Translation, Notes I*, 34.

10. Horses valued at more than 100 *asper*s were not to be confiscated. Mustafa Ali, *Mustafa Ali's Counsel for Sultans of 1581: Edition, Translation, Notes I*, 32; Mustafa Ali, *Mustafa Ali's Counsel for Sultans of 1581: Edition, Translation, Notes II*, trans. Andreas Tietze (Vienna: Verlag der österreichischen Akademie der Wissenschaften, 1982), 151.

11. Mustafa Ali, *Mustafa Ali's Counsel for Sultans of 1581: Edition, Translation, Notes I*, 33.

12. Robert Anhegger and Halil Inalcık, *Ḳānūnnāme-i Sulṭānī Ber Mūceb-i 'örf-i 'Osmānī: II. Mehmed ve II. Bayezid Devirlerine Ait Yasaḳnāme ve Ḳānūnnāmeler* (Ankara: Türk Tarih Kurumu Basımevi, 1956), 65–67.

13. V. L. Ménage and Colin Imber, *Ottoman Historical Documents: The Institutions of an Empire* (Edinburgh: Edinburgh University Press, 2021), 142, 150–151.

14. Lutfi Paşa b Abdülmuin Abdülhay Lutfi Paşa, *Âsafnâme*, ed. Ahmet Uğur (Ankara: Kültür ve Turizm Bakanlığı, 1982), 11–12.

15. Mustafa Ali, *Mustafa Ali's Counsel for Sultans of 1581: Edition, Translation, Notes I*, 33.

16. Some historians suggest he was keen to denounce the new imperial order that had passed him over for high office. Rifa'at Ali Abou-El-Haj, *Formation of the Modern State: The Ottoman Empire, Sixteenth to Eighteenth Centuries* (Albany: State University of New York Press, 1991), 25–28.

17. As cited in Silverstein, *Postal Systems in the Pre-modern Islamic World*, 109–110. Qutb al Din al-Nahrawali, *Kitab al-i'lam bi-a'lam bayt allah al-haram* (Leipzig, 1857), 299–300.

18. J. H. Mordtmann, "Die Jüdischen Kira Im Serai Der Sultane," *Mitteilungen des Seminars für Orientalische Sprachen: Westasiatische Studien* 32 (1929): 24.

19. Rıfat Günalan, Mehmet Canatar, and Mehmet Akman, *İstanbul Kadı Sicilleri Üsküdar Mahkemesi 84 Numaralı Sicil (H. 999–1000 / M. 1590–1591)* (Istanbul: İSAM Yayınları, 2010), 662, 664, 672.

20. For an example of a British traveler's participation in horse confiscation, see William Heude, *A Voyage up the Persian Gulf: And a Journey Overland from India to England, in 1817* (London: Strahn and Spottiswoode, 1819), 248. Other observations of tatar couriers obtaining horses and other resources by force may be found in Thomas Howel, *A Journal of the Passage from India: By a Route Partly Unfrequented, through Armenia and Natolia, or Asia Minor; To Which Are Added, Observations and Instructions, for the Use of Those Who Intend to Travel, Either to or from India, by That Route* (London: Printed for W. Clarke, 1791), 102; Sir John Macdonald Kinneir, *Journey through Asia Minor, Armenia, and Koordistan in the Years 1813 and 1814: With Remarks on the Marches of Alexander and Retreat of the Ten Thousand* (London: John Murray, 1818), 32, 36, 108–109; Broughton, *Travels in Albania and Other Provinces of Turkey in 1809 & 1810*, 67–68.

21. Abou-El-Haj, *Formation of the Modern State*, 9.

22. Ruy González de Clavijo, *Embassy to Tamerlane, 1403–1406*, trans. Guy Le Strange (London: Routledge Curzon, 2005), 95; Ruy González de Clavijo, *Historia del Gran Tamorlan*

e Itinerario y Enarracion del Viage, y Relacion de La Embajada Que Ruy Gonzalez de Clavijo Le Hizo por Mandado del Muy Poderoso Señor Rey Don Henrique El Tercero de Castilla, ed. Gonzalo Argote de Molina (Madrid: Don Antonio de Sancha, 1782), 125; Allsen, "Imperial Posts," 252–253; Joseph Needham, *Science and Civilization in China,* vol. 4: *Physics and Physical Technology, Pt. 3, Civil Engineering and Nautics* (Cambridge: Cambridge University Press, 1971), 17–18; John Randolph, "Communication and Obligation: The Postal System of the Russian Empire, 1700–1850," in *Information and Empire: Mechanisms of Communication in Russia, 1600–1854,* ed. Simon Franklin and Katherine Bowers (Cambridge, UK: Open Book Publishers, 2017), 155–183; Mahesh C. Regmi, *Imperial Gorkha: An Account of Gorkhali Rule in Kumaun (1791–1815)* (Delhi: Adroit Publishers, 1999), 26–37. I thank Shubhanga Pandey for this last reference.

23. Francesca Trivellato, "The Moral Economies of Early Modern Europe," *Humanity: An International Journal of Human Rights, Humanitarianism, and Development* 11, no. 2 (2020): 196.

24. Patricia Crone, *Pre-industrial Societies* (Oxford: Basil Blackwell, 1994), 27–33; Gül Şen, "Between Two Spaces: Enslavement and Labor in the Early Modern Ottoman Navy," in *Comparative and Global Framing of Enslavement,* ed. Jeannine Bischoff and Stephan Conermann, vol. 9 (Berlin: De Gruyter, 2023), 134–138; Mio Kishimoto, "Property Rights and Factor Markets," in *The Cambridge Economic History of China,* Volume I, *To 1800,* ed. Debin Ma and Richard Von Glahn (Cambridge: Cambridge University Press, 2022), 453–54.

25. Hendrik Spruyt, *The World Imagined: Collective Beliefs and Political Order in the Sino-centric, Islamic and Southeast Asian International Societies* (Cambridge: Cambridge University Press, 2020).

26. Halil Inalcık and Donald Quataert, eds., *An Economic and Social History of the Ottoman Empire, 1300–1914* (Cambridge: Cambridge University Press, 1994), 16–17; Abdurrahman Atçıl, *Scholars and Sultans in the Early Modern Ottoman Empire* (Cambridge: Cambridge University Press, 2017), 218.

27. Consider, too, Abou-El-Haj, *Formation of the Modern State,* 25–28; Zhang, *Power for a Price: The Purchase of Official Appointments in Qing China,* 130, 253–257.

28. Linda T. Darling, *A History of Social Justice and Political Power in the Middle East: The Circle of Justice from Mesopotamia to Globalization* (London: Routledge, 2013).

29. Nenad Moačanin, *Town and Country on the Middle Danube, 1526–1690,* Ottoman Empire and Its Heritage, vol. 35 (Leiden: Brill, 2006), 47–48.

30. David M. Robinson, *Korea and the Fall of the Mongol Empire: Alliance, Upheaval, and the Rise of a New East Asian Order* (Cambridge: Cambridge University Press, 2022), chap. 6.

31. Sixiang Wang, *Boundless Winds of Empire: Rhetoric and Ritual in Early Chosŏn Diplomacy with Ming China* (New York: Columbia University Press, 2023), 53.

32. Allsen, "Imperial Posts," 253–256; Ömer Bıyık, "124 numaralı Mühimme Defteri (H. 1128–1130)" (Master's thesis, Ege University, 2001), 203 (43/147), 305 (85/301); Kadir Güney, "190 Numaralı Mühimme Defteri'nin Özetli Transkripsyonu ve Değerlendirmesi (H. 1203–1204, M. 1789–1790. Sayfa 1–97)" (Master's thesis, Gaziantep University, 2012), 51–52 (12/23), 279–280 (86/187).

33. Personal correspondence with Mariusz Kaczka, November 2018, on Ottoman couriers traveling in the Polo-Lithuanian Empire. For an example of the delivery of an imperial letter from the Ottoman Empire to Moscow see, Yusuf Sarınay and Osman Yıldırım, *83*

numaralı Mühimme Defteri, 1036–1037 / 1626–1628: Özet, transkripsiyon, indeks ve tıpkıbasım (Ankara: T. C. Başbakanlık Devlet Arşivleri Genel Müdürlüğü, 2001), 29 (n.42), 63–64 (n.92).

34. John Bell, *Travels from St. Petersburg in Russia to Diverse Parts of Asia*, vol. 2 (Dublin: R. Bell, 1764), 428.

35. Abū Ṭālib Khān, *Travels of Mirza Abu Taleb Khan in Asia, Africa, and Europe, during the Years 1799, 1800, 1801, 1802, and 1803*, ed. Daniel O'Quinn, trans. Charles Stewart (Peterborough, Ontario: Broadview Press, 2009), 294.

36. Kinneir, *Journey through Asia Minor*, 31.

37. Kinneir, *Journey through Asia Minor*, 87.

38. Broughton, *Travels in Albania and Other Provinces of Turkey in 1809 & 1810*, 106–107.

39. On Barak, *On Time: Technology and Temporality in Modern Egypt* (Berkeley: University of California Press, 2013), 50; Abdelatif Mohammed al-Sabbagh, "Tanẓīm al-barīd fi al-shām ibbān al-ḥukm al-miṣri, 1831–1840," *Al-Majallah al-Tārīkhīyya al-Miṣriyya* 40 (1997–1999): 185–216. It is not true, as al-Sabbagh states, that Syria (al-Shām) did not have a postal system before the Egyptian occupation. Since al-Sabbagh's study is based on archival documents from the Egyptian National Archives (Dār al-Wathāʾiq), I suspect his findings reflect, rather, the perspective of Mehmed Ali Pasha's regime during a period of time when Mehmed was pushing for autonomy from Istanbul. For more information, see also *All about Postal Matters in Egypt* (*Egypt Maṣlaḥat al-Barīd*) (Florence: Landi Press, 1898).

40. Lauren A. Benton, *A Search for Sovereignty: Law and Geography in European Empires, 1400–1900* (New York: Cambridge University Press, 2010), 2.

41. Gottfried Hagen, "Kātip Çelebi's Maps and the Visualization of Space in Ottoman Culture," *Osmanlı Araştırmaları* 40 (2012): 288–292.

42. Halil Inalcık, "The Yürüks: Their Origins, Expansion and Economic Role," in *Oriental Carpet & Textile Studies II: Carpets of the Mediterranean Countries 1400–1600*, ed. Robert Pinner and Walter B. Denny (London: HALI Magazine, 1986), 47.

43. Anthony Greenwood, *Istanbul's Meat Provisioning: A Study of the Celep-Keşan System* (Chicago: Department of Near Eastern Languages and Civilizations, University of Chicago, 1988), 94–95, 97, 99, 124.

44. Compare with Xin Wen, *The King's Road: Diplomacy and the Remaking of the Silk Road* (Princeton, NJ: Princeton University Press, 2023), 102–103.

45. Gülrü Necipoğlu, *The Age of Sinan: Architectural Culture in the Ottoman Empire, 1539–1588* (London: Reaktion, 2005), 71–73; Zeitlian Watenpaugh, *Image of an Ottoman City*, 113; Halil Inalcık, *The Ottoman Empire: The Classical Age, 1300–1600* (New York: Praeger, 1973), 146–150.

46. Türkiye Cumhuriyeti Cumhurbaşkanlığı Devlet Arşivleri Başkanlığı, Osmanlı Arşivi [Presidential State Archives of the Republic of Turkey, Ottoman Archives], Istanbul (hereafter BOA), IE DH 34 2964.

47. Molly Greene, "History in High Places: Tatarna Monastery and the Pindus Mountains," *Journal of the Economic and Social History of the Orient* 64, nos. 1–2 (2021): 10–17.

48. This was the case of Karapınar, which lay between Ereğli and Konya. National Library of St. Cyril and St. Methodius, Sofia, Oriental Department, Bulgaria, F13167.

49. BOA, C.NF 30/1478.

50. This was the case for Üsküdar post station in 1759. Istanbul Şer'iyye Sicilleri, Evkâf-ı Hümāyūn Defter 162 Varak 80.

51. Faisal H. Husain, "Changes in the Euphrates River: Ecology and Politics in a Rural Ottoman Periphery, 1687–1702," *Journal of Interdisciplinary History* 47, no. 1 (2016): 1–25.

52. The pull-out map in Bozkurt features stations recorded in thirteen different registers that straddle at least eighty years. However, not all of them would have existed at the same time or for the entirety of that period. Bozkurt, *Osmanlı İmparatorluğunda Kollar, Ulak ve İaşe Menzilleri* [*Roads, Couriers, and Provisioning Stations in the Ottoman Empire*].

53. Robin Wimmel, "Architektur osmanischer Karawanseraien: Stationen des Fernverkehrs im Osmanischen Reich" (PhD diss., Technische Universität Berlin, 2016), https://depositonce.tu-berlin.de/handle/11303/5872; Robin Wimmel, "Edirne as a Stopover Destination. The Ekmekçioğlu Caravanserai and the Ottoman Road Network," in *The Heritage of Edirne in Ottoman and Turkish Times: Continuities, Disruptions and Reconnections,* ed. Birgit Krawietz and Florian Riedler, Studies in the History and Culture of the Middle East, vol. 34 (Berlin: De Gruyter, 2020), 152–204.

54. This same trip would take twenty-five days for an average horse-borne traveler and six weeks for the Ottoman imperial army. Peter Mundy, *The Travels of Peter Mundy in Europe and Asia, 1608–1667,* ed. Richard Carnac Temple and Lavinia Mary Anstey, vol. 1 (Cambridge, UK: Hakluyt Society, 1907), xxix–xxx; Caroline Finkel, *The Administration of Warfare: The Ottoman Military Campaigns in Hungary, 1593–1606* (Vienna: VWGÖ, 1988), 66; Bozkurt, *Osmanlı İmparatorluğunda Kollar, Ulak ve İaşe Menzilleri.*

55. Radner, "Introduction: Long-Distance Communication and the Cohesion of Early Empires," 7.

56. David French, "Pre- and Early-Roman Roads of Asia Minor: The Persian Royal Road," *Iran* 36 (1998): 15; Colin Heywood, "The Via Egnatia in the Ottoman Period: The Menzilhanes of the Sol Kol in the Late 17th / Early 18th Century," in *The Via Egnatia under Ottoman Rule, 1380–1699,* ed. Elizabeth Zachariadou (Rethymno: Crete University Press, 1996), 129–144; Fulya Ozkan, "Gravediggers of the Modern State: Highway Robbers on the Trabzon-Bayezid Road, 1850s–1910s," *Journal of Persianate Studies* 7 (2014): 222–223; Florian Riedler, "The Istanbul-Belgrade Route in the Ottoman Empire: Continuity and Discontinuity of an Imperial Mobility Space," in *The Balkan Route: Historical Transformations from Via Militaris to Autoput,* ed. Florian Riedler and Nenad Stefanov (Berlin: De Gruyter, 2021), 103–120.

57. r/DesirePath, accessed September 16 2023; https://www.reddit.com/r/DesirePath/ ("Dedicated to the paths that humans prefer, rather than the paths that humans create"). I thank Nicholas Ignelis for sharing this with me.

58. Allsen, "Imperial Posts," 243–244; Richard Bulliet, *The Camel and the Wheel* (New York: Columbia University Press, 1990), 19. See also this firsthand account of road construction for wagons and carts, Robert P. Blake and Richard N. Frye, "History of the Nation of the Archers (The Mongols) by Grigor of Akanc' Hitherto Ascribed to Matak'ia the Monk: The Armenian Text Edited with an English Translation and Notes," *Harvard Journal of Asiatic Studies* 12, no. 3/4 (1949): 327.

59. I found courier passes spanning the period from the 1670s to 1839, but there are too many other examples to list. Interested researchers should search for variations of "Istanbul'dan Mısır'a gidip gelecek iki nefere menzil hükmü verilmesi" in the Ottoman archives digital catalogue. Some examples: BOA, AE SMMD.IV 27/3098; BOA, C DH 13/601.

60. For a list of the stops from Egypt to Damascus, see BOA, TS.MA.d. 10477 (AH 1197 / 1782–1783 CE).

61. BOA, C NF 48/2385; BOA C ZB 4/154; Stephane Yerasimos, *Les Voyageurs Dans l'empire Ottoman (XIVe—XVIe Siècles): Bibliographie, Itinéraires et Inventaire Des Lieux Habités* (Ankara: Imprimerie de la société turque d'histoire, 1991), 67; Bıyık, "124 numaralı Mühimme Defteri (H. 1128–1130)," 341–342.

62. Khaled Fahmy, *All the Pasha's Men: Mehmed Ali, His Army, and the Making of Modern Egypt* (Cairo: American University in Cairo Press, 2002), 72.

63. Abdelatif Mohammed al-Sabbagh "Tanẓīm al-barīd fī al-shām ibbān al-ḥukm al-miṣri, 1831–1840," *Al-Majallah al-Tārīkhiyya al-Miṣriyya* 40 (1997–1999): 185.

64. National Library of St. Cyril and St. Methodius, Sofia, Oriental Department, Vidin Şer'iye Sicilleri S38, p. 16:—"Vech-i meşrūḥ üzere her kangıñuzuñ zīr-i ḥukūmetine dāhil olur ise bir sā'at eylendirmeyüb müretteb ve mukemmel menzil kayığı tedārik" (AH 1116 / 1702 CE).

65. Claude-Charles de Peyssonnel, *Traité sur le commerce de la Mer Noire,* vol. 2 (Paris: Cuchet, 1787), 299–300.

66. In Ottoman Turkish, "dörder çifte iki fener ḳayığı," "beş çifte piyāde ḳayığı," and "sefine," respectively; BOA, AE.SMST.III 259–20759; BOA, AE.SMST.III 259–20758; BOA, C.DH. 235/11708; BOA, C.NF. 39/1941.

67. Kinneir, *Journey through Asia Minor,* 319–333; Michael E. Meeker, *A Nation of Empire: The Ottoman Legacy of Turkish Modernity* (Oakland: University of California Press, 2002), 101.

68. In 1566, the Venetian bailo chose the overland route home from Istanbul as it was "more comfortable, and more abundant in the things needed to live and lodge." Jesse Cascade Howell, "The Ragusa Road: Mobility and Encounter in the Ottoman Balkans (1430–1700)" (PhD diss., Harvard University, 2017), 9.

69. Fernand Braudel, *The Mediterranean and the Mediterranean World in the Age of Philip II* (New York: Harper and Row, 1972), 103–107.

70. Ferdi Sönmez, "73 Numaralı Mühimme Defterinin Transkripsiyonu ve Değerlendirmesi (434–590) (Cilt I) / Tanscription and Evaluation of Muhimme Register Number 73 (434–590)" (Bitlis, Turkey, Bitlis Eren Üniversitesi, 2019), 49–50. Original document: BOA, A.DVNSMHM.d 73/987, 226.jpg.

71. Joshua M. White, *Piracy and Law in the Ottoman Mediterranean* (Stanford, CA: Stanford University Press, 2018), 61.

72. Sir William Foster, ed., *The Travels of John Sanderson in the Levant (1584–1602)* (London: Hakluyt Society, 1931), 39.

73. BOA, AE.SMST.II 110/11919 (AH 1112 / 1700–1 CE).

74. John Jackson, *Journey from India, towards England, in the Year 1797; By a Route Commonly Called Over-Land, through Countries Not Much Frequented, and Many of Them Hitherto*

Unknown to Europeans, Particularly between the Rivers Euphrates and Tigris through Curdistan, Diarbek, Armenia, and Natolia, in Asia and through Romalia, Bulgaria, Wallachia, Transylvania, &c. In Europe (London: Printed for T. Cadell, Jun. and W. Davies, Strand, 1799), 130; Kinneir, *Journey through Asia Minor*, 462.

75. Howel, *A Journal of the Passage from India*, 74.

76. Howel, *A Journal of the Passage from India*, 72.

77. Jackson, *Journey from India, towards England*, 128.

78. Howel, *A Journal of the Passage from India*, 72; Jackson, *Journey from India, towards England*, 128; Heude, *A Voyage up the Persian Gulf*, 214.

79. Heude, *A Voyage up the Persian Gulf*, 214, 78.

80. Needham, *Science and Civilization in China*, vol. 4: *Physics and Physical Technology*, Pt. 3, *Civil Engineering and Nautics*, 21, 29; Allsen, "Imperial Posts," 265–266.

81. Lane J. Harris, "The 'Arteries and Veins' of the Imperial Body: The Nature of the Relay and Post Station Systems in the Ming Dynasty, 1368–1644," *Journal of Early Modern History* 19, no. 4 (2015): 291.

82. Harris, "The 'Arteries and Veins' of the Imperial Body," 303.

83. Benjamin Braude, "Venture and Faith in the Commercial Life of the Ottoman Balkans, 1500–1650," *The International History Review* 7, no. 4 (1985): 528; Silverstein, *Postal Systems in the Pre-modern Islamic World*, 113–114; Youssef Ragheb, *Les Messagers Volants en Terre d'Islam* (Paris: CNRS éditions, 2002).

84. Çetin, *Ulak yol durak* [*Courier Stops*], 30–31.

85. KK 2695, 1.jpg shows the resources consumed by Salihiye station drawn from seventeen neighboring districts. I calculated the total cost of straw by using the price listed for Iznikmid district, where 5,000 *kıntar* of straw was valued at about 1,666 *guruş*. Accordingly, 32,000 *kıntar* of straw would be about 10,662 *guruş*; KK 2742, 2.jpg. For more information on military provisioning, see Finkel, *The Administration of Warfare*, 130–143. See also Chapter 5.

86. Çetin, *Ulak yol durak* [*Courier Stops*], 28–38; Suraiya Faroqhi, *Pilgrims and Sultans: The Hajj under the Ottomans, 1517–1683* (London: I. B. Tauris, 1994), 41.

87. Osman Turan, "Selçuk Kervansarayları," *Belleten* 39 (1946): 471–496; M. Kemal Özergin, "Anadolu'da Selçuklu Kervansarayları," *Tarih Dergisi* 15, no. 20 (1965): 141–170; Ayşıl Tükel Yavuz, "Anadolu Selçuklu Dönemi Hanları ve Posta-Menzil-Derbent Teşkilatları," in *Prof. Doğan Kuban'a armağan*, ed. Doğan Kuban et al., *Armağan dizisi*, no. 1 (Beyoğlu, Turkey: Istanbul: Eren, 1996), 25–38; Ayşıl Tükel Yavuz, "The Concepts That Shape Anatolian Seljuq Caravanserais," *Muqarnas* 14 (1997): 81.

88. Inalcık, *The Ottoman Empire*, 148; Mundy, *The Travels of Peter Mundy*, 1:45–46, 54, 70; Henry Maundrell, *A Journey from Aleppo to Jerusalem at Easter, A.D. 1697* (Oxford: The Theater, 1721), 5; Jackson, *Journey from India, towards England*, 122–123.

89. John Lewis Burckhardt, *Travels in Syria and the Holy Land* (Cambridge: Cambridge University Press, 2011), 36.

90. Heude, *A Voyage up the Persian Gulf*, 215–216.

91. Kinneir, *Journey through Asia Minor*, 19, 42, 84, 117, 148, 280–281, 321.

92. Howell, "The Ragusa Road," 194–195, 211; Mundy, *The Travels of Peter Mundy*, 1:66.

93. Howel, *A Journal of the Passage from India,* 64; Jackson, *Journey from India, towards England,* 114; Mundy, *The Travels of Peter Mundy,* 1:46, 52–53; Howell, "The Ragusa Road," 194.

CHAPTER 2. THE COURIER

1. I base my retelling of this chapter's opening scene on Seyit Ali Kahraman and Yücel Dağlı, eds., *Evliya Çelebi Seyahatnamesi 3: Topkapı Sarayı Bağdat 305 Yazmasının Traskripsiyonu—Dizini* (Istanbul: Yapı ve Kredi Bankası, 1993), 53–54.
2. This was the cavalry uprising led by Gürcü Abdülnebi Agha. For a brief overview of this uprising, please see Caroline Finkel, *Osman's Dream: The Story of the Ottoman Empire, 1300–1923* (New York: Basic Books, 2006), 236–239.
3. William J. Griswold, "Djalālī," in *Encyclopaedia of Islam Online,* 2nd ed., ed. P. Bearman (Brill: April 24, 2012); Suraiya Faroqhi, "Political Tensions in the Anatolian Countryside around 1600: An Attempt at Interpretation," in *Coping with the State: Political Conflict and Crime in the Ottoman Empire, 1550–1720* (Piscataway, NJ: Gorgias Press, 2010), 111–124; Suraiya Faroqhi, "Seeking Wisdom in China: An Attempt to Make Sense of the Celali Rebellions," in *Coping with the State: Political Conflict and Crime in the Ottoman Empire, 1550–1720* (Piscataway, NJ: Gorgias Press, 2010), 125–47; Sam White, *The Climate of Rebellion in the Early Modern Ottoman Empire* (New York: Cambridge University Press, 2011), esp chap. 7; Mücteba İlgürel, "Celâlî İsyanları," in *Türkiye Diyanet Vakfı İslâm Ansiklopedisi : Ca'fer Es-Sadık-Cilzzztçilik,* vol. 7 (Ankara: Türkiye Diyanet Vakfı, İslâm Ansiklopedisi Genel Müdürlüğü, 2019), 252–257; See also Karen Barkey, *Bandits and Bureaucrats: The Ottoman Route to State Centralization* (Ithaca, NY: Cornell University Press, 1994), Christopher Whitehead, "The Reluctant Pasha: Çerkes Dilaver and Elite Localization in the Seventeenth-Century Ottoman Empire," *Turcica* 53 (2022): 3–43.
4. I thank Zeynep Aydoğan for enlightening me about nose bags.
5. Robert Dankoff, "Evliya Çelebi and the *Seyahatname*," in *The Turks,* ed. Hasan Celâl Güzel, C. Cem Oğuz, and Osman Karatay, vol. 3 (Ankara: Yeni Türkiye, 2002), 605.
6. Robert Dankoff, *An Ottoman Mentality: The World of Evliya Çelebi,* 2nd Ed. Rev., Ottoman Empire and Its Heritage, vol. 31 (Leiden: Brill, 2006), xii, 2.
7. Robert Dankoff, "Turkic Languages and Turkish Dialects According to Evliya Çelebi," in *From Mahmud Kaşgari to Evliya Çelebi: Studies in Middle Turkic and Ottoman Literatures,* by Dankoff (Piscataway, NJ: Gorgias Press, 2009), 259–276; Özgen Felek, "Displaying Manhood and Masculinity at the Imperial Circumcision Festivity of 1582," *Journal of the Ottoman and Turkish Studies Association* 6, no. 1 (2019): 141–170; Suraiya Faroqhi, *Subjects of the Sultan: Culture and Daily Life in the Ottoman Empire* (London: I. B. Tauris, 2000), 101–104.

   Robert Dankoff's comprehensive study of the *Seyahatname* mentions that Evliya Çelebi worked as a courier, among the many hats he wore. Dankoff, *An Ottoman Mentality,* 2, 9, 133–134. Pakalın has also described Evliya Çelebi as a courier under his entry for the term, "Tatar." Mehmet Zeki Pakalın, *Osmanli Tarih Deyimleri ve Terimleri Sözlüğü 3* (Istanbul: Millî Eğitim Basımevi, 1983), 420–422. See also Çetin, *Ulak yol durak [Courier Stops],* 58.

8. Faroqhi, *Subjects of the Sultan: Culture and Daily Life in the Ottoman Empire,* 104.

9. Stephen C. Slota and Geoffrey C. Bowker, "How Infrastructures Matter," in *The Handbook of Science and Technology Studies,* ed. Ulrike Felt et al., 4th Ed. (Cambridge, MA: MIT Press, 2017), 529, 531; Star, "The Ethnography of Infrastructure," 380.

10. Geoffrey C. Bowker, "Information Mythology and Infrastructure," in *Information Acumen: The Understanding and Use of Knowledge in Modern Business,* ed. Lisa Bud-Frierman (London: Routledge, 1994), 245; Paul N. Edwards, *A Vast Machine: Computer Models, Climate Data, and the Politics of Global Warming* (Cambridge, MA: MIT Press, 2010), 20–23.

11. Kahraman and Dağlı, *Evliya Çelebi Seyahatnamesi 3: Topkapı Sarayı Bağdat 305 Yazmasının Traskripsiyonu—Dizini,* 3: 53–54.

12. Uyghur documents from the thirteenth and fourteenth centuries show that ulag referred to "any kind of livestock which was the property of or used by the postal system of the Mongol Empire." On the other hand, *ulagči,* with a suffix that still exists in Modern Turkish [c/ç][ı/i] denoting an occupation or profession, referred to the official attendants of the Mongol postal system. Allsen, "Imperial Posts," 253; Márton Vér, "Animal Terminology in the Uyghur Documents Concerning the Postal System of the Mongol Empire," *Turkic Languages* 23 (2019): 205.

13. All this was recorded in a chronicle of Xuanzang's travels by his biographer and fellow monk, Hui Li. Scholars regard this as the first written instance of the term *ulak.* "法师者是奴弟, 欲求法于婆罗门国, 愿可汗怜师如怜奴, 仍请敕以西诸国给邬落马递送出境." (慧立, 大慈恩寺三藏法師專) Hui Li, *Da Ci En Si San Zang Fa Shi Zhuan* (Beijing: Zhonghua Shuju, 2000), 21. The Yabghu Qaghan whom Xuangzang met is likely Yabghu Qaghan Si, son of Tong Yabghu Qaghan. Étienne de la Vaissière, "Note Sur La Chronologie Du Voyage de Xuanzang," *Journal Asiatique* 298, no. 1 (2010): 165; Paul Pelliot, "Neuf Notes Sur des Questions d'Asie Centrale," *T'oung Pao* 26, no. 4/5 (1929): 220; Denis Sinor, "Notes on the Equine Terminology of the Altaic Peoples," *Central Asiatic Journal* 10, no. 3/4 (1965): 315; Allsen, "Imperial Posts," 253; Vér, "Animal Terminology in the Uyghur Documents Concerning the Postal System of the Mongol Empire." According to Arakawa Masaharu, the term ulak referred not only to horses, but also to an accompanying guide who served as an escort and helped with navigation. Masaharu Arakawa, "トゥルファン出土漢文文書に見える Ulaɣ について [On a Turkic Term 'Ulaɣ' in Turfan Chinese Documents]," *内陸アジア言語の研究* [*Studies on Inner Asian Languages*] 9 (1994): 11.

14. Allsen, "Imperial Posts," 253.

15. The Ottoman Turkish term that I have translated as "agent" is *maṣlaḥatgüzār ādemi.* Kahraman and Dağlı, *Evliya Çelebi Seyahatnamesi 3: Topkapı Sarayı Bağdat 305 Yazmasının Traskripsiyonu—Dizini,* 54; Franciszek Meniński, *Thesaurus Linguarum Orientalium, Turcicæ, Arabicæ, Persicæ* (Vienna, 1680), 4704. In the nineteenth century, this term would be translated as "chargé d'affaires," a diplomat subordinate to the ambassador. Redhouse, *New Redhouse Turkish-English Dictionary,* 735.

16. I thank Evangeline Lin Mingen for her input on sociolinguistics.

17. Kahraman and Dağlı, *Evliya Çelebi Seyahatnamesi 3: Topkapı Sarayı Bağdat 305 Yazmasının Traskripsiyonu—Dizini,* 54.

18. Seyit Ali Kahraman and Yücel Dağlı, eds., *Evliya Çelebi Seyahatnamesi 9: Topkapı Sarayı Bağdat 305 Yazmasının Traskripsiyonu—Dizini* (Istanbul: Yapı ve Kredi Bankası, 1993), 266; Seyit Ali Kahraman and Yücel Dağlı, eds., *Evliya Çelebi Seyahatnamesi 10: Topkapı Sarayı Bağdat 305 Yazmasının Traskripsiyonu—Dizini* (Istanbul: Yapı ve Kredi Bankası, 1993), 370, 534.

19. Heyd, *Ottoman Documents on Palestine 1552–1615*, xv and 22.

20. "*Menzil: Âsitâne'den Üsküb-e varup gelince, Sipâhî Hasan ve iki nefer âdemlerine menzil [emri] yazılmışdur.*" Hacı Osman Yıldırım and Yusuf Sarınay, *85 numaralı Mühimme defteri: (1040–1041 (1042) / 1630–1631 (1632)): <özet—transkripsiyon—indeks>* (Ankara: T. C. Başbakanlık Devlet Arşivleri Genel Müdürlüğü, 2002), 402 (no. 662). (This is p. 402 of the hardcopy publication; for the PDF version downloadable through the official BOA website, the same entry 662 is found on pp. 407–408.)

21. This is my translation of Yıldırım and Sarınay, *85 numaralı Mühimme defteri*, 50 (no. 80); original document found in *Turkey Osmanlı Arşivi Daire Başkanlığı, 85 numarali mühimme defteri (1040/1630–1631): Tıpkıbasım* (Ankara: T. C. Başbakanlık Devlet Arşivleri Genel Müdürlüğü, 2001), 34 (no. 80); Heywood, "The Evolution of the Courier Order (Ulak Hükmi) in Ottoman Chancery Practice (Fifteenth to Eighteenth Centuries)," 292. *Çavuş* may also be translated as messenger; Gustav Bayerle, *Pashas, Begs, and Effendis: A Historical Dictionary of Titles and Terms in the Ottoman Empire* (Istanbul: Isis Press, 1997), 55.

22. One of the anonymous reviewers for this manuscript has argued that *çavuş* should be translated as "'messenger" rather than "marshal." I understand this perspective but have chosen to continue using "marshal" to minimize confusion for readers, since the point of this chapter is that many different officials performed the function of message delivery. Furthermore, for the past year (since January 2023) I have been translating seventeenth- and eighteenth-century Fee Waiver Registers compiled by provincial postmasters that reveal a wide variety of ranks engaged in message delivery—*çavuş* is just one among a range. My collaborator and I hope to publish our findings on this quantitative data (currently being transposed to a Microsoft Excel spreadsheet) about officials involved in courier duties and their respective titles and ranks in the near future. Ignatius Mouradgea d'Ohsson, *Tableau général de l'empire othoman: Divisé en deux parties, dont l'une comprend la législation mahométane; l'autre, l'histoire de l'empire othoman*, vol. 7 (Paris: De l'imprimerie de monsieur Firmin Didot, 1824), 324; Charles L. Wilkins, *Forging Urban Solidarities: Ottoman Aleppo 1640–1700* (Leiden: Brill, 2010), 86–87; Hathaway, *The Politics of Households in Ottoman Egypt*, 38–39.

23. *Turkey Osmanlı Arşivi Daire Başkanlığı, 3 numaralı Mühimme defteri (966–968 / 1558–1560)* (Ankara: T. C. Başbakanlık, Devlet Arşivleri Genel Müdürlüğü, 1993), 8.

24. Consider *Turkey Osmanlı Arşivi Daire Başkanlığı, 3 numaralı Mühimme defteri (966–968 / 1558–1560)* (Ankara: T. C. Başbakanlık, Devlet Arşivleri Genel Müdürlüğü, 1993), and Osman Yıldırım, ed., *6 numaralı mühimme defteri (972 / 1564–1565)* (Ankara: T. C. Başbakanlık, Devlet Arşivleri Genel Müdürlüğü, 1995). For the seventeenth century, see Choon Hwee Koh, "The Sublime Post: A History of Empire and Power through the Ottoman Post Station System, 1600–1839" (PhD diss., Yale University, 2020), chap. 2.

25. Yıldırım and Sarınay, *85 numaralı Mühimme defteri*, 11 (n. 15), 14 (n. 19), 17 (n. 25), 26 (n. 40), 26 (n. 41), 50 (n. 79), 69 (n. 108), 79 (n. 126), 81 (n. 132), 95–96 (n. 157), 96 (n. 158), 123 (n. 203), 154 (n. 253), 163 (n. 268), 164–165 (n. 270), 188 (n. 308), 253 (n. 415), 253 (n. 416), 307 (n. 507), 313 (n. 518), 313 (n. 519), 329 (n. 544), 352 (n. 580), 371 (n. 610), 371–372 (n. 612), 372 (n. 613), 390–391 (n. 641), 398 (n. 653), 434 (n. 716).

Yıldırım and Sarınay, *85 numaralı Mühimme defteri*, 6 (n. 6), 26 (n. 39), 50 (n. 80), 80 (n. 130), 95 (n. 156), 135 (n. 224), 160 (n. 263), 163 (n. 268), 165 (n. 271), 268 (n. 441), 268 (n. 442), 285 (n. 470), 313 (n. 519), 349 (n. 575), 371 (n. 611), 398 (n. 654), 402 (n. 663), 402 (n. 664).

Yıldırım and Sarınay, *85 numaralı Mühimme defteri*, 191 (n. 315) and 273 (n. 451).

26. Heude, *A Voyage up the Persian Gulf*, 198.

27. Jackson, *Journey from India, towards England*, 173.

28. Jackson, *Journey from India, towards England*, 114.

29. Jackson, *Journey from India, towards England*, 123.

30. Jackson, *Journey from India, towards England*, 130.

31. Howel, *A Journal of the Passage from India*, 104–105, 118; Jackson, *Journey from India, towards England*, 207–209, 214; Heude, *A Voyage up the Persian Gulf*, 225.

32. Babur, *The Baburnama: Memoirs of Babur, Prince and Emperor*, ed. and trans. Wheeler M. Thackston (Washington, DC: Freer Gallery of Art, Arthur M. Sackler Gallery, Smithsonian Institution, 1996), 53.

33. Heude, *A Voyage up the Persian Gulf*, 196.

34. Heude, *A Voyage up the Persian Gulf*, 204–205.

35. Seyit Ali Kahraman and Yücel Dağlı, eds., *Evliya Çelebi Seyahatnamesi 7: Topkapı Sarayı Bağdat 305 Yazmasının Traskripsiyonu—Dizini* (Istanbul: Yapı ve Kredi Bankası, 1993), 178.

36. Another image may be found in Peter Mundy's album titled *Miniatures from Turkish Manuscripts: A Catalogue and Subject Index of Paintings in the British Library and British Museum*, p. 21, no. 7 (25), https://www.britishmuseum.org/collection/object/W_1974 -0617-0-13-25, accessed online September 21, 2023.

37. St. Cyril and Methodius National Library in Sofia, Bulgaria, F13188, April 1686 (AH 1097); GRGSA IAM OJC 001 F51, 67.jpg (full decree on 67–68.jpg): "*ḥālā mevsim-i bahār olmaḳ ḥasebiyle ağaçlar yapraḳlanub ṭağlarda ḥaydūd ve sā'ir eşḳıyālar [var]*."

38. Heude, *A Voyage up the Persian Gulf*, 221–222.

39. Kinneir, *Journey through Asia Minor*, 442.

40. Jackson, *Journey from India, towards England*, 112, 142.

41. Jackson, *Journey from India, towards England*, 167.

42. Howel, *A Journal of the Passage from India*, 70.

43. Yahya Koç, "149 Numaralı Mühimme Defteri (1155–1156/1742–1743): İnceleme-Çeviriyazı-Dizin" (Master's thesis, Istanbul University, 2011), 582–584.

44. Kinneir, *Journey through Asia Minor*, 239; Howel, *A Journal of the Passage from India*, 104–105.

45. Jackson, *Journey from India, towards England*, xiv.

46. For the organizational structure of messengers in Safavid and Afsharid Iran, see the forthcoming article Willem Floor, "The Postal System in Safavid and Afsharid Iran,"

(unpublished manuscript, August 2023), .docx. I thank Willem Floor for sharing his article with me.

47. Jackson, *Journey from India, towards England,* xiv.

48. Kinneir, *Journey through Asia Minor,* 35.

49. Broughton, *Travels in Albania and Other Provinces of Turkey in 1809 & 1810,* 69.

50. Demetrius Cantemir, *The History of the Growth and Decay of the Othman Empire,* trans. N. Tindal (London: J. J. and P. Knapton, 1734), 414, n. 30; Rifa'at Ali Abou El Haj, "The Ottoman Vezir and Paşa Households 1683–1703: A Preliminary Report," *Journal of the American Oriental Society* 94, no. 4 (1974): 441, n.12; Mehmed Süreyya, Nuri Akbayar, and Seyit Ali Kahraman, *Sicill-i Osmani 4* (Istanbul: Kültür Bakanlığı ile Türkiye Ekonomik ve Toplumsal Tarih Vakfı, 1996), 1192–1193.

51. Mehmet Zeki Pakalın, *Osmanlı tarih deyimleri ve terimleri sözlüğü 2* (Istanbul: Millî Eğitim Basımevi, 1983), 198.

52. Jackson, *Journey from India, towards England,* 176.

53. Kahraman and Dağlı, *Evliya Çelebi Seyahatnamesi 3: Topkapı Sarayı Bağdat 305 Yazmasının Traskripsiyonu—Dizini,* 54.

54. Dankoff, *An Ottoman Mentality,* 2.

55. Evliya Çelebi, *The Intimate Life of an Ottoman Statesman,* 124–142.

56. Dankoff, *An Ottoman Mentality,* 22, 145–146; Kahraman and Dağlı, *Evliya Çelebi Seyahatnamesi 3: Topkapı Sarayı Bağdat 305 Yazmasının Traskripsiyonu—Dizini,* 282–285; Evliya Çelebi, *The Intimate Life of an Ottoman Statesman: Melek Ahmed Pasha (1588–1662): As Portrayed in Evliya Çelebi's Book of Travels (Seyahat-Name),* trans. Robert Dankoff (Albany: State University of New York Press, 1991), 124–129; Görkem Özizmirli, "Fear in Evliya Çelebi's *Seyahatnâme*: Politics and Historiography in a Seventeenth Century Ottoman Travelogue" (Master's thesis, Koç University, 2014), 65–72.

57. Evliya Çelebi, *The Intimate Life of an Ottoman Statesman,* 124–125.

58. Kahraman and Dağlı, *Evliya Çelebi Seyahatnamesi 3: Topkapı Sarayı Bağdat 305 Yazmasının Traskripsiyonu—Dizini,* 283; Seyit Ali Kahraman and Yücel Dağlı, eds., *Evliya Çelebi Seyahatnamesi 4: Topkapı Sarayı Bağdat 305 Yazmasının Traskripsiyonu—Dizini* (Istanbul: Yapı ve Kredi Bankası, 1993), 126.

59. Evliya Çelebi, *The Intimate Life of an Ottoman Statesman,* 127.

60. For other examples, see Kahraman and Dağlı, *Evliya Çelebi Seyahatnamesi 4: Topkapı Sarayı Bağdat 305 Yazmasının Traskripsiyonu—Dizini,* 197–198; Dankoff, *An Ottoman Mentality,* 100–101.

61. Sebouh Aslanian, *From the Indian Ocean to the Mediterranean: The Global Trade Networks of Armenian Merchants from New Julfa* (Berkeley, University of California Press, 2011), 102–110.

62. Seyit Ali Kahraman and Yücel Dağlı, eds., *Evliya Çelebi Seyahatnamesi 2: Topkapı Sarayı Bağdat 305 Yazmasının Traskripsiyonu—Dizini* (Istanbul: Yapı ve Kredi Bankası, 1993), 243.

63. Seyit Ali Kahraman and Yücel Dağlı, eds., *Evliya Çelebi Seyahatnamesi 5: Topkapı Sarayı Bağdat 305 Yazmasının Traskripsiyonu—Dizini* (Istanbul: Yapı ve Kredi Bankası, 1993), 7.

64. Kahraman and Dağlı, *Evliya Çelebi Seyahatnamesi 5,* 7; Seyit Ali Kahraman and Yücel Dağlı, eds., *Evliya Çelebi Seyahatnamesi 8: Topkapı Sarayı Bağdat 305 Yazmasının*

Traskripsiyonu—Dizini (Istanbul: Yapı ve Kredi Bankası, 1993), 28, 31. Kahraman and Dağlı, *Evliya Çelebi Seyahatnamesi 4: Topkapı Sarayı Bağdat 305 Yazmasının Traskripsiyonu—Dizini*, 360. Kahraman and Dağlı, 182; Kahraman and Dağlı, *Evliya Çelebi Seyahatnamesi 5: Topkapı Sarayı Bağdat 305 Yazmasının Traskripsiyonu—Dizini*, 12.

65. Jackson, *Journey from India, towards England,* 109.
66. Kahraman and Dağlı, *Evliya Çelebi Seyahatnamesi 3: Topkapı Sarayı Bağdat 305 Yazmasının Traskripsiyonu—Dizini,* 283.
67. Finkel, *Osman's Dream,* 203.
68. Eventually, Çomar Bölükbaşı was rehabilitated and became governor of Aintab (Gaziantep in modern Turkey) in 1650. There is a nineteenth-century analogue in the rebellious valley-lords (*derebey*) in Cilicia. After neutralizing their threat, the Ottoman government did not treat the rebels as criminals or bandits. Rather, they relocated the rebels to Istanbul, and awarded them government posts, land, and monthly salaries. Far from being viewed with animosity, these rebels were seen as "members of the ruling class—the Ottoman establishment—who had somehow become alienated from the capital and needed to be forcibly reintegrated." For an analysis of Evliya's nuanced position on the Celali revolts, see Erdem Sönmez, "Celaliler ve Üç Evliya Çelebi," *Kebikeç: İnsan Bilimleri İçin Kaynak Araştırmaları Dergisi* 33 (2012): 87–110; Gould, "Lords or Bandits? The Derebeys of Cilicia," 499–500.

CHAPTER 3. THE TATAR

1. BOA, MVL 859/88; 26 Receb 1280.
2. BOA, MVL 859/88; 26 Receb 1280, 5.jpg.
3. BOA, MVL 859/88; 26 Receb 1280, 11.jpg.
4. On the concepts of capacity, reach, and weight, see Soifer, "State Infrastructural Power."
5. During the thirteenth-century Mongol conquest, European sources referred to the Mongols as "Tartars," which, some scholars hypothesize, was related to Tartarus, an abyss of torment in Greek mythology. "Tartars" therefore referred to the "people of the hell," and the conquering Mongols were viewed as such in their time. David Morgan, *The Mongols* (Oxford: Blackwell, 2007), 51; Christopher P. Atwood, *The Rise of the Mongols: Five Chinese Sources* (Indianapolis: Hackett, 2021), 11; Finkel, *The Administration of Warfare,* 97–109, 203–204. I thank James Pickett for pointing me to Atwood's *Rise of the Mongols.*
6. For instance, a report from 1690 mentions one of the grand vizier's tatars, Tatar el-Haj Osman Ağa, who had personally delivered an imperial decree to Inecik, near the city of Izmir in modern Turkey. BOA, AE.SSÜL.II. 17/1750.
7. Unfortunately, the archival document C DH 33 / 16641 used by Nesim Yazıcı in his article regarding the reorganization of the Tatar Corps in 1775, during the reign of Abdülhamid I (1773–1789), was under restoration at the time of writing, and I was unable to access its contents. It may contain information about the founding date of the Tatar Corps. Yusuf Halaçoğlu suggests that the Tatar Corps was established by Abdülhamid I, but his work references only a secondary source by Şekip Esin that does not provide an archival source regarding the establishment of the Tatar Corps. Given that there are references to

tatar couriers in archival documents before Abdülhamid I's reign, I hold the view that the Tatar Corps had already existed before the reign of Abdülhamid I (1773–1789). Nesim Yazıcı, "Posta Nezaretinin Kuruluşu," in *Çağını Yakalayan Osmanlı!: Osmanlı Devleti'nde Modern Haberleşme ve Ulaştırma Teknikleri* (Istanbul: İslâm Tarih, Sanat, ve Kültür Araştırma Merkezi [IRCICA], 1995), 33. For the view that the Tatar Corps was established by Abdülhamid I, see Yusuf Halaçoğlu, *XVI–XVII. Yüzyıllarda Osmanlılarda Devlet Teşkilâtı ve Sosyal Yapı* (Ankara: Türk Tarih Kurumu, 2014), 174.

8. Howel, *A Journal of the Passage from India*, 60–61. See also Esmé Scott Stevenson, *Our Ride through Asia Minor* (London: Chapman and Hall, 1881), 292.

9. Mouradgea d'Ohsson, *Tableau général de l'empire othoman*, 7:173. Paul Rycaut's history did not use either ulak or tatar, but rather the term "messenger." Sir Paul Rycaut, *The History of the Present State of the Ottoman Empire: Containing the Maxims of the Turkish Polity, the Most Material Points of the Mahometan Religion, Their Sects and Heresies, Their Convents and Religious Votaries. Their Military Discipline, with an Exact Computation of Their Forces Both by Sea and Land . . . In Three Books* (London: R. Clavell, J. Robinson, and A. Churchill, 1686).

10. M. Hüdai Şentürk, "Osmanlılarda Haberleşme ve Menzil Teşkilatına Genel Bir Bakış," *Türkler* 14 (2000): 449; İsmail Hakkı Uzunçarşılı, *Osmanlı devletinin merkez ve bahriye teşkilatı* (Ankara: Türk Tarih Kurumu, 1984), 322. See also the entry for "tatar" and related compound words in Pakalın, *Osmanli Tarih Deyimleri ve Terimleri Sözlüğü 3*, 420–422.

11. In-person conversation with Iwamoto Keiko at Weekenders Café in Kyoto, Japan, March 26, 2023. On tatar migrants to Ottoman lands after the Crimean War and their becoming mounted couriers, see Lucy M. J. Garnett and John S. Stuart-Glennie, *The Women of Turkey and Their Folk-Lore*, vol. 2 (London: D. Nutt, 1890), 346–347. On various forms of nomadism in the Ottoman context, see Keiko Iwamoto, 帝国と遊牧民: 近世オスマン朝の視座より [*Nomads and the Early Modern Empire: Nomadic Peoples under Ottoman Rule from the 15th to the 18th Centuries*] (Kyoto: Kyōtodaigaku gakujutsu shuppankai, 2019), 21–41.

12. Michael Nizri, "Rethinking Center-Periphery Communication in the Ottoman Empire: The Kapı-Kethüdası," *Journal of the Economic and Social History of the Orient* 59 (2016): 477–478.

13. Ethan L. Menchinger, *The First of the Modern Ottomans: The Intellectual History of Ahmed Vasif* (Cambridge: Cambridge University Press, 2017), 41, 44, 144, 160. I am deeply grateful to Ethan Menchinger for his extraordinary generosity and collegiality in discussing his sources with me.

14. Canbakal, "Vows as Contract," 114.

15. Avner Wishnitzer, *Reading Clocks, Alla Turca: Time and Society in the Late Ottoman Empire* (Chicago: University of Chicago Press, 2015), 47.

16. Wishnitzer, *Reading Clocks, Alla Turca*, 50.

17. Carter Vaughn Findley, *Bureaucratic Reform in the Ottoman Empire: The Sublime Porte, 1789–1922* (Princeton, NJ: Princeton University Press, 1980), 98; Wishnitzer, *Reading Clocks, Alla Turca*, 46; Melis Hafez, *Inventing Laziness: The Culture of Productivity in Late Ottoman Society* (Cambridge: Cambridge University Press, 2022), 118.

18. Ahmed Akgündüz, "Shariʿah Courts and Shariʿah Records: The Application of Islamic Law in the Ottoman State," *Islamic Law and Society* 16, no. 2 (2009): 203; Uzunçarşılı, *Osmanlı devletinin merkez ve bahriye teşkilatı,* 249; Hafez, *Inventing Laziness,* 118–119, 112.

19. Leslie P. Peirce, *The Imperial Harem: Women and Sovereignty in the Ottoman Empire,* Studies in Middle Eastern History (New York: Oxford University Press, 1993), 8–9.

20. Hafez, *Inventing Laziness,* 98.

21. Hafez, *Inventing Laziness,* 124–146.

22. Kahraman and Dağlı, *Evliya Çelebi Seyahatnamesi 3: Topkapı Sarayı Bağdat 305 Yazmasının Traskripsiyonu—Dizini,* 53–54.

23. Jackson, *Journey from India, towards England,* 105–107.

24. See BOA, C. DH 33/1628; BOA, C. DH 42/2079; BOA, C. AS 1085/47843.

25. Jackson, *Journey from India, towards England,* 106–108.

26. See Chapter 8.

27. ISAM, DŞS 1B, 13–14.jpg (AH 1209 / 1794 CE) (Term for merchandise: *tüccār mālı*); GRGSA IAM OJC 001 F154, 18.jpg (AH 1201 / 1787 CE); ISAM, AŞS 71, 38.jpg (AH 1245 / 1830 CE) (term for merchandise: *tüccār yükü*); ISAM, DŞS 1B, 68.jpg (AH 1207 / 1793 CE).

28. BOA, MAD 3759.

29. Compare with Finkel, *The Administration of Warfare,* 73–74.

30. BOA, MAD 3759, 16.jpg: "*bāḳī ḳalan yüz altmış beş [165] neferiñ yevmiyyesi gelmek üzere āsitāne-i saʿādetde ve sāʾir maḥalde ve diyār-ı baʿidde olmağla henüz çeküb erişmemişlerdir.*"

31. Another possible roll-call register is BOA, D. KRZ.d. 33271 (AH 1158 / 1745 CE), especially pp. 6–7, 37 (5.jpg and 20.jpg).

32. Finkel, *The Administration of Warfare,* 49–50, 56; Rhoads Murphey, *Ottoman Warfare, 1500–1700* (London: UCL Press, 1999), 46–47; Gábor Ágoston, *The Last Muslim Conquest: The Ottoman Empire and Its Wars in Europe* (Princeton, NJ: Princeton University Press, 2021), 41, 324, 439.

33. Tatar reports are mostly found today in the Imperial Rescripts (*ḫaṭṭ-ı hümāyūn*) section of the Presidential Ottoman Archives in Istanbul, Türkiye. These reports generally feature the handwritten responses and instructions of the sultan at the top of the document; some scholars have described these as "top-priority correspondence." Mübahat S Kütükoğlu, *Osmanlı belgelerinin dili: (diplomatik)* (Istanbul: Kubbealtı akademisi Kültür ve sanʾat vakfı, 1994), 172–183; Tolga U. Esmer, "Notes on a Scandal: Transregional Networks of Violence, Gossip, and Imperial Sovereignty in the Late Eighteenth-Century Ottoman Empire," *Comparative Studies in Society and History* 58, no. 1 (2016): 103, 107.

34. BOA, HAT 4/122 (AH 1158 / 1745 CE).

35. See, for instance, the tatar reports in BOA, HAT 347/19748E which is also about the Egyptian invasion of Syria, and BOA, HAT 174/7515, which is about Cezzar Ahmed Pasha's battles with Abdullah Pasha in Tripoli and Damascus in 1803.

36. BOA, HAT 354/19887A.

37. For more information about the Syrian invasion, see Muhammad H. Kutluoğlu, *The Egyptian Question (1831–1841): The Expansionist Policy of Mehmed Ali Paşa in Syria and Asia Minor and the Reaction of the Sublime Porte* (Istanbul: Eren, 1998); Mikhail, *Nature and empire in Ottoman Egypt,* 124–169.

38. Esmer, "Notes on a Scandal," 118–120.
39. BOA, HAT 60/2677; Kara Feyzi gave Mustafa Pasha a bribe (*bahşiş*): *"ve merķūm Kara Feyzi Rumili / vālīsiniñ tatarını yanına çağırub Rodoslı Ahmed Ağanıñ ķapuçı ķarārı Mustafa-ya / virilmek içün bir ķıṭ'a kağıd (blank) ve on beş guruş bahşiş i'ṭā eylediğini."*
40. BOA, HAT 550/27126B.
41. *"Çöle ādemler göndererek bulunur ise mecrūḥen ķalan Ahmed tatara teslīm ideriz deyü."*
42. BOA, HAT 1392/55537 (AH 1204 / 1789–1790 CE); see Tolga U. Esmer, "Economies of Violence, Banditry and Governance in the Ottoman Empire around 1800," *Past & Present* 224, no. 1 (2014): 163–199.
43. I thank Edhem Eldem for generously sharing the original archival documents with me via email when I was unable to access the Ottoman archives during the first year of the pandemic. BOA, C. BLD 4/161 (AH 1207 / 1792 CE); BOA, C. BLD. 58/2897 (AH 1209 / 1795 CE); BOA, C. BLD. 130/6468 (AH 1210 / 1795 CE); BOA, C. BLD. 112/5583 (AH 1210 /1796 CE).
44. BOA, C. BLD 4/161 (1207 AH / 1792 CE); Edhem Eldem, "Of Bricks and Tiles: The History of a Local Industry in the Area of Mürefte (Thrace)," in *Living the Good Life: Consumption in the Qing and Ottoman Empires of the Eighteenth Century*, ed. Suraiya Faroqhi and Elif Akçetin (Leiden: Brill, 2017), 460.
45. BOA, MVL 529/68 (AH 1283).
46. BOA, MVL 536/50 (AH 1284)
47. BOA, MVL 807/92.
48. BOA, AE SMST III 83/6185.
49. Shaw, *The Financial and Administrative Organization and Development of Ottoman Egypt*, 187–188, 201–202; Christopher Whitehead, "The Veledeş Conflict: A Reassessment of the Mid-Seventeenth-Century Rebellions of the Altı Bölük Halkı," *Journal of the Ottoman and Turkish Studies Association* 8, no. 1 (2021): 303.
50. BOA, I.MVL 244/8839; BOA, I. MVL 246 / 8968; BOA, I. MVL. 254/9412; BOA, I.MVL. 258 / 9615; BOA, I.MVL.285/11247; BOA, I. MVL. 305 / 12543; BOA, I. MVL. 319/13502; BOA, I. MVL. 418/18311; BOA, I. MVL. 554/24876.
51. Sabri Yetkin, *Ege'de Eşkıyalar* (Istanbul: Tarih Vakfı Yurt Yayınları, 2003), 74.
52. Nadir Özbek, "Policing the Countryside: Gendarmes of the Late 19th-Century Ottoman Empire (1876–1908)," *International Journal of Middle East Studies* 40, no. 1 (2008): 55; Omri Paz, "Civil-Servant Aspirants: Ottoman Social Mobility in the Second Half of the Nineteenth Century," *Journal of the Economic and Social History of the Orient* 60, no. 4 (2017): 407; Yetkin, *Ege'de Eşkıyalar*, 74–76.
53. Metin Kunt, *The Sultan's Servants: The Transformation of Ottoman Provincial Government, 1550–1650* (New York: Columbia University Press, 1983), 41–44.

CHAPTER 4. THE DECREES

1. Colin Heywood, "Two Firmans of Mustafa II on the Reorganization of the Ottoman Courier System (1108/1696)," *Acta Orientalia Academiae Scientiarum Hungaricae* 54, no. 4 (2001): 490. I rely on Heywood's translation of the decrees in the rest of the chapter and have made only minor modifications.
2. Hughes, "Evolution of Large Technical Systems," 71–76.

3. For an overview of this period, see Finkel, *Osman's Dream*, chaps. 7–10; I also found the memoir of Osman of Timisoara a vivid and useful guide to understanding this unpredictable and uncertain period from the ground up. Osman of Timisoara, *Prisoner of the Infidels: The Memoirs of an Ottoman Muslim in Seventeenth-Century Europe*, trans. Giancarlo Casale (Oakland: University of California Press, 2021).

4. Salzmann, "Ancien Regime Revisited"; Cengiz Orhonlu, *Osmanlı İmparatorluğu'nda Aşiretleri İskanı* (Istanbul: Eren Yayıncılık, 1987); Linda T. Darling, "Ordering the Ottoman Elite: Ceremonial Lawcodes of the Late Seventeenth Century," *Turcica* 50 (2019): 355–382; Marinos Sariyannis, "Notes on the Ottoman Poll-Tax Reforms of the Late Seventeenth Century: The Case of Crete," *Journal of the Economic and Social History of the Orient* 54 (2011): 39–61; Hakan T. Karateke, *An Ottoman Protocol Register Containing Ceremonies from 1736 to 1808: BEO Sadaret Defterleri 350 in the Prime Ministry Ottoman State Archives, Istanbul* (Istanbul: Ottoman Bank Archives and Research Centre, 2007), 36; Tülay Artan, "The First, Hesitant Steps of Ottoman Protocol and Diplomacy into Modernity (1676–1725)," *The Court Historian* 26, no. 1 (2021): 29–43.

5. Heywood, "The Via Egnatia in the Ottoman Period," 135–136; Çetin, *Ulak yol durak* [*Courier Stops*], 292; Çınar, "Osmanlı Ulak-Menzilhane Sistemi ve XVIII Yüzyılın İlk Yarısında Antep Menzilleri [The Ottoman Post Station System and the Antep Post Station in the First Half of the Eighteenth Century]," 629.

6. Colin Heywood has transliterated and translated two of these decrees, which was a great help to me as I began research on this topic. Two decades after Heywood's article was published, I have transliterated and translated another two decrees in the same journal. Choon Hwee Koh, "Two More Firmans on the Reorganisation of the Ottoman Postal System (1101/1690 and 1209/1794): (Documents from the Amasya and Damascus Kadi Sicils)," *Acta Orientalia Academiae Scientiarum Hungaricae* 76, no. 1 (2023): 149–164.

7. ISAM, AŞS [Amasya Court Register] 19, p. 138 (74.jpg).

8. İzzet Sak, *37 Numaralı Konya Şer'iye Sicili (1102–1103/1691–1692): Transkripsiyon ve Dizin* [*Konya Judicial Records*, vol. 37] (Konya, Turkey: Konya Ticaret Odası, 2010), 475–476.

9. Sak, *37 numaralı Konya şer'iye sicili (1102–1103/1691–1692)*, 490–491.

10. Heywood, "Two Firmans," 488, 490–491.

11. Heywood, "Two Firmans," 487.

12. Heywood, "Two Firmans," 491.

13. Heywood, "Two Firmans," 490 (my italics).

14. Heywood, "Two Firmans," 493–495.

15. Records of these post stations existed from the 1590s. For instance, the Register of Ports and Stations, KK2555, lists all the ports and stations in the Ottoman Empire. However, its format differs greatly from the registers produced from the 1690s onward. The fact that Mustafa II requested these to be compiled anew suggests that the information recorded in KK2555 might not have been regularly used or updated.

16. Heywood, "Two Firmans," 490 (my italics).

17. I thank Linda Darling for her advice on this. BOA, MAD 3169, pp. 2–3.

18. I missed the detail of an assumed average of "ten hours per trip" in Choon Hwee Koh, "The Ottoman Postmaster: Contractors, Communication and Early Modern State Formation," *Past & Present* 251, no. 1 (2021): 126.

19. 354 (days in a *hijri* year) × 50 / 120 (120 *akçe* to 1 *guruş*) = 147.5 guruş. BOA, MAD 3169, p. 2.

20. William H. Sewell Jr., "A Strange Career: The Historical Study of Economic Life," *History and Theory* 49, no. 4 (2010): 151.

21. Theodore M. Porter, *Trust in Numbers: The Pursuit of Objectivity in Science and Public Life* (Princeton, NJ: Princeton University Press, 1995), ix.

22. See also Heywood, "Two Firmans."

23. BOA, MAD 3169, p. 3.

24. Abou El Haj, "The Ottoman Vezir and Paşa Households 1683–1703: A Preliminary Report"; Rifa'at Ali Abou El Haj, "The Narcissism of Mustafa II (1695–1703): A Psychohistorical Study," *Studia Islamica* 40 (1974): 115–131; Stanford J. Shaw, *History of the Ottoman Empire and Modern Turkey,* vol. 1: *Empire of the Gazis: The Rise and Decline of the Ottoman Empire 1280–1808* (Cambridge: Cambridge University Press, 1976), 223–228; Tezcan, *The Second Ottoman Empire,* 6; Cumhur Bekar, "The Rise of the Köprülü Household: The Transformation of Patronage in the Ottoman Empire in the Seventeenth Century," *Turkish Historical Review* 11, nos. 2–3 (2021): 229–256.

25. Findley, *Bureaucratic Reform in the Ottoman Empire,* 53, 65.

26. Joel Shinder, "Career Line Formation in the Ottoman Bureaucracy, 1648–1750: A New Perspective," *Journal of the Economic and Social History of the Orient* 16, no. 2/3 (1973): 222; Artan, "The First, Hesitant Steps of Ottoman Protocol and Diplomacy into Modernity (1676–1725)," 42.

27. Findley, *Bureaucratic Reform in the Ottoman Empire,* 58–63.

28. Compare the following two sections in Uzunçarşılı, *Osmanlı devletinin merkez ve bahriye teşkilatı,* 338–346 and 346–353.

29. Karateke, *An Ottoman Protocol Register Containing Ceremonies from 1736 to 1808,* 36.

30. Linda T. Darling, *Revenue-Raising and Legitimacy: Tax Collection and Finance Administration in the Ottoman Empire, 1560–1660* (Leiden: E. J. Brill, 1996), 249–260; Necati Aktaş, "Atik Şikâyet Defteri," in *Türkiye Diyanet Vakfı İslam Ansiklopedisi: Aşık Ömer-Bala Külliyesi,* vol. 4 (Üsküdar: Türkiye Diyanet Vakfı, İslâm Ansiklopedisi Genel Müdürlüğü, 1991), 68.

31. Başak Tuğ, *Politics of Honor in Ottoman Anatolia: Sexual Violence and Socio-Legal Surveillance in the Eighteenth Century* (Leiden: Brill, 2017), 86–93; Guy Burak, "Şeyhulislâm Feyzullah Efendi, the Ḥanafī Mufti of Jerusalem and the Rise of the Provincial Fatāwā Collections in the Eighteenth Century," *Journal of the Economic and Social History of the Orient* 64, no. 4 (2021): 377–403, quote from 395.

32. See also Abou-El-Haj, *Formation of the Modern State,* 66; Rifa'at Ali Abou-El-Haj, "The Reisülküttab and Ottoman Diplomacy at Karlowitz" (PhD diss., Princeton University, 1963).

33. It should be noted that documentary proliferation did not occur evenly across all arenas. For instance, some registers, such as pay lists of garrison soldiers (*mevācib defterleri*), decreased in quantity and quality of detail during this same time period. Klára Hegyi, *The Ottoman Military Organization in Hungary: Fortresses, Fortress Garrisons and Finances* (Berlin: Walter de Gruyter, 2018), 21, 29.

34. Heywood, "Two Firmans," 490.

35. See Chapter 8.

36. BOA, C NF 32/1577; BOA, HAT 488/23960; BOA, HAT 491 / 24036; Musa Çadırcı, "Posta Teşkilatı Kurulmadan Önce Osmanlı İmparatorluğu'nda Menzilhane ve Kiracıbaşılık [Post Stations and Postmasters in the Ottoman Empire before the Establishment of the Modern Postal System]," *VIII. Türk Tarihi Kongresi (11–15 Ekim 1976)* 2 (1981): 1359–1365.

37. BOA, C NF 32/1577; BOA, HAT 488 /23960; BOA, HAT 491/24036; Nesimi Yazıcı, "II. Mahmud Döneminde Menzilhaneler: 'Ref'-i Menzil Bedeli,'" in *İstanbul Üniversitesi Edebiyat Fakültesi Tarih Araştırma Merkezi Sultan II. Mahmud ve Reformları Semineri: 28–30 Haziran 1989* (Istanbul: Edebiyat Fakültesi Basımevi, 1990), 157–187; Halaçoğlu, *Osmanlılarda Ulaşım ve Haberleşme (Menziller) [Ottoman Transportation and Communications]*, 196–198. Also see BOA, C. DH 660; BOA, C. NF 464; BOA, C. NF 1769.

38. Anne Kolb, "Transport and Communication in the Roman State: The Cursus Publicus," in *Travel and Geography in the Roman Empire*, ed. Colin Adams and Ray Laurence (London: Routledge, 2001), 96–98; Igor de Rachewiltz, trans., *The Secret History of the Mongols: A Mongolian Epic Chronicle of the Thirteenth Century*, vol. 1 (Leiden: Brill, 2004), 214–215; Linnarsson, "Development of the Swedish Post," 35.

39. Yakup Bektas, "The Sultan's Messenger: Cultural Constructions of Ottoman Telegraphy, 1847–1880," *Technology and Culture* 41, no. 4 (2000): 669–696; Pauline Lewis, "Wired Ottomans: A Sociotechnical History of the Telegraph and the Modern Ottoman Empire, 1855–1911" (PhD diss., University of California, Los Angeles, 2018).

40. Heywood, "Two Firmans," 492.

CHAPTER 5. THE BOOKKEEPER

1. Uzunçarşılı, *Osmanlı devletinin merkez ve bahriye teşkilatı,* 348, 360, 372.

2. I thank Donna Landry for sharing this information with me and for helping me to understand the different practices of horseshoeing.

3. Although many of these must have been produced, I have found only a half dozen in the archives. Alpha is MAD 4030, Beta is KK 2742, Delta is MAD 3169, and Omicron is MAD 4106.

4. Douglas Howard, "Why Timars? Why Now? Ottoman Timars in the Light of Recent Historiography," *Turkish Historical Review* 8 (2017): 119–144.

5. For a useful summary of demographic studies, see Oktay Özel, "Population Changes in Ottoman Anatolia during the 16th and 17th Centuries: The 'Demographic Crisis' Reconsidered," *International Journal of Middle East Studies* 36, no. 2 (2004): 183–205. For a recent interdisciplinary effort between Ottoman defterology and archaeology, see Siriol Davies and Jack L. Davis, eds., *Between Venice and Istanbul: Colonial Landscapes in Early Modern Greece* (Princeton, NJ: American School of Classical Studies at Athens, 2007).

6. Colin Heywood, "Between Historical Myth and 'Mythohistory': The Limits of Ottoman History," *Byzantine and Modern Greek Studies* 12 (1988): 315–345; Halil Berktay, "The Search for the Peasant in Western and Turkish History/Historiography," in *New Approaches to State and Peasant in Ottoman History* (London: Frank Cass, 1992), 109–184; Heath Lowry, "The Ottoman Tahrir Defterleri as a Source for Social and Economic His-

tory: Pitfalls and Limitations," in *Türkische Wirtschafts-Und Sozialgeschichte (1071–1920)*, ed. Hans Georg Majer and Raoul Motika (Wiesbaden: Harrasowitz, 1995), 183–196.

7. Porter, *Trust in Numbers*; Daniel A. Stolz, "'Impossible to Provide an Accurate Estimate': The Interested Calculation of the Ottoman Public Debt, 1875–1881," *The British Journal for the History of Science* 55, no. 4 (2022): 477–493.

8. Anthony G. Hopwood, "On Trying to Study Accounting in the Contexts in Which It Operates," *Accounting, Organizations and Society* 8, no. 2 (1983): 287–305; Garry D. Carnegie, "The Present and Future of Accounting History," *Accounting, Auditing & Accountability Journal* 27, no. 8 (2014): 1241–1249; Alan Sangster, "The Genesis of Double Entry Bookkeeping," *The Accounting Review* 91, no. 1 (2016): 299–315; Angélica Vasconcelos, Alan Sangster, and Lúcia Lima Rodrigues, "Avoiding Whig Interpretations in Historical Research: An Illustrative Case Study," *Accounting, Auditing & Accountability Journal* 35, no. 6 (January 1, 2022): 1409.

9. "An analysis of the mind and world view of the compilers of tahrir registers remains a desideratum." Suraiya Faroqhi, *Approaching Ottoman History: An Introduction to the Sources* (New York: Cambridge University Press, 1999), 95.

10. Kathryn Burns, "Notaries, Truth, and Consequences," *American Historical Review* 110, no. 2 (2005): 350–379; Carolyn Dean, "Beyond Prescription: Notarial Doodles and Other Marks," *Word & Image* 25, no. 3 (2009): 293–316; Ann Laura Stoler, *Along the Archival Grain: Epistemic Anxieties and Colonial Common Sense* (Princeton, NJ: Princeton University Press, 2009); Paolo Sartori, "Authorized Lies: Colonial Agency and Legal Hybrids in Tashkent, c. 1881–1893," *Journal of the Economic and Social History of the Orient* 55 (2012): 688–717; Nandini Chatterjee, "Mahzar-Namas in the Mughal and British Empires: The Uses of an Indo-Islamic Legal Form," Comparative *Studies in Society and History* 58, no. 2 (2016): 379–406.

11. Geoffrey C. Bowker and Susan Leigh Star, *Sorting Things Out: Classification and Its Consequences* (Cambridge, MA: MIT Press, 1999), 3, 5, 9; Edward W. Constant II, "The Social Locus of Technological Practice: Community, System, or Organization?," in *The Social Construction of Technological Systems: New Directions in the Sociology and History of Technology,* ed. Wiebe E. Bijker, Thomas Parke Hughes, and Trevor Pinch (Cambridge, MA: MIT Press, 2012), 217–236.

12. Paul N. Edwards, *A Vast Machine: Computer Models, Climate Data, and the Politics of Global Warming* (Cambridge, MA: MIT Press, 2010), 17–20; Geoffrey C. Bowker, "Sustainable Knowledge Infrastructures," in *The Promise of Infrastructure,* ed. Nikhil Anand, Akhil Gupta, and Hannah Appel (Durham, NC: Duke University Press, 2018), 203.

13. Sometimes Edirne or Üsküdar post stations would be the first station of the route, not Istanbul.

14. In my counting, there were 64 pages in 1690 (BOA, MAD 4030) and 356 pages in the 1750s–1760s (BOA, MAD 4106).

15. There are other sorts of blank entries in BOA, MAD 4030, with idiosyncratic marginalia, but I have chosen to highlight the four most prevalent types here.

16. BOA, MAD 4030, p. 34; BOA, MAD 4030, p. 35; BOA, MAD 4030, p. 36; BOA, MAD 4030, p. 55—but Samakova and Pazarcık contain information; BOA, MAD 4030, p. 31.

17. BOA, MAD 4030, p. 46.

18. For example, see pp. 14–28 (5–12.jpg), 44–47 (18.jpg), 53–54 (20–21.jpg), and 58–60 (23–24.jpg) of BOA, MAD 4030. Sometimes, as in the Tolçi post station, the scribe merely scrawled "*Kifāyet miķdāri.*"

19. Heywood, "The Via Egnatia in the Ottoman Period," 133.

20. BOA, MAD 4030, p. 44; BOA, MAD 4030, p. 28; BOA, MAD 4030, p. 13; BOA, MAD 4030, p. 24; BOA, MAD 4030, pp. 16, 27, 28.

21. See BOA, MAD 4030, pp. 22–24, which shows the entries for Karacalar to Hacıköy.

22. An interesting comparison can be made with BOA, MAD 4108, another contemporary post station register with largely the same information but arranged in a different order. Note the resemblances, for example, between BOA, MAD 4108 2.jpg, and BOA, MAD 4030 17–18.jpg, as well as BOA, MAD 4108 3.jpg, and BOA, MAD 4030 19.jpg–21.jpg.

23. BOA, MAD 3844 (AH 1062 / 1651–1652 CE), 30, 46; BOA, MAD 2790 (AH 1082 / 1671–1672 CE), 31, 37–38, 46, 48, 102; MAD 3839 (AH 1097 / 1685–1686 CE), 25a, 29, 30b—31, 31a, 46, 57, 58–59 (also see 60.jpg and 61.jpg); BOA, MAD 2793 (AH 1103 / 1691–1692 CE), 41, 59, 66, 69–70, 74; BOA, MAD 2471 (AH 1104 / 1692–1693 CE), 26, 60–61, 64–65, 68, 72–73; BOA, MAD 3807 (AH 1108 / 1696–1697 CE), 30b, 31, 32b, 33a, 35a, 36b; BOA, MAD 3974 (AH 1110 / 1698–1699 CE), 26–27, 33–35, 53.

24. BOA, MAD 4030, p. 10. "*Eskişehir ķażāsı ahālīsi Edirne'de Dīvān-ı Hümāyūnuma ādam ve 'arżuḥāl gönderüb biz ķadīmden dört re's menzil bārgīri / Beslemek üzere Eskişehir menzile menzilcileri olub lakin iķtiżā ḥasebiyle menzil bārgīri ziyāde lāzım gelmeğin beynlerimizde mu'āvenat ile otuz / ķırķ re's bārgīr besler idi (?) lākin 'umūm üzere menzil bārgīri tertīb olunmağla bizden dahi tertīb olunmaķ üzere 'ināyet ricā ederiz / deyü i'lām eyledikleri ecilden ḥazīne-i 'āmiremde de maḥfūẓ olan menzil defterlerine naẓar olunduķta vech-i meşrūḥ üzere menzilci olduķları / mesṭūr ve naṣb olmağın imdi on re's menzil bārgīri beslemek üzere emr-i şerīf verile deyü fermān olub emr-i şerīf verildi. / Fī 4 C sene 1081* [October 19, 1670].

25. Some of these older sources were referred to by the Ottoman Turkish term *menzil defteri*, which is the same Ottoman Turkish name for the Comprehensive Post Station Register. However, the term *defter* could refer to records whether in the form of a bound register or of a simple paragraph written on a piece of paper. I suggest that the older sources referred to in Alpha (MAD 4030) were probably individual entries found in older Extraordinary Tax Registers, petitions, and other documents. Nejat Göyünç, "Defter," in *Türkiye Diyanet Vakfı İslam ansiklopedisi: Darüssaade-Dulkadıroğulları* (Üsküdar: Türkiye Diyanet Vakfı, İslâm Ansiklopedisi Genel Müdürlüğü, 1994), TDV İslâm Araştırmaları Merkezi. This phenomenon of using the same name for substantially different documents has precedents in the Ottoman world. In a similar vein, just because the same term *menzil defterleri* was used to refer to records prior to the 1670s and to fiscal registers from the 1690s does not indicate that they had to be substantially the same thing. See Molly Greene, "An Islamic Experiment? Ottoman Land Policy on Crete," *Mediterranean Historical Review* 11, no. 1 (1996): 70–72. See also Rifaʿat Abou El Haj, "Power and Social Order: The Uses of the Kanun," in *The Ottoman City and Its Parts: Urban Structure and Social Order,* ed. Irene A. Bierman, Rifaʿat Abou El Haj, and Donald Preziosi (New York: Aristide D. Caratzas, 1991), 91.

26. BOA, MAD 4030, p. 44.

27. BOA, MAD 4030, p. 9; firman dated AH 1057 / 1647 CE.

28. An imperial order declared that all 16.5 *hānes* (a kind of household unit for tax purposes) were to be exempted (*mu'āf*) from paying taxes. Instead, the villagers would be designated (*ta'yīn*) as "post station masters" (*menzilci*). According to two orders recorded in BOA, MAD 4030 and dated to 1643 CE, and pertaining to Tokat and Sivas post stations, 15 houses (*evler*) made up one taxable unit (*hāne*). BOA, MAD 4030, pp. 23, 26. See also Darling, *Revenue-Raising and Legitimacy*, 106–108.

29. BOA, MAD 4030, p. 17.

30. BOA, MAD 4030, p. 16. However, when villagers complained in a petition that the usual taxes had become insufficient to cover post station costs, an imperial order (*firmān*) dated to 1685 sanctioned the increase of *bedel-i nüzül* taxpayers by 26 households (*hāne*).

31. This was 268 *kile*s of wheat and 1,340 *kile*s of barley; 1 *kile* or bushel is roughly equivalent to 80½ pounds (36.5 kilograms). BOA, MAD 4030, p. 48.

32. BOA, KK 2742, p. 2.

33. Halil Sahillioğlu, "Dördüncü Marad'ın Bağdat Seferi Menzilnamesi—Bağdat Seferi Harp Jurnalı" *Belgeler* 2, nos. 3–4 (1965): 1–35.

34. BOA, MAD 4030, p. 45.

35. BOA, MAD 4030, p. 56. Other examples include Uzuncaabad (p. 54) and Divane Ali post station (p. 45).

36. This most probably referred to these expenses of equipment and salaries. BOA, KK 2742 4.jpg.

37. BOA, MAD 3169, 68.jpg–70.jpg. In addition, bookkeepers recorded several copies of orders issued to the judge of Galata relating to the contributions of bakeries to a local endowment and to Üsküdar post station. These orders concern lapses in the bakeries' payments to the endowments; their owners were accused of giving excuses (*'ilet ve bahāne*) for not fulfilling their financial obligations. This suggests that the funding structure for post stations overlapped and relied on existing contribution structures for endowments.

38. (Delta) BOA, MAD 3169, 70.jpg, p. 147. The bakery and aid were first mentioned in (Beta) BOA, KK 2742, 29.jpg, p. 60. For more information about the emergence and later legalization of the *imdād*, see Yavuz Cezar, *Osmanlı Maliyesinde Bunalım ve Değişim Dönemi* (Istanbul: Alan Yayıncılık, 1986), 53–60.

39. An *ocaklık* is a sum of money, usually derived from an assortment of tax revenues, that is assigned by the state to financially support a public function, such as the salaries of military personnel. Such funds were also used to finance other post stations in the empire. For a useful overview of this institution, see Michael Robert Hickok, *Ottoman Military Administration in Eighteenth-Century Bosnia* (Leiden: Brill, 1997), 42–53.

CHAPTER 6. THE POSTMASTER

1. ISAM, Adana Şer'iyye Sicilleri 39, 54.jpg as cited in Yağcı, "Hac ve Askeri Yol Üzerinde Bir Menzil: Adana Menzili [A Post Station on the Haj and Military Road: Adana Station]," 67.

2. Debts were a normal part of household realities in the early modern world; the average individual in Europe left behind unpaid debts upon their death, with some that exceeded the value of their property. Frank Trentmann, *Empire of Things: How We Became a World of*

Consumers, from the Fifteenth Century to the Twenty-First (New York: HarperCollins, 2016), 407. Trentmann's sources include Craig Muldrew, *The Economy of Obligation: The Culture of Credit and Social Relations in Early Modern England* (Basingstoke, UK: Palgrave, 1998), 68, 117–118; and Sheilagh Ogilvie, Markus Küpker, and Janine Maegraith, "Household Debt in Early Modern Germany: Evidence from Personal Inventories," *The Journal of Economic History* 72, no. 1 (2012): 134–167.

3. BOA, MAD 10492 8.jpg and D.MKF.d.31174 (17-02-1221); Çetin, *Ulak yol durak* [*Courier Stops*], 74–81; Baş, "XVIII–XIX Yüzyılın İlk Yarısında Gebze Menzilhanesi [The Gebze Post Station in the Eighteenth and First Half of the Nineteenth Century]," 106.

4. For the original use of the metaphor of thickening governance, see Greene, *The Edinburgh History of the Greeks, 1453 to 1774*, 182.

5. BOA, MAD 3169.

6. Güneş, "XVIII Yüzyılın İkinci Yarısında Osmanlı Menzil Teşkilatı ve Karahisar-ı Sahib Menzilleri [The Karahisar Post Station and the Ottoman Post Station System in the Second Half of the Eighteenth Century]," 40.

7. Yağcı, "Hac ve Askeri Yol Üzerinde Bir Menzil: Adana Menzili [A Post Station on the Haj and Military Road: Adana Station]," 70. For other examples, see Colin Heywood, "Some Turkish Archival Sources for the History of the Menzilhane Network in Rumeli during the Eighteenth Century (Notes and Documents on the Ottoman Ulak, I)," *Boğaziçi Üniversitesi Dergisi: Beşeri Bilimler-Humanities* 4–5 (July 1976): 44; Güneş, "XVIII Yüzyılın İkinci Yarısında Osmanlı Menzil Teşkilatı ve Karahisar-ı Sahib Menzilleri [The Karahisar Post Station and the Ottoman Post Station System in the Second Half of the Eighteenth Century]," 38; and Çetin, *Ulak yol durak* [*Courier Stops*], 208–209.

8. Arslan, son of Karz, undertook the office of the postmaster in Istanbul for a period of three years in the 1660s. Coşkun Yılmaz, ed., *İstanbul Kadı Sicilleri 51 İstanbul Mahkemesi 10 Numaralı Sicil (H. 1072–1073 / M. 1661–1663)*, trans. Yılmaz Karaca and Mehmet Akman, vol. 51 (Istanbul: Kültür AŞ, 2019), 284, 1035.

   Two non-Muslims (*zimmî*) Arslan, son of Gazal, and Toros, son of Haçok, were confirmed jointly as postmasters in Silivri in May 1676. Coşkun Yılmaz, ed., *İstanbul Kadı Sicilleri İstanbul Mahkemesi 18 Numaralı Sicil (H. 1086–1087 / M. 1675–1676)*, trans. Mehmet Akman (Istanbul: Türkiye Diyanet Vakfı İslâm Araştırmaları Merkezi (İSAM), 2010), 224, 776.

   BOA, AE.SAMD.III 57/5718 (AH 1133 / 1721 CE); BOA, AE.SABH.I 301/20227 (AH 1203 / 1789 CE) In 1694, the post stations of Istanbul, Silivri, and Edirne were managed by a *zimmî* named Sefer. Heywood, "Some Turkish Archival Sources for the History of the Menzilhane Network in Rumeli during the Eighteenth," 44; Colin Heywood, "The Ottoman Menzilhane and Ulak System in Rumeli in the 18th Century," in *Türkiye'nin Sosyal ve Ekonomik Tarihi, 1071–1920: Birinci Uluslararası Türkiye'nin Sosyal ve Ekonomik Tarihi Kongresi Tebliğleri*, ed. Osman Okyar and Halil İnalcık (Ankara: Meteksan Şirketi, 1980), 182; BOA, KK 2742, 2.jpg.

   BOA, AE.SAMD.III 189/18257 (AH 1121 / 1709 CE); BOA, AE.SAMD.III 1/84 (AH 1141 / 1729 CE); BOA, AE.SAMD.III 5/423 (AH 1139 / 1727 CE).

9. BOA, IE. ML 29/2810 (AH 1100 / 1689 CE); I thank Luke Yarbrough, Thomas Carlson, and George Kiraz for helping me to read these names and to identify their religious affiliations.

10. BOA, C.NF 11/520 (AH 1197 / 1783 CE). I thank Hratch Kestenian for identifying Krikor as Armenian and suggesting the Western Armenian transliteration.

11. BOA, AE.SAMD.III 64/6452 (AH 1136 /1724 CE).

12. BOA, AE.SAMD.III 5/423 (AH 1139 / 1727 CE); BOA, AE.SMHD.I 133/9839 (AH 1145 / 1733 CE) I thank Christine Philliou for identifying Christos as Greek Orthodox.

13. Ronald C. Jennings, "Kadi, Court, and Legal Procedure in 17th c. Ottoman Kayseri: The Kadi and the Legal System," *Studia Islamica* 48 (1978): 137–138. For a different view suggesting that Ottoman judges could also be locally appointed, see Leslie P. Peirce, *Morality Tales: Law and Gender in the Ottoman Court of Aintab* (Berkeley: University of California Press, 2003), 95.

14. Anastasopoulos, "Imperial Institutions and Local Communities: Ottoman Karaferye, 1758–1774," 29; Canbakal, "Vows as Contract," 109.

15. While these entries are sometimes titled *hüccet* by judicial scribes in the court records, the language of these entries also bears some similarities to *temessük* entries. Both terms may be translated into English as "deeds." See, for example, ISAM, KŞS 56, p. 1 (140.jpg) (June 18, 1743 / 25 R 1156); Ekrem Tak, "Diplomatik Bilimi Bakımından XVI.-XVII. Yüzyıl Kadı Sicilleri ve Bu Sicillerin Ihtiva Ettiği Belge Türlerinin Form Özellikleri ve Tanımlanması / 16th–17th Century Kadı Registers According to the Rules of Diplomatics and the Description and Structural Characteristics of the Document Types Recorded in These Registers" (PhD diss., Marmara University, 2009), 252–256.

16. For a critique of the overlooked administrative role of the Ottoman judge within the historiography, see Boğaç A. Ergene, *Local Court, Provincial Society, and Justice in the Ottoman Empire: Legal Practice and Dispute Resolution in Çankırı and Kastamonu (1652–1744)* (Leiden: Brill, 2003), 44.

17. İSAM, Amasya Şer'iye Sicilleri [Amasya Court Register] (hereafter AŞS) 19, varak 80 or p. 151 (AH 1100–1101 / 1688–1690 CE).

18. Even the longer entries from Amasya's judicial records, which may have spanned two to three pages, did not stipulate the postmaster's extensive duties and responsibilities, as seen in other entries such as those from Konya cited in notes 23 and 24. İSAM, AŞS 19, varak 80 or p. 151 (AH 1100–1101 / 1688–1690 CE); İSAM, AŞS 18, varak 75 (AH 1092–1093 / 1681–1682 CE); İSAM, AŞS 21, varak 2 or p. 1 (AH 1106–1107 / 1694–1696 CE); İSAM, AŞS 35, varak 2 or p. 1 (AH 1142–1144 / 1729–1732 CE); İSAM, AŞS 45, varak 2 or p. 1 (AH 1163–1164 / 1749–1751 CE); İSAM, AŞS 46, varak 9 (AH 1163–1168 / 1749–1755 CE); İSAM, AŞS 55, varak 2–3 (AH 1191–1192 / 1776–1777 CE).

19. Oriental Department of the National Library of St. Cyril and Methodius, Sofia, Vidin Şer'iye Sicilleri [Vidin Court Records] S8, p. 2.

20. This record uses an Arabic modification of the Ottoman Turkish term for courier in the plural: *al-ūlākāt* (as opposed to the Turkish plural, *ulaklar*). ISAM, HŞS 246, Defter 42, varak 169 (no. 655). This document is damaged and a part of it is missing.

21. Both terms originally came from the Arabic language.

22. ISAM, HŞS 246, Defter 40, varak 8 (p. 21) (1680–5 CE/ AH 1091–6); Fahad Ahmad Bishara, *A Sea of Debt: Law and Economic Life in the Western Indian Ocean, 1780–1950* (Cambridge: Cambridge University Press, 2017), 19–20, 58–59.

23. ISAM, KŞS 37, p. 5/148.jpg (7 Cemaziyelevvel 1103 / January 26, 1692); Transliterated in Sak, *37 Konya*, 5–6; also cited and used in Çetin, *Ulak yol durak* [*Courier Stops*], 206–207.

24. ISAM, KŞS 37, p. 3/149.jpg (10 Cemaziyelevvel 1103 / January 29, 1692); transliterated in Sak, *37 Konya*, 2–4; also cited and used in Çetin, *Ulak yol durak [Courier Stops]*, 206–207.

25. The term used here in the document is *icāreleri,* meaning "their renting of [the post station]."

26. İSAM, KŞS 37, p. 3 (10 Cemaziyelevvel 1103 / January 19, 1692); transliterated in Sak, *37 Konya*, 2–4; also cited and used in Çetin, *Ulak yol durak [Courier Stops]*, 206–207.

27. A typical description of a Fee Waiver Register in the digital catalogue of the Presidential Ottoman Archive in Istanbul reads as follows: "[this is a] register that shows the costs of the horses that were given to the couriers who passed through the Niš post station [*Niş menzilinden gelip geçen ulaklara verilen beygirlerin ücretlerini gösterir defter*]." BOA, D.MKF.d. 28800 (AH 1143).

28. Uzunçarşılı, *Osmanlı devletinin merkez ve bahriye teşkilatı*, 348, 372. In the modern cataloguing of these documents, however, not all of these Fee Waiver Registers ended up in the Mevkufat Kalemi (D.MKF) section of the Ottoman archives. The Ali Emiri (AE), Muallim Cevdet (C), and Kamil Kepeci (KK) sections of the archive also contain large numbers of these registers as they had been catalogued by the eponymous archivists, but a note is usually made in the description that these documents belonged to the Mevkufat Kalemi.

29. BOA, C.NF 25/1224. (1756–1758 CE / AH 1169–1171).

30. BOA, C.NF 25/1224, 5 (5.jpg). (1756–1758 CE / AH 1169–1171).

31. BOA, MAD 4106, 142 (55.jpg).

32. For Homs, see BOA, MAD 4106, 184–187 (76–7.jpg); for Mosul, BOA, MAD 4106, 254–256 (151–2.jpg); for Ereğli, BOA, MAD 4106, 100–105 (40–2.jpg); for Merzifon, BOA, MAD 4106, 288–292 (121–3.jpg).

33. BOA, D.MKF.d. 27918; MAD 3217, 21.jpg.

34. ISAM, AŞS 48, 39–40.jpg.

35. Wolfgang Behringer, "Communications Revolutions: A Historiographical Concept," *German History* 24, no. 3 (2006): 339.

36. Márton Vér and Isván Zimonyi, "Insights from the Inside: An Old Uyghur Register and the Administration of the Mongol Empire," in *Altaic and Chagatay Lectures. Studies in Honour of Éva Kincses-Nagy* (Szeged: Department of Altaistics, University of Szeged, 2021), 435–448; Márton Vér, *Old Uyghur Documents Concerning the Postal System of the Mongol Empire* (Turnhout: Brepols Publishers, 2019), 145–155.

37. Chelsea Zi Wang, "Dilemmas of Empire: Movement, Communication, and Information Management in Ming China, 1368–1644" (PhD diss., Columbia University, 2017), 40–51.

38. BOA, C.NF 13/602 (H.1271).

39. Güneş, "XVIII Yüzyılın İkinci Yarısında Osmanlı Menzil Teşkilatı ve Karahisar-ı Sahib Menzilleri [The Karahisar Post Station and the Ottoman Post Station System in the Second Half of the Eighteenth Century]"; Baş, "XVIII–XIX Yüzyılın İlk Yarısında Gebze Menzilhanesi [The Gebze Post Station in the Eighteenth and First Half of the Nineteenth Century]"; Çetin, *Ulak yol durak [Courier Stops]*.

40. Colin Heywood discusses these same classes of documents in detail but refers to them using different terminology. What I call Fee Waiver Registers (*inʿāmāt defteri*), he refers

to as *menzil defterleri,* and what I call the Comprehensive Post Station Registers (*menzil defteri*), he refers to as *niẓām defteri.* Heywood, "Some Turkish Archival Sources for the History of the Menzilhane Network in Rumeli during the Eighteenth," 42–44, 47. Methodologically, what I do here bears similarities to Takamatsu Yoichi's work. However, while he maps the administrative relations among a wide range of documents, I focus only on two types of documents. Yoichi Takamatsu, "Formation and Custody of the Ottoman Archives During the Pre-Tanzimat Period," *Memoirs of the Research Department of the Toyo Bunko* 64 (2006): 125–148.

41. Ed and G. Baer, "Iltizām," *Encyclopaedia of Islam,* 2nd ed., ed. P. Bearman et al.; F. Müge Göçek, "Mültezim," in *Encyclopaedia of Islam,* 2nd ed., ed. P. Bearman et al.

42. The term *taʿahhüd* has been used in reference to other voluntary undertakings of public duty, such as the appointment of guardians for orphans, see Hülya Canbakal, *Society and Politics in an Ottoman Town: ʿAyntāb in the 17th Century* (Leiden: Brill, 2007), 152–153; Wilkins, *Forging Urban Solidarities: Ottoman Aleppo 1640–1700,* 49; Redhouse, *New Redhouse Turkish-English Dictionary,* 1070.

43. Redhouse, *New Redhouse Turkish-English Dictionary,* 287. See also Michael Ursinus, "The Transformation of the Ottoman Fiscal Regime c. 1600–1850," in *The Ottoman World,* ed. Christine Woodhead (London: Routledge, 2011), 423–435.

44. Molly Greene, "An Islamic Experiment? Ottoman Land Policy on Crete," *Mediterranean Historical Review* 11, no. 1 (1996): 70–72; see also Rifaʿat Abou El Haj, "Power and Social Order: The Uses of the Kanun," in *The Ottoman City and Its Parts: Urban Structure and Social Order,* ed. Irene A. Bierman, Rifaʿat Abou El Haj, and Donald Preziosi (New York: Aristide D. Caratzas, 1991), 91.

45. Eugene N. White, "From Privatized to Government-Administered Tax Collection: Tax Farming in Eighteenth-Century France," *Economic History Review* 57, no. 4 (2004): 636–663; William Beik, *Absolutism and Society in Seventeenth-Century France: State Power and Provincial Aristocracy in Languedoc* (Cambridge: Cambridge University Press, 1985), 245–278; Ray Huang, *Taxation and Governmental Finance in Sixteenth-Century Ming China* (Cambridge: Cambridge University Press, 1974), 36–37; Susan Mann, *Local Merchants and the Chinese Bureaucracy, 1750–1950* (Stanford, CA: Stanford University Press, 1987); Irfan Habib, *The Agrarian System of Mughal India, 1556–1707* (Bombay: Asia Publishing House, 1963); John F. Richards, *Mughal Administration in Golconda* (Oxford: Clarendon Press, 1975), 141, 169; Muzaffar Alam, *The Crisis of Empire in Mughal North India: Awadh and the Punjab, 1707–1748,* 2nd ed. (New Delhi: Oxford University Press, 2013), 40–42; Farhat Hasan, *State and Locality in Mughal India: Power Relations in Western India, c. 1572–1730* (Cambridge: Cambridge University Press, 2004), 110–128; Paul Bushkovitch, "Taxation, Tax Farming, and Merchants in Sixteenth-Century Russia," *Slavic Review* 37, no. 3 (1978): 381–398; Hong Lysa, "The Tax Farming System in the Early Bangkok Period," *Journal of Southeast Asian Studies* 14, no. 2 (1983): 379–399; Max Weber, *Economy and Society: An Outline of Interpretive Sociology* (Berkeley: University of California Press, 1978), 965–966.

46. ISAM, HŞS 246, Defter 40, varak 8 (p. 21) (1680–5 CE / AH 1091–6); *Diyarbekir şerʿiyye sicilleri: Âmid mahkemesi Volume 2* [*Diyarbekir Judicial Records Vol. 2*], vol. 2 (Diyarbakır: Dicle Üniversitesi İlahiyat Fakültesi Yayınları, 2013), 149, 275; C. E. Bosworth and H. Gerber, "Muḳāṭaʿa," in Bearman et al., *Encyclopaedia of Islam,* 2nd ed.

47. See, for example, Amy Singer, *Palestinian Peasants and Ottoman Officials: Rural Administration around Sixteenth-Century Jerusalem* (Cambridge: Cambridge University Press, 1994), 74.

48. For details on how this functioned in the Dutch Republic, see Wantje Fritschy, *Public Finance of the Dutch Republic in Comparative Perspective: The Viability of an Early Modern Federal State (1570s–1795)* (Leiden: Brill, 2017), 339.

49. Stefan Winter, *The Shiites of Lebanon under Ottoman Rule, 1516–1788* (Cambridge: Cambridge University Press, 2010), 42.

50. Joseph Matuz, "Contributions to the Ottoman Institution of the Iltizam," *Osmanlı Araştırmaları* 11 (1991): 237–249.

51. For details on the sales and slaughter taxes on sheep in Istanbul, see Greenwood, "Istanbul's Meat Provisioning," 44–46.

52. Admittedly, the consequent hereditary nature of these contracts diminished the capability of the state to continue to extract wealth in later years. Mehmet Genç, "Osmanlı Maliyesinde Malikane Sistemi [The Ottoman Malikane System]," in *Osmanlı İmparatorluğunda Devlet ve Ekonomi [State and Economy in the Ottoman Empire]* (Istanbul: Ötüken Neşriyat A.Ş., 2000), 99–152; Ariel Salzmann, "Measures of Empire: Tax Farmers and the Ottoman Ancien Regime, 1695–1807" (PhD diss., Columbia University, 1995); Salzmann, "Ancien Regime Revisited."

53. Salzmann, "Measures of Empire," 147, 149–150, 414–415. There was another Esma Sultan (1778–1848), who was the daughter, not sister, of Abdülhamid I, and who also appears to have held substantial life-term tax farms. See Yaycıoğlu, *Partners of the Empire,* 146.

54. Salzmann, "Measures of Empire," 149, 414–415; Ariel Salzmann, "The Old Regime and the Ottoman Middle East," in *The Ottoman World,* ed. Christine Woodhead (London: Routledge, 2011), 417–419.

55. Yaycıoğlu, *Partners of the Empire,* 65–115.

56. Yaycıoğlu, *Partners of the Empire,* 68–78.

57. Canbakal, *Society and Politics in an Ottoman Town,* 127–130; İbrahim Solak and İzzet Sak, *38 numaralı Konya şer'iye sicili, 1103–1104 /1692–1693: Transkripsiyon ve dizin [Konya Judicial Records Vol. 38]* (Konya, Turkey: Selçuk Üniversitesi Basımevi, 2014), 348–349; Ibrahim Solak and İzzet Sak, *39 numaralı Konya ser'iye sicili (1113–1113 /1701–1702) (transkripsiyon ve dizin) [Konya Judicial Records Vol. 39]* (Konya, Turkey: Palet Yayınları, 2015), 25–26; İzzet Sak and İbrahim Solak, *53 Numaralı Konya Şer'iye Sicili (1148–1149/1736–1737): Transkripsiyon ve Dizin [Konya Judicial Records Vol. 53]* (Konya, Turkey: Selçuk Üniversitesi Basımevi, 2014), 327.

    Solak and Sak, *38 Konya,* 103; İzzet Sak and Cemal Çetin, *45 numaralı Konya şer'iye sicili, 1126–1127/1714–1715: transkripsiyon ve dizin [Konya Judicial Records Vol. 45]* (Konya, Turkey: Selçuklu Belediyesi Kültür Yayınları, 2008), 51–52; Solak and Sak, *38 Konya,* 103; Solak and Sak, *39 Konya,* 24.

58. Sak and Solak, *53 Konya,* 706–707; Marlene Kurz, *Das Sicill aus Skopje: kritische Edition und Kommentierung des einzigen vollständig erhaltenen Kadiamtsregisterbandes (Sicill) aus Üsküb (Skopje)* (Wiesbaden: Harrassowitz, 2003), 232–239.

59. Solak and Sak, *38 Konya,* 237, 260–261, 278–279.

60. Çetin, *Ulak yol durak [Courier Stops],* 207–209.

61. Yaycıoğlu, *Partners of the Empire*, 68, 76–77.

62. For more information on Ottoman craftsmen and guilds, see Faroqhi, "Ottoman Craftsmen."

CHAPTER 7. THE VILLAGER

1. Three petitions were submitted in the latter half of the month of (Zilhicce) in AH 1190, while one petition (Geyve) was submitted on the fifth day of the following month. BOA, C. NF 29/1411, 6.jpg (AH 17 Zilhicce 1190), 8.jpg (AH End Zilhicce 1190), 10.jpg (AH 27 Zilhicce 1190), and 12.jpg (AH 5 Muharrem 1191).

2. BOA, C. NF 29/1411, 16.jpg (also filed as C.NF 29/1411/3).

3. There were four muezzins, all called Mehmed.

4. There are some cases which may qualify as exceptions. In the fourteenth century, villagers inhabiting some lands were exempt from provisioning couriers thanks to privileges granted by sultans. In these cases, these privileges were granted to an individual but affected the collective status of other villager-inhabitants in that locality. V. L Ménage and Colin Imber, *Ottoman Historical Documents: The Institutions of an Empire* (Edinburgh: Edinburgh University Press, 2021), 150–151.

5. Büssow and Meier, "Ottoman Corporatism, Eighteenth to Twentieth Centuries," 87. On discussions regarding communalization that prefigure corporatism, see Inalcık, "Centralization and Decentralization in Ottoman Administration"; Canbakal, "Vows as Contract." For other examples of collective organizing, see Eleni Gara, "Çuha for the Janissaries—Velençe for the Poor: Competition for Raw Material and Workforce between Salonica and Veria, 1600–1650," in *Crafts and Craftsmen of the Middle East: Fashioning the Individual in the Muslim Mediterranean*, ed. Suraiya Faroqhi and Randi Deguilhem, The Islamic Mediterranean, vol. 4 (London: I. B. Tauris, 2005), 121–152.

6. For the original use of the metaphor of thickening governance, see Greene, *The Edinburgh History of the Greeks, 1453 to 1774*, 182.

7. Günalan, Canatar, and Akman, *İstanbul Kadı Sicilleri Üsküdar Mahkemesi 84 Numaralı Sicil*, 662, 672.

8. Günalan, Canatar, and Akman, *İstanbul Kadı Sicilleri Üsküdar Mahkemesi 84 Numaralı Sicil*, 664, 672.

9. Günalan, Canatar, and Akman, *İstanbul Kadı Sicilleri Üsküdar Mahkemesi 84 Numaralı Sicil*, 659, 662, 663, 669, 671, 672, 675.

10. Eventually, a man named Ahmed Agha appeared in court together with Mehmed and testified to Mehmed's innocence. The night when the horse was stolen, Ahmed Agha said, he and Mehmed were in a mountain post (*derbend*) in a valley between Ovacık and Akbıyık. While there, a Greek Orthodox Christian (*rum*) appeared riding the aforementioned horse with two saddles and one bridle. The saddle and bridle were brought to the court and given to a man named Cook Şirmerd (Asçı Şirmerd) for safekeeping. Mehmed was acquitted of any wrongdoing. Rifat Günalan et al., eds., *İstanbul kadı sicilleri Üsküdar mahkemesi 2 numaralı sicil (H. 924–927 / M. 1518–1521)*, İstanbul kadı sicilleri / [editör Coşkun Yılmaz] 2 (Istanbul: İslam Araştırmaları Merkezi, 2010), 134, 601.

11. Kenan Yıldız and Recep Ahıshalı, eds., *İstanbul Kadı Sicilleri Üsküdar Mahkemesi 9 Numaralı Sicil (H. 940–942 / M. 1534–1536)* (Istanbul: İSAM Yayınları, 2010), 207, 527.

12. James Grehan, "The Mysterious Power of Words: Language, Law, and Culture in Ottoman Damascus (17th–18th Centuries)," *Journal of Social History* 37, no. 4 (2004): 991–1015.

13. See also "kefâlet-i müteselsile" in Yetkin, *Ege'de Eşkıyalar,* 55.

14. Abdullah Saydam, "Kamu Hizmeti Yaptırma ve Suçu Önleme Yöntemi Olarak Osmanlılarda Kefâlet Usûlü," *Tarih ve Toplum* 164 (1997): 4–12; Nalan Turna, "Pandemonium and Order: Suretyship, Surveillance, and Taxation in Early Nineteenth-Century Istanbul," *New Perspectives on Turkey* 39 (2008): 167–189.

15. Anh Nga Longva, *Walls Built on Sand: Migration, Exclusion, and Society in Kuwait* (Boulder, CO: Routledge, 1997), 78–79. See also Neha Vora, *Impossible Citizens: Dubai's Indian Diaspora* (Durham, NC: Duke University Press, 2013); Attiya Ahmad, *Everyday Conversions: Islam, Domestic Work, and South Asian Migrant Women in Kuwait* (Durham, NC: Duke University Press, 2017).

16. Ronald C. Jennings, "Loans and Credit in Early 17th-Century Ottoman Judicial Records: The Sharia Court of Anatolian Kayseri," *Journal of the Economic and Social History of the Orient* 16, no. 2/3 (1973): 187; Ronald C. Jennings, "Women in Early 17th-Century Ottoman Judicial Records: The Sharia Court of Anatolian Kayseri," *Journal of the Economic and Social History of the Orient* 18, no. 1 (1975): 103; Ronald C. Jennings, "Zimmis (Non-Muslims) in Early 17th-Century Ottoman Judicial Records: The Sharia Court of Anatolian Kayseri," *Journal of the Economic and Social History of the Orient* 21, no. 3 (1978): 273–274; Canbakal, *Society and Politics in an Ottoman Town,* 171–172; Haim Gerber, "The Muslim Law of Partnerships in Ottoman Court Records," *Studia Islamica* 53 (1981): 113.

17. These credible individuals were not just men. Ronald Jennings has shown instances where women could be guarantors for loans taken by other parties, even without putting down any collateral. Jennings, "Women in Early 17th-Century Ottoman Judicial Records," 103.

18. See also Peirce, *Morality Tales,* 90; Canbakal, *Society and Politics in an Ottoman Town,* 123–149, 171–172; Özer Ergenç, "Osmanlı Şehrindeki Mahalle'nin İşlev ve Nitelikleri Üzerine," *Osmanlı Araştırmaları* 4 (1984): 73; H. Yunus Apaydın, "Kefalet," in *Türkiye Diyanet Vakfı İslam Ansiklopedisi: Kastilya-Kile,* vol. 25 (Üsküdar: Türkiye Diyanet Vakfı, İslâm Ansiklopedisi Genel Müdürlüğü, 2002), 168–177.

19. ISAM, AŞS 22, varak 39 (AH 1109 / 1698 CE).

20. For another example, see ISAM, AŞS 42, varak 32 (AH 1155 / 1742 CE).

21. This decree was addressed to all the officials situated along the left arm (*kol*) in Rumelia. GRGSA IAM OJC 001 F59, 18.jpg.

22. "*imdi Anaṭolınuñ ṣol ḳolunda vāḳi' menāzilden muḫtel-i niẓām olanlarıñ ma'rifet-i şer' ve cümle ittifāḳla mu'temedün-'aleyh kefilleri intihāb olunaraḳ kārgüzār ve mücerrebü'l-eṭvār menzilcileri naṣb ve ta'yīn.*" ISAM, AŞS 54, varak 74 (AH 1189 / 1775 CE).

23. This decree was addressed to all the post stations situated along the left arm (*kol*) of Anatolia. ISAM, AŞS 54, varak 74 (AH 1189 / 1775 CE).

24. ISAM, AŞS 54, varak 99 (AH 1190 / 1776 CE); ISAM, AŞS 55, varak 31–32 (AH 1190 / 1777 CE).

25. See Canbakal, "Vows as Contract," 111–112.

26. St. Cyril and Methodius National Library in Sofia, Bulgaria, F13188. (AH 1097 / 1686 CE).

27. For example, see the explanation given in another court record GRGSA IAM OJC 001 F51, 67.jpg (full decree on 67–68.jpg): "*ḥālā mevsim-i bahār olmaḳ ḥasebiyle ağaçlar yapraḳlanub ṭağlarda ḥaydūd ve sā'ir eşḳıyālar [var]*."

28. "*Bağdād ve Erzurum ve Kürdistān ṭaraflarından gelen ulaḳ ve Ḳasṭamonu üzerinden gelen ulaḳ cümleden bizim ḳażāmıza uğrarlar.*"

29. Uğur Ünal and Murat Cebecioğlu, *91 numaralı Mühimme defteri (H.1056 / M.1646–1647): özet, çeviri yazı, tıpkıbasım* (Istanbul: T. C. Başbakanlık Devlet Arşivleri Genel Müdürlüğü, 2015), 244.

30. Koç, "149 Numaralı Mühimme Defteri (1155–1156 / 1742–1743)," 305–307.

31. St. Cyril and Methodius National Library in Sofia, Bulgaria, F13167. (AH 1104 / 1693 CE).

32. For more information on *ḥāṣ* lands, please see Orhonlu, Cengiz, "Khāṣṣ," in *Encyclopaedia of Islam*, 2nd ed., ed. P. Bearman et al.

33. AE. SMST. II 89/9550 (AH 1109 / 1698 CE).

34. For a study of such direct appeals in the case of Ottoman Egypt, see James Baldwin, "Petitioning the Sultan in Ottoman Egypt," *Bulletin of the School of Oriental and African Studies* 75, no. 3 (2012): 499–524.

35. For other similar examples, see TS.MA.e 697 / 64 3 R 1227. Canbakal shares several examples from seventeenth-century Ayntab. Unfortunately, I was unable to locate the original source because of the discrepancy in cataloguing system that Canbakal used and the system currently in use in ISAM. Canbakal, *Society and Politics in an Ottoman Town*, 175.

36. See also Eunjeong Yi, *Guild Dynamics in Seventeenth-Century Istanbul: Fluidity and Leverage*, The Ottoman Empire and Its Heritage, vol. 27 (Leiden: Brill, 2004), 198.

37. Greenwood, "Istanbul's Meat Provisioning," 87.

38. Although the literal translation of *kefālet defteri* would be "suretyship register," scholars working on this subject tend to use the term "inspection register." Başaran, *Selim III, Social Control and Policing in Istanbul at the End of the Eighteenth Century,* especially 106–167; Cengiz Kırlı, "The Struggle over Space: Coffeehouses of Ottoman Istanbul, 1780–1845" (PhD diss., State University of New York at Binghamton, 2000), especially 67–111; Cengiz Kırlı, "A Profile of the Labor Force in Early Nineteenth-Century Istanbul," *International Labor and Working-Class History* 60 (2001): 125–140.

39. Morita, "Between Hostility and Hospitality."

40. Nina Ergin, "The Albanian Tellâk Connection: Labor Migration to the Hammams of 18th-Century Istanbul, Based on the 1752 Istanbul Hamâmları Defterleri," *Turcica* 43 (2011): 231–256.

41. Masayuki Ueno, "In Pursuit of Laicized Urban Administration: The Muhtar System in Istanbul and Ottoman Attitudes toward Non-Muslim Religious Authorities in the Nineteenth Century," *International Journal of Middle East Studies* 54, no. 2 (2022): 302–318.

42. These stations were İznikmid, Şapanca, Ḥendeḳ, Düzce, Bolu, Gerede, Bayındır, Karacalar, Karacaviran, Hacı Hamza, Osmancık, Merzifon, Amasya, Turhal, Tokat, Sivas, Divriği, Kangal, Hasan Çelebi, Hasan Patrik, Malatya, İzoli, Kars, and two others (as yet undeciphered place-names). MAD 10492, 225.jpg and 226.jpg.

43. In some cases, the judge from one locality composed deeds for multiple villages. The judge from Malatya, for instance, penned deeds for the villages of Hasan Çelebi, Hasan Patrik, Malatya, and İzoli. Each entry for these locations ended with *Malaṭya ḳāżīsiniñ verdiği ḥüccet-i şer'iyyedir*. MAD 10492, 226.jpg.

44. The title of this section of the fiscal register tells us that "these are summaries of the deeds and reports collected by Hasan Agha who was assigned [to the task of] post station administration." "*Menāzil niẓāmına me'mūr dergāh-ı 'ālī gediklü müteferriḳalarından Ḥasan Ağanıñ getürdiği ḥucec ve 'arżlarıñ hulāṣasıdır*." BOA, MAD 10492, 225.jpg.

45. BOA, MAD 10492, 220.jpg, 222.jpg, and 223.jpg. (AH 1138–1139 / 1726–1727 CE).

46. Although I was unable to locate collective contracts for non-Anatolian provinces in the archives, it is highly probable that similar public oaths were written up as deeds for other regions of the empire.

47. The full text is transliterated here and may be found on BOA, MAD 10492, 225.jpg. "*Bu āna değin menzil-i mezbūrden mürūr-i 'ubūr iden ulaḳlar meks̱ olunmayub ba'de'l-yevm dahi meks̱ ve te'hīr itdirilmemek üzere ahālī-i ḳażā birbirlerine tekeffül eylediklerine ḥüccet-i şer'iyye virdiklerin ḳāżısı 'arż ider*."

48. Canbakal, *Society and Politics in an Ottoman Town*, 93.

49. BOA, MAD 10492, 220.jpg. "*Menzilhānede tuvānā bārgīrler ḥāżır ve ulaḳlar meks̱ itmeyüb bu vecih üzere niẓām ve menzilcileriñ müddeti tamāmında (?) kifāyet miḳdārı bārgīrler tedārik ideriz deyü ahālī-i ḳażā birbirlerine kefīl olub ta'ahhüd ve ḥüccet virdiklerine Aḳşehir ḳāżısı 'arż eder*."

50. BOA, MAD 10492, 220.jpg. "*Lefke ḳaṣabası ahālīleri meclis-i şer'de menzilhānemizde olan bārgīrleriñ bir miḳdārı ta'dīl ile niẓām ve ba'de'l-yevm mürūr ve 'ubūr iden ulaḳları meks̱ itdirmemek üzere cümle ma'rifetiyle niẓām virildüği ḥüccet-i şer'iyyedir*."

51. BOA, MAD 10492, 223.jpg.

52. See, for instance, BOA, MAD 10492 222.jpg and 223.jpg.

53. On face-to-face communication in Ottoman corporatist villages, see Büssow and Meier, "Ottoman Corporatism, Eighteenth to Twentieth Centuries," 94. As scholars ranging from archaeologists to organizational scientists have observed, much of the organizational work of large states involves political communities that are so dispersed and large that they cannot convene in person. William Honeychurch, "Alternative Complexities: The Archaeology of Pastoral Nomadic States," *Journal of Archaeological Research* 22, no. 4 (2014): 284.

54. The full text is transliterated here and may be found on BOA, MAD 10492, 225.jpg. "*Menzilkeşān ve re'āyāları yüz yirmi miḳdāri menzil bārgīri tedārik ve her birleri evlerinde beslyüb mürūr iden ulaḳlara żarūret çekdirilmeyüb menzil-i mezbūri vech-i meşrūḥ üzere işledüp iki ṭarafında olan menzilleriñ bārgīrlerini menzil-i āhara geçurmeziz deyü tekeffül eylediklerine virdikleri bir ḳıṭa ḥüccet-i şer'iyyedir*."

   The key phrase here, "*iki ṭarafında olan menzilleriñ bārgīrlerini menzil-i āhara geçurmeziz*," may be understood as "we will never let the horses pass from one menzil to the next," with "*geçurmeziz*" being the negative form of the aorist in the first person plural. I thank Morita Madoka for confirming my interpretation and clarifying the grammar at work here.

55. Jane Myers, *Horse Safe: A Complete Guide to Equine Safety* (Collingwood, Australia: Landlinks Press, 2005), 10.

56. Elke Hartmann, Eva Søndergaard, and Linda J. Keeling, "Keeping Horses in Groups: A Review," *Applied Animal Behaviour Science* 136 (2012): 77–87. For more information, see also L. J. Keeling et al., "Injury Incidence, Reactivity and Ease of Handling of Horses Kept in Groups: A Matched Case Control Study in Four Nordic Countries," *Applied Animal Behaviour Science* 185 (2016): 59–65.

57. Honeychurch, "Alternative Complexities," 289.

58. Daniel G. Bates, *Nomads and Farmers; A Study of the Yörük of Southeastern Turkey* (Ann Arbor: Museum of Anthropology, University of Michigan, 1973), 123–124.

59. Kenneth Shapiro and Margo DeMello, "The State of Human-Animal Studies," *Society and Animals* 18 (2010): 307–3018; William Honeychurch and Cheryl A. Makarewicz, "The Archaeology of Pastoral Nomadism," *Annual Review of Anthropology* 45 (2016): 341–359; Gala Argent, "Do the Clothes Make the Horse? Relationality, Roles, and Statuses in Iron Age Inner Asia," *World Archaeology* 42, no. 2 (2010): 157–174.

60. For more information on pastoralists and animals, see Nora Barakat, "Marginal Actors? The Role of Bedouin in the Ottoman Administration of Animals as Property in the District of Salt, 1870–1912," *Journal of the Economic and Social History of the Orient* 58, no. 1/2 (2015): 105–134; Reşat Kasaba, *A Moveable Empire: Ottoman Nomads, Migrants, and Refugees* (Seattle: University of Washington Press, 2009), 87–88.

61. Elinor Ostrom, *Governing the Commons: The Evolution of Institutions for Collective Action* (Cambridge: Cambridge University Press, 2017), 30.

62. Ostrom, *Governing the Commons*, 18.

63. Ostrom, *Governing the Commons*, 216.

64. I have encountered Registers of Apportionment (*tevzî' defterleri*) that mentioned postal expenses in my research but I need to spend more time with them to fully grasp their logic. For now, please see the excellent work of Sevinç Küçükoğlu (I thank Canay Şahin for informing me of this article.) L. Sevinç Küçükoğlu, "New Fiscal Actors to Control Provincial Expenditures at the End of 18th Century," *Osmanlı Araştırmaları* 54 (2019): 241–76; see also Evgenij Radušev, "Les Dépenses locales dans l'Empire Ottoman au XVIIIe siècle (Selon les Données de Registres de Cadi de Ruse, Vidin et Sofia)," *Études Balkaniques* 16, no. 3 (1980): 87–88. For more information on these registers, see Halil Inalcık, "Military and Fiscal Transformation in the Ottoman Empire, 1600–1700," *Archivum Ottomanicum* 6 (1980): 335–337; Michael Ursinus, "The Transformation of the Ottoman Fiscal Regime c. 1600–1850," in *The Ottoman World,* ed. Christine Woodhead (London: Routledge, 2011), 423–435; Yannis Spyropoulos, Stefanos Poulios, and Antonis Anastasopoulos, "Çiftliks, Landed Elites, and Tax Allocation in Eighteenth-Century Ottoman Veroia," *European Journal of Turkish Studies: Social Sciences on Contemporary Turkey* 30 (2020): 1–35. For examples of how the commons has been studied in other fields, see Alvaro Carvajal Castro, "Early Medieval Commons? Or How the History of Early Medieval Europe Could Benefit from a Necessary Conversation: The Case from NW Iberia," *International Journal of the Commons* 15, no. 1 (2021): 338–353; M. Laborda Peman and T. De Moor, "History and the Commons: A Necessary Conversation," *International Journal of the Commons* 10, no. 2 (2016): 517–528; Tina L. Thurston and Manuel Fernández-Götz, eds., *Power from Below in Premodern Societies: The Dynamics of Political Complexity in the Archaeological Record* (Cambridge: Cambridge University Press, 2021).

65. Büssow and Meier, "Ottoman Corporatism, Eighteenth to Twentieth Centuries," 94–95; Astrid Meier, "The Materiality of Ottoman Water Administration in Eighteenth-Century Rural Damascus," in *Landscapes of the Islamic World: Archaeology, History, and Ethnography,* ed. Stephen McPhillips and Paul D. Wordsworth (Philadelphia: University of Pennsylvania Press, 2016), 19–33.

66. Phanish Puranam and Dorthe Døjbak Håkonsson, "Valve's Way," *Journal of Organization Design (Aarhus)* 4, no. 2 (2015): 2–4; Vivianna Fang He and Phanish Puranam, "Collaborative Conflict Management," SSRN Scholarly Paper (Rochester, NY, November 16, 2021), 8.

67. Meeker, *A Nation of Empire,* 149, 152, 203, 389. Meeker's discussion of Ottoman social structure deserves longer and closer examination than I have been able to accomplish here. I have been thinking through his insights alongside David Faure's in *Emperor and Ancestor: State and Lineage in South China* (Stanford, CA: Stanford University Press, 2007) and Martin Van Bruinessen's *Agha, Shaikh, and State: The Social and Political Structures of Kurdistan* (London: Zed Books, 1992).

68. Here is another potential example: the late geographer Michael E. Bonine studied irrigation systems in 1970s Iran and uncovered remarkable sophistication in water-sharing arrangements. Michael E. Bonine, "From Qanāt to Kort: Traditional Irrigation Terminology and Practices in Central Iran," *Iran* 20 (1982): 145–159.

69. J. Stephen Lansing, *Perfect Order: Recognizing Complexity in Bali* (Princeton, NJ: Princeton University Press, 2006), 87; J. Stephen Lansing, *Priests and Programmers: Technologies of Power in the Engineered Landscape of Bali* (Princeton, NJ: Princeton University Press, 2007), xx–xxi, 14.

70. Melanie Mitchell, *Complexity: A Guided Tour* (New York: Oxford University Press, 2009), 13. For further reading, see Mitchel Resnick, *Turtles, Termites, and Traffic Jams: Explorations in Massively Parallel Microworlds* (Cambridge, MA: MIT Press, 2001); Steven Johnson, *Emergence: The Connected Lives of Ants, Brains, Cities, and Software* (New York: Scribner, 2001); Steven Strogatz, *Sync: How Order Emerges from Chaos in the Universe, Nature and Daily Life* (New York: Hyperion, 2003); Nicholas A. Christakis and James H. Fowler, *Connected: The Surprising Power of Our Social Networks and How They Shape Our Lives* (New York: Little, Brown, 2009). Although not yet a rigorous notion, some neural networks that underlie the deep learning technology developed by Geoffrey Hinton are believed to exhibit characteristics of "emergent computation." Melanie Mitchell, email, December 29, 2020. For a good introduction to AI technology, its recent history, and its implementation in the business world, see Kai-Fu Lee, *AI Superpowers: China, Silicon Valley and the New World Order* (Boston: Houghton Mifflin Harcourt, 2018).

71. Mehdi Moussaïd, Dirk Helbing, and Guy Theraulaz, "How Simple Rules Determine Pedestrian Behavior and Crowd Disasters," *Proceedings of the National Academy of Sciences* 108, no. 17 (2011): 6884–6888.

72. Lansing, *Perfect Order,* 88–121.

73. Lansing, *Perfect Order,* 88–89, 121.

74. Ostrom, *Governing the Commons,* 29.

75. Greene, *The Edinburgh History of the Greeks, 1453 to 1774,* chap. 7; Winter, *A History of the ʿAlawis,* chap. 4.

76. Winter, *A History of the 'Alawis,* 120. Consider also the anthropologist Martin Van Bruinessen's observation about Kurdish tribes, albeit in a different time frame. "The conception of the tribe as a creation of the state, rather than as a social and political formation preceding it, gradually imposed itself on me in the course of my fieldwork, and more forcefully during my subsequent reading of historical sources. Certain tribal confederacies that I came across seemed to owe their very existence to deliberate interventions by one of the large states." Martin Van Bruinessen, *Agha, Shaikh, and State: The Social and Political Structures of Kurdistan* (London: Zed Books, 1992), 134.

77. Deborah Boucoyannis presents a fascinating synthetic study that will surely provoke many new research questions. Deborah Boucoyannis, *Kings as Judges: Power, Justice, and the Origins of Parliaments* (Cambridge: Cambridge University Press, 2021), 22, 283–285.

CHAPTER 8. BREAKDOWN

1. This is a fictionalized imagining taken from a few sources: a copy of an imperial order dated to 1763 found in BOA, MAD 4106, 3.jpg, as well as a series of imperial decrees regarding the shortages of horses at post stations examined later in this chapter.

2. Graham and Thrift, "Out of Order," 2–8; Russell and Vinsel, "After Innovation, Turn to Maintenance."

3. Stephen Graham, "When Infrastructures Fail," in *Disrupted Cities: When Infrastructure Fails,* ed. Stephen Graham (New York: Routledge, 2010), 3.

4. Paul N. Edwards et al., "AHR Conversation: Historical Perspectives on the Circulation of Information," *American Historical Review* 116, no. 5 (2011): 1409. Also consider the following in a pre-industrial context: Charles Perrow, *Normal Accidents: Living with High-Risk Technologies* (Princeton, NJ: Princeton University Press, 1999).

5. It probably took a few years of lag time for this two-tier courier order system to be implemented; it is unlikely that Mustafa II's decrees of 1696 were immediately implemented.

6. See, for instance, BOA, AE SABH I 118/7977 and BOA, AE SABH I 129 / 8688.

7. I follow Edhem Eldem in translating *peşin* as "immediate payment." Edhem Eldem, *French Trade in Istanbul in the Eighteenth Century* (Leiden: Brill, 1999), 132.

8. Heywood, "The Evolution of the Courier Order (Ulak Hükmi) in Ottoman Chancery Practice (Fifteenth to Eighteenth Centuries)," 291; Çetin, *Ulak yol durak [Courier Stops],* 216–217.

9. BOA, MAD 4106, 1–3.jpg. For a deep dive into the technical details of this system, see Choon Hwee Koh, "An Ottoman Liquidity Crunch: Immediate and Deferred Payments at Post Stations (Menzilhane), 1713–1763," *Turcica* 54 (2023): 355–375.

10. It is not clear how these numbers were arrived at; the internal memo does not explain them, but simply states them. BOA, MAD 4106, 2.jpg; Koh, "An Ottoman Liquidity Crunch."

11. On decision-making in the Ottoman Empire, see Caesar E. Farah, ed., *Decision Making and Change in the Ottoman Empire* (Kirksville: Thomas Jefferson University Press at Northeast Missouri State University, 1993).

12. BOA, MAD 4106, 2.jpg, line 14: *"akçe yetişdirmeğe ṭāḳat getürilmeyeceğinden nāşî";* lines 16–17: *"hazīne-i 'āmireden küll-i yevm akçe virilmek hasāretinden ve verilecek akçeniñ tedāriki meşaḳḳatından vāreste."*

13. Açıkel, "Osmanlı Ulak-Menzilhane Sistemi Çerçevesinde Tokat Menzilhanesi (1690–1840) [Tokat Post Station in the Framework of the Ottoman Postal System, 1690–1840]," 7.

14. BOA, MAD 4106, 3.jpg.

15. Koh, "An Ottoman Liquidity Crunch."

16. James Mahoney and Kathleen Thelen, "A Theory of Gradual Institutional Change," in *Explaining Institutional Change: Ambiguity, Agency, and Power,* ed. James Mahoney and Kathleen Thelen (Cambridge: Cambridge University Press, 2009), 17; Jacob S. Hacker, Paul Pierson, and Kathleen Thelen, "Drift and Conversion: Hidden Faces of Institutional Change," in *Advances in Comparative-Historical Analysis,* ed. James Mahoney and Kathleen Thelen (Cambridge: Cambridge University Press, 2015), 184. I thank Kathleen Thelen for kindly corresponding with me on this issue and giving me the confidence to apply the concept of institutional drift to an eighteenth-century context (March–April 2022).

17. After reading and rereading these imperial orders for five years, it is still not clear to me why bureaucrats were unable to return to the fee waiver system.

18. Elena Frangakis-Syrett, "The Ottoman Monetary System in the Second Half of the Eighteenth and in the Early Nineteenth Centuries: A View from the Provinces," in *Trade and Money: The Ottoman Economy in the Eighteenth and Early Nineteenth Centuries* (Istanbul: Isis Press, 2007), 75–96; Elena Frangakis-Syrett, "Money Shortage and the Ottoman Economy: Late Seventeenth to the Late Eighteenth Centuries," in *Trade and Money,* 49–73.

19. Stanford J. Shaw, *The Budget of Ottoman Egypt 1005–1006 / 1596–1597* (The Hague: Mouton, 1968), 10; Shaw, *The Financial and Administrative Organization and Development of Ottoman Egypt, 1517–1798,* 202–208.

20. Aysel Yıldız, *Crisis and Rebellion in the Ottoman Empire: The Downfall of a Sultan in the Age of Revolution* (London: I. B. Tauris, 2017), 57–59, 63–64.

21. Francesca Trivellato, *The Promise and Peril of Credit: What a Forgotten Legend about Jews and Finance Tells Us about the Making of European Commercial Society* (Princeton, NJ: Princeton University Press, 2019), 2–3.

22. André Raymond, *Artisans et commerçants au Caire au XVIIIe siècle. Tome I* (Damas, Syria: Presses de l'Ifpo, 1973), 298–301; Eldem, *French Trade in Istanbul in the Eighteenth Century,* 113–47; Matthias B. Lehmann, *Emissaries from the Holy Land: The Sephardic Diaspora and the Practice of Pan-Judaism in the Eighteenth Century* (Stanford, CA: Stanford University Press, 2014), 43, 66–69.

23. Eldem, *French Trade in Istanbul in the Eighteenth Century,* 133.

24. Mehmet Genç, "Esham: İç Borçlanma," in *Osmanlı İmparatorluğunda Devlet ve Ekonomi* [*State and Economy in the Ottoman Empire*] (Istanbul: Ötüken Neşriyat A.Ş., 2000), 186–195.

25. Ali Akyıldız, *Para Pul Oldu: Osmanlı'da Kağıt Para, Maliye ve Toplum* (Istanbul: İletişim, 2003), 35–40; Ali Coşkun Tunçer and Şevket Pamuk, "Ottoman Empire: From 1830 to 1914," in *South-Eastern European Monetary and Economic Statistics from the Nineteenth Century to World War II* (Athens, Sofia, Bucharest, and Vienna: Bank of Greece, Bulgarian National Bank, National Bank of Romania, and Oesterreichische Nationalbank, 2014), 171–197.

26. Roderic H. Davison, *Essays in Ottoman and Turkish History, 1774–1923: The Impact of the West* (Austin: University of Texas Press, 1990), 60, 63–68; Akyıldız, *Para Pul Oldu,* 48–54.

27. Akinobu Kuroda, "Concurrent but Non-integrable Currency Circuits: Complementary Relationships among Monies in Modern China and Other Regions," *Financial History Review* 15, no. 1 (2008): 19. And see Debendra Bijoy Mitra, *Monetary System in the Bengal Presidency, 1757–1835* (Calcutta: K. P. Bagchi, 1991), 81: "A striking feature of the monetary system of Bengal was the use of different types of coins for particular commodities. . . . In Jessore, trade in rice and other grains was carried on in siccas, but cloth, ghee, and oil were purchased in Murshidabad sonauts whereas French arcots were used for salt trade."

28. Akinobu Kuroda, *A Global History of Money* (New York: Routledge, 2020), 60; Jane I. Guyer, *Marginal Gains: Monetary Transactions in Atlantic Africa* (Chicago: University of Chicago Press, 2004), 37.

29. Davison, *Essays,* 63–68; Akinobu Kuroda, *A Global History of Money* (New York: Routledge, 2020), 10–14, 58–62. Also see Akinobu Kuroda, "What Is the Complementarity among Monies? An Introductory Note," *Financial History Review* 15, no. 1 (2008): 7–15.

30. Matthew Mosca, *From Frontier Policy to Foreign Policy: The Question of India and the Transformation of Geopolitics in Qing China* (Stanford, CA: Stanford University Press, 2013).

31. I thank Bin Wong for first raising the question of horse supply.

32. William G. Clarence-Smith, "Animal Power as a Factor in Ottoman Military Decline, 1683–1918," Paper presented at the "War Horses of the World" conference, SOAS, University of London, May 3, 2014. The primary sources are accounts by Luigi Marsigli and Baron de Tott.

33. Peyssonnel, *Traité sur le commerce de la Mer Noire,* 2:339; Alan W. Fisher, *A Precarious Balance: Conflict, Trade, And Diplomacy on The Russian Ottoman Frontier* (Istanbul: Isis Press, 1999), 181.

34. Edward Louis Keenan, "Muscovy and Kazan: Some Introductory Remarks on the Patterns of Steppe Diplomacy," *Slavic Review* 26, no. 4 (1967): 552.

35. Halil İnalcık, *Sources and Studies on the Ottoman Black Sea,* vol. 1: *The Customs Register of Caffa, 1487–1490,* Studies in Ottoman Documents Pertaining to Ukraine and the Black Sea Countries, vol. 2 (Cambridge, MA: Distributed by Harvard University Press for the Ukrainian Research Institute, Harvard University, 1996), 32, 60, 99–108, 133–139; Peyssonnel, *Traité sur le commerce de la Mer Noire,* 2:27, 49, 51; Stella Ghervas, "The Black Sea," in *Oceanic Histories,* ed. David Armitage, Alison Bashford, and Sujit Sivasundaram (New York: Cambridge University Press, 2017), 238–239.

36. Peyssonnel, *Traité sur le commerce de la Mer Noire,* 2:170; Clarence-Smith, "Animal Power as a Factor in Ottoman Military Decline, 1683–1918."

37. Clarence-Smith, "Animal Power as a Factor in Ottoman Military Decline, 1683–1918."

38. Kasaba, *A Moveable Empire,* 87.

39. Clarence-Smith, "Animal Power as a Factor in Ottoman Military Decline, 1683–1918."

40. Irène Beldiceanu-Steinherr, "A Propos des Tribus Atčeken (XVe–XVIe Siècles)," *Journal of the Economic and Social History of the Orient* 30, no. 2 (1987): 159; Hala Mundhir

Fattah, *The Politics of Regional Trade in Iraq, Arabia, and the Gulf, 1745–1900* (Albany: State University of New York Press, 1997), 163.

41. Clarence-Smith, " "Animal Power as a Factor in Ottoman Military Decline, 1683–1918."

42. Ottoman military histories rarely tell us about how horses were procured, which appears to be an honest reflection of available archival records on the subject. Sometimes we learn more about horsemen (cavalry) than horses. Murphey, *Ottoman Warfare, 1500–1700;* Ágoston, *The Last Muslim Conquest;* Virginia H. Aksan, *The Ottomans 1700–1923: An Empire Besieged,* 2nd ed. (Abingdon, UK: Routledge, Taylor and Francis, 2022); The Ottomans certainly had the language to describe horses, but such descriptions are found in manuscripts about horses, rather than in administrative documents about horses. Tülay Artan, "Ahmed I and 'Tuhfet'ül-Mülûk ve's-Selâtin'': A Period Manuscript on Horses, Horsemanship and Hunting," in *Animals and People in the Ottoman Empire,* ed. Suraiya Faroqhi (Istanbul: Eren, 2010), 256.

43. These were called *yaddasht-i tashiha* (memorandum of verification), *daghnama* (branding certificate), and *saqtinama* (death certificate), respectively. I examined original copies of each in the Telangana State Archives (Hyderabad) in the summer of 2016. Interested researchers will find that they appear frequently in all volumes of M. A. Nayeem et al., eds., *Mughal Documents: Catalogue of Aurangzeb's Reign* (Hyderabad: State Archives, Govt. of Andhra Pradesh, 1980). Also see Yusuf Husain Khan, *Selected Documents of Aurangzeb's Reign, 1659–1706 A. D* (Central Records Office, Government of Andhra Pradesh, 1958).

44. H. G. Creel, "The Role of the Horse in Chinese History," *The American Historical Review* 70, no. 3 (1965): 669; Morris Rossabi, "The Tea and Horse Trade with Inner Asia during the Ming," *The Journal of Asian Studies* 4, no. 2 (1970): 138. See also Paul J. Smith, *Taxing Heaven's Storehouse: Horses, Bureaucrats, and the Destruction of the Sichuan Tea Industry 1074–1224* (Cambridge, MA: Harvard University Asia Center, 1991).

45. Morris Rossabi, "The Tea and Horse Trade with Inner Asia during the Ming," *The Journal of Asian Studies* 4, no. 2 (1970): 136–168.

46. BOA, MAD 8464, p. 9, 4.jpg; ISAM, KŞS 47 250–252.jpg; İzzet Sak, *47 Numaralı Konya Şer'iye Sicili, 1128–1129/1716–1717: Transkripsiyon ve Dizin* [*Konya Judicial Records Vol. 47*] (Konya, Istanbul: Tablet, 2006), 574–555.

47. ISAM, AŞS 24, 26.jpg (AH 1114 / 1702 CE).

48. ISAM, AŞS 29, 13.jpg. (AH 1131 / 1719 CE).

49. ISAM, AŞS 31, 103.jpg (AH 1135 / 1723 CE).

50. *Diyarbekir şer'iyye sicilleri: Âmid mahkemesi Volume 2* [*Diyarbekir Judicial Records Vol. 2*] (Diyarbakır, Turkey: Dicle Üniversitesi İlahiyat Fakültesi Yayınları, 2013), 218. For another example, see GRGSA IAM OJC 001 F127, 38–39.jpg (AH 1188 / 1774 CE).

51. Keywords: *tama'-ı hâm, cerr-i nef' ve celb-i menfa'atlar.* BOA, C.NF. 9/411.

52. These 22 stations were Turhal, Tokat, Kangal, Alacahan, Hasan Çelebi, Hasan Patrik (Hısnıpatrik), Malatya, İzoli, Harput, Ergani, Diyarbekir, Mardin, Nusaybin, Cizre, Musul, Karakuş, Erbil (Andava), Altınsuyu bridge, Kirkük, Tavuk, Tuzhurmatı, and Kefri. Keywords: *kendü havâlarına harc u sarf. Diyarbekir şer'iyye sicilleri: Âmid mahkemesi Volume 2* [*Diyarbekir Judicial Records Vol. 2*] (Diyarbakır, Turkey: Dicle Üniversitesi İlahiyat Fakültesi Yayınları, 2013, 207–209. ISAM, AŞS 37, 22–23.jpg (AH 1146 / 1733 CE).

53. Keywords: *müflis, kallāş;* ISAM, AŞS 41, 40.jpg. (AH 1153 / 1740 CE).

54. For an overview of these wars, see Donald Quataert, *The Ottoman Empire, 1700–1922* (Cambridge: Cambridge University Press, 2005), 37–41.

55. Recep Karacakaya, İsmail Yücedağ, and Nazım Yılmaz, eds., *Safranbolu Şer'iyye Sicili 2116 Numaralı Defter* (Istanbul: Safranbolu Belediye Başkanlığı, 2013), 46–51; *Diyarbekir şer'iyye sicilleri: Âmid mahkemesi Volume 1* [*Diyarbekir Judicial Records Vol. 1*] (Diyarbakır, Turkey: Dicle Üniversitesi İlahiyat Fakültesi Yayınları, 2013), 410–411.

56. ISAM, AŞS 72, 14–15.jpg (AH 1241 / 1826 CE); *Diyarbekir şer'iyye sicilleri,* 381–385; ISAM, DŞS 4, 43.jpg (AH 1246 / 1830 CE).

57. Şevket Pamuk, "Prices in the Ottoman Empire, 1469–1914," *International Journal of Middle East Studies* 36 (2004): 455.

58. Keywords: *ḥazele, kār-ı mekr.* GRGSA IAM OJC 001 F160, 48.jpg (AH 1207 / 1793 CE); this is the same as Kurz, *Das Sicill aus Skopje,* 499–501.

59. While camels were typically used for long-distance transportation of bulky goods, horses were also included in caravans. Suraiya Faroqhi, "Camels, Wagons, and the Ottoman State in the Sixteenth and Seventeenth Centuries," *International Journal of Middle East Studies* 14, no. 4 (1982): 532–533.

60. ISAM, DŞS 1B, 13–14.jpg (AH 1209 / 1794 CE) (Term for merchandise: *tüccār mālı*); GRGSA IAM OJC 001 F154, 18.jpg (AH 1201 / 1787 CE); AŞS 71, 38.jpg (AH 1245 / 1830 CE) (Term for merchandise: *tüccār yükü*); ISAM, DŞS 1B, 68.jpg (AH 1207 / 1793 CE).

61. BOA, HAT 491/ 24036 (AH 1250 / 1834–5 CE); 1 vükkiye = 1.2828 kg, Walther Hinz, *İslam'da Ölçü Sistemleri,* trans. Açar Sevim (Istanbul: Edebiyat Fakültesi Basımevi, 1990), 30, 44.

62. ISAM, DŞS 1B, 37–38.jpg (AH 1210 / 1796 CE). See also BOA, HAT 665 / 32327F, and 1411–57441. For condemnations of fake couriers wearing courier costumes, see BOA, C. AS 1085–47843; BOA, C.DH 42/2079; and BOA, C.DH 33/1628.

63. GRGSA IAM OJC 001 F167, 15–16.jpg (AH 1210 / 1795 CE); *"voyvoda ve mültezim maķūleleriniñ ve sā'ir o mişillüleriñ teba'a ve ḫidmetkārları."*

64. BOA, MVL 6–22.

65. GRGSA IAM OJC 001 F160, 48.jpg (AH 1207 / 1793 CE); this is the same as Kurz, *Das Sicill aus Skopje,* 499–501.

66. Mehmet Genç, "L'Économie Ottomane et La Guerre au XVIIIème Siècle," *Turcica* 27 (1995): 177–196; Elena Frangakis-Syrett, "The Economic Activities of Ottoman and Western Communities in Eighteenth-Century Izmir," *Oriente Moderno* 79, no. 1 (1999): 11–26; Şevket Pamuk, *A Monetary History of the Ottoman Empire* (Cambridge: Cambridge University Press, 2000), 159.

67. On interlinked goods such as sugar, tea, coffee, chocolate, and maté that are better understood collectively rather than individually, in terms of a "hot beverages" market that ushered in new sociabilities that recursively intensified their demand, see Frank Trentmann, *Empire of Things: How We Became a World of Consumers, from the Fifteenth Century to the Twenty-First* (New York: HarperCollins, 2016), 78–94.

68. For a sweeping overview of the changing economic geography of the Mediterranean circa 1550–1650, see Faruk Tabak, *The Waning of the Mediterranean, 1550–1870* (Baltimore,

MD: Johns Hopkins University Press, 2008), 175–185; Masters, *Origins of Western Economic Dominance*, 27–28; McGowan, *Economic Life in Ottoman Europe*, 15–16.

69. McGowan, *Economic Life in Ottoman Europe*, 20; Carter, "Commerce of the Dubrovnik Republic," 389–390; Faroqhi, "The Early History of the Balkan Fairs," 50.

70. Stoianovich, "The Conquering Balkan Orthodox Merchant," 261–262, 281–282, 287, 299, 301; Masters, *Origins of Western Economic Dominance*, 174–175.

71. Doumani, *Rediscovering Palestine*; Faroqhi, "Ottoman Craftsmen," 90; Genç, "Ottoman Industry in the Eighteenth Century," 64, 67.

72. Philippe Pétriat, "Caravan Trade in the Late Ottoman Empire: The 'Aqil Network and the Institutionalization of Overland Trade," *Journal of the Economic and Social History of the Orient* 63 (2020): 44 (n11), 51–52.

73. André Raymond, "Soldiers in Trade: The Case of Ottoman Cairo," *British Journal of Middle Eastern Studies* 18, no. 1 (1991): 16–37; Tezcan, *The Second Ottoman Empire*, 199–212.

74. Metin Kunt, *The Sultan's Servants: The Transformation of Ottoman Provincial Government, 1550–1650* (New York: Columbia University Press, 1983), chap. 5.

75. Doumani, *Rediscovering Palestine*, chap. 5; Aysel Yıldız and İrfan Kokdaş, "Peasantry in a Well-Protected Domain: Wallachian Peasantry and Muslim Çiftlik/Kışlaks under Ottoman Rule," *Journal of Balkan and Near Eastern Studies* 22, no. 1 (2020): 180–184.

76. Tezcan, *The Second Ottoman Empire*, 36–40; Marios Hadjianastasis, "Crossing the Line in the Sand: Regional Officials, Monopolisation of State Power and 'Rebellion.' The Case of Mehmed Ağa Boyacıoğlu in Cyprus, 1685–1690," *Turkish Historical Review* 2, no. 2 (2011): 155–176; Sophia Laiou, "Economic Networks in the Eastern Mediterranean: Kâtiboğlu Mehmed Efendi of Izmir and His Christian Partner," *Mediterranean Historical Review* 34, no. 2 (2019): 181–194.

77. Metin Kunt, "Derviş Mehmed Paşa, Vezir and Entrepreneur: A Study in Ottoman Political Economic Theory and Practice," *Turcica* 9 (1977): 211.

78. Menchinger, *The First of the Modern Ottomans*, 180–182.

79. ISAM, AŞS 19, p. 138, 74.jpg (AH 1101 / 1690 CE).

80. Heywood, "Two Firmans," 488–491.

81. BOA, MAD 3179, s.3 or 1.jpg; GRGSA IAM OJC 001, F145, 75–76.jpg (AH 1197 / 1783 CE); GRGSA IAM OJC 001 F154, 15.jpg (AH 1201 / 1787 CE); GRGSA IAM OJC 001 F154, 18.jpg (AH 1201 / 1787 CE); GRGSA IAM OJC 001 F157, 6–7.jpg (AH 1204 / 1789 CE); AŞS 72, 14–15.jpg (AH 1241 / 1826 CE); ISAM, DŞS 4, 43.jpg (AH 1246 / 1830 CE)

82. "*kendü maṣāliḥler ile īyāb ve ẕehāb iden yolcı ve mültezim ve tüccār maḳūlelerini.*" GRGSA IAM OJC 001 F154, 18.jpg. (AH 1201 / 1787 CE).

83. Two other decrees, dated to 1783 and 1787, associated those who obtained horses while carrying out their own affairs with officials who obtained more horses than their authentic courier orders actually allowed them to have, without punishing either group. GRGSA IAM OJC 001 F145, 75–76.jpg (AH 1197 / 1783 CE); F154, 15.jpg. (AH 1201 / 1787 CE).

84. "*Maṣāliḥ-i mühimme-i devlet-i ʿāliyye ile āmedşüd idenlere mahṣūṣ ve münḥaṣır iken giderek maṣlaḥatlı maṣlaḥatsız ve belki serserī ve tüccāra varıncaya ḳadar herkes birer taḳrīb inʿām menzil aḥkāmı aḥẕiyle ve baʿzen dahi menzil aḥkāmı olmayarak ṭaşralarda şunuñ*

bunuñ ḥimāyesiyle cümlesi menzile süvār olmaḳda olduḳlarından menzilleriñ maṣārifi dahi refte refte çoğallaraḳ." BOA, HAT 491 / 24036. (AH 1250 / 1834 CE).

85. I borrowed these images and phrases from Andrew Shryock, who wrote, "So, you isolated this recurrent pattern of missing horses. It's there from 1690 to 1833. But you also show how an entire world is changing around this pattern." Andrew Shryock, "Meticulous Sleuthing" *Comparative Studies in Society and History Forum,* September 12 2023, https://sites.lsa.umich.edu/cssh/2023/09/12/meticulous-sleuthing-a-conversation -with-koh-choon-hwee/.

86. William Sewell Jr. was expanding on Caroline Arni's point about the reconceptualization of the fetus in late eighteenth-century physiology, when "what had been the unborn became the not-yet-born." Emmanuel Akyeampong et al., "AHR Conversation: Explaining Historical Change; or, The Lost History of Causes," *American Historical Review* 120, no. 4 (2015): 1407, 1409–1410.

87. Mosca, *From Frontier Policy to Foreign Policy,* 2–3, 19, 127–160, 187–189. On the concept of the "information order," see Bayly, *Empire and Information: Intelligence Gathering and Social Communication in India, 1780–1870,* 3–6, chapter 9.

88. Findley, *Bureaucratic Reform in the Ottoman Empire,* 85, 88, 90, 96, 110.

89. Daniel Kahneman, Jack L. Knetsch, and Richard H. Thaler, "Anomalies: The Endowment Effect, Loss Aversion, and Status Quo Bias," *Journal of Economic Perspectives* 5, no. 1 (1991): 193–206. For examples of how such cognitive biases operate in public policies today, see Donald Low, ed., *Behavioural Economics and Policy Design: Examples from Singapore* (Singapore: World Scientific, 2011). For an analogy with grade inflation in the United States, on why individuals might persist in collectively doing something that is "wrong" and why organizations might not take action, see Andrew Shryock, "Meticulous Sleuthing," *Comparative Studies in Society and History Forum* (University of Michigan), September 12, 2023, https://sites.lsa.umich.edu/cssh/2023/09/12/meticulous-sleuthing-a-conversation -with-koh-choon-hwee/. The statement that the postal system cost only 1 percent of the empire's annual budget is based on information gleaned from Mehmet Genç and Erol Özvar, eds., *Osmanlı Maliyesi Kurumlar ve Bütçeler 1* (Istanbul: Osmanlı Bankası Arşiv ve Araştırma Merkezi, 2006), and discussion with Professor Ali Coşkun Tunçer. We hope to have something published in the next few years that will strengthen this claim.

90. Açıkel, "Osmanlı Ulak-Menzilhane Sistemi Çerçevesinde Tokat Menzilhanesi (1690–1840) [Tokat Post Station in the Framework of the Ottoman Postal System, 1690–1840]," 8; Tokat Court Register 21, s.149/150/1. There is an earlier decree dated to Rebiülahir AH 1204 (1790 CE) which mentions that non-officials were allowed to use post station horses by rent (*kirā*). However, the earlier decree lacks the specific details that the later decree has and does not detail the fees that non-officials had to pay. GRGSA IAM OJC 001 F157, 15.jpg. (AH 1204 / 1790 CE).

91. ISAM, DŞS 4, 86.jpg. (AH 1247 / 1832 CE).

92. BOA, HAT 491/ 24036. (AH 1250 / 1834–5 CE).

CONCLUSION

1. Ostrom, *Governing the Commons,* 26.

2. I have borrowed the concept of coevolution from Ang Yuen Yuen, *How China Escaped the Poverty Trap* (Ithaca, NY: Cornell University Press, 2016), 3.

3. On infrastructural power, see Mann, "Autonomous Power of the State," 113. For one view on how the meaning of how *ahālī* changed during the Tanzimat era, see Ussama Samir Makdisi, "Corrupting the Sublime Sultanate: The Revolt of Tanyus Shahin in Nineteenth-Century Ottoman Lebanon," *Comparative Studies in Society and History* 42, no. 1 (2000): 201.

4. "In Ottoman studies too, we commonly use the term 'community' to characterize diverse collectivities without taking into account variation over the lifespan of the Ottoman Empire. . . . Nevertheless, we need to recognize that the dynamism we observe in the seventeenth and eighteenth centuries may not have rested on primeval communities that simply became stronger due, according to Inalcik, mainly to changes in the taxation system. If we begin to draw more freely on what we already know about economic change during this period, it becomes clear that dynamism in public life coexisted with increased social differentiation." Canbakal, "Vows as Contract," 111–112.

5. Asaf Tanrıkut, *Türkiye Posta ve Telgraf ve Telefon Tarihi ve Teşkilat ve Mevzuatı* (Ankara: PTT Genel Müdürlüğü, 1984), 42–44, 29–42.

6. "Le courrier partira de Constantinople tous les lundis et y sera de retour tous les samedis. Il arrivera à Andrinople tous les mercredis et en repartira tous les jeudis." Turhan Turgut, *Osmanlı İmparatorluğu Posta Tarihi: Tarifeler ve Posta Yolları 1840–1922 / Postal History of the Ottoman Empire: Rates and Routes 1840–1922* (Istanbul: Alfa, 2018), 23.

7. Şekip Eskin, *Türk Posta Tarihi* (Ankara: Ulusal Matbaa, 1942), 16–17.

8. Eskin, *Türk Posta Tarihi*, 18.

9. Roderic H. Davison, "The Advent of the Electric Telegraph in the Ottoman Empire," in *Essays in Ottoman and Turkish History, 1774–1923: The Impact of the West* (Austin: University of Texas Press, 1990), 136. On the Ottoman telegraph, see also Yakup Bektas, "The Sultan's Messenger: Cultural Constructions of Ottoman Telegraphy, 1847–1880," *Technology and Culture* 41, no. 4 (2000): 669–696; Pauline Lewis, "Wired Ottomans: A Sociotechnical History of the Telegraph and the Modern Ottoman Empire, 1855–1911" (PhD diss., University of California, Los Angeles, 2018); Diren Çakılcı, *Rumeli Telgraf Hatları (1854–1876)* (Ankara: Türk Tarih Kurumu, 2019).

10. John, "Recasting the Information Infrastructure for the Industrial Age," 58–59.

11. Richard R. John, *Spreading the News: The American Postal System from Franklin to Morse* (Cambridge, MA: Harvard University Press, 1995), 4, 51.

12. Behringer, "Communications Revolutions," 341–342.

13. Whereas royal courts were not the main producers of source material regarding travel and courier itineraries in Europe, the imperial bureaucracy was the dominant source of historical information in the Ottoman case, at least to my knowledge. (Future researchers may revise this claim.) To give an example, a recent study of 81 European itinerary books mostly produced outside royal courts between 1545 and 1761 revealed 3,655 routes that connected 1,587 cities in Europe. In contrast, fiscal registers prepared by Ottoman government bureaucrats reveal that there were only about 200 official post stations in the empire in the 1700s. It is not unreasonable to suggest, then, that there had to be more unofficial stations and routes used by Ottoman subjects than were entered into the government-produced written record. Juraj Kittler, "Capitalism and Communications: The Rise of Commercial Courier Networks in the Context of the Champagne Fairs," *Capitalism: A Journal of History and Economics* 4, no. 1 (2023): 109–152; Rachel Midura,

"Itinerating Europe: Early Modern Spatial Networks in Printed Itineraries, 1545–1700," *Journal of Social History* 54, no. 4 (2021): 1023–1063.

14. Robert G. Albion, "The 'Communication Revolution,'" *The American Historical Review* 37, no. 4 (1932): 718–720; Richard R. John, "American Historians and the Concept of the Communications Revolution," in *Information Acumen: The Understanding and Use of Knowledge in Modern Business*, ed. Lisa Bud-Frierman (London: Routledge, 1994), 98–110.

15. Behringer, "Communications Revolutions: A Historiographical Concept," 337, 339.

16. See Chapter 6.

17. Shaw, *Between Old and New*, 185–186; Mehmed Efendi and Yirmisekiz Çelebi, *Relation de l'ambassade de Mehemet-Effendi, a la cour de France, en M. DCC. XXI. écrite par lui-meme, et traduite du turc* (Constantinople, 1757), 20, http://ark.bnf.fr/ark:/12148 /bpt6k97744781; Seyyid Abdürrahim Muhibb Efendi and Seyyid Ali Efendi Moralı, *Deux ottomans à Paris sous le Directoire et l'Empire: Relations d'ambassade*, trans. Stefanos Yerasimos (Arles: Actes Sud, 1998), 190–194; Also see Niyazi Berkes, *The Development of Secularism in Turkey* (Montreal: McGill University Press, 1964), 82–85.

18. I am unable to list all the studies that exemplify this point, but these are the studies that left the deepest impression on me at the time of writing: Yonca Köksal, *The Ottoman Empire in the Tanzimat Era: Provincial Perspectives from Ankara to Edirne* (New York: Routledge, 2019); Derin Terzioğlu, "How to Conceptualize Ottoman Sunnitization: A Historiographical Discussion," *Turcica* 44 (2013): 321–322; Ayfer Karakaya-Stump, *The Kizilbash-Alevis in Ottoman Anatolia: Sufism, Politics and Community*, Edinburgh Studies on the Ottoman Empire (Edinburgh: Edinburgh University Press, 2020), 259, 289; Hülya Canbakal, "Vows as Contract in Ottoman Public Life (17th–18th Centuries)," *Islamic Law and Society* 18, no. 1 (2011): 85–115.

19. Ussama Samir Makdisi, "Corrupting the Sublime Sultanate: The Revolt of Tanyus Shahin in Nineteenth-Century Ottoman Lebanon," Comparative *Studies in Society and History* 42, no. 1 (2000): 201; Yaycıoğlu, *Partners of the Empire*. See also Stanford J. Shaw, *Between Old and New: The Ottoman Empire under Sultan Selim III, 1789–1807* (Cambridge, MA: Harvard University Press, 1971), chaps. 21–23.

20. This percentage (1 percent) is based on information gleaned from Mehmet Genç and Erol Özvar, eds., *Osmanlı Maliyesi Kurumlar ve Bütçeler 1* (Istanbul: Osmanlı Bankası Arşiv ve Araştırma Merkezi, 2006) and through discussion with Professor Ali Coşkun Tunçer. We hope to have something published in the next few years that will strengthen this claim.

21. On "transformation," see Olivier Bouquet, "From Decline to Transformation: Reflections on a New Paradigm in Ottoman History," *Osmanlı Araştırmaları* 60 (2022): 27–60.

22. "Infrastructure is fundamentally a relational concept." Star, "The Ethnography of Infrastructure," 380.

Bibliography

ARCHIVAL SOURCES

Istanbul, Turkey

Türkiye Cumhuriyeti Cumhurbaşkanlığı Devlet Arşivleri Başkanlığı, Osmanlı Arşivi [Presidential State Archives of the Republic of Türkiye, Ottoman Archives], Istanbul (BOA)

İslam Araştırmaları Merkezi [Centre for Islamic Studies], Istanbul (ISAM)

Sofia, Bulgaria

National Library of St. Cyril and St. Methodius, Sofia, Oriental Department

Thessaloniki, Greece

Greece General State Archives, Historical Archives of Macedonia (Thessaloniki), Ottoman Islamic Courts 001 (GRGSA IAM OJC 001)

PUBLISHED SOURCES

3 numaralı Mühimme defteri (966–968/1558–1560). Ankara: T. C. Başbakanlık, Devlet Arşivleri Genel Müdürlüğü, 1993.

Abou El Haj, Rifaʿat Ali. *Formation of the Modern State: The Ottoman Empire, Sixteenth to Eighteenth Centuries*. Albany: State University of New York Press, 1991.

———. "The Narcissism of Mustafa II (1695–1703): A Psychohistorical Study." *Studia Islamica* 40 (1974): 115–131.

———. "The Ottoman Vezir and Paşa Households 1683–1703: A Preliminary Report." *Journal of the American Oriental Society* 94, no. 4 (1974): 438–447.

———. "Power and Social Order: The Uses of the Kanun." In *The Ottoman City and Its Parts: Urban Structure and Social Order,* edited by Irene A. Bierman, Rifa'at Abou El Haj, and Donald Preziosi, 77–99. New York: Aristide D. Caratzas, 1991.

———. "The Social Uses of the Past: Recent Arab Historiography of Ottoman Rule."

Abū Ṭālib Khān. *Travels of Mirza Abu Taleb Khan in Asia, Africa, and Europe, during the Years 1799, 1800, 1801, 1802, and 1803.* Edited by Daniel O'Quinn. Translated by Charles Stewart. Peterborough, Ontario: Broadview Press, 2009.

Açıkel, Ali. "Osmanlı Ulak-Menzilhane Sistemi Çerçevesinde Tokat Menzilhanesi (1690–1840) [Tokat Post Station in the Framework of the Ottoman Postal System, 1690–1840]." *Ege Üniversitesi Edebiyat Fakültesi Tarih İncelemeleri Dergisi* 19, no. 2 (2004): 1–33.

Ágoston, Gábor. *The Last Muslim Conquest: The Ottoman Empire and Its Wars in Europe.* Princeton, NJ: Princeton University Press, 2021.

Ağır, Seven, and Onur Yıldırım. "Gedik: What's in a Name?" In *Bread from the Lion's Mouth: Artisans Struggling for a Livelihood in Ottoman Cities,* edited by Suraiya Faroqhi, 217–236. Oxford, NY: Berghahn Books, 2015.

Ahmad, Attiya. *Everyday Conversions: Islam, Domestic Work, and South Asian Migrant Women in Kuwait.* Durham, NC: Duke University Press, 2017.

Akarlı, Engin. "Gedik: A Bundle of Rights and Obligations for Istanbul Artisans and Traders, 1750–1840." In *Law, Anthropology and the Constitution of the Social: Making Persons and Things,* edited by Alain Pottage and Martha Mundy, 166–200. Cambridge: Cambridge University Press, 2004.

Akgündüz, Ahmed. "Shari'ah Courts and Shari'ah Records: The Application of Islamic Law in the Ottoman State." *Islamic Law and Society* 16, no. 2 (2009): 202–230.

Akın, Yiğit. *When the War Came Home: The Ottomans' Great War and the Devastation of an Empire.* Stanford, CA: Stanford University Press, 2018.

Aksan, Virginia H. *The Ottomans, 1700–1923: An Empire Besieged.* 2nd ed. Abingdon, UK: Routledge, Taylor and Francis, 2022.

———. *An Ottoman Statesman in War and Peace: Ahmed Resmi Efendi, 1700–1783.* Leiden: Brill, 1995.

Aktaş, Necati. "Atik Şikâyet Defteri." In *Türkiye Diyanet Vakfı İslam Ansiklopedisi: Aşık Ömer-Bala Külliyesi.* 4:68. Üsküdar: Türkiye Diyanet Vakfı, İslâm Ansiklopedisi Genel Müdürlüğü, 1991.

Akyeampong, Emmanuel, Caroline Arni, Pamela Kyle Crossley, Mark Hewitson, and William H. Sewell, Jr. "AHR Conversation: Explaining Historical Change; or, The Lost History of Causes." *American Historical Review* 120, no. 4 (2015): 1369–1422.

Akyıldız, Ali. *Para Pul Oldu: Osmanlı'da Kağıt Para, Maliye ve Toplum.* Istanbul: İletişim, 2003.

Akyüz, Jülide. "Anadolu'nun Orta Kolu Üzerinde Bir Menzil: Amasya Menzili, İşleyişi, Sorunları [A Post Station on the Anatolian Middle Road: Amasya Post Station]." *Askeri Tarih Araştırmaları Dergisi* 8 (2006): 45–53.

Alam, Muzaffar. *The Crisis of Empire in Mughal North India: Awadh and the Punjab, 1707–1748.* 2nd ed. New Delhi: Oxford University Press, 2013.

Albion, Robert G. "The 'Communication Revolution.'" *The American Historical Review* 37, no. 4 (1932): 718–720.

All about Postal Matters in Egypt (Egypt Maṣlaḥat al-Barīd). Florence: Landi Press, 1898.

Allsen, Thomas. "Imperial Posts, West, East and North: A Review Article: Adam J. Silverstein, *Postal Systems in the Pre-modern Islamic World.*" *Archivum Eurasiae Medii Aevi* 17 (2011): 237–276.

Anastasopoulos, Antonis. "Imperial Institutions and Local Communities: Ottoman Karaferye, 1758–1774." PhD diss., Cambridge University, 1999.

Ang, Yuen Yuen. *How China Escaped the Poverty Trap.* Ithaca, NY: Cornell University Press, 2016.

Anhegger, Robert, and Halil Inalcık. *Ḳānūnnāme-i Sulṭānī Ber Mūceb-i ʿörf-i ʿOsmānī: II. Mehmed ve II. Bayezid Devirlerine Ait Yasaḳnāme ve Ḳānūnnāmeler.* Ankara: Türk Tarih Kurumu Basımevi, 1956.

Apaydın, H. Yunus. "Kefalet." In *Türkiye Diyanet Vakfı İslam Ansiklopedisi: Kastilya-Kile,* 25:168–177. Üsküdar: Türkiye Diyanet Vakfı, İslâm Ansiklopedisi Genel Müdürlüğü, 2002.

Arakawa, Masaharu. "トゥルファン出土漢文文書に見える Ulaɣ について [On a Turkic Term "Ulaɣ" in Turfan Chinese Documents]." 内陸アジア言語の研究 [*Studies on Inner Asian Languages*] 9 (1994): 1–25.

Argent, Gala. "Do the Clothes Make the Horse? Relationality, Roles and Statuses in Iron Age Inner Asia." *World Archaeology* 42, no. 2 (2010): 157–174.

Artan, Tülay. "Ahmed I and 'Tuhfetü'l-Mülûk ve's-Selâtin: A Period Manuscript on Horses, Horsemanship and Hunting." In *Animals and People in the Ottoman Empire.* Edited by Suraiya Faroqhi, 235–270. Istanbul: Eren, 2010.

———. "The First, Hesitant Steps of Ottoman Protocol and Diplomacy into Modernity (1676–1725)." *The Court Historian* 26, no. 1 (2021): 29–43.

Aslanian, Sebouh. *From the Indian Ocean to the Mediterranean: The Global Trade Networks of Armenian Merchants from New Julfa.* Berkeley, CA: University of California Press, 2011.

Atçıl, Abdurrahman. *Scholars and Sultans in the Early Modern Ottoman Empire.* Cambridge: Cambridge University Press, 2017.

Atwood, Christopher P. *The Rise of the Mongols: Five Chinese Sources.* Indianapolis, IN: Hackett, 2021.

Aynur, Hatice. "Ottoman Literature." In *The Cambridge History of Turkey,* edited by Suraiya Faroqhi, 3:481–520. Cambridge: Cambridge University Press, 2006.

Babur. *The Baburnama: Memoirs of Babur, Prince and Emperor.* Edited and translated by Wheeler M. Thackston. Washington, DC: Smithsonian Institution, 1996.

Baer, Ed. and G. "Iltizām." *Encyclopaedia of Islam,* 2nd ed., edited by P. Bearman, Th. Bianquis, C. E. Bosworth, E. van Donzel and W. P. Heinrichs. Consulted online on April 24, 2012. https://referenceworks.brillonline.com/entries/encyclopaedia-of-islam-2/iltizam-COM_0367?s.num=0&s.f.s2_parent=s.f.book.encyclopaedia-of-islam-2&s.q=iltizam.

Baldwin, James. "Petitioning the Sultan in Ottoman Egypt." *Bulletin of the School of Oriental and African Studies* 75, no. 3 (2012): 499–524.

Barak, On. *On Time: Technology and Temporality in Modern Egypt.* Berkeley: University of California Press, 2013.

Barakat, Nora. "Marginal Actors? The Role of Bedouin in the Ottoman Administration of Animals as Property in the District of Salt, 1870–1912." *Journal of the Economic and Social History of the Orient* 58, no. 1/2 (2015): 105–134.

Barkey, Karen. *Bandits and Bureaucrats: The Ottoman Route to State Centralization.* Ithaca, NY: Cornell University Press, 1994.

Baş, Yaşar. "XVIII-XIX Yüzyılın İlk Yarısında Gebze Menzilhanesi [The Gebze Post Station in the Eighteenth and First Half of the Nineteenth Century]." *International Periodical for the Languages, Literature and History of Turkish or Turkic* 8, no. 5 (2013): 101–126.

Başaran, Betül. *Selim III, Social Control and Policing in Istanbul at the End of the Eighteenth Century: Between Crisis and Order.* Leiden: Brill, 2014.

Bates, Daniel G. *Nomads and Farmers; A Study of the Yörük of Southeastern Turkey.* Ann Arbor: Museum of Anthropology, University of Michigan, 1973.

Bayerle, Gustav. *Pashas, Begs, and Effendis: A Historical Dictionary of Titles and Terms in the Ottoman Empire.* Istanbul: Isis Press, 1997.

Bayly, C. A. *Empire and Information: Intelligence Gathering and Social Communication in India, 1780–1870.* Cambridge: Cambridge University Press, 1996.

Behringer, Wolfgang. "Communications Revolutions: A Historiographical Concept." *German History* 24, no. 3 (2006): 333–374.

Beik, William. *Absolutism and Society in Seventeenth-Century France: State Power and Provincial Aristocracy in Languedoc.* Cambridge: Cambridge University Press, 1985.

Bekar, Cumhur. "The Rise of the Köprülü Household: The Transformation of Patronage in the Ottoman Empire in the Seventeenth Century." *Turkish Historical Review* 11, nos. 2–3 (2021): 229–256.

Bektas, Yakup. "The Sultan's Messenger: Cultural Constructions of Ottoman Telegraphy, 1847–1880." *Technology and Culture* 41, no. 4 (2000): 669–696.

Beldiceanu-Steinherr, Irène. "A Propos Des Tribus Atčeken (XVe-XVIe Siècles)." *Journal of the Economic and Social History of the Orient* 30, no. 2 (1987): 121–195.

Bell, John. *Travels from St. Petersburg in Russia to Diverse Parts of Asia.* Vol. 2. Dublin: R. Bell, 1764.

Berkes, Niyazi. *The Development of Secularism in Turkey.* Montreal: McGill University Press, 1964.

Berktay, Halil. "The 'Other' Feudalism: A Critique of 20th Century Turkish Historiography and Its Particularisation of Ottoman Society." PhD diss., University of Birmingham, 1990.

———. "The Search for the Peasant in Western and Turkish History / Historiography." In *New Approaches to State and Peasant in Ottoman History,* 109–184. London: Frank Cass, 1992.

Bilgin, Arif. "From Artichoke to Corn: New Fruits and Vegetables in the Istanbul Market (Seventeenth to Nineteenth Centuries)." In *Living the Good Life: Consumption in the Qing and Ottoman Empires of the Eighteenth Century,* edited by Suraiya Faroqhi and Elif Akçetin, 259–282. Leiden: Brill, 2017

Bishara, Fahad Ahmad. *A Sea of Debt: Law and Economic Life in the Western Indian Ocean, 1780–1950.* Cambridge: Cambridge University Press, 2017.

Bıyık, Ömer. "124 numaralı Mühimme Defteri (H. 1128–1130)." Master's thesis, Ege University, 2001.

Blake, Robert P., and Richard N. Frye. "History of the Nation of the Archers (The Mongols) by Grigor of Akancʻ Hitherto Ascribed to Matakʻia the Monk: The Armenian Text Edited with an English Translation and Notes." *Harvard Journal of Asiatic Studies* 12, no. 3/4 (1949): 269–399.

Bloom, Harold. *The Western Canon: The Books and School of the Ages.* New York: Harcourt Brace, 1994.

Bonine, Michael E. "From Qanāt to Kort: Traditional Irrigation Terminology and Practices in Central Iran." *Iran* 20 (1982): 145–159.

Boucoyannis, Deborah. *Kings as Judges: Power, Justice, and the Origins of Parliaments.* Cambridge: Cambridge University Press, 2021.

Bouquet, Olivier. "From Decline to Transformation: Reflections on a New Paradigm in Ottoman History." *Osmanlı Araştırmaları* 60 (2022): 27–60.

Bowker, Geoffrey C. "Information Mythology and Infrastructure." In *Information Acumen: The Understanding and Use of Knowledge in Modern Business,* edited by Lisa Bud-Frierman, 231–247. London: Routledge, 1994.

———. "Sustainable Knowledge Infrastructures." In *The Promise of Infrastructure,* edited by Nikhil Anand, Akhil Gupta, and Hannah Appel, 203–222. Durham, NC: Duke University Press, 2018.

Bowker, Geoffrey C. and Susan Leigh Star. *Sorting Things Out: Classification and Its Consequences.* Cambridge, MA: MIT Press, 1999.

Bozkurt, Rıza. *Osmanlı İmparatorluğunda Kollar, Ulak ve İaşe Menzilleri [Roads, Couriers, and Provisioning Stations in the Ottoman Empire].* Ankara: Genelkurmay Başkanlığı Harp Tarihi Dairesi, 1966.

Braude, Benjamin. "Venture and Faith in the Commercial Life of the Ottoman Balkans, 1500–1650." *The International History Review* 7, no. 4 (1985): 519–452.

Braudel, Fernand. *The Mediterranean and the Mediterranean World in the Age of Philip II*. New York: Harper and Row, 1972.

Broughton, John Cam Hobhouse. *Travels in Albania and Other Provinces of Turkey in 1809 & 1810. Journey through Albania*. London: J. Murray, 1855. https://catalog .hathitrust.org/Record/101677626.

Bulliet, Richard. *The Camel and the Wheel*. New York: Columbia University Press, 1990.

Burak, Guy. "Şeyhulislâm Feyzullah Efendi, the Ḥanafī Mufti of Jerusalem and the Rise of the Provincial Fatāwā Collections in the Eighteenth Century." *Journal of the Economic and Social History of the Orient* 64, no. 4 (2021): 377–403.

Burckhardt, John Lewis. *Travels in Syria and the Holy Land*. Cambridge: Cambridge University Press, 2011.

Burns, Kathryn. "Notaries, Truth and Consequences." *American Historical Review* 110, no. 2 (2005): 350–379.

Bushkovitch, Paul. "Taxation, Tax Farming, and Merchants in Sixteenth-Century Russia." *Slavic Review* 37, no. 3 (1978): 381–398.

Büssow, Johann, and Astrid Meier. "Ottoman Corporatism, Eighteenth to Twentieth Centuries: Beyond the State-Society Paradigm in Middle Eastern History." In *Ways of Knowing Muslim Cultures and Societies: Studies in Honour of Gudrun Krämer*, edited by Bettina Gräf, Birgit Krawietz, and Schirin Amir-Moazami, 81–110. Leiden: Brill, 2019.

Çadırcı, Musa. "Posta Teşkilatı Kurulmadan Önce Osmanlı İmparatorluğu'nda Menzilhane ve Kiracıbaşılık [Post Stations and Postmasters in the Ottoman Empire before the Establishment of the Modern Postal System]." *VIII. Türk Tarihi Kongresi (11–15 Ekim 1976)* 2 (1981): 1359–1365.

Çakılcı, Diren. *Rumeli Telgraf Hatları (1854–1876)*. Ankara: Türk Tarih Kurumu, 2019.

Canbakal, Hülya. *Society and Politics in an Ottoman Town: 'Ayntāb in the 17th Century*. Leiden: Brill, 2007.

———. "Vows as Contract in Ottoman Public Life (17th–18th Centuries)." *Islamic Law and Society* 18, no. 1 (2011): 85–115.

Cantemir, Demetrius. *The History of the Growth and Decay of the Othman Empire*. Translated by N. Tindal. London: J. J. and P. Knapton, 1734.

Carnegie, Garry D. "The Present and Future of Accounting History." *Accounting, Auditing & Accountability Journal* 27, no. 8 (2014): 1241–1249.

Carter, F. W. "The Commerce of the Dubrovnik Republic, 1500–1700." *The Economic History Review* 24, no. 3 (1971): 370–394.

Castro, Alvaro Carvajal. "Early Medieval Commons? Or How the History of Early Medieval Europe Could Benefit from a Necessary Conversation: The Case from NW Iberia." *International Journal of the Commons* 15, no. 1 (2021): 338–353.

Çetin, Cemal. *Ulak yol durak: Anadolu yollarında padişah postaları (Menzilhaneler)*. Istanbul: Hikmetevi Yayınları, 2013.

———. "XVIII. Yüzyılda Çorum Menzilhaneleri." In *Uluslar Arası Osmanlı'dan Cumhuriyete Çorum Sempozyumu (Bildiriler 23–25 Kasım 2007)*, vol. III, pp. 1573–1593. Çorum: Çorum Belediyesi Kültür Yayınları, 2008.

Cezar, Yavuz. *Osmanlı Maliyesinde Bunalım ve Değişim Dönemi*. Istanbul: Alan Yayıncılık, 1986.

Chatterjee, Nandini. "Mahzar-Namas in the Mughal and British Empires: The Uses of an Indo-Islamic Legal Form." *Comparative Studies in Society and History* 58, no. 2 (2016): 379–406.

Christakis, Nicholas A., and James H. Fowler. *Connected: The Surprising Power of Our Social Networks and How They Shape Our Lives*. New York: Little, Brown, 2009.

Çınar, Hüseyin. "Osmanlı Ulak-Menzilhane Sistemi ve XVIII Yüzyılın İlk Yarısında Antep Menzilleri [The Ottoman Post Station System and the Antep Post Station in the First Half of the Eighteenth Century]." *Osmanlı* 3 (1999): 627–637.

Clarence-Smith, William G. "Animal Power as a Factor in Ottoman Military Decline, 1683–1918." Paper presented at the "War Horses of the World" conference, SOAS, University of London, May 3, 2014.

Clavijo, Ruy González de. *Embassy to Tamerlane, 1403–1406*. Translated by Guy Le Strange. London: Routledge Curzon, 2005.

———. *Historia Del Gran Tamorlan e Itinerario y Enarracion del Viage, y Relacion de La Embajada Que Ruy Gonzalez de Clavijo Le Hizo Por Mandado Del Muy Poderoso Señor Rey Don Henrique El Tercero de Castilla*. Edited by Gonzalo Argote de Molina. Madrid: Don Antonio de Sancha, 1782.

Collaço, Gwendolyn. "'World-Seizing' Albums: Imported Paintings from ʿAcem and Hindūstān in an Eclectic Ottoman Market." *Ars Orientalis* 51 (2021): 133–187.

Constant II, Edward W. "The Social Locus of Technological Practice: Community, System, or Organization?" In *The Social Construction of Technological Systems: New Directions in the Sociology and History of Technology*, edited by Wiebe E. Bijker, Thomas Parke Hughes, and Trevor Pinch, 217–236. Cambridge, MA: MIT Press, 2012.

Cowen, Deborah. *The Deadly Life of Logistics*. Minneapolis: University of Minnesota Press, 2014.

Creel, H. G. "The Role of the Horse in Chinese History." *The American Historical Review* 70, no. 3 (1965): 647–672.

Crone, Patricia. *Pre-industrial Societies*. Oxford: Basil Blackwell, 1994.

Dai, Yingcong. "The Qing State, Merchants, and the Military Labor Force in the Jinchuan Campaigns." *Late Imperial China* 22, no. 2 (2001): 35–90.

———. "Yingyung Shengxi: Military Entrepreneurship in the High Qing Period, 1700–1800." *Late Imperial China* 26, no. 2 (2005): 1–67.

Dankoff, Robert. *An Ottoman Mentality: The World of Evliya Çelebi*. 2 ed. rev. Ottoman Empire and Its Heritage, vol. 31. Leiden: Brill, 2006.

———. "Evliya Çelebi and the Seyahatname." In *The Turks*, edited by Hasan Celâl Güzel, C. Cem Oğuz, and Osman Karatay, 3:605–626. Ankara: Yeni Türkiye, 2002.

————. "Turkic Languages and Turkish Dialects According to Evliya Çelebi." In *From Mahmud Kaşgari to Evliya Çelebi: Studies in Middle Turkic and Ottoman Literatures,* edited by Robert Dankoff, 259–276. Piscataway, NJ: Gorgias Press, 2009.

Darling, Linda T. *A History of Social Justice and Political Power in the Middle East: The Circle of Justice from Mesopotamia to Globalization.* London: Routledge, 2013.

————. "Ordering the Ottoman Elite: Ceremonial Lawcodes of the Late Seventeenth Century." *Turcica* 50 (2019): 355–382.

————. *Revenue-Raising and Legitimacy: Tax Collection and Finance Administration in the Ottoman Empire, 1560–1660.* Leiden: E. J. Brill, 1996.

Davies, Siriol, and Jack L. Davis, eds. *Between Venice and Istanbul: Colonial Landscapes in Early Modern Greece.* Princeton, NJ: American School of Classical Studies at Athens, 2007.

Davison, Roderic H. *Essays in Ottoman and Turkish History, 1774–1923: The Impact of the West.* Austin: University of Texas Press, 1990.

————. "The Advent of the Electric Telegraph in the Ottoman Empire." In *Essays in Ottoman and Turkish History, 1774–1923: The Impact of the West,* 133–165. Austin: University of Texas Press, 1990.

Dean, Carolyn. "Beyond Prescription: Notarial Doodles and Other Marks." *Word & Image* 25, no. 3 (2009): 293–316.

Deringil, Selim. *Conversion and Apostasy in the Late Ottoman Empire.* New York: Cambridge University Press, 2012.

Diyarbekir şer'iyye sicilleri: Âmid mahkemesi Volume 1 [*Diyarbekir Judicial Records Vol. 1*]. Diyarbakır: Dicle Üniversitesi İlahiyat Fakültesi Yayınları, 2013.

Diyarbekir şer'iyye sicilleri: Âmid mahkemesi Volume 2 [*Diyarbekir Judicial Records Vol. 2*]. Diyarbakır: Dicle Üniversitesi İlahiyat Fakültesi Yayınları, 2013.

Doumani, Beshara. *Family Life in the Ottoman Empire: A Social History.* Cambridge: Cambridge University Press, 2017.

————. *Rediscovering Palestine: Merchants and Peasants in Jabal Nablus, 1700–1900.* Berkeley: University of California Press, 1995.

Easterling, Keller. *Extrastatecraft: The Power of Infrastructure Space.* London: Verso, 2014.

Edwards, Paul N. "Infrastructure and Modernity: Force, Time, and Social Organization in the History of Sociotechnical Systems." In *Modernity and Technology,* edited by Thomas J. Misa, Philip Brey, and Andrew Feenberg, 185–225. Cambridge, MA: MIT Press, 2003.

————. *A Vast Machine: Computer Models, Climate Data, and the Politics of Global Warming.* Cambridge, MA: MIT Press, 2010.

Edwards, Paul N., Geoffrey C. Bowker, Steven J. Jackson, and Robin Williams. "Introduction: An Agenda for Infrastructure Studies." *Journal of the Association for Information Systems* 10, no. 5 (2009): 364–374.

Edwards, Paul N., Lisa Gitelman, Gabrielle Hecht, Adrian Johns, Brian Larkin, and Neil Safier. "AHR Conversation: Historical Perspectives on the Circulation of Information." *American Historical Review* 116, no. 5 (2011): 1393–1435.

Eldem, Edhem. *French Trade in Istanbul in the Eighteenth Century.* Leiden: Brill, 1999.

———. "Of Bricks and Tiles: The History of a Local Industry in the Area of Mürefte (Thrace)." In *Living the Good Life: Consumption in the Qing and Ottoman Empires of the Eighteenth Century,* edited by Suraiya Faroqhi and Elif Akçetin, 433–473. Leiden: Brill, 2017.

Ensmenger, Nathan. "The Environmental History of Computing." *Technology and Culture* 59, no. 4 (2018): S7–33.

Ergenç, Özer. "Osmanlı Şehrindeki Mahalle'nin İşlev ve Nitelikleri Üzerine." *Osmanlı Araştırmaları* 4 (1984): 69–78.

Ergene, Boğaç A. *Local Court, Provincial Society, and Justice in the Ottoman Empire: Legal Practice and Dispute Resolution in Çankırı and Kastamonu (1652–1744).* Leiden: Brill, 2003.

Ergin, Nina. "The Albanian Tellâk Connection: Labor Migration to the Hammams of 18th-Century Istanbul, Based on the 1752 Istanbul Hamâmları Defterleri." *Turcica* 43 (2011): 231–256.

Ertuğ, Nejdet. *Osmanlı döneminde İstanbul deniz ulaşımı ve kayıkçılar* [Istanbul sea transportation and boatmen in the Ottoman period]. Ankara: Kültür Bakanlığı, 2001.

Erünsal, İsmail. *Osmanlılarda Kütüphaneler ve Kütüphanecilik: Tarihi Gelişimi ve Organizasyonu.* Istanbul: Timaş Yayınları, 2015.

Eskin, Şekip. *Türk Posta Tarihi.* Ankara: Ulusal Matbaa, 1942.

Esmer, Tolga U. "Economies of Violence, Banditry and Governance in the Ottoman Empire Around 1800." *Past & Present* 224, no. 1 (2014): 163–199.

Evliya Çelebi. *The Intimate Life of an Ottoman Statesman: Melek Ahmed Pasha (1588–1662): As Portrayed in Evliya Çelebi's Book of Travels (Seyahat-name).* Translated by Robert Dankoff. Albany: State University of New York Press, 1991.

Fahmy, Khaled. *All the Pasha's Men: Mehmed Ali, His Army, and the Making of Modern Egypt.* Cairo: American University in Cairo Press, 2002.

Farah, Caesar E., ed. *Decision Making and Change in the Ottoman Empire.* Kirksville: Thomas Jefferson University Press at Northeast Missouri State University, 1993.

Faroqhi, Suraiya. *Approaching Ottoman History: An Introduction to the Sources.* New York: Cambridge University Press, 1999.

———. "Camels, Wagons, and the Ottoman State in the Sixteenth and Seventeenth Centuries." *International Journal of Middle East Studies* 14, no. 4 (1982): 523–539.

———. "The Early History of the Balkan Fairs." *Südost Forschungen* 37 (1978): 50–67.

———. "Ottoman Craftsmen: Problematic and Sources with Special Emphasis on the Eighteenth Century." In *Crafts and Craftsmen of the Middle East,* edited by Suraiya Faroqhi and Randi Deguilhem, 84–118. London: I. B. Tauris, 2005.

———. *Pilgrims And Sultans: The Hajj under the Ottomans 1517–1683.* London: I. B. Tauris, 1994.

———. "Political Tensions in the Anatolian Countryside around 1600: An Attempt at Interpretation." In *Coping with the State: Political Conflict and Crime in the Ottoman Empire, 1550–1720*. United States: Gorgias Press, 2010, 111–124.

———. "Seeking Wisdom in China: An Attempt to Make Sense of the Celali Rebellions." In *Coping with the State: Political Conflict and Crime in the Ottoman Empire, 1550–1720*. United States: Gorgias Press, 2010: 125–147.

———. *Subjects of the Sultan: Culture and Daily Life in the Ottoman Empire*. London: I. B. Tauris, 2000.

———. "Women, Wealth and Textiles in 1730s Bursa." In *Living the Good Life: Consumption in the Qing and Ottoman Empires of the Eighteenth Century*, edited by Suraiya Faroqhi and Elif Akçetin, 213–235. Leiden: Brill, 2017.

Faruqui, Munis D. *The Princes of the Mughal Empire, 1504–1719*. Cambridge: Cambridge University Press, 2012.

Fattah, Hala Mundhir. *The Politics of Regional Trade in Iraq, Arabia, and the Gulf, 1745–1900*. SUNY Series in the Social and Economic History of the Middle East. Albany: State University of New York Press, 1997.

Faure, David. *Emperor and Ancestor: State and Lineage in South China*. Stanford, CA: Stanford University Press, 2007.

Felek, Özgen. "Displaying Manhood and Masculinity at the Imperial Circumcision Festivity of 1582." *Journal of the Ottoman and Turkish Studies Association* 6, no. 1 (2019): 141–170.

Findley, Carter Vaughn. *Bureaucratic Reform in the Ottoman Empire: The Sublime Porte, 1789–1922*. Princeton, NJ: Princeton University Press, 1980.

Finkel, Caroline. *Osman's Dream: The Story of the Ottoman Empire, 1300–1923*. New York: Basic Books, 2006.

———. *The Administration of Warfare: The Ottoman Military Campaigns in Hungary, 1593–1606.* Vienna: VWGÖ, 1988.

Fisher, Alan W. *A Precarious Balance: Conflict, Trade, and Diplomacy on the Russian-Ottoman Frontier*. Istanbul: Isis Press, 1999.

Fleischer, Cornell. *Bureaucrat and Intellectual in the Ottoman Empire: The Historian Mustafa Âli (1541–1600)*. Princeton, NJ: Princeton University Press, 1986.

Fletcher, Joseph. "Turco-Mongolian Monarchic Tradition in the Ottoman Empire." *Harvard Ukrainian Studies* 3/4 (1979–1980): 236–251.

Floor, Willem. "The Postal System in Safavid and Afsharid Iran." Unpublished manuscript, last modified May 26 2023, .docx.

Fortna, Benjamin C. *Imperial Classroom: Islam, the State, and Education in the Late Ottoman Empire*. Oxford: Oxford University Press, 2002.

Fossella, Jason Curtis. "The Emperor's Eyes: The Dromos and Byzantine Communications, Diplomacy and Bureaucracy, 518–1204." PhD diss., Saint Louis University, 2014.

Foster, Sir William, ed. *The Travels of John Sanderson in The Levant (1584–1602)*. London: Hakluyt Society, 1931.

Frangakis-Syrett, Elena. "Money Shortage and the Ottoman Economy: Late Seventeenth to the Late Eighteenth Centuries." In *Trade and Money: The Ottoman Economy in the Eighteenth and Early Nineteenth Centuries,* 49–73. Istanbul: Isis Press, 2007.

———. "The Economic Activities of Ottoman and Western Communities in Eighteenth-Century Izmir." *Oriente Moderno* 79, no. 1 (1999): 11–26.

———. "The Ottoman Monetary System in the Second Half of the Eighteenth and in the Early Nineteenth Centuries: A View from the Provinces." In *Trade and Money: The Ottoman Economy in the Eighteenth and Early Nineteenth Centuries,* 75–96. Analecta Isisiana 93. Istanbul: Isis Press, 2007.

Franz, Kurt. "Handlist of Stations of the Ayyubid and Mamluk Communication Systems." In *Egypt and Syria under Mamluk Rule Political, Social and Cultural Aspects,* edited by Amalia Levanoni, 295–396. Leiden: Brill, 2021.

French, David. "Pre-and Early-Roman Roads of Asia Minor: The Persian Royal Road." *Iran* 36 (1998): 15–43.

Fritschy, Wantje. *Public Finance of the Dutch Republic in Comparative Perspective: The Viability of an Early Modern Federal State (1570s–1795)*. Leiden: Brill, 2017.

Fynn-Paul, Jeff ed. *War, Entrepreneurs, and the State in Europe and the Mediterranean, 1300–1800*. Leiden: Brill, 2014.

Gara, Eleni. "Çuha for the Janissaries—Velençe for the Poor: Competition for Raw Material and Workforce between Salonica and Veria, 1600–1650." In *Crafts and Craftsmen of the Middle East: Fashioning the Individual in the Muslim Mediterranean,* edited by Suraiya Faroqhi and Randi Deguilhem, 121–152. The Islamic Mediterranean, vol. 4. London: I. B. Tauris, 2005.

Garnett, Lucy Mary Jane and John Stuart Stuart Glennie. *The Women of Turkey and Their Folk-Lore.* Vol. 2. London: D. Nutt, 1890.

Gelvin, James. "The 'Politics of Notables' Forty Years After." *MESA Bulletin* 40, no. 1 (2006): 19–29.

Genç, Mehmet. "Esham: İç Borçlanma." In *Osmanlı İmparatorluğunda Devlet ve Ekonomi* [*State and Economy in the Ottoman Empire*], 186–195. Istanbul: Ötüken Neşriyat A.Ş., 2000.

———. "L'Économie Ottomane et La Guerre Au XVIIIème Siècle." *Turcica* 27 (1995): 177–196.

———. "Osmanlı Maliyesinde Malikane Sistemi [The Ottoman Malikane System]." In *Osmanlı İmparatorluğunda Devlet ve Ekonomi* [*State and Economy in the Ottoman Empire*], 99–152.

———. "Ottoman Industry in the Eighteenth Century: General Framework, Characteristics, and Main Trends." In *Manufacturing in the Ottoman Empire and Turkey,*

1500–1950, edited by Donald Quataert, 59–86. Albany: State University of New York Press, 1994.

Genç, Mehmet, and Erol Özvar, eds. *Osmanlı Maliyesi Kurumlar ve Bütçeler 1.* Istanbul: Osmanlı Bankası Arşiv ve Araştırma Merkezi, 2006.

Gerber, Haim. "The Muslim Law of Partnerships in Ottoman Court Records." *Studia Islamica* 53 (1981): 109–119.

Ghervas, Stella. "The Black Sea." In *Oceanic Histories,* edited by David Armitage, Alison Bashford, and Sujit Sivasundaram, 234–266. Cambridge Oceanic Histories. New York: Cambridge University Press, 2017.

Gleick, James. *The Information: A History, a Theory, a Flood.* New York: Pantheon Books, 2011.

Goldsworthy, Vesna. *Inventing Ruritania: The Imperialism of the Imagination.* New Haven, CT: Yale University Press, 1998.

Gould, Andrew G. "Lords or Bandits? The Derebeys of Cilicia." *International Journal of Middle East Studies* 7 (1976): 485–506.

Göçek, Fatma Müge. "Mültezim." In *Encyclopaedia of Islam,* 2nd ed., edited by P. Bearman, Th. Bianquis, C. E. Bosworth, E. van Donzel, and W. P. Heinrichs. Leiden: Brill, 2012.

Göyünç, Nejat. "Defter." In *Türkiye Diyanet Vakfı İslam ansiklopedisi: Darüssaade-Dulkadıroğulları,* 9:88–90. Istanbul: Türkiye Diyanet Vakfı, İslâm Ansiklopedisi Genel Müdürlüğü, 1994.

Graham, Stephen, ed. *Disrupted Cities: When Infrastructure Fails.* New York: Routledge, 2010.

———. "When Infrastructures Fail." In *Disrupted Cities: When Infrastructure Fails,* edited by Stephen Graham, 1–26. New York: Routledge, 2010.

Graham, Stephen, and Nigel Thrift. "Out of Order: Understanding Repair and Maintenance." *Theory, Culture & Society* 24, no. 3 (2007): 1–25.

Greene, Molly. "An Islamic Experiment? Ottoman Land Policy on Crete." *Mediterranean Historical Review* 11, no. 1 (1996): 60–78.

———. *The Edinburgh History of the Greeks, 1453 to 1774: The Ottoman Empire.* Edinburgh: Edinburgh University Press, 2015.

———. "History in High Places: Tatarna Monastery and the Pindus Mountains." *Journal of the Economic and Social History of the Orient* 64, nos. 1–2 (2021): 1–24.

Greenwood, Anthony. "Istanbul's Meat Provisioning: A Study of the Celep-Keşan System." PhD diss., University of Chicago, 1988.

Grehan, James. "The Mysterious Power of Words: Language, Law, and Culture in Ottoman Damascus (17th–18th Centuries)." *Journal of Social History* 37, no. 4 (2004): 991–1015.

———. "Smoking and 'Early Modern' Sociability: The Great Tobacco Debate in the Ottoman Middle East (Seventeenth to Eighteenth Centuries)." *American Historical Review* 111, no. 5 (2006): 1352–1377.

Griswold, W. J. " Djalālī." In *Encyclopaedia of Islam,* 2nd ed., edited by P. Bearman, Th. Bianquis, C. E. Bosworth, E. van Donzel and W. P. Heinrichs. Leiden: Brill, 2012.

Günalan, Rifat, Vildan Kemal, Özlem Altıntop, Hatice Ayyıldız Bahadır, Mahmut Ak, and Mustafa Oğuz, eds. *İstanbul kadı sicilleri Üsküdar mahkemesi 2 numaralı sicil (H. 924–927 / M. 1518–1521).* İstanbul kadı sicilleri [editör Coşkun Yılmaz] 2. Istanbul: İslam Araştırmaları Merkezi, 2010.

Günalan, Rifat, Mehmet Canatar, and Mehmet Akman. *İstanbul Kadı Sicilleri Üsküdar Mahkemesi 84 Numaralı Sicil (H. 999–1000 / M. 1590–1591).* Istanbul: İSAM Yayınları, 2010.

Güneş, Mehmet. "XVIII Yüzyılın İkinci Yarısında Osmanlı Menzil Teşkilatı ve Karahisar-ı Sahib Menzilleri [The Karahisar Post Station and the Ottoman Post Station System in the Second Half of the Eighteenth Century]." *Afyon Kocatepe Üniversitesi Sosyal Bilimler Enstitüsü Dergisi* 3, no. 3 (2008): 35–63.

Güney, Kadir. "190 Numaralı Mühimme Defteri'nin Özetli Transkripsyonu ve Değerlendirmesi (H. 1203–1204, M. 1789–1790. Sayfa 1–97)." Master's thesis, Gaziantep University, 2012.

Guyer, Jane I. *Marginal Gains: Monetary Transactions in Atlantic Africa.* Chicago: University of Chicago Press, 2004.

Habib, Irfan. *The Agrarian System of Mughal India, 1556–1707.* Bombay: Asia Publishing House, 1963.

Hacker, Jacob S., Paul Pierson, and Kathleen Thelen. "Drift and Conversion: Hidden Faces of Institutional Change." In *Advances in Comparative-Historical Analysis,* edited by James Mahoney and Kathleen Thelen, 180–208. Cambridge: Cambridge University Press, 2015.

Hadjianastasis, Marios. "Crossing the Line in the Sand: Regional Officials, Monopolisation of State Power and 'Rebellion.' The Case of Mehmed Ağa Boyacıoğlu in Cyprus, 1685–1690." *Turkish Historical Review* 2, no. 2 (2011): 155–176.

Hafez, Melis. *Inventing Laziness: The Culture of Productivity in Late Ottoman Society.* Cambridge: Cambridge University Press, 2022.

Hagen, Gottfried. "Kātip Çelebi's Maps and the Visualization of Space in Ottoman Culture." *Osmanlı Araştırmaları* 40 (2012): 283–293.

Halaçoğlu, Yusuf. *Osmanlılarda Ulaşım ve Haberleşme (Menziller) [Ottoman Transportation and Communications].* Ankara: PTT Genel Müdürlüğü, 2002.

———. *XVI-XVII. Yüzyıllarda Osmanlılarda Devlet Teşkilâtı ve Sosyal Yapı.* Ankara: Türk Tarih Kurumu, 2014.

Hamadeh, Shirine. *The City's Pleasures: Istanbul in the Eighteenth Century.* Seattle: University of Washington Press, 2008.

Hanna, Nelly. *In Praise of Books: A Cultural History of Cairo's Middle Class, Sixteenth to the Eighteenth Century.* Syracuse, NY: Syracuse University Press, 2003.

Harris, Lane J. "The 'Arteries and Veins' of the Imperial Body: The Nature of the Relay and Post Station Systems in the Ming Dynasty, 1368–1644." *Journal of Early Modern History* 19, no. 4 (2015): 287–310.

Hartmann, Elke, Eva Søndergaard, and Linda J. Keeling. "Keeping Horses in Groups: A Review." *Applied Animal Behaviour Science* 136 (2012): 77–87.

Hasan, Farhat. *State and Locality in Mughal India: Power Relations in Western India, c. 1572–1730.* Cambridge: Cambridge University Press, 2004.

Hathaway, Jane. *The Politics of Households in Ottoman Egypt: The Rise of the Qazdaglis.* Cambridge: Cambridge University Press, 1997.

He, Vivianna Fang, and Phanish Puranam. "Collaborative Conflict Management." SSRN Scholarly Paper. Rochester, NY, November 16, 2021. https://doi.org/10.2139/ssrn.3964840.

Hegyi, Klára. *The Ottoman Military Organization in Hungary: Fortresses, Fortress Garrisons and Finances.* Berlin: Walter de Gruyter, 2018.

Heude, William. *A Voyage up the Persian Gulf: And a Journey Overland from India to England, in 1817.* London: Strahn and Spottiswoode, 1819.

Heyd, Uriel. *Ottoman Documents on Palestine 1552–1615: A Study of the Firman According to the Mühimme Defteri.* Oxford: Clarendon Press, 1960.

Heywood, Colin. "Between Historical Myth and 'Mythohistory': The Limits of Ottoman History." *Byzantine and Modern Greek Studies* 12 (1988): 315–345.

———. "The Evolution of the Courier Order (Ulak Hükmi) in Ottoman Chancery Practice (Fifteenth to Eighteenth Centuries)." In *Osmanische Welten: Quellen Und Fallstudien. Festschrift Für Michael Ursinus,* edited by Johannes Zimmermann, Cristoph Herzog, and Raoul Motika, 269–312. Bamberg: University of Bamberg Press, 2016.

———. "The Ottoman Menzilhane and Ulak System in Rumeli in the Eighteenth Century." In *Birinci Ulusarası Türkiye'nin Sosyal ve Ekonomik Tarihi Kongresi Tebliğleri (Social and Economic History of Turkey),* edited by Osman Okyar, and Halil İnalcık, 179–186. Ankara: Meteksan, 1980.

———. "Some Turkish Archival Sources for the History of the Menzilhane Network in Rumeli during the Eighteenth Century (Notes and Documents on the Ottoman Ulak, I)." *Boğaziçi Üniversitesi Dergisi: Beşeri Bilimler-Humanities* 4–5 (July 1976): 39–54.

———. "Two Firmans of Mustafa II on the Reorganization of the Ottoman Courier System (1108/1696)." *Acta Orientalia Academiae Scientiarum Hungaricae* 54, no. 4 (2001): 485–496.

———. "The Via Egnatia in the Ottoman Period: The Menzilhanes of the Sol Kol in the Late 17th / Early 18th Century." In *The Via Egnatia under Ottoman Rule, 1380–1699,* edited by Elizabeth Zachariadou, 129–144. Rethymno: Crete University Press, 1996.

Hickok, Michael Robert. *Ottoman Military Administration in Eighteenth-Century Bosnia.* Leiden: Brill, 1997.

Hinz, Walther. *İslam'da Ölçü Sistemleri.* Translated by Açar Sevim. Istanbul: Edebiyat Fakültesi Basımevi, 1990.

Honeychurch, William. "Alternative Complexities: The Archaeology of Pastoral Nomadic States." *Journal of Archaeological Research* 22, no. 4 (2014): 277–326.

Honeychurch, William, and Cheryl A. Makarewicz. "The Archaeology of Pastoral Nomadism." *Annual Review of Anthropology* 45 (2016): 341–359.

Hopwood, Anthony G. "On Trying to Study Accounting in the Contexts in Which It Operates." *Accounting, Organizations and Society* 8, no. 2 (1983): 287–305.

Hourani, Albert. "Ottoman Reform and the Politics of Notables." In *The Modern Middle East: A Reader,* edited by Albert Hourani, Philip S. Khoury, and Mary C. Wilson, 83–109. London: I. B. Tauris, 1993.

Howard, Douglas. "Why Timars? Why Now? Ottoman Timars in the Light of Recent Historiography." *Turkish Historical Review* 8 (2017): 119–144.

Howel, Thomas. *A Journal of the Passage from India: By a Route Partly Unfrequented, through Armenia and Natolia, or Asia Minor; To Which Are Added, Observations and Instructions, for the Use of Those Who Intend to Travel, Either to or from India, by That Route.* London: Printed for W. Clarke, 1791.

Howell, Jesse Cascade. "The Ragusa Road: Mobility and Encounter in the Ottoman Balkans (1430–1700)." PhD diss., Harvard University, 2017.

Huang, Ray. *Taxation and Governmental Finance in Sixteenth-Century Ming China.* Cambridge: Cambridge University Press, 1974.

Hughes, Thomas P. "The Evolution of Large Technical Systems." In *The Social Construction of Technological Systems: New Directions in the Sociology and History of Technology,* edited by Wiebe E. Bijker, Thomas P. Hughes, and Trevor Pinch, 51–82. Cambridge, MA: MIT Press, 1987.

———. *Networks of Power: Electrification in Western Society, 1880–1930.* Baltimore, MD: Johns Hopkins University Press, 1983.

Hui Li. *Da Ci En Si San Zang Fa Shi Zhuan.* Beijing: Zhonghua Shuju, 2000.

Husain, Faisal H. "Changes in the Euphrates River: Ecology and Politics in a Rural Ottoman Periphery, 1687–1702." *Journal of Interdisciplinary History* 47, no. 1 (2016): 1–25.

İlgürel, Mücteba. "Celâlî İsyanları," in *Türkiye Diyanet Vakfı İslam Ansiklopedisi: Ca'fer Es-Sadık-Ciltçilik,* vol. 7. Ankara: Türkiye Diyanet Vakfı, İslâm Ansiklopedisi Genel Müdürlüğü, 2019: 252–257.

Inalcık, Halil. "Centralization and Decentralization in Ottoman Administration." In *Studies in Eighteenth Century Islamic History,* edited by Thomas Naff and Roger Owen, 27–52. Carbondale: Southern Illinois University Press, 1977.

———. "Military and Fiscal Transformation in the Ottoman Empire, 1600–1700." *Archivum Ottomanicum* 6 (1980): 283–337.

———. *The Ottoman Empire: The Classical Age, 1300–1600.* New York: Praeger, 1973.

———. *Sources and Studies on the Ottoman Black Sea.* Vol. 1: *The Customs Register of Caffa, 1487–1490.* Studies in Ottoman Documents Pertaining to Ukraine and the Black Sea Countries 2. Cambridge, MA: Distributed by Harvard University Press for the Ukrainian Research Institute, Harvard University, 1996.

———. "The Yürüks: Their Origins, Expansion and Economic Role." In *Oriental Carpet & Textile Studies II: Carpets of the Mediterranean Countries 1400–1600,* edited by Robert Pinner and Walter B. Denny, 39–66. London: HALI Magazine, 1986.

Inalcık, Halil, and Donald Quataert, eds. *An Economic and Social History of the Ottoman Empire, 1300–1914.* Cambridge: Cambridge University Press, 1994.

Islamoğlu, Huri, and Çağlar Keyder. "Agenda for Ottoman History." *Review* 1, no. 1 (1977): 31–55.

Iwamoto, Keiko. 帝国と遊牧民: 近世オスマン朝の視座より [*Nomads and the Early Modern Empire: Nomadic Peoples under Ottoman Rule from the 15th to the 18th Centuries*]. Kyoto: Kyōtodaigaku gakujutsu shuppankai, 2019.

Jackson, John. *Journey from India, towards England, in the Year 1797; By a Route Commonly Called Over-Land, through Countries Not Much Frequented, and Many of Them Hitherto Unknown to Europeans, Particularly between the Rivers Euphrates and Tigris through Curdistan, Diarbek, Armenia, and Natolia, in Asia and through Romalia, Bulgaria, Wallachia, Transylvania, &c. In Europe.* London: Printed for T. Cadell, Jun. and W. Davies, Strand, 1799.

Jennings, Ronald C. "Loans and Credit in Early 17th-Century Ottoman Judicial Records: The Sharia Court of Anatolian Kayseri." *Journal of the Economic and Social History of the Orient* 16, no. 2/3 (1973): 168–216.

———. "Kadi, Court, and Legal Procedure in 17th c. Ottoman Kayseri: The Kadi and the Legal System." *Studia Islamica,* no. 48 (1978): 133–172.

———. "Women in Early 17th-Century Ottoman Judicial Records: The Sharia Court of Anatolian Kayseri." *Journal of the Economic and Social History of the Orient* 18, no. 1 (1975): 53–114.

———. "Zimmis (Non-Muslims)in Early 17th-Century Ottoman Judicial Records: The Sharia Court of Anatolian Kayseri." *Journal of the Economic and Social History of the Orient* 21, no. 3 (1978): 225–293.

John, Richard R. "American Historians and the Concept of the Communications Revolution." In *Information Acumen: The Understanding and Use of Knowledge in Modern Business,* edited by Lisa Bud-Frierman, 98–110. London: Routledge, 1994.

———. "Recasting the Information Infrastructure for the Industrial Age." In *A Nation Transformed by Information: How Information Has Shaped the United States from Colonial Times to the Present,* edited by Alfred D. Chandler and James W. Cortada, 55–106. Oxford: Oxford University Press, 2000.

———. *Spreading the News: The American Postal System from Franklin to Morse.* Cambridge, MA: Harvard University Press, 1995.

Johnson, Steven. *Emergence: The Connected Lives of Ants, Brains, Cities and Software.* New York: Scribner, 2001.

Kahneman, Daniel, Jack L. Knetsch, and Richard H. Thaler. "Anomalies: The Endowment Effect, Loss Aversion, and Status Quo Bias." *Journal of Economic Perspectives* 5, no. 1 (1991): 193–206.

Kahraman, Seyit Ali, and Yücel Dağlı, eds. *Evliya Çelebi Seyahatnamesi 2: Topkapı Sarayı Bağdat 305 Yazmasının Traskripsiyonu—Dizini.* Istanbul: Yapı ve Kredi Bankası, 1993.

———, eds. *Evliya Çelebi Seyahatnamesi 3: Topkapı Sarayı Bağdat 305 Yazmasının Traskripsiyonu—Dizini.* Istanbul: Yapı ve Kredi Bankası, 1993.

———, eds. *Evliya Çelebi Seyahatnamesi 4: Topkapı Sarayı Bağdat 305 Yazmasının Traskripsiyonu—Dizini.* Istanbul: Yapı ve Kredi Bankası, 1993.

———, eds. *Evliya Çelebi Seyahatnamesi 5: Topkapı Sarayı Bağdat 305 Yazmasının Traskripsiyonu—Dizini.* Istanbul: Yapı ve Kredi Bankası, 1993.

———, eds. *Evliya Çelebi Seyahatnamesi 7: Topkapı Sarayı Bağdat 305 Yazmasının Traskripsiyonu—Dizini.* Istanbul: Yapı ve Kredi Bankası, 1993.

———, eds. *Evliya Çelebi Seyahatnamesi 8: Topkapı Sarayı Bağdat 305 Yazmasının Traskripsiyonu—Dizini.* Istanbul: Yapı ve Kredi Bankası, 1993.

———, eds. *Evliya Çelebi Seyahatnamesi 9: Topkapı Sarayı Bağdat 305 Yazmasının Traskripsiyonu—Dizini.* Istanbul: Yapı ve Kredi Bankası, 1993.

———, eds. *Evliya Çelebi Seyahatnamesi 10: Topkapı Sarayı Bağdat 305 Yazmasının Traskripsiyonu—Dizini.* Istanbul: Yapı ve Kredi Bankası, 1993.

Karacakaya, Recep, İsmail Yücedağ, and Nazım Yılmaz, eds. *Safranbolu Şer'iyye Sicili 2116 Numaralı Defter.* Istanbul: Safranbolu Belediye Başkanlığı, 2013.

Karakaya-Stump, Ayfer. *The Kizilbash-Alevis in Ottoman Anatolia: Sufism, Politics and Community.* Edinburgh Studies on the Ottoman Empire. Edinburgh: Edinburgh University Press, 2020.

Karateke, Hakan T. *An Ottoman Protocol Register Containing Ceremonies from 1736 to 1808: BEO Sadaret Defterleri 350 in the Prime Ministry Ottoman State Archives, Istanbul.* Istanbul: Ottoman Bank Archives and Research Centre, 2007.

Kasaba, Reşat. *A Moveable Empire: Ottoman Nomads, Migrants, and Refugees.* Seattle: University of Washington Press, 2009.

Keeling, L. J., K. E. Bøe, J. W. Christensen, S. Hyyppä, H. Jansson, G. H. M. Jørgensen, and J. Ladewig. "Injury Incidence, Reactivity and Ease of Handling of Horses Kept in Groups: A Matched Case Control Study in Four Nordic Countries." *Applied Animal Behaviour Science* 185 (2016): 59–65.

Keenan, Edward Louis. "Muscovy and Kazan: Some Introductory Remarks on the Patterns of Steppe Diplomacy." *Slavic Review* 26, no. 4 (1967): 548–558.

Khoury, Dina Rizk. *State and provincial society in the Ottoman Empire: Mosul, 1540–1834.* Cambridge: Cambridge University, 1997.

———. "The Ottoman Centre versus Provincial Power-Holders: An Analysis of the Historiography." In *The Cambridge History of Turkey: The Later Ottoman Empire,*

1603–1839, edited by Suraiya Faroqhi, 3:135–156. Cambridge: Cambridge University Press, 2006.

Kinneir, Sir John Macdonald. *Journey through Asia Minor, Armenia, and Koordistan in the Years 1813 and 1814: With Remarks on the Marches of Alexander and Retreat of the Ten Thousand.* London: John Murray, 1818.

Kishimoto, Mio. "Property Rights and Factor Markets." In *The Cambridge Economic History of China.* Volume I, *To 1800,* edited by Debin Ma and Richard Von Glahn, 448–483. Cambridge: Cambridge University Press, 2022.

Kittler, Juraj. "Capitalism and Communications: The Rise of Commercial Courier Networks in the Context of the Champagne Fairs." *Capitalism: A Journal of History and Economics* 4, no. 1 (2023): 109–152.

Kırlı, Cengiz. "A Profile of the Labor Force in Early Nineteenth-Century Istanbul." *International Labor and Working-Class History* 60 (2001): 125–140.

———. "The Struggle over Space: Coffeehouses of Ottoman Istanbul, 1780–1845." PhD diss, Binghamton University, State University of New York, 2000. "A Profile of the Labor Force in Early Nineteenth-Century Istanbul." *International Labor and Working-Class History* 60 (2001): 125–140.

Koç, Yahya. "149 Numaralı Mühimme Defteri (1155–1156 / 1742–1743): İnceleme-Çeviriyazı-Dizin." Master's thesis, Istanbul University, 2011.

Koh, Choon Hwee. "The Mystery of the Missing Horses: How to Uncover an Ottoman Shadow Economy." *Comparative Studies in Society and History* 64, no. 3 (2022): 576–610.

———. "An Ottoman Liquidity Crunch: Immediate and Deferred Payments at Post Stations (Menzilhane), 1713–1763." *Turcica* 54 (2023): 355–375.

———. "The Ottoman Postmaster: Contractors, Communication and Early Modern State Formation." *Past & Present* 251, no. 1 (2021): 113–152.

———. "The Sublime Post: A History of Empire and Power through the Ottoman Post Station System, 1600–1839." PhD diss., Yale University, 2020.

———. "Two More Firmans on the Reorganisation of the Ottoman Postal System (1101/1690 and 1209/1794): (Documents from the Amasya and Damascus Kadi Sicils)." *Acta Orientalia Academiae Scientiarum Hungaricae* 76, no. 1 (2023): 149–164.

Köksal, Yonca. *The Ottoman Empire in the Tanzimat Era: Provincial Perspectives from Ankara to Edirne.* New York: Routledge, 2019.

Kolb, Anne. "Transport and Communication in the Roman State: The Cursus Publicus." In *Travel and Geography in the Roman Empire,* edited by Colin Adams and Ray Laurence, 95–105. London: Routledge, 2001.

Kraelitz-Greifenhorst, Friedrich. *Osmanische Urkunden in Türkischer Sprache aus der Zweiten Hälfte des 15. Jahrhunderts: Ein Beitrag zur Osmanischen Diplomatik.* Vienna: Alfred Hölder, 1921.

Krstić, Tijana. *Contested Conversions to Islam: Narratives of Religious Change in the Early Modern Ottoman Empire.* Stanford, CA: Stanford University Press, 2011.

Küçükoğlu, L. Sevinç. "New Fiscal Actors to Control Provincial Expenditures at the End of 18th Century." *Osmanlı Araştırmaları* 2019, no. 54 (2019): 241–276.

Kunt, Metin. "Derviş Mehmed Paşa, Vezir and Entrepreneur: A Study in Ottoman Political Economic Theory and Practice." *Turcica* 9 (1977): 197–214.

———. *The Sultan's Servants: The Transformation of Ottoman Provincial Government, 1550–1650.* New York: Columbia University Press, 1983.

Kuroda, Akinobu. "Concurrent but Non-integrable Currency Circuits: Complementary Relationships among Monies in Modern China and Other Regions." *Financial History Review* 15, no. 1 (2008): 17–36.

———. *A Global History of Money.* New York: Routledge, 2020.

———. "What Is the Complementarity among Monies? An Introductory Note." *Financial History Review* 15, no. 1 (2008): 7–15.

Kurz, Marlene. *Das Sicill aus Skopje: Kritische Edition und Kommentierung des einzigen vollständig erhaltenen Kadiamtsregisterbandes (Sicill) aus Üsküb (Skopje).* Wiesbaden: Harrassowitz, 2003.

Laborda Peman, M., and T. De Moor. "History and the Commons: A Necessary Conversation." *International Journal of the Commons* 10, no. 2 (2016): 517–528.

Laiou, Sophia. "Economic Networks in the Eastern Mediterranean: Kâtiboğlu Mehmed Efendi of Izmir and His Christian Partner." *Mediterranean Historical Review* 34, no. 2 (2019): 181–194.

Lansing, J. Stephen. *Perfect Order: Recognizing Complexity in Bali.* Princeton, NJ: Princeton University Press, 2006.

———. *Priests and Programmers: Technologies of Power in the Engineered Landscape of Bali.* Princeton, NJ: Princeton University Press, 2007.

Larkin, Brian. "The Politics and Poetics of Infrastructure." *Annual Review of Anthropology* 42 (2013): 327–343.

Lee, Kai-Fu. *AI Superpowers: China, Silicon Valley and the New World Order.* Boston: Houghton Mifflin Harcourt, 2018.

Lehmann, Matthias B. *Emissaries from the Holy Land: The Sephardic Diaspora and the Practice of Pan-Judaism in the Eighteenth Century.* Stanford, CA: Stanford University Press, 2014.

Lewis, Pauline. "Wired Ottomans: A Sociotechnical History of the Telegraph and the Modern Ottoman Empire, 1855–1911." PhD diss., University of California, Los Angeles, 2018.

Linnarsson, Magnus. "The Development of the Swedish Post Office c. 1600–1718." In *Connecting the Baltic Area: The Swedish Postal System in the Seventeenth Century,* edited by Heiko Droste, 25–47. Huddinge, Sweden: Södertörns högskola, 2011.

Longva, Anh Nga. *Walls Built on Sand: Migration, Exclusion, and Society in Kuwait.* Boulder, CO: Routledge, 1997.

Low, Donald, ed. *Behavioural Economics and Policy Design: Examples from Singapore.* Singapore: World Scientific, 2011.

Lowry, Heath. "The Ottoman Tahrir Defterleri as a Source for Social and Economic History: Pitfalls and Limitations." In *Türkische Wirtschafts-Und Sozialgeschichte (1071–1920)*, edited by Hans Georg Majer and Raoul Motika, 183–196. Wiesbaden: Harrasowitz, 1995.

Lysa, Hong. "The Tax Farming System in the Early Bangkok Period." *Journal of Southeast Asian Studies* 14, no. 2 (1983): 379–399.

Mahoney, James, and Kathleen Thelen. "A Theory of Gradual Institutional Change." In *Explaining Institutional Change: Ambiguity, Agency, and Power,* edited by James Mahoney and Kathleen Thelen, 1–37. Cambridge: Cambridge University Press, 2009.

Makdisi, Ussama Samir. "Corrupting the Sublime Sultanate: The Revolt of Tanyus Shahin in Nineteenth-Century Ottoman Lebanon." *Comparative Studies in Society and History* 42, no. 1 (2000): 180–208.

Mann, Michael. "The Autonomous Power of the State: Its Origins, Mechanisms and Results." In *States in History,* edited by John A. Hall, 109–136. Oxford: Basil Blackwell, 1986.

Mann, Susan. *Local Merchants and the Chinese Bureaucracy, 1750–1950.* Stanford, CA: Stanford University Press, 1987.

Martins, O., Luiza Prado de, and Pedro J. S. Vieira de Oliveira. "Designer/Shapeshifter: A Decolonizing Redirection for Speculative and Critical Design." In *Tricky Design: The Ethics of Things*, edited by Tom Fisher and Lorraine Gamman, 103–114. London: Bloomsbury Visual Arts, 2019.

Masters, Bruce. *Origins of Western Economic Dominance in the Middle East: Mercantilism and the Islamic Economy in Aleppo, 1600–1750.* New York: New York University Press, 1988.

Matuz, Joseph. "Contributions to the Ottoman Institution of the Iltizam." *Osmanlı Araştırmaları* 11 (1991): 237–249.

Maundrell, Henry. *A Journey from Aleppo to Jerusalem at Easter, A.D. 1697.* Oxford: The Theater, 1721.

Maurer, Petra. "The Tibetan Governmental Transport and Postal System: Horse Services and Other Taxes from the 13th to the 20th Centuries." *Buddhism, Law & Society* 5 (2019): 1–58.

McGowan, Bruce. *Economic Life in Ottoman Europe: Taxation, Trade and the Struggle for Land, 1600–1800.* Cambridge: Cambridge University Press, 1981.

McLuhan, Marshall. *Understanding Media: The Extensions of Man.* Cambridge, MA: MIT Press, 1994.

Meadows, Donella H. *Thinking in Systems: A Primer.* Edited by Diana Wright. London: Earthscan, 2008.

Meeker, Michael E. *A Nation of Empire: The Ottoman Legacy of Turkish Modernity.* Oakland, CA: University of California Press, 2002.

Mehmed Efendi and Yirmisekiz Çelebi. *Relation de l'ambassade de Mehemet-Effendi, a la cour de France, en M. DCC. XXI. écrite par lui-meme, et traduite du turc.* Constantinople,1757. http://ark.bnf.fr/ark:/12148/bpt6k9774478r.

Meier, Astrid. "The Materiality of Ottoman Water Administration in Eighteenth-Century Rural Damascus." In *Landscapes of the Islamic World: Archaeology, History, and Ethnography,* edited by Stephen McPhillips and Paul D. Wordsworth, 19–33. Philadelphia: University of Pennsylvania Press, 2016.

Meiton, Frederik. *Electrical Palestine: Capital and Technology from Empire to Nation.* Berkeley, CA: University of California Press, 2019.

Ménage, V. L., and Colin Imber. *Ottoman Historical Documents: The Institutions of an Empire.* Edinburgh: Edinburgh University Press, 2021.

Menchinger, Ethan L. *The First of the Modern Ottomans: The Intellectual History of Ahmed Vasif.* Cambridge: Cambridge University Press, 2017.

Meniński, Franciszek. *Thesaurus Linguarum Orientalium, Turcicæ, Arabicæ, Persicæ.* Vienna, 1680.

Messick, Brinkley. *The Calligraphic State: Textual Domination and History in a Muslim Society.* Berkeley University of California, 1993.

Meyer, John W., and Brian Rowan. "Institutionalized Organizations: Formal Structure as Myth and Ceremony." *The American Journal of Sociology* 83, no. 2 (1977): 340–63.

Midura, Rachel. "Itinerating Europe: Early Modern Spatial Networks in Printed Itineraries, 1545–1700." *Journal of Social History* 54, no. 4 (2021): 1023–1063.

———. "Princes of the Post: Power, Publicity, and Europe's Communications Revolution (1500–1700)." Unpublished manuscript, last modified January 2023, .docx.

Mikhail, Alan. *Nature and Empire in Ottoman Egypt: An Environmental History.* Cambridge: Cambridge University Press, 2011.

Mitchell, Melanie. *Complexity: A Guided Tour.* New York: Oxford University Press, 2009.

Mitchell, Peter. *Horse Nations: The Worldwide Impact of the Horse on Indigenous Societies Post-1492.* Oxford: Oxford University Press, 2015.

Mitchell, Timothy. *Carbon Democracy: Political Power in the Age of Oil.* Brooklyn: Verso, 2011.

Mitra, Debendra Bijoy. *Monetary System in the Bengal Presidency, 1757–1835.* Calcutta: K. P. Bagchi, 1991.

Moačanin, Nenad. *Town and Country on the Middle Danube, 1526–1690.* Ottoman Empire and Its Heritage, vol. 35. Leiden: Brill, 2006.

Mordtmann, J. H. "Die Jüdischen Kira im Serai der Sultane." *Mitteilungen des Seminars für Orientalische Sprachen: Westasiatische Studien* 32 (1929): 1–38.

Morgan, David. *The Mongols.* Oxford: Basil Blackwell, 2007.

Morita, Madoka. "Between Hostility and Hospitality: Neighbourhoods and Dynamics of Urban Migration in Istanbul (1730–54)." *Turkish Historical Review* 7 (2016): 58–85.

Mosca, Matthew. *From Frontier Policy to Foreign Policy: The Question of India and the Transformation of Geopolitics in Qing China.* Stanford, CA: Stanford University Press, 2013.

Mouradgea d'Ohsson, Ignatius. *Tableau général de l'empire othoman: Divisé en deux parties, dont l'une comprend la législation mahométane; l'autre, l'histoire de l'empire othoman.* Vol. 7. Paris: De l'imprimerie de monsieur Firmin Didot, 1824.

Moussaïd, Mehdi, Dirk Helbing, and Guy Theraulaz. "How Simple Rules Determine Pedestrian Behavior and Crowd Disasters." *Proceedings of the National Academy of Sciences* 108, no. 17 (2011): 6884–6888. https://doi.org/10.1073/pnas.1016507108.

Muldrew, Craig. *The Economy of Obligation: The Culture of Credit and Social Relations in Early Modern England.* Basingstoke, UK: Palgrave, 1998.

Mundy, Peter. *The Travels of Peter Mundy in Europe and Asia, 1608–1667.* Edited by Richard Carnac Temple and Lavinia Mary Anstey. Vol. 1. Cambridge, UK: Hakluyt Society, 1907.

Murphey, Rhoads. *Ottoman Warfare, 1500–1700.* London: UCL Press, 1999.

———. "Mustafa Ali and the Politics of Cultural Despair." *International Journal of Middle East Studies* 21, no. 2 (1989): 243–255.

Mustafa Ali. *Mustafa Ali's Counsel for Sultans of 1581: Edition, Translation, Notes I.* Translated by Andreas Tietze.Vienna: Verlag der österreichischen Akademie der Wissenschaften, 1979.

———. *Mustafa Ali's Counsel for Sultans of 1581: Edition, Translation, Notes II.* Translated by Andreas Tietze.Vienna: Verlag der österreichischen Akademie der Wissenschaften, 1982.

Myers, Jane. *Horse Safe: A Complete Guide to Equine Safety.* Collingwood, Victoria, Australia: Landlinks Press, 2005.

Nayeem, M. A. Sayyid Dā'ūd Ashraf, P. Sitapati, and H. Rajendra Prasad, eds. *Mughal Documents: Catalogue of Aurangzeb's Reign.* Hyderabad: State Archives, Government of Andhra Pradesh, 1980.

Necipoğlu, Gülru. *The Age of Sinan: Architectural Culture in the Ottoman Empire, 1539–1588.* London: Reaktion, 2005.

Needham, Joseph. *Science and Civilization in China.* Vol. 4: *Physics and Physical Technology,* Part 3, *Civil Engineering and Nautics.* Cambridge: Cambridge University Press, 1971.

Nizri, Michael. "Rethinking Center-Periphery Communication in the Ottoman Empire: The Kapı-Kethüdası." *Journal of the Economic and Social History of the Orient* 59 (2016): 473–498.

Ogilvie, Sheilagh. "State Capacity and Economic Growth: Cautionary Tales from History." *National Institute Economic Review* 262 (2022): 28–50.

Ogilvie, Sheilagh, Markus Küpker, and Janine Maegraith. "Household Debt in Early Modern Germany: Evidence from Personal Inventories." *The Journal of Economic History* 72, no. 1 (2012): 134–167.

Orhonlu, Cengiz. *Osmanlı İmparatorluğu'nda Aşiretleri İskanı.* Istanbul: Eren Yayıncılık, 1987.

———. *Osmanlı İmparatorluğunda şehircilik ve ulaşım üzerine araştırmalar: şehir mimarları, kaldırımcılık, köprücülük, su-yolculuk, kayıkçılık, gemicilik, nehir nakliyatı, kervan, kervan yolları.* İzmir: Ege Üniversitesi Edebiyat Fakültesi Yayınları, 1984.

Osmanlı İmparatorluğu'nda Aşiretleri İskanı. Istanbul: Eren Yayıncılık, 1987.

Osman of Timisoara. *Prisoner of the Infidels: The Memoirs of an Ottoman Muslim in Seventeenth-Century Europe.* Translated by Giancarlo Casale. Oakland: University of California Press, 2021.

Ostrom, Elinor. *Governing the Commons: The Evolution of Institutions for Collective Action.* Cambridge: Cambridge University Press, 2017.

Özbek, Nadir. "Policing the Countryside: Gendarmes of the Late 19th-Century Ottoman Empire (1876–1908)." *International Journal of Middle East Studies* 40, no. 1 (2008): 47–67.

Özel, Oktay. "Population Changes in Ottoman Anatolia during the 16th and 17th Centuries: The 'Demographic Crisis' Reconsidered." *International Journal of Middle East Studies* 36, no. 2 (2004): 183–205.

Özergin, M. Kemal. "Anadolu'da Selçuklu Kervansarayları." *Tarih Dergisi* 15, no. 20 (1965): 141–170.

Özizmirli, Görkem. "Fear in Evliya Çelebi's Seyahatnâme: Politics and Historiography in a Seventeenth Century Ottoman Travelogue." Master's thesis, Koç University, 2014.

Ozkan, Fulya. "Gravediggers of the Modem State: Highway Robbers on the Trabzon-Bayezid Road, 1850s–1910s." *Journal of Persianate Studies* 7 (2014): 219–250.

Özkaya, Yücel. "XVIII Yüzyılda Menzilhane Sorunu." *Ankara Üniversitesi Dil ve Tarih Coğrafya Fakültesi Dergisi* 28, nos. 3–4 (1970): 339–367.

Pakalın, Mehmet Zeki. *Osmanli Tarih Deyimleri ve Terimleri Sözlüğü 3.* Istanbul: Millî Eğitim Basımevi, 1983.

———. *Osmanlı tarih deyimleri ve terimleri sözlüğü 2.* Istanbul: Millî Eğitim Basımevi, 1983.

Pamuk, Şevket. *A Monetary History of the Ottoman Empire.* Cambridge: Cambridge University Press, 2000.

———. "Prices in the Ottoman Empire, 1469–1914." *International Journal of Middle East Studies* 36 (2004): 451–468.

Parker, Geoffrey. *The Military Revolution: Military Innovation and the Rise of the West, 1500–1800.* Cambridge: Cambridge University Press, 1988.

Parrott, David. *The Business of War: Military Enterprise and Military Revolution in Early Modern Europe.* Cambridge: Cambridge University Press, 2012.

Paşa, Lutfi Paşa b Abdülmuin Abdülhay Lutfi. *Âsafnâme.* Edited by Ahmet Uğur. Ankara: Kültür ve Turizm Bakanlığı, 1982.

Paz, Omri. "Civil-Servant Aspirants: Ottoman Social Mobility in the Second Half of the Nineteenth Century." *Journal of the Economic and Social History of the Orient* 60, no. 4 (2017): 381–419.

Peirce, Leslie P. *The Imperial Harem: Women and Sovereignty in the Ottoman Empire.* New York: Oxford University Press, 1993.

———. *Morality Tales: Law and Gender in the Ottoman Court of Aintab.* Berkeley: University of California Press, 2003.

Pelliot, Paul. "Neuf Notes sur des Questions d'Asie Centrale." *T'oung Pao* 26, no. 4/5 (1929): 201–266.

Perrow, Charles. *Normal Accidents: Living with High-Risk Technologies.* Princeton, NJ: Princeton University Press, 1999.

Pétriat, Philippe. "Caravan Trade in the Late Ottoman Empire: The 'Aqil Network and the Institutionalization of Overland Trade." *Journal of the Economic and Social History of the Orient* 63 (2020): 38–72.

Peyssonnel, Claude-Charles de. *Traité sur le commerce de la Mer Noire.* Vol. 2. Paris: Cuchet, 1787.

Philliou, Christine. "Communities on the Verge: Unraveling the Phanariot Ascendancy in Ottoman Governance." *Comparative Studies in Society and History* 51, no. 1 (2009): 151–181.

Phillips, Amanda. *Sea Change: Ottoman Textiles between the Mediterranean and the Indian Ocean.* Oakland: University of California Press, 2021.

Porter, Theodore M. *Trust in Numbers: The Pursuit of Objectivity in Science and Public Life.* Princeton, NJ: Princeton University Press, 1995.

Puranam, Phanish, and Dorthe Døjbak Håkonsson. "Valve's Way." *Journal of Organization Design (Aarhus)* 4, no. 2 (2015): 2–4.

Quataert, Donald. *The Ottoman Empire, 1700–1922.* Cambridge: Cambridge University Press, 2005.

Rachewiltz, Igor de, trans. *The Secret History of the Mongols: A Mongolian Epic Chronicle of the Thirteenth Century.* Vol. 1. Leiden: Brill, 2004.

Radner, Karen. "Introduction: Long-Distance Communication and the Cohesion of Early Empires." In *State Correspondence in the Ancient World: From New Kingdom Egypt to the Roman Empire,* edited by Karen Radner, 1–9. Oxford Studies in Early Empires. Oxford: Oxford University Press, 2014.

Radušev, Evgenij. "Les Dépenses Locales dans l'Empire Ottoman au XVIIIe Siècle (Selon les Données de Registres de Cadi de Ruse, Vidin et Sofia)." *Études Balkaniques* 16, no. 3 (1980): 74–94.

Ragheb, Youssef. *Les Messagers Volants en Terre d'Islam.* Paris: CNRS éditions, 2002.

Randolph, John. "Communication and Obligation: The Postal System of the Russian Empire, 1700–1850." In *Information and Empire: Mechanisms of Communication in Russia, 1600–1854,* edited by Simon Franklin and Katherine Bowers, 155–183. Cambridge, UK: Open Book Publishers, 2017.

Raymond, André. *Artisans et commerçants au Caire au XVIIIe siècle.* Vol. 1. Damas: Presses de l'Ifpo, 1973.

———. "Soldiers in Trade: The Case of Ottoman Cairo." *British Journal of Middle Eastern Studies* 18, no. 1 (1991): 16–37.

r/DesirePath, https://www.reddit.com/r/DesirePath/ ("Dedicated to the paths that humans prefer, rather than the paths that humans create").

Redhouse, Sir James. *Ne Redhouse Turkish-English Dictionary.* Istanbul: Redhouse Yayınevi, 1986.

———. *A Turkish and English Lexicon Shewing in English the Significations of the Turkish Terms.* Beirut: Librairie du Liban, 1987.

Regmi, Mahesh C. *Imperial Gorkha: An Account of Gorkhali Rule in Kumaun (1791–1815).* Delhi: Adroit Publishers, 1999.

Reinhart, A. Kevin. *Lived Islam: Colloquial Religion in a Cosmopolitan Tradition.* Cambridge: Cambridge University Press, 2020.

Resnick, Mitchel. *Turtles, Termites, and Traffic Jams: Explorations in Massively Parallel Microworlds.* Cambridge, MA: MIT Press, 2001.

Richards, John F. *Mughal Administration in Golconda.* Oxford: Clarendon Press, 1975.

Riedler, Florian. "The Istanbul-Belgrade Route in the Ottoman Empire: Continuity and Discontinuity of an Imperial Mobility Space." In *The Balkan Route: Historical Transformations from Via Militaris to Autoput,* edited by Florian Riedler and Nenad Stefanov, 103–120. Berlin: De Gruyter, 2021.

Roberts, Michael. *Essays in Swedish History.* London: Weidenfeld and Nicolson, 1967.

Robinson, David M. *Korea and the Fall of the Mongol Empire: Alliance, Upheaval, and the Rise of a New East Asian Order.* Cambridge: Cambridge University Press, 2022.

Rogan, Eugene. "Instant Communication: The Impact of the Telegraph in Ottoman Syria." In *The Syrian Land: Processes of Integration and Fragmentation,* edited by Thomas Philipp and Birgit Schaebler, 113–128. Stuttgart: F. Steiner, 1998.

Rosner, Daniela. *Critical Fabulations: Reworking the Methods and Margins of Design.* Cambridge, MA: MIT Press, 2018.

Rossabi, Morris. "The Tea and Horse Trade with Inner Asia during the Ming." *The Journal of Asian Studies* 4, no. 2 (1970): 136–168.

Rowe, John Howland. "Inca Culture at the Time of the Spanish Conquest." In *Handbook of South American Indians,* edited by Julian Haynes Steward, Vol. 2: *The Andean Civilizations,* 183–330. Washington, DC: U.S. Government Publishing Office, 1946.

Russell, Andrew L., and Lee Vinsel. "After Innovation, Turn to Maintenance." *Technology and Culture* 59, no. 1 (2018): 1–25.

Rüstem, Ünver. *Ottoman Baroque: The Architectural Refashioning of Eighteenth-Century Istanbul.* Princeton, NJ: Princeton University Press, 2019.

Rycaut, Sir Paul. *The History of the Present State of the Ottoman Empire: Containing the Maxims of the Turkish Polity, the Most Material Points of the Mahometan Religion,*

Their Sects and Heresies, Their Convents and Religious Votaries. Their Military Discipline, with an Exact Computation of Their Forces Both by Sea and Land . . . In Three Books. London: R. Clavell, J. Robinson and A. Churchill, 1686.

(al-)Sabbagh, Abdelatif Mohammed. "Tanẓīm Al-Barīd Fī al-Shām Ibbān al-Ḥukm al-Miṣri, 1831–1840." *Al-Majallah al-Tārīkhīyya al-Miṣriyya* 40 (1997–1999): 185–216.

Sahillioğlu, Halil. "Dördüncü Marad'ın Bağdat Seferi Menzilnamesi—Bağdat Seferi Harp Jurnalı." *Belgeler* 2, nos. 3–4 (1965): 1–35.

Şahin, Canay. "The Economic Power of Anatolian Ayans of the Late Eighteenth Century: The Case of the Caniklizades." *International Journal of Turkish Studies* 11, nos. 1–2 (2005): 29–49.

———. "The Rise and Fall of an Ayan Family in Eighteenth Century Anatolia: The Caniklizades (1737–1808)." PhD diss., Bilkent University, 2004.

Sajdi, Dana. *The Barber of Damascus: Nouveau Literacy in the Eighteenth-Century Ottoman Levant.* Stanford, CA: Stanford University Press, 2013.

Sak, İzzet. *11 Numaralı Konya Şer'iye Sicili [Konya Judicial Records Vol. 11].* Konya: Kömen Yayınları, 2007.

———. *37 numaralı Konya şer'iye sicili (1102–1103 / 1691–1692): Transkripsiyon ve dizin [Konya Judicial Records Vol. 37].* Konya: Konya Ticaret Odası, 2010.

———. *47 Numaralı Konya Şer'iye Sicili, 1128–1129/1716–1717: Transkripsiyon ve Dizin [Konya Judicial Records Vol. 47].* Konya: Tablet, 2006.

Sak, İzzet, and Cemal Çetin. *45 numaralı Konya şer'iye sicili, 1126–1127/1714–1715: transkripsiyon ve dizin [Konya Judicial Records Vol. 45].* Konya: Selçuklu Belediyesi Kültür Yayınları, 2008.

Sak, İzzet, and İbrahim Solak. *53 Numaralı Konya Şer'iye Sicili (1148–1149/1736–1737): Transkripsiyon ve Dizin [Konya Judicial Records Vol. 53].* Konya: Selçuk Üniversitesi Basımevi, 2014.

Salzmann, Ariel. "An Ancien Regime Revisited: 'Privatization' and Political Economy in the Eighteenth-Century Ottoman Empire." *Politics & Society* 21, no. 4 (1993): 393–423.

———. "Measures of Empire: Tax Farmers and the Ottoman Ancien Regime, 1695–1807." PhD diss., Columbia University, 1995.

———. "The Old Regime and the Ottoman Middle East." In *The Ottoman World,* edited by Christine Woodhead, 409–422. London: Routledge, 2011.

Sangster, Alan. "The Genesis of Double Entry Bookkeeping." *The Accounting Review* 91, no. 1 (2016): 299–315.

Sariyannis, Marinos. "Notes on the Ottoman Poll-Tax Reforms of the Late Seventeenth Century: The Case of Crete." *Journal of the Economic and Social History of the Orient* 54 (2011): 39–61.

Sarınay, Yusuf, and Osman Yıldırım. *83 numaralı Mühimme Defteri, 1036–1037/1626–1628: Özet, transkripsiyon, indeks ve tıpkıbasım.* Ankara: T. C. Başbakanlık Devlet Arşivleri Genel Müdürlüğü, 2001.

Sartori, Paolo. "Authorized Lies: Colonial Agency and Legal Hybrids in Tashkent, c. 1881–1893." *Journal of the Economic and Social History of the Orient* 55 (2012): 688–717.

Saydam, Abdullah. "Kamu Hizmeti Yaptırma ve Suçu Önleme Yöntemi Olarak Osmanlılarda Kefâlet Usûlü." *Tarih ve Toplum* 164 (1997): 4–12.

Schultz, Tristan, Danah Abdulla, Ahmed Ansari, Ece Canlı, Mahmoud Keshavarz, Matthew Kiem, Luiza Prado de O. Martins, and Pedro J. S. Vieira de Oliveira. "What Is at Stake with Decolonizing Design? A Roundtable." *The Journal of the Design Studies Forum* 10, no. 1 (2018): 81–101.

Şentürk, M. Hüdai. "Osmanlılarda Haberleşme ve Menzil Teşkilatına Genel Bir Bakış." *Türkler* 14 (2000): 446–461.

Sewell Jr., William H. "A Strange Career: The Historical Study of Economic Life." *History and Theory* 49, no. 4 (2010): 146–166.

Seyyid Abdürrahim Muhibb Efendi, and Seyyid Ali Efendi Moralı. *Deux ottomans à Paris sous le Directoire et l'Empire: Relations d'ambassade.* Translated by Stefanos Yerasimos. Arles: Actes Sud, 1998.

Shafiee, Katayoun. *Machineries of Oil: An Infrastructural History of BP in Iran.* Cambridge, MA: MIT Press, 2018.

Shapiro, Kenneth, and Margo DeMello. "The State of Human-Animal Studies." *Society and Animals* 18 (2010): 307–318.

Shaw, Stanford J. *Between Old and New: The Ottoman Empire under Sultan Selim III, 1789–1807.* Cambridge, MA Harvard University Press, 1971.

———. *The Budget of Ottoman Egypt, 1005–1006/1596–1597.* The Hague: Mouton, 1968.

———. *The Financial and Administrative Organization and Development of Ottoman Egypt, 1517–1798.* Princeton, NJ: Princeton University Press, 1962.

———. *History of the Ottoman Empire and Modern Turkey.* Vol. 1: *Empire of the Gazis: The Rise and Decline of the Ottoman Empire 1280–1808.* Cambridge: Cambridge University Press, 1976.

Shinder, Joel. "Career Line Formation in the Ottoman Bureaucracy, 1648–1750: A New Perspective." *Journal of the Economic and Social History of the Orient* 16, no. 2 / 3 (1973): 217–237.

Shryock, Andrew. "Meticulous Sleuthing. A Conversation with Koh Choon Hwee." *Comparative Studies in Society and History Forum,* September 12 2023, https://sites.lsa.umich.edu/cssh/2023/09/12/meticulous-sleuthing-a-conversation-with-koh-choon-hwee/.

Silverstein, Adam J. *Postal Systems in the Pre-modern Islamic world.* Cambridge: Cambridge University Press, 2007.

Singer, Amy. *Palestinian Peasants and Ottoman Officials: Rural Administration around Sixteenth-Century Jerusalem.* Cambridge: Cambridge University Press, 1994.

Sinor, Denis. "Notes on the Equine Terminology of the Altaic Peoples." *Central Asiatic Journal* 10, no. 3/4 (1965): 307–315.

Skiotis, Dennis N. "From Bandit to Pasha: First Steps in the Rise to Power of Ali of Tepelen, 1750–1784." *International Journal of Middle East Studies* 2 (1971): 219–244.

Slota, Stephen C., and Geoffrey C. Bowker. "How Infrastructures Matter." In *The Handbook of Science and Technology Studies,* 4th ed., edited by Ulrike Felt, Rayvon Fouché, Clark A. Miller, and Laurel Smith-Doerr. 529–554. Cambridge, MA: MIT Press, 2017.

Smith, Paul J. *Taxing Heaven's Storehouse: Horses, Bureaucrats, and the Destruction of the Sichuan Tea Industry, 1074–1224.* Boston, MA: Council on East Asian Studies, Harvard University; distributed by Harvard University Press, 1991.

Soifer, Hillel. "State Infrastructural Power: Approaches to Conceptualization and Measurement." *Studies in Comparative International Development* 43, nos. 3–4 (2008): 231–251.

Solak, İbrahim, and İzzet Sak. *38 numaralı Konya şer'iye sicili, 1103–1104 /1692–1693: Transkripsiyon ve dizin [Konya Judicial Records Vol. 38].* Konya: Selçuk Üniversitesi Basımevi, 2014.

———. *39 numarali Konya ser'iye sicili (1113–1113 /1701–1702) (transkripsiyon ve dizin) [Konya Judicial Records Vol. 39].* Konya: Palet Yayınları, 2015.

Sönmez, Erdem. "Celaliler ve Üç Evliya Çelebi." *Kebikeç: İnsan Bilimleri İçin Kaynak Araştırmaları Dergisi* 33 (2012): 87–110.

Sönmez, Ferdi. "73 Numaralı Mühimme Defterinin Transkripsiyonu ve Değerlendirmesi (434–590)(Cilt I) / Transcription and Evaluation of Muhimme Register Number 73 (434–590)." Master's thesis, Bitlis Eren Üniversitesi, 2019.

Spruyt, Hendrik. *The World Imagined: Collective Beliefs and Political Order in the Sino-centric, Islamic and Southeast Asian International Societies.* Cambridge: Cambridge University Press, 2020.

Spyropoulos, Yannis, Stefanos Poulios, and Antonis Anastasopoulos. "Çiftliks, Landed Elites, and Tax Allocation in Eighteenth-Century Ottoman Veroia." *European Journal of Turkish Studies. Social Sciences on Contemporary Turkey* 30 (2020): 1–35.

Star, Susan Leigh. "The Ethnography of Infrastructure." *American Behavioral Scientist* 43, no. 3 (1999): 377–391.

Stevenson, Esmé Scott. *Our Ride through Asia Minor.* London: Chapman and Hall, 1881.

Stoianovich, Traian. "The Conquering Balkan Orthodox Merchant." *The Journal of Economic History* 20 (1960): 234–313.

Stoler, Ann Laura. *Along the Archival Grain: Epistemic Anxieties and Colonial Common Sense.* Princeton, NJ: Princeton University Press, 2009.

Stolz, Daniel A. "'Impossible to Provide an Accurate Estimate': The Interested Calculation of the Ottoman Public Debt, 1875–1881." *The British Journal for the History of Science* 55 (2022): 477–493.

Strogatz, Steven. *Sync: How Order Emerges from Chaos in the Universe, Nature and Daily Life.* New York: Hyperion, 2003.

Süreyya, Mehmed, Nuri Akbayar, and Seyit Ali Kahraman. *Sicill-i Osmani 4.* Istanbul: Kültür Bakanlığı ile Türkiye Ekonomik ve Toplumsal Tarih Vakfı, 1996.

Şen, Gül. "Between Two Spaces: Enslavement and Labor in the Early Modern Ottoman Navy." In *Comparative and Global Framing of Enslavement,* edited by Jeannine Bischoff and Stephan Conermann, 9:133–166. Berlin: De Gruyter, 2023.

Şimşek, Veysel. "The First 'Little Mehmeds': Conscripts for the Ottoman Army, 1826–53." *Osmanlı Araştırmaları* 44, no. 44 (2014): 265–311.

Tabak, Faruk. *The Waning of the Mediterranean, 1550–1870.* Baltimore, MD: Johns Hopkins University Press, 2008.

Tak, Ekrem. "Diplomatik Bilimi Bakımından XVI.-XVII. Yüzyıl Kadı Sicilleri ve Bu Sicillerin Ihtiva Ettiği Belge Türlerinin Form Özellikleri ve Tanımlanması / 16th-17th Century Kadı Registers According to the Rules of Diplomatics Science and the Description and Structural Characteristics of the Document Types Recorded in These Registers." PhD diss., Marmara University, 2009.

Takamatsu, Yoichi. "Formation and Custody of the Ottoman Archives During the Pre-Tanzimat Period." *Memoirs of the Research Department of the Toyo Bunko* 64 (2006): 125–148.

Talbert, Richard J. A. *Rome's World: The Peutinger Map Reconsidered.* Cambridge: Cambridge University Press, 2010.

Tamdoğan, Işık. "The Ottoman Political Community in the Process of Justice Making in the 18th-Century Adana." In *Forms and Institutions of Justice: Legal Actions in Ottoman Contexts,* edited by Yavuz Aykan and Işık Tamdoğan, 9–18. Istanbul: Institut français d'études anatoliennes, 2018.

Tanrıkut, Asaf. *Türkiye Posta ve Telgraf ve Telefon Tarihi ve Teşkilat ve Mevzuatı.* Ankara: PTT Genel Müdürlüğü, 1984.

Terzioğlu, Derin. "How to Conceptualize Ottoman Sunnitization: A Historiographical Discussion." *Turcica* 44 (2013): 301–338.

———. "Where İlm-i Hal Meets Catechism: Islamic Manuals of Religious Instruction in the Ottoman Empire in the Age of Confessionalization." *Past & Present* 220 (2013): 79–114.

Tezcan, Baki. *The Second Ottoman Empire: Political and Social Transformation in the Early Modern World.* New York: Cambridge University Press, 2010.

———. "Ethnicity, Race, Religion and Social Class: Ottoman Markers of Difference." In *The Ottoman World,* edited by Christine Woodhead, 159–170. London: Routledge, 2011.

Thompson, Irving A. A. *War and Government in Habsburg Spain, 1560–1620.* London: Athlone Press, 1976.

Thurston, Tina L., and Manuel Fernández-Götz, eds. *Power from below in Premodern Societies: The Dynamics of Political Complexity in the Archaeological Record.* Cambridge: Cambridge University Press, 2021.

Tilly, Charles. *Coercion, Capital, and European States, AD 990–1992.* Cambridge, MA.: Blackwell, 1992.

Todorova, Maria. *Imagining the Balkans.* Oxford: Oxford University Press, 2009.

Torres Sánchez, Rafael. *Military Entrepreneurs and the Spanish Contractor State in the Eighteenth Century.* Oxford: Oxford University Press, 2016.

Trentmann, Frank. *Empire of Things: How We Became a World of Consumers, from the Fifteenth Century to the Twenty-First.* New York: HarperCollins, 2016.

Trivellato, Francesca. "The Moral Economies of Early Modern Europe." *Humanity: An International Journal of Human Rights, Humanitarianism, and Development* 11, no. 2 (2020): 193–201.

——. *The Promise and Peril of Credit: What a Forgotten Legend about Jews and Finance Tells Us about the Making of European Commercial Society.* Princeton, NJ: Princeton University Press, 2019.

"The Moral Economies of Europe." *Humanity: An International Journal of Human Rights, Humanitarianism, and Development* 11, no. 2 (2020): 193–201.

Tuğ, Başak. *Politics of Honor in Ottoman Anatolia: Sexual Violence and Socio-Legal Surveillance in the Eighteenth Century.* Leiden: Brill, 2017.

Tunçer, Ali Coşkun, and Şevket Pamuk. "Ottoman Empire: From 1830 to 1914." In *South-Eastern European Monetary and Economic Statistics from the Nineteenth Century to World War II,* 171–197. Athens, Sofia, Bucharest, and Vienna: Bank of Greece, Bulgarian National Bank, National Bank of Romania, and Oesterreichische Nationalbank, 2014.

Turan, Osman. "Selçuk Kervansarayları." *Belleten* 39 (1946): 471–496.

Turgut, Turhan. *Osmanlı İmparatorluğu Posta Tarihi: Tarifeler ve Posta Yolları 1840–1922 / Postal History of the Ottoman Empire: Rates and Routes 1840–1922.* Istanbul: Alfa, 2018.

Turna, Nalan. "Pandemonium and Order: Suretyship, Surveillance, and Taxation in Early Nineteenth-Century Istanbul." *New Perspectives on Turkey* 39 (2008): 167–189.

Ueno, Masayuki. "In Pursuit of Laicized Urban Administration: The Muhtar System in Istanbul and Ottoman Attitudes toward Non-Muslim Religious Authorities in the Nineteenth Century." *International Journal of Middle East Studies* 54, no. 2 (May 2022): 302–318.

Ünal, Uğur, and Murat Cebecioğlu. *91 numaralı Mühimme defteri (H. 1056 / M. 1646–1647): Özet, çeviri yazı, tıpkıbasım.* Istanbul: T. C. Başbakanlık Devlet Arşivleri Genel Müdürlüğü, 2015.

Ursinus, Michael. "The Transformation of the Ottoman Fiscal Regime c. 1600–1850." In *The Ottoman World,* edited by Christine Woodhead, 423–435. London: Routledge, 2011.

Uzunçarşılı, İsmail Hakkı. *Osmanlı devletinin merkez ve bahriye teşkilatı.* Ankara: Türk Tarih Kurumu, 1984.

Vaissière, Étienne de la. "Note sur la Chronologie du Voyage de Xuanzang." *Journal Asiatique* 298, no. 1 (2010): 157–168.

Van Bruinessen, Martin. *Agha, Shaikh, and State: The Social and Political Structures of Kurdistan.* London: Zed Books, 1992.

Vasconcelos, Angélica, Alan Sangster, and Lúcia Lima Rodrigues. "Avoiding Whig Interpretations in Historical Research: An Illustrative Case Study." *Accounting, Auditing & Accountability Journal* 35, no. 6 (2022): 1402–1430.

Vér, Márton. "Animal Terminology in the Uyghur Documents Concerning the Postal System of the Mongol Empire." *Turkic Languages* 23 (2019): 192–210.

—–. "The Postal System of the Mongol Empire in Northeastern Turkestan." PhD diss., University of Szeged, 2016.

———. *Old Uyghur Documents Concerning the Postal System of the Mongol Empire.* Turnhout, Bengium: Brepols, 2019.

"Animal Terminology in the Uyghur Documents Concerning the Postal System of the Mongol Empire." *Turkic Languages* 23 (2019): 192–210.

Vér, Márton, and Isván Zimonyi. "Insights from the Inside: An Old Uyghur Register and the Administration of the Mongol Empire." In *Altaic and Chagatay Lectures. Studies in Honour of Éva Kincses-Nagy,* 435–448. Szeged, Hungary: Department of Altaic Studies, University of Szeged, 2021.

Vezenkov, Alexander. "Entangled Geographies of the Balkans: The Boundaries of the Region and the Limits of the Discipline." In *Entangled Histories of the Balkans: Concepts, Approaches, and (Self-)Representations,* edited by Roumen Daskalov, Diana Mishkova, Tchavdar Marinov, and Alexander Vezenkov, 4:115–256. Leiden: Brill, 2017.

Vora, Neha. *Impossible Citizens: Dubai's Indian Diaspora.* Durham, NC: Duke University Press, 2013.

Wang, Chelsea Zi. "Dilemmas of Empire: Movement, Communication, and Information Management in Ming China, 1368–1644." PhD diss., Columbia University, 2017.

———."More Haste, Less Speed: Sources of Friction in the Ming Postal System." *Late Imperial China* 40, no. 2 (2019): 89–140.

Wang, Sixiang. *Boundless Winds of Empire: Rhetoric and Ritual in Early Chosŏn Diplomacy with Ming China.* New York: Columbia University Press, 2023.

Weber, Max. *Economy and Society: An Outline of Interpretive Sociology.* Berkeley: University of California Press, 1978.

Wen, Xin. *The King's Road: Diplomacy and the Remaking of the Silk Road.* Princeton, NJ: Princeton University Press, 2023.

White, Eugene N. "From Privatized to Government-Administered Tax Collection: Tax Farming in Eighteenth-Century France." *Economic History Review* 57, no. 4 (2004): 636–663.

White, Joshua M. *Piracy and Law in the Ottoman Mediterranean.* Stanford, CA: Stanford University Press, 2018.

White, Sam. *The Climate of Rebellion in the Early Modern Ottoman Empire.* Studies in Environment and History. New York: Cambridge University Press, 2011.

Whitehead, Christopher. "The Reluctant Pasha: Çerkes Dilaver and Elite Localization in the Seventeenth-Century Ottoman Empire." *Turcica* 53 (2022): 3–43.

———. "The Veledeş Conflict: A Reassessment of the Mid-Seventeenth-Century Rebellions of the Altı Bölük Halkı." *Journal of the Ottoman and Turkish Studies Association* 8, no. 1 (2021): 291–310.

Wilkins, Charles L. *Forging Urban Solidarities: Ottoman Aleppo 1640–1700.* Leiden: Brill, 2010.

Wimmel, Robin. "Architektur osmanischer Karawanseraien: Stationen des Fernverkehrs im Osmanischen Reich." PhD diss., Technische Universität Berlin, 2016. https://depositonce.tu-berlin.de/handle/11303/5872.

———. "Edirne as a Stopover Destination. The Ekmekçioğlu Caravanserai and the Ottoman Road Network." In *The Heritage of Edirne in Ottoman and Turkish Times: Continuities, Disruptions and Reconnections,* edited by Birgit Krawietz and Florian Riedler, 152–204. Studies in the History and Culture of the Middle East, vol. 34. Berlin: De Gruyter, 2020.

Winter, Stefan. *A History of the 'Alawis: From Medieval Aleppo to the Turkish Republic.* Princeton, NJ: Princeton University Press, 2016.

———. *The Shiites of Lebanon under Ottoman Rule, 1516–1788.* Cambridge: Cambridge University Press, 2010.

Wishnitzer, Avner. *Reading Clocks, Alla Turca: Time and Society in the Late Ottoman Empire.* Chicago: University of Chicago Press, 2015.

Yağcı, Zübeyde Güneş. "Hac ve Askeri Yol Üzerinde Bir Menzil: Adana Menzili [A Post Station on the Haj and Military Road: Adana Station]." *Çukurova Araştırmaları Dergisi* 1, no. 1 (2015): 58–74.

Yapp, Malcolm E. "Europe in the Turkish Mirror." *Past & Present* 137, no. 1 (1992): 134–155.

Yavuz, Ayşıl Tükel. "Anadolu Selçuklu Dönemi Hanları ve Posta-Menzil-Derbent Teşkilatları." In *Prof. Doğan Kuban'a armağan,* edited by Doğan Kuban, Zeynep Ahunbay, Deniz Mazlum, and Kutgün Eyüpgiller, 25–38. Armağan dizisi, no. 1. Beyoğlu, Turkey: Eren, 1996.

———. "The Concepts That Shape Anatolian Seljuq Caravanserais." *Muqarnas* 14 (1997): 80–95.

Yaycıoğlu, Ali. *Partners of the Empire: The Crisis of the Ottoman Order in the Age of Revolutions.* Stanford, CA: Stanford University Press, 2016.

Yazıcı, Nesimi. "II. Mahmud Döneminde Menzilhaneler: 'Ref'-i Menzil Bedeli.'" In *İstanbul Üniversitesi Edebiyat Fakültesi Tarih Araştırma Merkezi Sultan II. Mahmud ve Reformları Semineri: 28–30 Haziran 1989*, 157–187. Istanbul: Edebiyat Fakültesi Basımevi, 1990.

———. "Posta Nezaretinin Kuruluşu." In *Çağını Yakalayan Osmanlı!: Osmanlı Devleti'nde Modern Haberleşme ve Ulaştırma Teknikleri*, edited by Mustafa Kaçar and Ekmeleddin İhsanoğlu, 23–45. Istanbul: IRCICA Yayınları, 1995.

Yerasimos, Stephane. *Les Voyageurs dans l'empire Ottoman (XIVe—XVIe Siècles): Bibliographie, Itinéraires et Inventaire Des Lieux Habités.* Ankara: Imprimerie de la société turque d'histoire, 1991.

Yetkin, Sabri. *Ege'de Eşkıyalar.* Istanbul: Tarih Vakfı Yurt Yayınları, 2003.

Yi, Eunjeong. *Guild Dynamics in Seventeenth-Century Istanbul: Fluidity and Leverage.* The Ottoman Empire and Its Heritage, vol. 27. Leiden: Brill, 2004.

Yıldırım, Hacı Osman, and Yusuf Sarınay. *85 numaralı Mühimme defteri: (1040–1041 (1042)/1630–1631 (1632). Özet—transkripsiyon—indeks.* Ankara: T. C. Başbakanlık Devlet Arşivleri Genel Müdürlüğü, 2002.

Yıldırım, Osman, ed. *6 numaralı mühimme defteri (972/1564–1565).* Ankara: T. C. Başbakanlık, Devlet Arşivleri Genel Müdürlüğü, 1995.

Yıldız, Aysel. *Crisis and Rebellion in the Ottoman Empire: The Downfall of a Sultan in the Age of Revolution.* London: I. B. Tauris, 2017.

———., and İrfan Kokdaş. "Peasantry in a Well-Protected Domain: Wallachian Peasantry and Muslim Çiftlik / Kışlaks under Ottoman Rule." *Journal of Balkan and Near Eastern Studies* 22, no. 1 (2020): 175–190.

Yıldız, Kenan, and Recep Ahıshalı, eds. *İstanbul Kadı Sicilleri Üsküdar Mahkemesi 9 Numaralı Sicil (H. 940–942 / M. 1534–1536).* Istanbul: İSAM Yayınları, 2010.

Yılmaz, Coşkun, ed. *İstanbul Kadı Sicilleri 51 İstanbul Mahkemesi 10 Numaralı Sicil (H. 1072–1073 / M. 1661–1663).* Translated by Yılmaz Karaca and Mehmet Akman. Vol. 51. Istanbul: Kültür AŞ, 2019.

———, ed. *İstanbul Kadı Sicilleri İstanbul Mahkemesi 18 Numaralı Sicil (H. 1086–1087 / M. 1675–1676).* Translated by Mehmet Akman. Istanbul: Türkiye Diyanet Vakfı İslâm Araştırmaları Merkezi (İSAM), 2010.

Yusuf Husain Khan. *Selected Documents of Aurangzeb's Reign, 1659–1706 A. D.* Central Records Office, Government of Andhra Pradesh, 1958.

Zdraveva, Milka. "The Menzil Service in Macedonia, Particularly around Bitolj, in the Period of Turkish Domination." *Études Balkaniques* 31, no. 2 (1995): 82–88.

Zeitlian Watenpaugh, Heghnar. *The Image of an Ottoman City: Imperial Architecture and Urban Experience in Aleppo in the 16th and 17th Centuries.* Leiden: Brill, 2004.

Zhao, Xiaoxuan. *Songdai Yizhan Zhidu* [*The Relay System during the Song Dynasty*]. Taipei: Lian jing chu ban shi ye gong si, 1983.

Zhang, Lawrence. *Power for a Price: The Purchase of Official Appointments in Qing China.* Cambridge, MA: Harvard University Asia Center, 2022.

Acknowledgments

In July 2006, Singapore played host to hundreds of kids from eighty-two countries who came to compete in the International Physics Olympiad. I was assigned to chaperone five Iranian teenagers. I was eighteen at the time. They were probably fifteen or sixteen. I spoke no Persian; only one student, Ehsan, spoke a bit of English so he translated for Hasan, Shahab, Nima, and Tavaf. We stayed in a university dorm for ten days, kids taking care of kids. I remember running around campus at night with other chaperones to stop our guests from exploding Pepsi bottles (and other material) for fun. I remember anxiously counting heads at the Night Safari to make sure I didn't lose anybody, because another team had "wandered" into an enclosure. These were young physicists with strong empirical inclinations. Ten days flew by, and soon it was farewell at the airport. Standing at the departure hall, I remember wondering why I had not learned anything about Iran in school, or much about the Middle East. This small question soon took over my life. Nearly two decades later, after several twists, turns, births, and deaths, this book exists.

Many people helped me build this research project, which began as a dissertation supervised by Alan Mikhail, Francesca Trivellato, Peter Perdue, and Richard M. Eaton. I thank them for training me to read, write, and think. For their meticulously written feedback on various versions of the book manuscript, part or whole, I thank the six anonymous reviewers engaged by the press and Suraiya Faroqhi, Mitchell Tan Wei Liang, Ben Fortna, Molly Greene, Shashi

Jayakumar, Victor Lieberman, Samson Lim, Colin Heywood, Kim Soo Yong, Uluğ Kuzuoğlu, Tamara Maatouk, Madoka Morita, Selin Ünlüönen, Yong Cho, Richard Von Glahn, Wang Sixiang, Luke Yarbrough, and Serkan Yolaçan. Heartfelt thanks to friends outside of academia who gave detailed feedback on several chapter drafts: Doruk Baykal, Matthias Chew Yong Peng, Chye Shu Wen, and Letitia Lew.

Many colleagues helped to decipher Ottoman Turkish words I could not read, especially personal names and place-names. I have thanked them individually in the relevant endnotes. In addition, Ceyhun Arslan, Özgen Felek, Rossitsa Gradeva, Hratch Kestenian, Tamara Maatouk, Madoka Morita, Milena Petkova, Mesut Sayan, Selin Ünlüönen, and Stefan Winter either helped me many times or generously helped with paleographic puzzles that could not be solved (and hence I could not thank them in the endnotes and am thanking them here).

For corresponding with me on the smallest of questions and/or for their helpful comments during this writing journey, I thank Majed Akhter, Yiğit Akın, David Akin, Syed Farid Alatas, Begüm Adalet, Fahad Bishara, Linda Darling, Sam Dolbee, William Clarence Gervase-Smith, Dina Rizk Khoury, Koh Tong Kai, Akinobu Kuroda, Donna Landry, Liew Han Hsien, Michael Meeker, Ellen Nye, Tommaso Stefini, Daniel Stolz, Baki Tezcan, Işın Taylan, Ali Coşkun Tunçer, Richard Von Glahn, and Jeff Wasserstrom. At the final stages of revision an extended email conversation with Andrew Shryock helped me see several things clearly. I am most indebted to Suraiya Faroqhi for mentoring me and for answering my numerous questions. Edhem Eldem, Ethan Menchinger, and Eugene Rogan generously hunted down the archival and manuscript sources which they had cited in their publications and shared them with me over email during the pandemic. Şenay Döner passed along relevant sources she had encountered—even if I did not ultimately use these in this book, I am grateful for her collegiality and hope to use them elsewhere.

I thank everyone who generously shared their book proposals with me and gave advice on the publishing process, especially Emma Flatt. Gwendolyn Collaço and Selin Ünlüönen gave advice on using images from Ottoman manuscripts. Tamara Maatouk, Madoka Morita, Mitchell Harris, and Tong Hien Chi helped with proofreading and index-making. Nimet İpek helped with archival access during the pandemic.

I thank everyone at all these places and venues who gave me the opportunity to present my work and get feedback, as well as all audience members who engaged with my ideas: SUNY Binghamton (especially Nathaneal Andrade's insightful question); MADCAP on Zoom, University of Virginia (Fahad

Bishara); Economic and Social History of the World Seminar, Institute of Historical Research, School of Advanced Study, University of London (Ali Coşkun Tunçer); Stanford University's Eurasian Empires workshop (Nora Barakat); Society for the Social Studies of Quantification (SSSQ) Data Deluges Conference (Ted Porter); the Financial History Seminar (Sebastian Felten); the Ottoman Political Economy seminar; Financial History Network (Paula Vedoveli); the MESA and CIEPO conferences (thanks to panel chairs Fredrik Meiton, Carter Vaughn Findley, and others); the Premodern Postal Systems Working Group (William Gervase Clarence-Smith, Willem Floor, Magnus Linnarsson, Petra Maurer, Rachel Midura, Felice Physioc, John Randolph, Richard Talbert, Márton Vér, Chelsea Wang Zi, and others); Pacific Rim Ottomanists' Conference 2023 at Tobunken Institute for Advanced Studies on Asia, Tokyo University (Akiba Jun) and Doshisha University (Horii Yutaka). Special thanks to Ueno Masayuki, who attended every paper presentation and asked questions at every session all the way from Istanbul via Zoom—his engagement greatly enriched the conferences from which I learned a lot.

Archivists and librarians provided crucial help. I would like to thank Gabriela Angelova at the St. Cyril and Methodius National Library in Sofia, Bulgaria, and Nestor Mpampidis at the Greece General State Archives, Historical Archives of Macedonia (Thessaloniki). I thank the staff at the Presidential State Archives of the Republic of Turkey, Ottoman Archives, as well as Kenan Yıldız, Esra Karayel Muhacır, Neslihan Aracı Güler, Nuray Urkaç Güler, Büşra Atmaca, Hatice Aldemir, and Şüheda Tokat at İslam Araştırmaları Merkezi (İSAM). At İSAM I was also a beneficiary of the hospitality, tea, sweets, and conversation (*sohbet*) in Kenan hoca's office.

I would like to acknowledge the work of numerous graduate students, teams of archivists, historians, and professors based mostly in Türkiye who published transcriptions of court records (*şer'iye sicilleri*), Registers of Important Affairs (*mühimme defteri*), and other kinds of archival records as dissertations, edited volumes, or online databases (especially kadisicilleri.org). These were either keyword searchable or had a useful index. Without these resources, I could not have hoped to access the range of archival material used in this study and to attempt to see the postal system as a system.

I am grateful for logistical help from friends and colleagues. Free housing was provided by Maria Vassileva in Sofia, Bulgaria; by Abdelrahman Mahmoud, his mother Laila, and his family in Cairo, Egypt; by Helga Seeden and Lorma Maatouk (and the whole Beit Maatouk) in Lebanon; by Hratch Kestenian and Chee Wai May in New York; and by Richard M. Eaton in Tucson, AZ, USA. Richard

Eaton brought me to explore the old Pony Express route, the Butterfield Over-land Mail Trail, and to find Dragoon Springs Stage Station. At Yale, librarians Ahmed Ramadan and Rich Richie kindly kept our belongings in their respec-tive houses when we had to leave New Haven. For procuring multiple PDFs, es-pecially during the pandemic, I thank Joane Chaker, Daria Kovaleva, Hratch Kestenian, Tamara Maatouk, Li Yan McCurdy, and Işın Taylan. Financial help came from the Social Science Research Council, the Research Center for Ana-tolian Civilizations (Koç University), the American Research Institute in Tür-kiye, the MacMillan Center (Yale University), as well as the Faculty Development Office (Academic Personnel Office) and the Center for Early Global Studies (CMRS-CEGS) at the University of California, Los Angeles (UCLA). I thank all these institutions for supporting this research and the humanities more generally.

Although my research eventually went down other paths, I want to thank those who helped me during my archival stints in Delhi, Hyderabad, Cairo, and Tehran: [Delhi] Masanda Magdalin, Himani Upadhyaya, Shivangi Pareek, and Richa Singh [Hyderabad] Benjamin Cohen (University of Utah) and Profes-sor A. Karunaker (Osmania University); [Cairo] even though I was ultimately unsuccessful I thank Motani Yusuke, who took the trouble to vet my petition letter to the authorities at the Dar al-Watha'iq (Egyptian National Archive); [Iran] Zehra Eviz, Mizukami Ryo, and Reyhaneh Asgari and her family; Azar Rahimi and her family.

Training for the research undertaken in this book took many years. I thank [for Ottoman and Modern Turkish] Alexis Wick, the late Etem Erol, Himmet Taşkömür, Özgen Felek, Ahmet Okal (who named me Çiğdem), Sevde Felek; [for Classical and Modern Persian] Amr Ahmed, Sheida Dayani, Justine Lan-dau, Azar Rahimi, and all my teachers at Dehkhoda; [for Classical and Modern Arabic] Dahlia Abo-Haggar, Ahmadiyya al-Nassan, John Meloy, Tarek Abuhu-sayn, and al-Markaz Center in Singapore. Special thanks to Justine Landau for making me memorize poems by Hafez and Rumi in our classical Persian classes; they came in handy when the Mughal archivist at Telangana State Archives, Hy-derabad, refused to give me access to the documents unless I recited a Persian poem a day for him and let him film me on his smartphone doing so. Fortunately for my limited repertoire, he soon settled on a favourite poem (by Rumi), so for the rest of my time there I only had to recite that one for archival access each morning.

For Ottoman documents training, I thank Ali Akyıldız, the late Mehmet Genç, Orhan Sakin, and Kenan Yıldız. They generously allowed me to audit their

Ottoman documents classes at 29 May University, the former Istanbul Şehir University, and even sat with me to read my documents the few times that I asked. John Meloy taught me to read Mamluk-era chronicles in Arabic. My teachers at Yale taught me how to read Tang, Song, Yuan, Qing, and Qajar-era documents; although I did not expect to, I eventually applied the methods I had learned from them to understand Ottoman documents. Selçuk Aydın taught me to ride a horse and introduced me to the naughty Halil Bey and the gentle Turkish Delight. Münir Beken invited me to join the UCLA Ottoman Music ensemble and, together with Mr. Ian Price, taught me to play the derbeke (darbouka). I count these two latter skills part of my ongoing training to becoming a better Ottoman historian.

The American University of Beirut's Department of History and Archaeology taught me how to do research and became my surrogate family in the process. I thank John Meloy, Clare Leader, Helga Seeden, Samir Seikaly, Zein Seikaly, Alexis Wick, Tamara Maatouk, Hratch Kestenian, the late Abdelrahman Abuhusayn, Paul Newson, Helene Sader, Jack Nurpetlian, Lyall Armstrong, Nadia El-Cheikh, Tariq Tell, Tylor Brand, and Nabeeha Osailly. Tamara and Hratch taught me, among other things, Lebanese manners. My gratitude also to Raja Abu Hassan, Berivan Aydın, Troy Carter, Sahar Naim, and Rami el-Ojaimi for their friendship, as well as Amale Feghali and other colleagues at the AUB Archaeological Museum for their kindness while I was a student worker there.

The University of Arizona gave me my first training in Middle East Studies. I am grateful to the late Michael Bonine and the extraordinary community of graduate students and faculty there in AY 2010–2011. Professors Bonine and Anne Betteridge opened up the world of Iran to me. He brought a water clock to class and showed us how it was used to distribute *qanat* water shares in Iranian villages; she screened a documentary that showed how the Bakhtiari used inflated goat skins to cross rivers. Richard M. Eaton was my very first mentor and remains one to this day. Heartfelt thanks to Dina Jadallah, Farzin Vejdani, Ben Fortna, Ahmet Okal, and all the graduate students who were there that year. Before Tucson, I spent an eventful year at Lady Shri Ram College, Delhi University; it was there when I was first inspired by my brilliant classmates to consider research as a vocation.

The National University of Singapore (NUS) opened up the whole world to me. It is thanks to the exchange opportunities and scholarships made available to my generation that I was able to study abroad in Delhi University and the University of Arizona. In AY 2011–2012 I interned under the late Michael C. Hudson, then Director, and Rana B. Khoury, then Executive Assistant of the Middle

East Institute (MEI), NUS; it was Hudson who told me about the American University of Beirut and its MA programs.

Things came full circle back to NUS after I received my PhD in 2020. During the pandemic, I worked as an adjunct lecturer at the Lee Kuan Yew School of Public Policy (LKYSPP), NUS. I thank Kartini Binte Abdul Rahman, Andrew Francis-Tan, Mehmet Akif Demircioğlu, Terence Ho, Suzaina Kadir, Leong Ching, Danny Quah, and, most importantly, the students from my Politics of Infrastructure course for a wonderful year. (Shoutout to the White Pepper WhatsApp group.) After this stint ended in 2021, the Asia Research Institute, NUS, kindly accommodated me as a Visiting Researcher with library privileges. For this I thank Tim Bunnell and Tan Tai Yong. Michelle Miller, Lin Hongxuan, Ashawari Chaudhuri, Canay Özden-Schilling, and other colleagues and staff gave me a sense of community during those isolating times. Above all, Syed Farid Alatas included me in various events and working groups and invited me for countless coffee chats, where his curiosity about Ottoman studies spurred me to read more and more.

I am grateful to the Department of History at the University of California, Los Angeles (UCLA), for support. To my senior colleagues in the Middle East field, Jim Gelvin and Sebouh Aslanian. A shoutout to all the faculty on the fifth floor of Bunche Hall, with hugs to all my fellow assistant professors. Huge thanks to the incredible History Department staff. Aslı Bâli, Kara Cooney, Kevin Terraciano, Richard Antaramian, and Eva Nguyen went above and beyond to help me during an extremely difficult period. Sheida Dayani, George Dutton, Andrea Goldman, Nile Green, Toby Higbie, Pete Stacey, Stefania Tutino, and Kaya Menteşeoğlu made time to give me important advice. Wendy Shaw kindly gifted me with old books and dictionaries in the summer of 2022. For other crucial advice between 2014 and 2020, I thank CJ Huang, Cho Wonhee, Park Hyunhee, Veysel Şimşek, James Pickett, Denise Y. Ho, Michael Montesano, Jack Chia, Winston Chow, Ramazan Hakkı Öztan, and Francesca Trivellato.

I thank Jaya Chatterjee, Amanda Gerstenfeld, and Mary Pasti from Yale University Press for guiding me through the publishing, peer review, and copyediting processes. I took longer than I was supposed to in manually revising the endnotes due to my decision to reorder several chunks of text; I thank the team for their infinite patience with me and their accommodations made to the timeline.

All mistakes are mine.

Everyone is a potential friend. For reciprocating my attempts at friendship and keeping me sane during those monastic years of research, I thank: [at Yale] Li

Yan, the Persian calligraphy group, the Turco-Mongol Quriltai, the late Zeng Lingyi, Yong, Selin, Işın, Bayan, Dinnie, Bo, Özgen hoca, Barbara di Gennaro and her family, Shivangi, Mike, James, Tse Yang, CT, Faizah, George, Arina, Yong Le, Nichole Nelson, Elly Toyoda; [at Harvard] Chloe, Han Hsien, Ceyhun, Daria, Farah, Joane; [at Hyderabad 2019] "Be danand ke" WhatsApp group, Pia Maria, Amrita, Stan, James; [in Iran] Zehra; [in Türkiye] Nimet İpek, the nearly-all-female graduate student working group where we took turns to cook, chat, and workshop papers; my ANAMED cohort, especially Julien Boucly, Robert Coates-Stephens (who started the conversation that led to the title of this book and who took us to hunt for Roman cisterns in Istanbul), and Zeynep Aydoğan (for her kindness and sage advice when I needed it); Ananya Vajpeyi, Marjorie Verley, Madoka, Shivangi, Letitia, Koh Choon Min, Koh Choon Yee, Marcus Kho, Fabian Lee, Koh Leng Leng, and Arnaud, all of whom helped me enjoy my time in Istanbul and Beirut. The deepest friendships I made on this monastic path of doctoral research were forged in Beirut—flashback to the department in the mornings, with Hratch already at his computer terminal and Seikaly shuffling up behind him to boil water. He'd lay out the *kaak* on a tissue paper and tell me to fetch the milk, and then others would start emerging from their offices. Seeden would bark something. Abu Husayn would emerge saying something else. The bantering would start. Tamara would stand beside me, and we would get ready to listen to them (re)tell their stories.

I am grateful to the friends who continue to choose to be in my life: Andrea Ong, Toh Bao En, Matthias Chew (who taught me the term "learned helplessness"); Letitia Lew, Grace Chew Ming Xian, Imran bin Mustapha, Kevin Lee Soong Yan, Lim Tse Yang, Claire Ho Shu Fen, Dhaneswery Makentharan, Bridget Shoo, Wee Jun Kai, Ng Kexian, the LeMoNs WhatsApp group (plus Pak), the Markaz Babes (Norham Erlyna Binte Abdul Hamid [Tipah], Nurhidayah Ameer Hamzah [Yot], Zatul Himmah [Aton], Tengku Sri Melati [Me'on], Rabi'ah Bte Ghazali [Pe'ah]), the Board Games group (Nathan Wangliao Yinan, Angela Chai, Yap Leong Gen), Momo Ong, Friends Who Reciprocate WhatsApp group (do you really, though?), the Nabih Faris Library WhatsApp group, and the Kent Ridge Common online student newspaper crew (Lester Lim, Anirudh Krishnan, Salima Nadira, Sharifah Nabilah Binte Syed Omar, Tan Xiang Yeow). Shoutouts to Philip Holden, Ng Yun Sian, Michael C. Yeo, and Shannon Ang and to Shu Wen's Singapore-based Faction Press, an independent non-fiction micropress dedicated to bringing stories from Southeast Asia to the world.

I apologize for not being able to name everybody who has helped me over the past decade.

My deepest love and appreciation to Koh Piak Huat, Chin Ngiok Pah, Koh Choon Yee, Koh Choon Min, the late Zhang Meowyin, Mitchell Tan Wei Liang, Tan Kim Lam, and Jody Wong, especially during the past few years of never-ending medical appointments, surgeries, procedures, and medications. Only they know the true cost of my ambition to try to understand those glimpses of a wider, unfamiliar world I saw in those ten days in 2006.

Index